The Gospel of Sri Ramakrishna and its Relevance

The Gospel of Sri Ramakrishna and its Relevance

Edited by

Projit Kumar Palit
and
Swami Kamalasthananda

Kaveri Books
New Delhi - 110002

First Published in 2017
ISBN : 978-93-86463-00-5

Published by
Kaveri Books
4832/24, Ansari Road, Daryaganj,
New Delhi - 110 002 (India)
Ph. : 011-2328 8140, 4707 2321
E-mail : info@kaveribooks.com
kaveribooks@gmail.com
Website : www.kaveribooks.com

Typesetting at Creative Graphics, Delhi

PRINTED IN INDIA

Dedication

To
Prof. Tapodhir Bhattacharjee,
Former Vice Chancellor,
Assam University,
Silchar.

Acknowledgement

Sri Sri Rāmakrishna Kathāmrita is the soul of the Ramakrishna-Vivekananda movement in the nineteenth century in India. Mahendranath Gupta recorded his daily interactions with Ramakrishna in his diary which were subsequently published as Sri-Sri-Ramakrishna-Kathamrta in five Volumes in Bengali language during 1902CE, 1905CE, 1908CE, 1910CE and 1932 CE. It is an important religious Book in the 20th Century and it has created a new spiritual culture in India.

We are expressing deep regards and gratitude to Most Revered Srimat Swami Prabhanandaji Maharaj, Vice President, Ramakrishna Math and mission, Belur Math for his valuable 'Foreword'.

We are sincerely grateful and indebted to all authors who have contributed their research papers for this volume. We are also sincerely thankful and obliged to the President, Sri Ma Trust, Chandigarh – 160018 for giving consent to publish two articles which are - Personality Of Sri Ramakrishna As It Emerges From The Gospel - Swami Mukhyananda and Sri Ramakrishna Kathamrita: Sri M.'S Unique Contribution To Bengali Literature - Pranab Ranjan Ghosh in our edited volume. We are also sincerely thankful and obliged to the president, Advaita Ashrama, Mayavati, Uttarakhand for giving consent to publish one article which is – The Gospel of Sri Ramakrishana and the life of M- Swami Prabhananda in our edited volume.

We are thankful to Mr. Rakesh Goel , Kaveri Books, New Delhi for publishing this volume within a very short time.

Projit Kumar Palit &
Swami Kamalasthananda

Ramakrishna Math
P.O. Belur Math, Dist. Howrah
West Bengal : 711202, India

Ph. No. 033-2654-5700/5701/5702
Fax : 91-033-2654-4346
E-mail: prabhananda@rkmm.org
Website : www.belurmath.org

Foreword

I am delighted to introduce the present volume entitled, 'The Gospel of Sri Ramakrishna and its relevance' edited by two scholars Dr. Projit Kumar Palit, Professor and Head in the Department of History, Assam University, (A Central University), Silchar, Assam and Swami Kamalasthananda, Principal, Ramkrishna Mission Vivekananda Centenary College, Rahara, West Bengal. As many as twenty distinguished scholars have articulated on various aspects of the Gospel of Sri Ramakrishna and its significance in the present society. I hope the readers would be immensely benefited from the learned exposition of the Gospel. Eventually, the Gospel of Sri Ramakrishna has become an authentic symbol of the Ramakrishna-Vivekananda Movement in India and abroad.

Mahendranath Gupta recorded his daily interactions with Ramakrishna in his diary which were subsequently published under the title, Sri Sri Ramakrishna-Kathamrita in five Volumes in Bengali language (1902 CE, 1905 CE, 1908 CE, 1910 CE and 1932 CE). Some praised its "stenographic precision", another described it as a "historical record of a saint" of nineteenth century in Bengal, again someone mentioned the Gospel as a well-documented record of not only the teachings of Sri Ramakrishna, as also indirectly recorded the political, social values of the nineteenth century in Bengal. There is another point quite fascinating: M tried hard to keep himself hidden by using about a dozen pseudonyms here and there. There you get fleshes of his autobiography.

'M' first met Sri Ramakrishna in 1882. Sri Ramakrishna passed away on the 16th August, 1886. Thus 'M's record covers last four years after meeting his master; 'M' claims that he simply recorded the teachings of Sri Ramakrishna. The Gospel was not his creation. It was not a product of his imagination. 'M' humbly submitted that it was a report only of his own understanding. 'M' wrote to Pramada Das Mitra, 'My object has been to present scenes from his daily life as well as his teachings as I understand them.' I am confident that this volume will be well accepted by scholars and readers in the academic world. I congratulate the editors for their sincerity and successful efforts.

Swami Prabhananda
Vice-President
Ramakrishna Math and Mission,
Belur Math, West Bengal

Introduction

The nineteenth century was a very important period of Indian politics, when the British imperialism was expanding rapidly and Indian nationalism was on the rise. The Ramakrishna-Vivekananda Movement was played an important role for the developing of the Indian nationalism. Sri Rāmakrishna was the central figure of the Movement and he was one of the most significant spiritual leaders of the modern world and a great lover of humanity.

Ramakrishna (February 18, 1836 – August 16, 1886) was born in a poor Brahmin family in rural Bengal. He was staying in Kolkata from 1852 CE, first in *Jhamapukur* and then as a priest of the Kali temple in Dakshineswar, dedicated to the goddess Kali, which had the influence of the main strands of Bengali bhakti tradition. Sri Ramakrishna practised different paths of Hinduism and experienced the same reality. He also experimented with other religions, notably Islam and Christianity, and said that they all lead to the same God. His deep meditative knowledge was expressed by his simple words *"yato mat tato path"* i.e. "as many faiths, so many paths." which became the popular sign of interfaith understanding. Sri Ramakrishna, though conventionally uneducated, he attracted the attention of the middle class and numerous Bengali intellectuals. Through his God-intoxicated life Sri Ramakrishna proved that the revelation of God takes place at all times and that God-realization is not the monopoly of any particular age, country, or people. In him, deepest spirituality and broadest catholicity stood side by side. The God-man of nineteenth-century India did not found any cult, nor did he show a new path to salvation. His message was his God-consciousness. When God-consciousness falls short, traditions become dogmatic and oppressive and religious teachings lose their transforming power. At a time when the very foundation of religion, faith in God, was crumbling under the relentless blows of materialism and scepticism, Sri Ramakrishna, through his burning spiritual realizations, demonstrated beyond doubt the reality of God and the validity of the time-honoured teachings of all the prophets and saviours of the past, and thus restored the falling edifice of religion on a secure foundation.

The greatest contribution of Sri Ramakrishna to the modern world is his message of the harmony of religions. To Sri Ramakrishna all religions are the revelation of God in His diverse aspects to satisfy the manifold demands of human minds. Like different photographs of a building taken from different angles, different religions give us the pictures of one truth from different standpoints. They are not contradictory but complementary. Sri Ramakrishna faithfully practiced the spiritual disciplines of different religions and came to the realization that all of them lead to the same goal. ***His one of the important contribution is that the paths may vary, but the goal remains the same. Harmony of religions is not uniformity; it is unity in diversity. It is not a fusion of religions, but a fellowship of religions based on their common goal—communion with God. This harmony is to be realized by deepening our individual God-consciousness.*** In the present-day world, threatened by nuclear war and torn by religious intolerance, Sri Ramakrishna's message of harmony gives us hope and shows the way. The life and experiences of the Indian saint Sri Ramakrishna afford us an opportunity to understand the nature of mystic experiences. In a religious context, Sri Ramakrishna's experiences were varied and spontaneous, as well as induced, and they had a profound impact on his life as well as that of his culture. This is illustrated by Ramakrishna describing God as a mother who cooks fish differently for her children according to their tastes, temperaments and their ability to digest different types of food. For Ramakrishna, God is both the Mother of the universe and also of individual souls of the children. In India, a mother is considered as one who sacrifices herself for her children and goes to great lengths to satisfy them and bring them happiness. According to Ramakrishna, God as a Mother therefore makes different religions and belief systems according to each person's needs and tastes. Through his experimental inferences Ramakrishna was successful in resuscitating the lost faith in the Indian national ideals of spirituality, renunciation and service. On the other hand, he was the pioneer of setting forth a global culture, uniting the East and West, the different sects and sections of the society based on his experience of the universality of the supreme truth manifesting through varied modes. Thus the advent of Sri Ramakrishna was a turning point ushering a new age of hope, unity and greatness which was never dreamt before not only for India but for the entire world at large. However his impact is still to be assessed with only a few voices of recognition of the fact. Many prominent persons like Debendranath Tagore, Ishwar Chandra Vidyasagar, Swami Dayananda, Pratap Chandra Mazumdar, Shivanath Shastri, Trailokyanath Sanyal and

Kesab Chandra Sen interacted with him and all accepted his genius and greatness. Many young and educated persons accepted him as their preceptor. One of them, Sri Mahendranath Gupta noted down the dialogues of Sri Ramakrishna in his diary when he visited the Master. Later he wrote down these dialogues elaborately through intense meditation and contemplation. It was published in a book named *Sri Sri Ramakrishna Kathamrita*. He had noted down all the dialogues in a stenographic style. He had no intention of publishing these in a book form. His way of writing the book is mentioned by him as –

> *I wrote everything from memory after I returned home. ......Sometimes I would keep on writing the events of one sitting for seven days........I used to meditate on every scene for more than thousand times. As a result the events which had occurred many days back were revealed to me in a lively manner by the grace of the Master...Many a time I did not feel satisfied with my description of the events; I would then immediately plunge myself in deep meditation ...Then the correct image would arise...That is why in spite of the big gap in the physical sense, this story remains so fresh and lifelike in my mind as if it happened just now*[1].

After reading his book in its initial pamphlet form, Swami Vivekananda wrote a letter with inspiring words –

> *Many thanks for your publication. Only, I am afraid it will not pay its way in a pamphlet form. . . . Never mind, pay or no pay -- let it see the blaze of daylight. You will have many blessings on you ....!*[2]

Swami Vivekananda wrote another letter to Mahendranath Gupta where he mentioned that Sri Ramakrishna is vividly expressed through the entire writing and the writer scrupulously hides himself throughout the description.

> *It is indeed wonderful. The move is quite original, and never was the life of a great Teacher brought before the public untarnished by the writer's mind, as you are presenting this one. The language also is beyond all praise, so fresh, so pointed, and withal so plain and easy...... I now understand why none of us attempted his life before. It has been reserved for you, this great work. He*

1. Swami Chetanananda (1999). *Sri Ramakrishner Sannidhye*. Kolkata, Udbodhan. p.256
2. Swami Vivekananda, The Complete works of Swami Vivekananda, Vol.6, Advaita Ashrama, Kolkata, p.412.

is with you evidently....... The Socratic dialogues are Plato all over; you are entirely hidden. Moreover, the dramatic part is infinitely beautiful.[1]

In the above letter Swamiji has compared the work of Mahendranath Gupta with Plato's work. Plato has written a book on Socrates - '*Dialogues of Plato*'. The complete monumental work is nothing but the expression of the genius of Plato but it hardly expresses the teacher, Socrates. In the Apology portion of the book Plato mentions three types of apologies *1st. The defence properly so called; 2nd. The shorter address in mitigation of the penalty; 3rd. The last words of prophetic rebuke and exhortation*[2]. These apologies apparently appear as the dialogues of Socrates but careful readings reveal that these are nothing but the ideas of Socrates expressed by Plato in his own style.

On the whole we arrive at the conclusion that the Apology is true to the character of Socrates, but we cannot show that any single sentence in it was actually spoken by him. It breathes the spirit of Socrates, but has been cast anew in the mould of Plato[3].

Moreover the middle and the last dialogues clearly express the ideas of Plato and his philosophy. Here the writer establishes his ideas in his own style and expression.

In these dialogues, Plato begins expressing his own views, in the guise of Socrates. .... The later dialogues are deeper developments of the philosophy expressed in the earlier ones; these are the most difficult of Plato's works[4].

Another book on dialogue is by Gregory, the *Great Dialogues, Book 2: Life of Benedict*. Here author Gregory's account of Benedict, which forms Book 2 of the Dialogues, is regarded by many modern scholars as historically reliable in its biographical outline, even if much of its detailed matter is taken up with the miracles of the saint. But this narration has some characteristics where the author of the book is frequently questioned by his disciple for interpretation of the fact of narration in the texts. So here the dialogue is mainly for greater explanation of the facts related to the saint's life depicted in the narration. The dialogue is not between the character of the saint and the author, but the author and his disciple.

---

1. Swami Vivekananda, The Complete works of Swami Vivekananda, Vol.5, Advaita Ashrama, Kolkata, p.140.
2. http://holybooks.lichtenbergpress.netdna-cdn.com/wp-content/uploads/plato-complete-works.pdf?351736, p.30
3. Ibid. p.30
4. http://www.sacred-texts.com/cla/plato/

Another of the Dialogues' departures from the Eastern model is its use of frequent dialogic interludes between narrative episodes, in which Gregory the "author" is questioned by his disciple, the deacon Peter, giving Gregory a chance to comment on and interpret some of the implications of the narratives themselves. Gregory probably adapted this dialogic device from Sulpicius Severus, whose lengthy supplement (404-06) to his Life of Martin of Tours was cast in dialogue form, although the dialogue was common enough in Latin literature in general[1].

The work of Mahendranath is unique compared to the two great works i.e. the works of Plato and the works of Gregory in the following aspects :

1. Mahendranath has taken notes on the very day of the meeting with the Master in his own way of stenographic style.
2. Later while meditating he visualized all the incidents of that very day in a sense to get spiritual lessons from that day's scene. So in his writing he depicted the very scene of the day as a spectator not as a writer or interpreter. So instead of calling himself an author who colours facts in his own peculiar way, Mahendranath Gupta calls himself a recorder. So on the title page we find mentioned 'Recorded by 'M".
3. In the very scene where he himself is present, at the time of writing he disguises himself in the pseudonym '*M*' or '*Master Mahashaya*' or '*Mahim*'. This unique mode of description of the scene highlights effectively the main character of the scene i.e. Sri Ramakrishna.
4. His meticulous writing describes the other related matters like the description of the site, the descriptions of the people present, natural scenery, and other minute details.
5. His writings in the *Kathamrita* are a useful tool for studying the geographical, ecological, social and demographical idea of the then society.

Another type of incidence of narrating the scene is found in the Mahabharata where *Sanjay*, the charioteer and minister of King *Dhritarashtra* narrates the whole Kurukshetra war to the king. As the king is blind, he wants to know the news of the war. *Sanjay* who is gifted with power of seeing events at a distance, granted by the Rishi Vyasa, is employed for describing the details of the war held between *Kauravas* and *Pandavas*. But in the whole process he is only the spectator and narrator. In no way he is involved in the

1. http://d.lib.rochester.edu/teams/text/whatley-saints-lives-in-middle-english-collections-life-of-st-benedict-introduction

whole scene. He is completely away from the whole scene. His narration of the war to *Dhritarashtra* no way adds any extra flavour to the main facts and incidents of Mahabharata. So in this respect the narration of the scene by Mahendranath is somewhat different from that of *Sanjay.*

At the very outset of Mahendranath's writings one verse from the Bhagavatam is quoted which gives the motto of the writing to the reader. -

Tava kathāmrtam tapta-jīvanam
kavibhir īditam kalmasāpaham
śravana-mańgalam śrīmad ātatam
bhuvi grnanti ye bhūri-dā janāh

The nectar of Your words and the descriptions of Your activities are the life and soul of those suffering in this material world. These narrations, transmitted by learned sages, eradicate one's sinful reactions and bestow good fortune upon whoever hears them. These narrations are broadcast all over the world and are filled with spiritual power. Certainly those who spread the message of Godhead are most munificent[1].

The very beginning of the narration gives a lofty message to humanity. It is not only helpful to remove the sufferings of the humanity but also bestow good fortune and blessings to all for leading a life of an enlightened citizen. The word *Kathamrita* is collected from the above verse by the writer. In the name *Sri Sri Ramakrishna Kathamrita* two words *Ramakrishna* and *Kathamrita* are present. Here both the words are duly significant for the formation of the title of the book. According to the Sanskrit grammar the two words are joined by *Tatpurusha samasa* i.e. as a Determinative Compound by the rule *shashthi samarthena.* So it implies *Ramakrishnasya Kathamritam* meaning 'Nectarine words of Ramakrishna'. Here the emphasis is on the *uttarapada* i.e. *Kathamritam.* Thus it is Mahendranath Gupta's emphasis on the ideas of Ramakrishna and not just the person. So it is not a biography but a verbatim record of his ideas. This is a serious attempt on the part of the Ramakrishna Movement to safeguard the ideas preached by the man and not to make a hype of the personality alone which would have weakened the power otherwise. On the other hand, Mahendranath Gupta did not exclude the very word *Ramakrishna* from the title and name it just *Kathamrita.* This too has a well thought reason behind. The ideas, experiences and goals which Ramakrishna speaks of in the *Kathamrita* are very much embodied in his personality. In

1. http://kksongs.org/songs/t/tavakathamrtamtapta.html

fact if Ramakrishna is the source of a river high on the top of the mountains, *Kathamrita* is the river which flows down to the plains. Just as the source and the river are inseparable so are Ramakrishna and his *Kathamrita.* Moreover the lofty personality of Sri Ramakrishna would have remained inaccessible to the common masses if it did not melt down as the river of *Kathamrita.* In addition the lay person needs a personality where the ideas are fructified without which the theoretical ideas do not appeal much. Thus Mahendranath Gupta presents both the man and his message, both *Ramakrishna* and his *Kathamrita* in the very title of his book so that on one hand the ideas are broadcast and on the other hand the practicability and verity of these ideas are verified from the very life of Ramakrishna presented in his various moods and expressions in the dramatic scenes of the *Kathamrita.* Thus in this wonderful book we find Ramakrishna explaining various states of *Samadhi*, and himself merging in that state while describing it as a live demonstration of his words. Or he gives references to his direct experiences to illustrate a point. Thus the title though primarily focuses the ideas of Ramakrishna but consequentially pulls in the life, experiences and personality of Ramakrishna with the same weightage.

Highlighting the uniqueness of Mahendranath Gupta in the history of Hagiography Aldous Huxley, the renowned historian writes in his foreword to 'The Gospel of Sri Ramakrishna' the English translation of "*Sri Sri Ramakrishna Kathamrita*" by Swami Nikhilananda, where he demarcates Mahendranath Gupta from the prevalent trends of omitting details by auto-biographers, introducing interpretations by the reporters and incompetence in recording, presenting and comprehending the facts by the followers –

> *When we leave the field of art for that of spiritual religion, the scarcity of competent reporters becomes even more strongly marked. Of the day-to-day life of the great theocentric saints and contemplatives we know, in the great majority of cases, nothing whatever. Many, it is true, have recorded their doctrines in writing, and a few, such as St. Augustine, Suso and St. Teresa, have left us autobiographies of the greatest value. But, all doctrinal writing is in some measure formal and impersonal, while the autobiographer tends to omit what he regards as trifling matters and suffers from the further disadvantage of being unable to say how he strikes other people and in what way he affects their lives. Moreover, most saints have left neither writings nor self-portraits, and for knowledge of their lives, their characters and their teachings, we are forced to rely upon the records made by their disciples who,*

> *in most cases, have proved themselves singularly incompetent as reporters and biographers. Hence the special interest attaching to this enormously detailed account of the daily life and conversations of Sri Ramakrishna*[1].

With this background Aldous Huxley mentions the special characteristics of Mahendranath Gupta, which makes him an exceptional and gifted recorder–

> *"M", as the author modestly styles himself, was peculiarly qualified for his task. To a reverent love for his master, to a deep and experiential knowledge of that master's teaching, he added a prodigious memory for the small happenings of each day and a happy gift for recording them in an interesting and realistic way. Making good use of his natural gifts and of the circumstances in which he found himself, "M" produced a book unique, so far as my knowledge goes, in the literature of hagiography. No other saint has had so able and indefatigable a Boswell*[2].

Our attempt is to illustrate different aspects of the novel book Sri Rāmakrishna Kathāmrita through some thoughtful research papers from different Scholars. The Scholars in this monograph belong to different fields and they have analyzed many significant issues of the monograph through their thoughtful research papers. Through all the research papers the two pivots i.e. *Ramakrishna* and his teachings which have depicted in the *Kathamrita* have come again and again to give the reader a comprehensive understanding about theme of the book.

---

1. http://www.wearesentience.com/uploads/7/2/9/3/7293936/gospel_srk.pdf
2. http://www.wearesentience.com/uploads/7/2/9/3/7293936/gospel_srk.pdf

Contents

1 The Gospel of Sri Ramakrishna and the life of M

Swami Prabhananda

We learn from the diary of M. that on 2 April 1905, Holy Mother told Nikunja Devi, the wife of M., in the presence of Golap Ma, 'I bless that this book (the *Kathamrita)* may spread very widely so that all people may know the Master.' Again, on the day previous to the Kali puja day that year, Holy Mother said to Nikunja Devi, 'Daughter-in-law, tell your husband that I am blessing him from the core of my heart.' We wonder if M. ever dreamt that Holy Mother's blessings would bear fruit in the way they have done in recent times which have been witnessing an unprecedented spurt in the sale of the Bengali edition of the book, with one of the new single volume editions of the book alone registering sales of a quarter million copies in the first month and a half of its publication.

Many people celebrated the *Kathamrita* centenary during 1982-83; and Sri Ma Trust, Chandigarh, published a commemorative volume entitled *Sri Sri Ramakrishna Kathamrita Centenary Memorial,* although the first volume of the Kathamrita was published first on March, 1902. Here it must be noted that the *Kathamrita* is not a reproduction of M.'s diary, and that M. did not even think of the word 'Kathamrita' as the title of his articles or book before 1898. M. met his Master, Sri Ramakrishna, on a Sunday in the month of February, 1882. Unfortunately M. did not remember the exact date of this meeting. It was certainly not 26 February 1882, as is popularly held. Among the three probable dates M. has mentioned in his diary, circumstantial evidence almost conclusively points to 19 February 1882 as the date of his first meeting. Evidently, M. did not record immediately the proceedings of this meeting, nor of the next six meetings which he had with Sri Ramakrishna, in quick succession. Of these, the proceedings of the first five only have been reported in the *Gospel;* the remaining two have been left out.

However, soon thereafter, perhaps six weeks following the first meeting, M. started recording the proceedings of these meetings in his diary. Being the headmaster of a school, he could be with the Master only on Sundays and other holidays. He kept short diary notes of the incidents, discussions, and discourses that took place in the course of his association with Sri Ramakrishna. Evidently he kept these diaries for his personal use. Once M. said:

> I used to note down the Master's words in order to think about them in the intervals before I met him again, so that the impressions made on my mind might not be overlaid by the stress of worldly work and responsibilities. It was thus for my own benefit that I first made the notes so that 1 might comprehend his teachings more perfectly.

When a great devotee of Sri Ramakrishna, Girish Chandra Ghosh, wanted to glance through the diary, M. declined, saying that its contents could be disclosed only after his death. But circumstances forced M. to change his decision. He devoted himself to transcribing his diary into a biographical narrative, and he did it in four stages.

First, he published a collection of Sri Ramakrishna's teachings under the title *Paramhamsadever Ukti.* Only its third edition, published in 1892 by Satchidananda Gitaratna, has been traced. The collection was done with the help of one Sadhu Mahindranath Gupta. Recent research clearly suggests that both Satchidananda Gitaratna and Sadhu Mahindranath Gupta were pseudonyms of M. On seeing the first edition of this publication in Bengali, Swami Vivekananda congratulated M. on 7 February 1889, writing. 'Thanks a million! You have hit Ramkristo in the right point. Few, alas, few understand him.'

Second, repeatedly inspired by Holy Mother, Sri Sarada Devi, and by some instruction he received from Sri Ramakrishna in a dream, M. launched upon a daring enterprise. Instead of presenting Sri Ramakrishna's teachings in isolation, he now decided to present Sri Ramakrishna and his words in a realistic setting. Holding those diary notes in front of him, M. would meditate on them for hours to reconstruct the scenes, the dialogues, and the atmosphere he had witnessed so long ago. He was not merely recalling the past but was actually reliving those blessed hours. One of the outcomes of this exercise was the *Gospel.* Around 1897, M. published in English four booklets under the titled *Leaf from the Gospel of Sri Ramakrishna.* On reading the second leaflet, Swami Vivekananda wrote him on 24 November 1897, 'Now you are doing just the thing. .. You will have many blessings on you and many more curses but *vaisahi sab kal banta saheb* (That is always the way of the world, Sir.)' M. read his manuscripts, some in English and others in Bengali, at the Sunday meetings of the Ramakrishna Mission Association held at Balaram Bose's house in Calcutta. The Bengali monthly *Tattvamanjari* demanded that the words of the Master should be published in the vernacular. As prophesied by Swami Vivekananda, M.'s work was hailed by many as a precious gift; but there were some hostile criticisms too. Some dubbed the *Gospel* as a mere Sunday report of M., and said that the Master had other superior teachings which he did not reveal to M. Hurt by such uncharitable remarks from some familiar quarters, M. felt discouraged. However, the appreciation of persons like Swami Vivekananda and Holy Mother dispelled all his doubts. Holy Mother wrote him from Jayrambati, 'Once he (Sri Ramakrishna) had kept all that in safe custody with you; now, as he thinks necessary, he is getting it published... All that you have recorded is true. One day when I was listening to what you had recorded, I thought that he himself was speaking.' Thus being assured, M. hurriedly started publishing instalments of the *Kathamrita* in seventeen popular Bengali journals like *Udbodhan, Tattvamanjari, Nababharat, Sahitya, Hindu Patrika,* etc. from 1897 onwards.

Third, Swami Trigunatitananda, editor of the *Udbodhan,* the Bengali organ of the Ramakrishna Order, published in one volume everything M. had already published in various journals. Thus, on 11 March 1902, the first volume of *Sri Sri Ramakrishna Kathamrita* came out. This brought heaps of praise for M. Still, he could not summon enough self-confidence to proceed further. At such a moment Sri Ramakrishna guided him through a dream. On 14 October 1902, M. saw the Master in a dream. M. touched his feet. The Master assured him saying, I have taken your responsibility. I am holding you. Why do you worry so much?' M. begged pardon of the Master. The Master then repeatedly assured him. Henceforward, M. assumed a rather aggressive posture. He himself took the initiative, and published the second, third, and fourth volumes of the *Kathamrita* in 1904,1908, and 1910 respectively. The year 1925 saw the publication of its appendices in the form of a booklet. And the fifth volume was with the printers when M. passed away on 4 June 1932.

Fourth, to meet the growing demand of the readers Vol. I of the *Gospel,* translated into English by the author himself, was published in 1907 by the Brahmavadin Office, Madras. Again, based on the English translation of some of M.'s diary notes, Swami Abhedananda published Vol. I of the *Gospel* in December 1907, from the Vedanta Society, New York. A second edition of the

'M' (Mahendra Nath Gupta)

first one, revised by M. himself, was brought out by the Ramakrishna Math, Madras in 1911. The following year the Vedanta Society of San Francisco brought out a reprint of the Madras edition. Its second part was published by the Madras Math in 1922. And the full translation of the entire *Kathamrita,* by Swami Nikhilananda, appeared first in 1942.

The *Gospel* created a stir, particularly among intellectuals. Aldous Huxley observed, 'No other saint has had so able and indefatigable a Boswell. Never have the small events of a contemplative's daily life been described with such wealth of intimate details. Never have the casual and unstudied utterances of a great religious teacher been set down with so minute a fidelity.' On reading a part of the English *Gospel* that was published at that time, Monsieur Romain Rolland wrote to M. on 10 October 1928, 'Thank you for having transmitted to us the benefit of the benign smile of your Master.' The well-known modern novelist Christopher Isherwood, who wrote a popular biography of Sri Ramakrishna, finds in the atmosphere of the *Gospel* narrative the quality of 'nowness'. Being in the occasional company of Sri Ramakrishna, M. was aware of this and tried to narrate it with a 'thankful wonder'. The style of the *Gospel* is Biblical in its simplicity. It is as simple as Sri Ramakrishna himself. It takes the readers straight to the truth, and not through any metaphysical maze.

Though the *Gospel* is mainly a record of the teachings of Sri Ramakrishna, it is also a biography of the great Master in the last and most important phase of his life. According to Harold Nicholson, an authentic biography must have the three elements of truth, individuality and art.[1] The *Gospel* has all these and something more. But what is the real 'gospel' (or glad tidings, as the word literally means) that the *Kathamrita* has brought to humanity? It is the message of the One Eternal Religion discovered and vitalized by Sri Ramakrishna. This special feature was pointed out by Swami Vivekananda when he said, 'Other teachers have taught special religions which bear their names, but this great teacher of the nineteenth century made no claim for himself. He left every religion undisturbed because he had realized that in reality, they are all part and parcel of one eternal religion.'[2] Into whatever category we may put it, this piece of hagiographic literature has a great charm for it can certainly help men to find peace and happiness even in the midst of the antireligious philosophies of today.

The act of writing about a real person, whether in a biography or in a memoir, instantly deprives his personality of several dimensions, instantly transforms him through print into a limited image. M. minimized this shortcoming by combining annotative and analytical methods with the synthetic method. When questioned about his portrayal of his Master, M. explained, 'We have tried to take different photographs of the Master. Every shot provides details of Sri Ramakrishna in a different setting.' More significant than this is the fact that M.'s creative genius enabled him to project Sri Ramakrishna's detached photographs with such continuity and speed that the effect produced combines motion and life. We find in front of us, as it were, a living Sri Ramakrishna smiling, talking, cracking jokes, singing, dancing, and occasionally diving into the ocean of bliss—always with a bewitching smile on his lips. The whole book is filled, through and through, with the loftiness, tranquility, and gravity of the highest spiritual experiences. But this is harmoniously blended with the naturalness and spontaneity of real life, including the apparently trivial incidents of day-to-day life. Some even suspected that M. had foisted his own ideas on the illiterate priest of Dakshineswar. One such person was N. Bangarayya of Madras. He came to Calcutta, talked with M. for three days, and was convinced that the disciple's style of speaking was entirely different from that of the Master.[3] Sri Ramakrishna was unique, and unique were his words. N. N. Gupta, an eyewitness, truly remarked, 'No other man within the memory of man spoke as Ramakrishna spoke.' And M. had the unique credit of presenting those words undistorted.

Unlike other scriptures, the *Gospel* does not demand any preparation on the part of the reader. The teachings are of universal application. They satisfy the learned and the ignorant alike. A man of devotion, a man of work, a man of knowledge—all are inspired equally, not excluding the atheist. Realizing the frailties and inadequacies of human beings, Sri Ramakrishna assured everyone of the glad tidings'; and M. has brought that message of hope within the reach of all.

We now turn to another important aspect of the *Gospel*. Notwithstanding his great literary talent, the production of the *Kathamrita* was but a by-product of M.'s Ramakrishna-*sadhana* to which he had committed himself ever since his first meeting with Sri Ramakrishna in February 1882. Academically the most brilliant among the Master's disciples, M. was then serving as the headmaster of a high school. By that time he had had four children, three sons and a daughter. Bitter family squabbles made the peace loving M. so despondent that he actually walked out one night into the wide world with the thought of putting an end to his life. Circumstances brought him, however, to Sri Ramakrishna at Dakshineswar. M. considered this meeting the greatest event' of his life. Sri Ramakrishna welcomed him saying, 'I can see from the signs of your eyes, brows, and face that you are a yogi. You look like a yogi who has just left his seat of meditation.' Deeply moved by Sri Ramakrishna's magically plastic and sensitive disposition, attractive smile, charming voice, and deep spiritual experiences, M. opened himself freely to his presence and influence. His rudderless life found a new creative direction and mission. M. accepted Sri Ramakrishnaas his mentor and saviour in crossing the ocean of life. He would often repeat the salutation prayer:

Samsararnava ghoreyah karnadhara svarupakah
Namostu Ramakrishnaya tasmai Sri Gurave namah

(Composed by Swami Abhedananda)

'Salutations to Ramakrishna, the Guru, who stands firm as the helmsman while ferrying people across the dangerous ocean of worldliness.'

From that moment M. had a new lease of life. Moreover, he gradually blossomed into an evangelist of the Godman.

Sri Ramakrishna, who could see into the depths of M. made some significant statements about him. M. regarded them as *mahavakyas.* They were fifty-two in number. He recorded them reverentially in his diary. Among them we find Sri Ramakrishna's saying, 'I recognized you on hearing you read *Chaitanya Bhagavatam.* You are my own. The same substance, like father and son... Before you came here, you didn't know who you were. Now you will know.' In the presence of Ishwarchandra Vidyasagar, Sri Ramakrishna said of him, 'He is a nice young man and is sound at the core. He is like the river Phalgu. The surface is covered with sand; but if you dig a little, you will find water flowing underneath.' He also said: 'Once (in a vision) I saw Gauranga and his devotees singing kirtan in the Panchavati. I think I saw Balaram there, and you too.' Referring to M. the Master once told Devendra Majumdar, 'The inundated water has united the drain with the pond. Now the water is quivering a little— He and I have become one.' The thirty-sixth *mahavakya* states, 'Illumine him, Mother, otherwise how will he illumine others in turn? Why have you thrown him into the world? Otherwise, had this firework been ignited, how it would have excelled!' However, in another *mahavakya* the Master assured M. by praying to the Mother, 'Mother, please reveal yourself to him now and then. Let him pursue both. What will it do by making him give up everything at once, Mother! Well, you may do whatever you like in the end. If you want him to give up everything, do so.'

From the very beginning, Sri Ramakrishna taught M., 'Do all your duties, but keep your mind on God. Live with all—with wife and children, father and mother—and serve them. Treat them as if they were very dear to you, but you know in your heart of hearts that they do not belong to you.' While M. practised the spiritual disciplines prescribed by the Master, the latter protected him as a mother bird protects her fledglings from rain and wind by spreading her wings over them. As M. proceeded, he became diluted in the ocean of thought of Sri Ramakrishna. Sri Ramakrishna once said to M., 'You don't want anything from me, but you love to see me and hear my words. My mind also dwells on you. I wonder how you are and why you don't come.' According to the science of homeopathy, the strength of a medicine increases as its dilution increases. As M.'s dilution in the thought of Sri Ramakrishna increased, he became richer in his spiritual attainments.

If those fifty-two statements of Sri Ramakrishna be regarded as *shruti,* Sri Ramakrishna's specific commands to him, eighty-five in number, were held by him as *smriti.* Here are a few examples of them. 'Meditate on God, you have much work to do'; 'Visit this place, just as one cleanses a brass pot daily'; 'Advise the youths who call upon you'; 'Bring Bankim (a boy devotee) here, otherwise you instruct him; your words will bring him illumination'; 'Whenever you fail to visit here, write me a postcard'; 'Massage my feet.'

M. not only carefully shifted and catalogued the *mahavakyas* and *adeshas* (commands) from the sayings of the Master, but he sincerely followed them in letter and spirit. He served the Master in his humble way. Moreover, in spite of his natural modesty, he was persuaded by the Master to sing devotional songs and even to participate in devotional dances along with other devotees. And his endeavours were amply rewarded. Even as late as 1 March 1899, M. dreamt that he was passionately singing, 'O Lord, must all my days pass by so utterly in vain?' and that on hearing this, the Master passed into deep *samadhi.*

Thus the process of being and becoming went on in M. Like a sunflower with its face always turned towards the sun, M., depending entirely on Sri

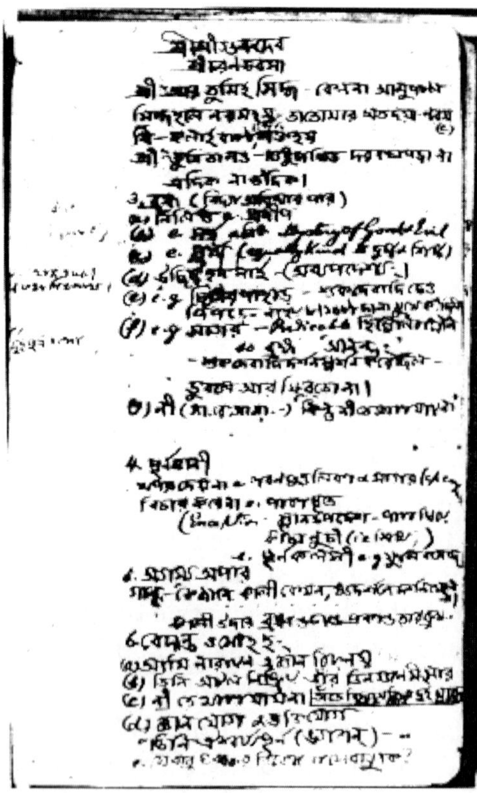

A page from M.'s Diary of the Kathamrita

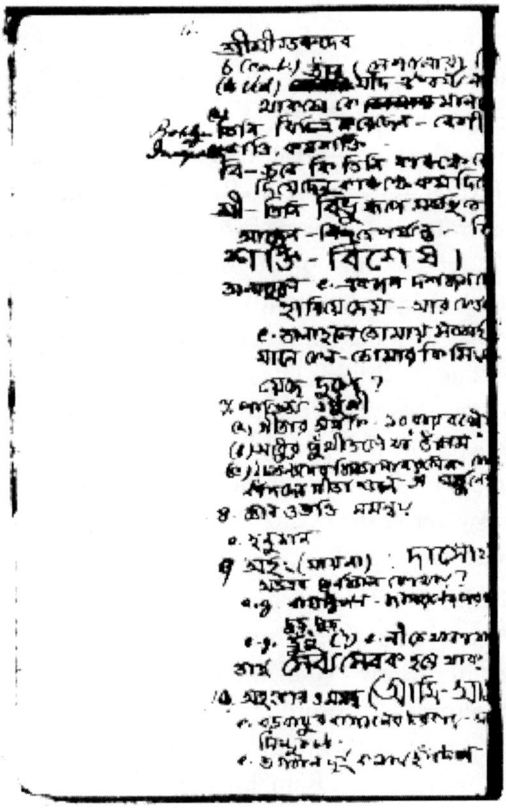

A page from M.'s Diary of the Kathamrita

Ramakrishna, moved forward in the path to the divine. He felt an urge to renounce family life and become a monk. Sri Ramakrishna prevented him, saying, 'Mother has told me that you have to do a little of Her work—you will have to teach "Bhagavata", the word of God, to humanity. The Mother keeps a *Bhagavata* pundit bound to the world.' But even this could not fully pacify him. Then, one evening when M. was alone with him at Dakshineswar, Sri Ramakrishna said in an ecstatic mood, 'Let nobody think that if he does not do Mother's work, it would remain undone. The Mother can turn even a straw into a teacher.' This settled once and for all M.'s hesitation and doubt. In obedience to his guru's command, M. lived outwardly as a householder but inwardly all-absorbed in the Divine. His life exemplified the Master's teaching that an ideal householder must be a *grihastha sannyasi* who practises inner renunciation. He must live like a good maidservant of a rich family, loving and caring properly for the children of the house but knowing always that her real house and children are elsewhere. Sri Ramakrishna kept a loving watch on M., who sincerely followed the Master's advice in handling the worldly problems as well as the spiritual disciplines prescribed by him.

One day Sri Ramakrishna was heard to utter in an ecstatic mood, 'Mother, I cannot talk any further—give power to Ram, Mahendra, Vijay, and others; let them do your work from now onwards.' Sri Ramakrishna chose Mahendra (M.) as his faithful recorder, commissioned him to keep a record of his teachings, tutored him in the art, and frequently discussed with him what had been spoken. Thus the Master guided him in keeping a correct and authentic record of his ideas, views, and teachings. The fiftieth *mahavakya* of Sri Ramakrishna was, 'He has no trace of ego'. True to this, this humble messenger, when someone approached him for spiritual guidance, would often say, 'I am an insignificant person. But I live by the side of an ocean and I keep with me a few pitchers of the water of the ocean. When a visitor comes, I entertain him with that. What else can I speak but his words?'

The evangelist M. gradually turned into a living gospel. His life, so long centred on the Master, became full of the thought of the Master. Like St. Paul, he could say, 'The life I now live in the flesh, I live by the faith in the Son of God.' One eyewitness has recorded: 'Though his exterior was Mahendra Gupta, his interior was united with Sri Ramakrishna through his deliberating, thinking, and meditating on Sri Ramakrishna and continuously practising in life, his teachings... He did not retain what is called the 'fiery independent spirit of self-assertion'.

He completely gave up his inherent, fiery, independent thinking and desire for self-assertion. Sri Ramakrishna had filled his heart to the full. The purpose of his living was only to serve as a reflection of Sri Ramakrishna.[4]

He considered himself a mere machine driven by Sri Ramakrishna. It was from this firm faith he used to defend himself, saying, 'Have I composed this [the *Gospel*]? The Master himself has done his work. Appearing in me as the intellect and will-power, the Master made me write. He is the Master; he is the doer—whether we understand this or not.'[5] Toward the last phase of his life when some admirer of his attributed the production of the *Gospel* to his talent, M. protested, saying, 'He [the Master] is everything. So long as the tram car is connected to the live wire, the car moves, the lamps burn, and the fans work. But the moment the car is detached, nothing works. Now I fully realize that, taking me by the hand, he is prodding me forward, and surely he will lead me for the rest of my life.'[6]

As M. advanced in his journey to the temple of the Divine, one could notice another development in him. The seed of great possibilities that was sown in his heart gradually germinated and sprouted forth into a plant. As it grew into a fine tree, there appeared besides the rich foliage a beautiful bloom, rich in colour and fragrance. The story of this development is quite fascinating. During the early days, when his mental horizon had just turned crimson with the rise of the Ramakrishna-sun, he declared that he had never before seen such knowledge, ecstatic love, faith in God, renunciation, and catholicity in anybody other than Sri Ramakrishna. As his inner life deepened further, it dawned on him that Christ, Sri Chaitanya and Sri Ramakrishna—all the three were one and the same. After he had drunk a few sips of the nectar of divine bliss in the company of Sri Ramakrishna, he one day submitted to Sri Ramakrishna, 'You are as infinite as He, of whom we have been talking. Truly, no one can fathom your depth.' His poetic temperament found nice expression when M. said to the Master, 'God sports through you. This I have realized, that you are the instrument and God is the Master. God has created other beings as if with a machine, but yourself with His own hand.' As M. progressed in his Ramakrishna-sadhana, his inner life continued to blossom forth. On 28 July 1885, M., at his Master's behest, repeated before him, 'You told us to imagine a field extending to the horizon and beyond. It extends without any obstruction; but we cannot see it on account of a wall in front of us. In that wall there is a round hole. Through the hole we see a part of that infinite field.' The Master asked him, 'Tell me what that hole is.' M. replied, 'You are that hole. Through you can be seen everything—that Infinite meadow without any end.' The Master patted the disciple's back, expressing his pleasure at his understanding. The disciple's understanding continued to grow deeper. He finally set up in his heart a perennial 'Dakshineswar' where Sri Ramakrishna, the God-incarnate, sported eternally with his loving devotee. He further shared with the worldly people the bliss he derived through his regular communion with the God-incarnate.

From being a chronicler, M. gradually changed into an evangelist dedicated to the cause of the Master. But for what? An idealist as he was, he dreamt of a golden future. In a letter addressed to a swami of the Ramakrishna Order in 1928, M. wrote:

This time the Godman of modern times has appeared in this

> country.....Henceforth the foreign culture, that is, the so-called material civilization of the West, will not be adored for long. Sex-worship and dollar-worship, it is hoped, will disappear by the grace of the Lord. 'Pure devotion', 'Human life's aim is God-realization', etc., as upheld by the Master, will henceforth be pursued. And your life and character, and not mere lectures, will arouse the consciousness of the people, no doubt.

Thus, in his daily life, M. caught the glint of his Master's splendour and glory. It shone through all he said, all he did, all he was.

Sri Ramakrishna had noticed the coexistence of the attitudes of 'servant-I' and 'I-am-That' in M. Though these two constituted his personality, only the attitude of 'servant-I' found predominance in the life and deeds of M. as the chronicler of the Master. Bathed in the glorious light of Ramakrishna, 'Master Mahashay', as M. was popularly called, was a typical Indian *rishi* who used to draw crowds of spiritual seekers, as well as strangers, around him. One such person, an Englishman, has left on record his impression of him. He wrote:

> Night after night I come, less to hear the pious utterances of Master Mahashaya than to bask in the spiritual sunshine of his presence. The atmosphere around him is tender and beautiful, gentle and loving; he has found some inner bliss, and the radiation of it seems palpable. Often I forget his words, but I cannot forget his benignant personality. That which drew him again to Ramakrishna seems to draw me to Mahashaya also, and I begin to understand how potent must have been the influence of the teacher when the pupil exercises such a fascination upon me.[7]

With his own individuality lost in the light of Sri Ramakrishna, M.'s true nature shone in the glory of his Master. His true life which began as the chronicler soon became a glorious commentary on the *Gospel* itself. His thoughts, actions, and utterings—all these reflected Sri Ramakrishna and his glory. Spiritual aspirants felt attracted by the angelic appearance of M. with his silky, white beard and large lustrous eyes. They regarded him as 'his Master's voice.' In him they could also see his Master's reflection. He was a true evangelist of the first order, and his words and actions evoked nothing but the thoughts of his Master and the image of his Master. Thus brilliantly shone the Mahendra-moon, a satellite of the Ramakrishna-sun, till 4 June 1932, when he offered his last prayer, 'Mother—Gurudev—take me in your arms.' His prayer was granted. The disciple's spirit reunited with the Master. Nevertheless, M., as the chronicler and evangelist, continues to live in the *Gospel* side by side with his Master—he as *anoraniyan* (smaller than the smallest) and his Master as *mahatomahiyan* (greater than the greatest). They have for all practical purposes become one for eternity.

REFERENCES

1. Harold Nicholson, *The Development of English Biography,* 1959, P. 157
2. *Complete Works,* Vol. IV, p. 187
3. *Prabuddha Bharata,* June 1949, pp. 228-29
4. Mahendranath Dutta, *Mastermasayer Anudhyan* (Bengali), p. 19
5. *Udbodhan,* Vol. 67, No. 8, p. 434
6. Ibid., p. 316
7. Paul Brunton, *A Search in Secret India,* 1934, p.133

• • •

2

Personality of Sri Ramakrishna as it emerges from the Gospel

Swami Mukhyananda

Sri Ramakrishna has been, as Christopher Isherwood has termed it in his biography of Sri Ramakrishna, "a phenomenon"[1] in the religion-spiritual firmament of the world. He rose on the horizon like a spiritual sun whose morning glory enveloped the world within a few decades of his appearance. Those who had the poetic vision and sage insight to catch the beauty of that glorious dawn hailed it in wondrous words and announced it to mankind both in the East and the West.

Keshab Chandra Sen in the East and Max Müller in the West were among the earliest to scatter the brilliant rays of the life of Sri Ramakrishna over a wide circle by their writings and speeches. However, it was Swami Vivekananda, the illustrious disciple of Sri Ramakrishna, who understood the full grandeur and vast scope of his seraphic Master's great and profound life and its immense meaning and lasting significance for the religious life of India and of humanity at large. Exclaimed Vivekananda:

> "The time was ripe for one to be born, who in one body would have the brilliant intellect of Shankara and the wonderfully expansive, infinite heart of Chaitanya; one who would see in every sect the same spirit working, the same God; one who would see God in every being, one whose heart would weep for the poor, for the weak, for the outcast, for the downtrodden, for everyone in this world, inside India or outside India; and at the same time whose grand brilliant intellect would conceive of such noble thoughts as would harmonize all conflicting sects, not only in India, but outside India, and bring a marvelous harmony, the universal religion of head and heart into existence. Such a man was born, and I had the good fortune to sit at his feet for years. There he lived, without any book learning whatsoever;

> this great intellect never learnt even to write his own name, but the most brilliant graduates of our university found in him an intellectual giant. He was a strange man, this Sri Ramakrishna Paramhamsa, the great Sri Ramakrishna, the fulfillment of the Indian sages; the sage for the time, one whose teaching is just now, in the present time, most beneficial."[2]

"Without studying Ramakrishna Paramhamsa first, one can never understand the real import of the Vedas, the Vedanta, of the Bhagavata and the other Puranas. His life is a searchlight of infinite power thrown upon the whole mass of Indian religious thought. He was the living commentary to the Vedas and to their aim. He lived in one life the whole cycle of the national religious existence in India... This man had in fifty years lived the five thousand years of national spiritual life and so raised himself to be an object-lesson for future generations... His life is the living commentary to the Vedas of all nations. People will come to know him by degrees... He is the latest and the most perfect (of the Avatars) – the concentrated embodiment of knowledge, love, renunciation, catholicity and the desire to serve mankind."[3]

Romain Rolland, the eminent sage and savant of France, was the best interpreter to the West of the profound message of Ramakrishna-Vivekananda through his immortal study on them in two volumes: 'Ramakrishna the Man-God and the Universal Gospel of Vivekananda' (1926). Writes he:

> "I am bringing to Europe, as yet unaware of it, the fruit of a new autumn, a new message of the Soul, the symphony of India, bearing the name of Ramakrishna. It can be shown (and we shall not fail to point out) that this symphony, like those of our classical masters, is built up of a hundred different musical elements emanating from the past...

The man whose image I here evoke was the consummation of two thousand years of the spiritual life of three hundred million people... He was a little village Brahmin of Bengal, whose outer life was set in a limited frame without striking incident, outside the political and social activities of his time. But his inner life embraced the whole multiplicity of men and gods. It was a part of the very source of Energy, the Divine Shakti."[4]

While the limited and scattered utterances of Vivekananda about Sri Ramakrishna are profound and reveal the Great Master at his best, and the biography of Romain Rolland interprets the Life and Message of the Master superbly in the world-wide religious context, equating Sri Ramakrishna with Jesus Christ, it is in The Gospel of Sri Ramakrishna, originally recorded by M. (Mahendranath Gupta) in Bengali, that we get the minute details of his varied moods and movements, his acts and attitudes, and his teachings and trances. Here the Great Master comes alive before us in all vividness; scene after scene of his ecstatic life unfolds itself before our mental vision, and we feel as one of the participants in the great drama of his life, in his sportfull lila.

In his Foreword to the Gospel, the English translation of M.'s Bengali 'Sri Sri Ramakrishna Kathamrita' by Swami Nikhilananda, which we make use of for the purpose of this study,[5] Aldous Huxley writes:

> "Never have the small events of a contemplative's daily life been described with such wealth of intimate detail. Never have the casual and unstudied utterances of a great religious teacher been set down with so minute a fidelity… what a scholastic philosopher would call the 'accidents' of Ramakrishna's life were intensely Hindu and, therefore, so far as we in the West are concerned, unfamiliar and hard to understand; its 'essence', however, was intensely mystical and therefore universal. To read through these conversations in which mystical doctrine alternates with an unfamiliar kind of humour, and where discussions of the oddest aspects of Hindu mythology give place to the most profound and subtle utterances about the nature of Ultimate Reality, is in itself a liberal education in humility, tolerance, and suspense of judgment."

Nikhilananda says in his preface to the translation:

> "Sri Ramakrishna was almost illiterate. He never clothed his thoughts in formal language. His words sought to convey his direct realisation of Truth. His conversation was in a village patois (of Bengal). Therein lies its charm. In order to explain to his listeners an abstruse philosophy, he like Christ before him, used with telling effect homely parables and illustrations culled from his observation of the daily life around him... The words of Sri Ramakrishna have already exerted a tremendous influence in the land of his birth. Savants of Europe have found in his words the ring of universal truth. But these words were not the product of intellectual cognition; they were rooted in direct experience. Hence, to students of religion, psychology, and physical science, these experiences of the Master are of immense value for the understanding of religious phenomena in general. No doubt, Sri Ramakrishna was

> a Hindu of the Hindus; yet his experiences transcended the limits of the dogmas and creeds of Hinduism. Mystics of religions other than Hinduism will find in Sri Ramakrishna's experiences a corroboration of the experiences of their own prophets and seers. And this is very important today for the resuscitation of religious values."

Many people know fairly Sri Ramakrishna as the Prophet of harmony of religions; some people comprehend his universal dimensions and his great role in the spiritual regeneration of mankind; may be a few realize that he has opened up new vistas and horizons for spiritual attainments; but very few know the different aspects of his versatile, living, vibrant, divine personality. For Sri Ramakrishna samadhi (spiritual trance) was a constant and natural mode of divine knowledge and wisdom, (p. 175).[6] In the Gospel, he is often seen to go into indrawn moods, ecstasies, and trances.[7] An atmosphere of devotion, singing and dancing in divine emotion, and conversation centred on God and bhakti, pervades the Gospel, though other aspects are not lacking, as we shall see.[8] But most people, devoid of broad understanding and keen insight, form the idea of Sri Ramakrishna only as a great bhakta of the Divine Mother, childlike, always soft and indrawn, and little aware of, or unconcerned with, the world and its affairs. While such a view is partly true, this estimate overlooks the rather important dimensions of Sri Ramakrishna's many-faceted great personality and it shows lack of understanding of Sri Ramakrishna's deep interest in the spiritual welfare of mankind.[9] We find in several speeches, write-ups and films on Sri Ramakrishna, that he is depicted as a goody-goody bhakta and we miss there the inner strength of his personality in his dealings with vastly varied types of people, and his leonine character. We get only the मृदूनि कुसुमादपि (softer than a flower) aspect of his great mind, but not the वज्रादपि कठोराणि (harder than diamond) aspect.

We may get some corrective to the above partial views of people from the presentation of the Master's personality in 'Sri Ramakrishna, the Great Master'[10] (Sri Sri Ramakrishna-lila-prasanga in Bengali) by Swami Saradananda. Further, as Vivekananda has said:

> "According to one's own capacity one has understood Sri Ramakrishna and so is discussing about him. It is not bad either to do so... But if any of his devotees has concluded that what he has understood of him is the only truth, then he is an object of pity... But do not listen to such one-sided estimates. What he was, the concentrated embodiment of how many previous avataras – we could not understand a bit even

spending the whole life in religious austerity. Therefore one has to speak about him with caution and restraint. As are one's capacities, to that extent has he filled one with ideas. One spray from the full ocean of his spirituality, if realized, will make gods of men. Such a synthesis of universal ideas you will not find in the history of the world again. Understand from this who was born in the person of Sri Ramakrishna. When he used to instruct his sannyasin disciples, he would rise from his seat and look about if any householder was coming that way or not. If he found none, then in glowing words he would depict the glory of renunciation and tapasya. As a result of the rousing power of that fiery dispassion, we have renounced the world and become averse to worldliness."[11]

What the Bhagavata (XI.8.5) says about the Avadhuta applies to Sri Ramakrishna very aptly in certain respects:

Munih prasannagambhiro durvigähyo duratyayah,
Anantapäro hyaksobhyah stimitoda ivärnavah.

– The holy sage, his mind fixed in the Self, is placid and profound, difficult to fathom and cross over; he is illimitable and imperturbable, like the ocean with calm waters.

However, if we delve deep into the Gospel, scan it intelligently, and piece together the various incidents and events connected with Sri Ramakrishna and ponder on his words and attitudes, we can get a very vivid, colourful, and balanced picture of Sri Ramakrishna in life. Let us, therefore, address ourselves to this task and see how Sri Ramakrishna emerges before our vision. As the Gospel is a huge work of over a thousand, recording the events of over four years (1882-1886) we shall primarily survey in detail the first chapter which treats of the first meetings of M. with, and his impressions of, the Master[12] and refer to some other events and incidents in other chapters in a general way.

The First Chapter, entitled 'Master and Disciple', records four visits of M. to the Master at Dakshineshwar (near Calcutta), between February 26th (probable date of his first visit) and March 6th, 1882 (probable date of his fourth visit), covering about eight days in which M. unfolds the picture of the Master as he appeared to him. When M. entered Sri Ramakrishna's room at Dakshineshwar with his companion Sidhu for the first time:

"They found him seated on a wooden couch, facing the east. With a smile on his face he was talking of God.[13] The room was full of people, all seated on the floor, drinking in his words in deep silence."

M. stood there speechless and looked on:

> "It was as if he were standing where all the holy places met and as if Sukadeva himself were speaking the word of God, or as if Sri Chaitanya were singing the name and glories of the Lord in Puri with Ramananda, Swarup and other devotees."

"M. looked around him with wonder and said to himself: What a beautiful place! What a charming man! How beautiful his words are! I have no wish to move from this spot."

M., however, goes round the temple-garden and returns to the room and finds the doors shut. Seeing Brinde, the maid, outside, he enquires of her about the Master and learns that he had been living there for a long time. The Master has no need to go on lecture tours. He had a commission from God. He spreads his fragrance from where he is. "The lotus opens and the bees come by themselves,"[14] M. asked her, "Does he read many books?" "Books? Oh dear, no! They are all on his tongue."[15] M. was amazed that Sri Ramakrishna read no books. Sri Ramakrishna was no scholar or pandit. But yet, spiritual wisdom flowed through his lips spontaneously from the depths of truth. M. thought it perhaps was time for evening devotions of the Master. He asked Brinde to seek permission from the Master for himself and Sidhu to meet him. But Brinde replied, "Go right in, children, go in and sit down." The Great Master had no pretensions. He was simple and easy of access to all; no formalities. He did not consider himself a guru.[16]

M. and Sidhu salute the Master on entering. The Master bids them to sit and asks M. about his whereabouts. But M. noticed that:

> "Now and then the Master seemed to become absent-minded. Later he learnt that this mood is called bhava, ecstasy. It is like the state of the angler who has been sitting with his rod: the fish comes and swallows the bait, and the float begins to tremble; the angler is on the alert; he grips the rod and watches the float steadily and eagerly; he will not speak to anyone. Such was the state of Sri Ramakrishna's mind. Later M. heard, and himself noticed, that Sri Ramakrishna would often go into this mood after dusk, sometimes becoming totally unconscious of the outer world."

After a little conversation M. saluted the Master and took his leave. But Sri Ramakrishna did not fail to ask, "Come again", even though his mind was absorbed in the divine mood. It was not to show mere courtesy. It was affection towards those who went to him and his interest in their welfare.[17] On his way home M. began to wonder:

> "Who is this serene-looking man who is drawing me back to him? Is it possible for a man to be great without being a scholar? How wonderful it is! I should like to see him again. He himself said, 'Come again.' "

There was something ethereally attractive in the Master's personality. We find record of it in the Gospel on several occasions. The Master himself reminisces:

> "Can you tell me why all these youngsters, and you people too, visit me? There must be something in me; or why should you all feel such a pull, such an attraction? Once I visited Hriday's house at Sihore. From there I was taken to Shyambazar. I had a vision of Gauranga before I entered the village, and I realised that I should meet Gauranga's devotees there. For seven days and nights I was surrounded by a huge crowd of people. Such attraction! Nothing but kirtan and dancing day and night. People stood in rows on the walls and even were on the trees. I stayed at Natavar Goswami's house. It was crowded day and night. In the morning I would run away to the house of a weaver for a little rest. There too I found that people would gather after a few minutes." (p. 495).

On his second visit, one or two days later, M. found the Master just like an ordinary man. As it was still winter (end of February) the Master had put on a moleskin shawl bordered with red.[18] The barber had come and he was about to be shaved.[19] The Master welcomed M. smiling. He stammered a little when he spoke. The Master showed keen interest and enquired where M. was staying and so on. He even knew Ishan Kaviraj, who he learnt was M.'s brother-in-law. Suddenly the Master's eager interest switched over from Kaviraj (Ayurvedic physician) to Keshab Chandra Sen, who was ill and made anxious enquiries about his health. With utter simplicity the Master revealed:

> "I made a vow to worship the Mother with green coconut and sugar on Keshab's recovery. Sometimes, in the early hours of the morning, I would wake up and cry before Her: 'Mother, please make Keshab well again. If Keshab doesn't live, whom shall I talk with when I go to Calcutta?' And so it was that I resolved to offer Her the green coconut and sugar."

Then the Master's interest moves on to a foreigner, and he asks M.

"Tell me, do you know of a certain Mr. Cook who has come to Calcutta? Is it true that he is giving lectures? Once Keshab took me on a steamer, and this Mr. Cook, too, was in the party."

The Master notices everything and remembers it; he brings it out at the appropriate time.[20] Next the Master bestows his attention on one Pratap's brother. The Divine Master is not all sweet. He could be stern and critical too when the occasion needed it. He narrates:

> "Pratap's brother came here. He stayed a few days. He had nothing to do and said he wanted to live here. I came to know that he had left his wife and children with his father-in-law. He has a whole brood of them! So I took him to task. Just fancy! He is the father of so many children! Will people from the neighbourhood feed them and bring them up? He isn't even ashamed that someone else is feeding his wife and children, and that they have been left at his father-in-law's house. I scolded him very hard and asked him to look for a job. Then he was willing to leave here."

The Master knew propriety well, and what course was appropriate for whom. "Man should possess dignity and alertness", he said, (p. 830). Renunciation was not escapism from duties and responsibilities and one must have self-respect.[21]

Then comes M.'s own turn. Some searching questions follow to gauge the ins and outs of M. The Master's keen eye examined all those who came to him, and he took persons into his inner circle or as disciples only after thorough testing.[22]

Master: "Are you married?"

M.: "Yes, Sir."

Master (with a shudder): "Oh, Ramlal! Ramlal! Alas, he is married." The Master continued, "Have you children?"

M. whispered in a trembling voice: "Yes, Sir, I have children." Master (very sadly): "Ah me! He even has children."

But the Master, to soothe M., explained his remarks affectionately, looking at M. kindly: "You see, you have certain good signs. I know them by looking at a person's forehead, his eyes and so on."[23]

Master (continuing): "Tell me, now, what kind of person is your wife? Has she spiritual attributes, or is she under power of avidya?"

M.: "She is all right. But I am afraid she is ignorant."

Master (with evident displeasure): "And you are a man of knowledge?"

The Master did not mince words where correction was necessary. But it was all for good; there was no malice in it. He did not like to unsettle people's minds, but only make them liberal.

When, next, the question turned on God with form and without form, M. said, he would like to think of God as formless. The Master emphasized. "Remember that God with form is just as true as God without form. But hold fast to your own conviction."

M. ventured: "Sir, suppose one believes in God with form. Certainly He is not the clay image!"

Master (interrupting): "But why clay? It is an image of Spirit."

M. argued: "But Sir, one should explain to those who worship the clay image that it is not God, and that, while worshipping it, they should have God in view and not the clay image. One should not worship clay."

The Master did not spare. He said sharply: "That is the one hobby of you Calcutta people – giving lectures and bringing light to others! Nobody ever stops to consider how to get the light himself. Who are you to teach others?"[24]

However, the Master explained the significance of image worship satisfactorily and said; "God is our Inner Guide. He will be the teacher," and admonished M.: "Why should you get a headache over it (image worship)? You had better try for knowledge and devotion yourself."[25]

This time M. felt his ego completely crushed. He concludes: "What a shame! How foolish I am! This is not mathematics or history or literature, that one can teach it to others. No, this is the deep mystery of God. What he says appeals to me."

Then with what simplicity and wealth of common illustrations does the Master elucidate, without ambiguity, the questions of spiritual seekers, which engenders conviction in their minds! And how practical they are!

M. asked: "How ought we to live in the world?"

Master: "Do all your duties, but keep your mind on God. Live with all – with wife and children, father and mother – and serve them. Treat them as if they were very dear to you, but know in your heart of hearts that they do not belong to you."

The Master supplements the answer with four more apt illustrations:

1. A maid-servant serving in the house of a rich man doing all her work diligently, but with her mind on her own children in the village;

2. The tortoise moving about in the water but with her thoughts on her eggs;
3. Breaking opens the jackfruit after smearing the hands with oil;
4. Preparing first butter from milk and then putting it in water so that it will not mix with the water.

Then he further elaborates it with instruction on the means of fixing the mind on God, by resorting to solitude occasionally and by the use of discrimination about the Real and the unreal etc.[26]

The next question of M. was: "Is it possible to see God?" The Master answers assuringly without the least ambiguity: "Yes, certainly,"[27] and then in his own inimitable way explains how one can obtain God vision through longing, comparing it with the intense longing of the worldly people for worldly things, and giving other apt illustrations, like that of the kitten mewing for its mother with complete dependence on her. He interspersed the reply with a soul stirring song (which is a general characteristic of the Master's way of instruction, and very effective) in his charming voice, and pointed out:

"Longing is like the rosy dawn. Afar the dawn, out comes the sun. Longing is followed by the vision of God."

M. had been profoundly impressed by the first two visits to this wonderful man. He had been thinking of the Master constantly, and of the utterly simple way he explained the deep truths of spiritual life. Never before had he met such a man.

M. came on his third visit the next Sunday (5th March). The room was filled with devotees. The Master smiled as he talked and the conversation was about worldly men and how to deal with them. "They speak ill of the spiritually minded", he said, and compared the latter's attitude to that of an elephant which moves along the street without caring to look at the curs that bark at it.

The Master asked the spirited Narendra, about nineteen then (later Swami Vivekananda): "If people speak ill of you, what will you think of them?"

Narendra replied: "I shall think that dogs are barking at me."

The Master smilingly corrected him, "Oh, no, you must not go that far, my child. (laughter). God dwells in all beings. But you may be intimate only with good people; you must keep away from the evil-minded. God is even in the tiger; but you cannot embrace the tiger on that account." (laughter).

Then, the Master elucidated its implications with the parables of the

'Mahout-Narayana and Elephant-Narayana' to keep away from the wicked, and with that of 'the Brahmachari and the Snake', to hiss at the wicked people to scare them away, but not to inject poison into, or to injure, them.

We see Sri Ramakrishna was an expert storyteller and used the parables with telling effect to the utmost advantage to drive home in simple way spiritual truths and their practical application in life. There is no dearth of parables, common telling illustrations and similes, and wit and wisdom to suit every occasion aptly.[28] They flow out spontaneously as he talks in a natural unaffected way. He does not pose as a teacher or a Guru standing on a high pedestal. He is the Great Master without being conscious of it.[29] All feel at ease in his company, whether rich or poor, high or low, young or old, and men or women. Wherever he is there is a mart of joy.

The Master is fully aware of the nature of the worldly persons,[30] and very graphically describes their mentality comparing them to the fish caught in the net, which burrow themselves into the mud with the net in their mouths thinking they are quite safe. But he assures, replying to a question, that there is certainly hope for even these if they keep holy company, etc. and pray to God saying, 'Give me faith and devotion.' The Master does not reject anyone. He finds a way for all. He declares, "Everybody will surely be liberated. But one should follow the instructions of the Guru." (p. 23). "Once a person has faith, he has achieved everything. There is nothing greater than faith." Then he goes on to recount the miracles worked by faith in the name of God and makes all laugh saying that even God Rama had to build a bridge to cross the sea, but Hanuman with one bound cleared it with Rama's name on his lips. He then sings a song in his charming voice to the Divine Mother glorifying the power of Her name.

The Master was an expert connoisseur of persons.[31] He knows not only the nature of worldly-minded, but of great ones, and of spiritual geniuses too, and even of naughty boys. Pointing to Narendra, he said:

> "You all see this boy. He behaves that way here. A naughty boy seems very gentle when with his father. But he is quite another when he plays in the chandni. Narendra and people of his type belong to the class of the ever-free. They are never entangled in the world. When they grow a little older they feel the awakening of inner consciousness and go directly towards God. They come to the world only to teach others. They never care for anything of the world. They are never attached to 'woman and gold'." (p. 12)

Then he illustrated the ever-free nature of Narendra with the legend of the 'Homa Bird', which always flies high up in the sky and whose young ones, newly hatched, develop wings before they touch the ground and fly up to the mother-bird in the sky. What an apt illustration! Then the Master extolled Narendra's talents:

> "You see, Narendra excels in singing, playing on instruments, study and everything. The other day he had a discussion with Kedar and tore his arguments to shreds." (All laugh).[32]

Here we come upon another aspect of the Master. He shows interest even in reasoning, though he is against vain argumentation. He asked M.: "Is there any book in English on reasoning? Tell me what it says."[33] M. explained; but while listening, the mood suddenly changed and the Master became absent-minded. M. sauntered in the garden and after a while returned to the Master's room. He describes the scene:

> "There, on the small north verandah, he (M.) witnessed an amazing sight. Sri Ramakrishna was standing still, surrounded by a few devotees, and Narendra was singing. M. had never heard anyone except the Master sing so sweetly. When he looked at Sri Ramakrishna he was struck with wonder; for the Master stood motionless, with eyes transfixed. He seemed not even to breathe. A devotee told M. that the Master was in samadhi. M. had never before seen or heard of such a thing. Silent with wonder, he thought: "Is it possible for a man to be so oblivious of the outer world in the consciousness of God? How deep his faith and devotion must be to bring about such a state!' "

Narendra was singing a song on Lord Hari which described His peerless beauty. The Master was reflecting the sentiments in his person like a delicate spiritual instrument. Narendra sang:

> 'Meditate, O my mind, on the Lord Hari,
>
> ......
>
> Ever more beauteous in fresh-blossoming love
> That shames the splendour of a million moons,
> Like lightning gleams the glory of His form,
> Raising erect the hair for very joy.'

"The Master shuddered when the last line was sung. His hair stood on end, and tears of joy streamed down his cheeks. Now and then his lips parted in a smile. Was he seeing the peerless beauty of God, 'that shames the splendour of a million moons'? Was this the vision of God, the Essence of Spirit?"

The song continued:

> 'Worship His feet in the lotus of your heart;
> With heavenly love, behold that matchless sight.'

"Again that bewitching smile. The body motionless as before, the eyes half shut, as if beholding a strange inner vision."

Next day when M. comes in the afternoon, quite a different scene opens. The Master (then about 46) is sitting on the small couch and with a smile is talking with Narendra, Bhavanath, and other young men, all about nineteen or twenty.

"The Master was having great fun with the boys, treating them as if they were his most intimate friends. Peals of side-splitting laughter filled the room as if it were a mart of joy. The whole thing was a revelation to M. He thought: "Didn't I see him only yesterday intoxicated with God? Wasn't he swimming then in the Ocean of Divine Love – a sight I had never seen before? And today the same person is behaving like an ordinary man! Wasn't it he who scolded me on the first day of my coming here? Didn't he admonish me, saying, 'And you are a man of knowledge!'?"

Though Sri Ramakrishna was having great fun with the boys, no sooner M. entered the room, the Master laughed aloud and said to the boys: "There! He has come again." They all joined in the laughter.[34] The Master explained the cause of the laughter:

"A man once fed a peacock with a pill of opium at four o' clock in the afternoon. The next day, exactly at that time, the peacock came back. It had felt the intoxication of the drug and returned just in time to have another dose." (All laugh).

M. thought this a very apt illustration. Even at home he had been unable to banish the thought of Sri Ramakrishna for a moment. His mind was constantly at Dakshineshwar and he had counted the minutes until he should go again.

While the Master and the boys were having fun, his glance did not miss M. who was sitting in silence. The Master remarked to Ramlal: "You see, he is a little advanced in years (about 28), and therefore somewhat serious. He sits quiet while the youngsters are making merry."

From the great fun, suddenly the Master's mood changed and he drew their attention to Hanuman's intense longing for Sri Rama:

"Just imagine Hanuman's state of mind. He didn't care for money, honour, creature comforts, or anything else. He longed only for God."

The Master sang a song about Hanuman, and even as he was singing he went into samadhi.

"Again the half-closed eyes and motionless body that one sees in his photograph. Just a minute before, the devotees had been making merry in his company. After a long time the Master came back to ordinary consciousness. His face lighted up with a smile and his body relaxed; his senses began to function in a normal way. He shed tears of joy as he repeated the holy name of Rama. M. wondered whether this very saint was the person who a few minutes earlier had been behaving like a child of five!"

Note the quick and complete change in the moods and attitudes of the Master. Again the scene changes – The Master said to Narendra and M. "I should like to hear you speak and argue in English." "They both laughed… It was impossible for M. to argue any more before the Master." And yet M. was a learned man and Sri Ramakrishna an illiterate! Behold the power of the Master's personality!

In the afternoon M. suddenly came upon the Master talking to Narendra. He was saying:

> "Look here. Come a little more often. You are a new-comer. On first acquaintance people visit each other quite often, as is the case with a lover and his sweetheart." (Narendra and M. laugh).

Nothing escapes the Master, though he was always intoxicated with God. He even knows the ways of the sweethearts and uses the illustration aptly.[35] Then he told M. about how the peasants select bullocks with mettle and spirit by touching their tails. Those, which meekly lie down, they reject, and those that frisk about and show their spirit they select. And he continued, "Narendra is like a bullock of this latter class. He is full of spirit within." The Master liked such spirit. He did not like namby-pamby fellows. He continued:

> "There are some people who have no grit whatever. They are like flattened rice soaked in milk – soft and mushy. No inner strength."[36]

The Master had a scientific mind. He did not depend entirely on his own views. He always sought confirmation. He said to M. "Go and talk to Narendra. Then tell me what you think of him."[37]

M. had been fascinated by Sri Ramakrishna's personality[38] and had been enchanted by the Master's sweet music. When the time for departure came, he felt reluctant to go and instead went in search of Sri Ramakrishna. M. saw him in the Natmandir (hall in front of the Kali temple), pacing up and down, and asked him with hesitation if there would be any more singing that evening. The Master replied, "No, not tonight." But he added, "I am going to Balaram Bose's house in Calcutta. Come there and you will hear me sing." The Master was keenly interested in the welfare of the devotees. He was not content that they come to him at Dakshineshwar. He himself graced their places and this also provided opportunities for the neighbouring people and those who could not go so far to Dakshineshwar to meet him. When M. felt some hesitation whether he would be welcome at a stranger's place, the Master assured him, "Oh no, why should you think that? Just mention my name. Say that you want to see me; then someone will take you to me." The Lord is very easy of approach.

Again, like a scientist, he wanted to know what M. felt about himself, since he appeared to be so fascinated.

Master: "Let me ask you something. What do you think of me?" When M. remained silent the Master repeated, "What do you think of me? How many annas of knowledge of God have I?"

M. replied. "I do not understand what you mean by 'annas'. But of this I am sure. I have never before seen such knowledge, ecstatic love, faith in God, renunciation, and catholicity anywhere."[39]

The Master laughed like a child. M. bowed low before him and took his leave.

He had gone up to the gate but remembering, he came back to Sri Ramakrishna who was still in the Natmandir, and saw:

> "In the dim light the Master, all alone, was pacing the hall, rejoicing in the Self as the lion lives and roams alone in the forest."
>
> "In silent wonder M. surveyed that great soul."

* * *

We see from the foregoing that a wonderful many-faceted personality of the Master stands out before us even in the account of the first few days of M.'s visit to the Master. If we survey the whole Gospel on the lines of the First Chapter, we can see a good number of other important aspects of the Master's personality emerging, and those which we have already come across reinforced and enriched.[40] Swami Vivekananda used to say that the Master's moods were inexhaustible:

"Sri Ramakrishna had an infinite breadth of feeling. He had infinite moods and phases. Even if you might form an idea of the limits of Brahma-jnana, the knowledge of the Absolute, you could not do the same with the unfathomable depths of his mind. Thousands of Vivekanandas may spring forth through one gracious glance of his eyes! Sri Ramakrishna is not exactly what the ordinary followers have comprehended him to be... He only knows what he himself really was; his frame was only a human one, but everything else about him was entirely different from that of others. Truly, I tell you, I have understood him very little."

Note what even the great Vivekananda says!

Consider the great spiritual power and inner strength of the person who could hold the sustained interest and devotion of so large a number of persons of high calibre and varied natures that we come across in the Gospel. There was the great and learned Keshab Chandra Sen, who was held in high esteem even in the West, an admired leader of the Brahmo Samaj, a great orator, and considered the idol of 'Young Bengal', and yet he came under the sway of the Master, and became the first instrument in spreading the Master's divine life and message. Then pursue his visit and the brilliant and profound conversation with so eminent a person and so great a Pandit as Ishwar Chandra Vidyasagar. The unlearned priest of Kali is in his natural elements. Wit, humour, and divine wisdom flow out of him spontaneously. Never for once is he in hesitation for words or ideas or quick repartee. He is in divine intoxication, and yet quite appreciative of the greatness of Vidyasagar.[41] Even the Pandit admitted openly that he learnt something new from Sri Ramakrishna, which he had not heard before: that of all entities Brahman alone is not made ucchishta (defiled).

Then see the variety of other eminent personalities that flit across the pages of the Gospel who were like little boys before the Master. To name only a few – Rani Rasmani, Mathur Nath Biswas, Pandit Narayana Shastri, Pandit Padmalochan, Pandits Shashadhara Tarkachudamani and Samadhyayi, Vijaya Krishna Goswami, Trailokya Nath Sanyal, Col. Viswanath, Bankim Chandra Chatterji, Ashwini Kumar Datta, Hirananda of Sindh, Nitya Gopal, Dr. Rajendra Lal, Dr. Bhadhuri, Adhar, Jadulal Mullick, Shambhulal Mullick, Pratap Chandra Mazumdar, Wiliams, etc.[42] And how even a rationalist and a man of science like Dr. Mahendra Lal Sarkar, who founded the Indian Association for the cultivation of science, was captivated by Sri Ramakrishna! The number of persons of all ages and classes who find place in the Gospel in association with Sri Ramakrishna is legion, and we find that a host of devotees from all sects and creeds and of all stations in life came to him for inspiration. There are also those who became his famous householder disciples such as Ramachandra Dutta, Manamohan Mitra, Suresh Kumar Mitra (Surendra), Durgacharan Nag, Akshaya Kumar Sen (who wrote the Ramakrishna Punthi), Devendra, Kalipada Ghosh, Balaram Bose, and M. himself, the author of the Gospel, and several others who spread the message of the Master and advanced his divine mission.

Above all, is it the work of any but a great spiritual dynamo to tame and hold together about a score of the intelligent and spirited youths of the University, well versed in modern sciences and rationalism, and inspire them with renunciation and dedication to the service of God and man? See the Gospel, how he gradually built up the cluster of his future great sannyasin disciples like Rakhal, Baburam, Shashi, Sarat, Tarak, and others and made a Vivekananda of Narendra and an Adbhutananda of an illiterate servant boy, Latu. And how he subdued that terrible Bhairava, the dramatist genius Girish Chandra Ghosh, the father of Bengali stage, but an inveterate drunkard who led a fast life, and transform him into one of the greatest devotees endowed with unflinching faith, so much so that he hailed openly Sri Ramakrishna as an Incarnation of God!

Sri Ramakrishna's moulding of persons into greatness was not confined to men only. His greatest gift to the world is the Holy Mother. He transformed the simple Saradamani, his wife, into his first sannyasini disciple and into the Holy Mother of the Ramakrishna-world, who guided his great disciples and the destinies of the Ramakrishna Order and ministered to a large number of devotees, for thirty-four long years after the passing away of the Master. Then there was Gopal-Ma, who had the living experience of Bala-Gopala (Child Krishna) playing with her, due to the Master's blessings. Many were the other women devotees whom the Master guided who find reference in the Gospel. Gauri-Ma later started an ashrama for women and schools for girls. Though Sri Ramakrishna emphasized on the 'kamini-kanchana tyaga' and advocated that spiritual aspirants of either sex should not mix closely with each other, we find in the Gospel Sri Ramakrishna held all women as the embodiments of the Divine Mother and commended this attitude to all.[43]

Sri Ramakrishna's moods varied from that of a feminine one (p. 780) to that of a child. He would sometimes throw off his clothes and pace up and down like a five-year old child (p. 818). Then, he could perfectly mimic several types of male and female characters and send the young devotees into roars of laughter.[44] Sometimes, he would be in the heroic mood. When Adhar mentioned to him the cause of the grief of his friend who was bereaved (p. 143), the Master sang the song:

> "To arms! to arms! O Man! Death storms your house in battle array!
> Bearing the quiver of knowledge, mount the chariot of devotion;"
> ...
> Bend the bow of your tongue with the bow-string of love, . . .
> Fight your foe from the Ganges' bank and he is easily slain."

And then said, "What can you do? Be ready for Death. Death has entered the house. You must fight him with the weapon of God's holy name."

Then what a variety of songs does the Master sing! From the light and frivolous song to entertain children (p. 477), with whom he was very happy:

> Come; let me braid your hair,
> Lest your husband should scold you,
> When he beholds you!

to the most intoxicating devotional songs! Every sentiment is represented: there are those depicting the pangs of separation, and those inculcating intense renunciation, highest discrimination, and supreme knowledge; and those describing the union of Shakti in the Muladhara with Shiva in the Sahasrara, passing through the six Chakras. And there are songs for every occasion. Songs are there in the name of Shiva, Shakti, Kali, Durga, Rama, Krishna, Hanuman, Gauranga and Nityananda, etc. There are more than 200 songs of all types recorded in the Gospel sung by the Master and others composed by Ramaprasad, Kamalakanta, Premadasa, Trailokya, Madan, Nareshchandra, Meerabhai, Nanak and others. All this wide variety reveals the versatility and breadth of Master's mind and talents. The Master's singing was unusually melodious and charming, often interspersed with his improvisations and accompanied by his ecstatic trances and inspiring dances.

And what to speak of his tireless dancing, intoxicated with the divine mood, often going into rapturous samadhi! You meet these scenes often in the Gospel. At the festival of Panihati, M. records (p. 193):

> "Sri Ramakrishna entered by turns into all the moods of ecstasy. In deep samadhi he stood still, his face radiating a divine glow. In the state

of partial consciousness he danced, sometimes gently and sometimes with the vigour of a lion."

"Again, regaining consciousness of the world, he sang, himself leading the chorus:

'Behold, the two brothers have come, who weep while chanting Hari's name,... See how all Nadia is shaking under the waves of Gauranga's love!...'

"The crowd, with the Master in the centre, surged toward the temple of Radha-Krishna. Only a small number could enter. The rest stood outside the portal and jostled with one another to have a look at Sri Ramakrishna. In a mood of intoxication he began to dance in the courtyard of the shrine. Every now and then his body stood transfixed in deep samadhi. Hundreds of people around him shouted the name of God, and thousands outside caught the strain and raised the cry with full-throated voices."[45]

Does this not remind one of the 'Rasa-dance' of Sri Krishna! We also find in the Gospel that Sri Ramakrishna's knowledge of the various religious sects, of saints and seers, and the various Yogas and other religious disciplines was quite wide (see the Index). There are also references to Ramayanas of Valmiki and Tulsidas, Adhyatma Ramayana, Ashtavakra Samhita, Bhaktamala, Bhagavata, Gita, Chandi, Tantras, Manu Samhita, Narada Pancharatra, Panchadashi, Panini, Puranas, Smritis, Prabodhachandrodaya, Vivekachudamani, Yogavasishtha, and other works, all of which go to show the wide interest and horizon of the Master.

Then we find that the Master witnesses the religious dramas at the Star Theatre (of Girish Ghosh), goes to see a circus, and is interested how a photograph is taken. He knows the Maidan, Museum, Zoo, Asiatic Society, Bengal Bank, Fort William, and is interested in visiting even the Science Association of Dr. Sarkar. And every one of his experiences provides him enough material to draw spiritual lessons to communicate in his brilliant conversations. The Master is ever active visiting the houses of devotees, participates in Brahmo festivals, goes on a boat-trip on the Ganges with Keshab and his Brahmo party, and attends Ratha-yatra at Balaram Bose's house, etc. Everywhere he creates a surcharged divine atmosphere. No page of the Gospel is drab or dull. We have the whole gamut of human emotions of a higher type displayed there by Sri Ramakrishna. We see the high states of the Master, his intense detachment and his joyful moods in spite of his fractured arm or the intense pain in the throat. To the very end we see his interest in the spiritual development of all those who came to him and his deep sympathy and love for all."[46] And he is particularly interested in pure youngsters.

Here he advises the householders how to live in the world, and there he expatiates on the glories of renunciation. He is at home with the young and the old, the learned and the ignorant, children and women, the poor and the rich, ordinary clerks and high officers, doctors and scientists, artists and philosophers, devotees and saints. Here he discusses with the Vedantists, there with the Vaishnavas or Shaktas or again about different sects and religions. He brings God face to face to us, exhorts us to consider Him as our very own and very near to us and to strive to realize Him in life. Nowhere anything is jarring, nowhere anything narrow, and nowhere the interest slackens. One is lifted up into an ethereal atmosphere of divine harmony. Verily he was the personification of all the yogas and the spiritual life of all mankind.[47] No wonder Vivekananda sang in a hymn composed by him on Sri Ramakrishna, who was the combined incarnation of Sri Rama and Sri Krishna:

Advayatattvasamähitacittam
projjvalabhaktipatävottam ,
Karmakalevaramadbhutacestam
yämi gurum saranam bhavavaidyam.
Naradeva deva jaya jaya naradeva!

– I surrender myself to the Guru, the Man-God, the physician for the malady of this samsara (relative existence), whose mind ever dwelt on the Non-dualistic Truth (Advaita), whose personality was covered by the cloth of supreme devotion, who was ever active (for the good of humanity) and whose actions were all super-human.

Victory unto that God of all mankind!
Victory unto that Man-God!
Om Sriramakrsnarpanamastu!

REFERENCES

1. It is Swami Vivekananda who first used the word, though in a slightly different way, regarding Sri Ramakrishna. Says he: "But here is a man in whose company we have been day and night and yet consider him to be a far greater personality than any of them (Krishna, Buddha, Christ, etc.), Can you understand this phenomenon?" (Complete Works of Vivekananda, Vol. VII, 8th Edn. 1972, p. 484).
2. Ibid., Vol, III, 11th Edn. 1973 pp. 267-8. 'Sages of India.'

3. Letters of Swami Vivekananda, Advaita Ashrama, IV Edn. 1948, pp. 187, 155, 254.
4. Vol. I Life of Sri Ramakrishna, Advaita Ashrama, 'To My Western Readers'.
5. The Gospel of Sri Ramakrishna, Sri Ramakrishna Math, Madras; 6th Edition 1974.
6. The page numbers in brackets refer to The Gospel of Sri Ramakrishna.
7. While even great saints strive hard to attain samadhi and ecstasy, we find Sri Ramakrishna striving to bring down the mind to the normal plane. He said to the Divine Mother, "Mother, I want to be normal. Please don't make me unconscious. I should like to talk to the sadhu about Satchidananda. Mother, I want to be merry talking about Satchidananda." (p. 320). "The Master's natural tendency of mind was to soar into the plane of God-consciousness. He would force his mind to be conscious of the body." (p. 828).
8. The master was a Vijnani. He accepted both the Absolute and the Relative. He says: "A mere jnani trembles with fear. He is like the amateur satranja player. He is anxious to move his pieces somehow to the safety zone, where they won't be overtaken by his opponent. But a Vijnani is not afraid of anything. He has realized both aspects of God – Personal and Impersonal. He has talked with God. He has enjoyed the bliss of God… I don't press my arm to my side. Both my hands are free. I am not afraid of anything. I accept both the Nitya and the Lila, both the Absolute and the Relative." (p. 435) cf. Sri Krishna says in the Gita (XIII.2): क्षेत्रक्षेत्रज्ञोर्ज्ञानं यतज्ज्ञानं मतं मम. (The Knowledge of both the Inner Reality – Self or God – and the universe is considered by Me as full Knowledge).
9. The Master says, "it is being revealed to me that there is a greater manifestation of God in man than in other created beings." God is telling me, as it were: 'I dwell in men. Be merry with men'. (p. 356). "Man is Narayana Himself. If God can manifest Himself through an image, then why not through man also? God is born as man for the purpose of sporting as man."(p. 356). "I have been feeling much inclined to the Naralila (sport of God as man). It is God Himself who plays about as human beings. If God can be worshipped through a clay image, then why not through man?" (p. 358)
10. Published by Sri Ramakrishna Math, Madras.
11. The Holy Mother recognized the quality of supreme renunciation in Sri Ramakrishna as the highest and placed it above his achievement of the Harmony of all Religions.
12. Since this Memorial Volume is intended to commemorate the Centenary of M.'s first visit to the Master, from which date the record of the Gospel begins, it is apt that we should treat the First Chapter in detail. Further, it throws light on some of the salient aspects of the Master's personality.

13. We find the Master in the Gospel always with his beatific smile, 'with his usual beaming countenance'. (p. 19). Even during the days of his fractured arm and his last prolonged fatal illness, the smile never left him. The Master had two desires: "First, that I should be the king of the devotees, and second, that I should not be a dry sadhu." (p. 797). He was always full of joy and filled others also with joy. He laughed and made others also laugh. (p. 335).
14. The master said to Vijay Krishna Goswami: "The task of a religious teacher is indeed difficult. One cannot teach man without a direct command from God. People won't listen to you if you teach without such authority. Such teaching has no force behind it. One must first of all attain God through spiritual discipline or some other means. Thus armed with authority from God, one can be a teacher and give lectures anywhere. He who receives authority from God also receives power from Him. Only then can he perform the difficult task of a teacher." (p. 100). Nobody can confound a preacher who teaches people after having received the command of God. Getting a ray of light from the goddess of learning, a man becomes so powerful that before him big scholars seem mere earthworms... Such a preacher may not be a scholarly person, but don't conclude from it that he has any lack of wisdom. Does book-learning make one wise? He who has commission from God never runs short of wisdom... As he teaches people, the Divine Mother Herself supplies him with fresh knowledge from behind. That knowledge never comes to an end." (p. 420).
15. The master did not read books. "But how many scriptures I have heard!" he said. (p. 899). "During my boyhood I could understand what the sadhus read at the Lahas' house at Kamarpukur, although I would miss a little here and there. If a Pandit speaks to me in Sanskrit I can follow him, but I cannot speak it myself." (p. 358). The Master could also converse in Hindustani (pp. 605-6). He quotes a Hindi couplet from Tulsidas regarding sticking to truth (p. 238) (cf. also p. 252 regarding Tulsi). "I have heard a great deal about Buddha" (p. 382). The Divine Mother also revealed to him "everything that is in the Vedas, the Vedanta, Puranas, Tantras, etc." (p. 542). He also knew something of Nyaya and Panini (p. 607). He tells Bankim: "Analogy is one-sided. You are a Pandit; haven't you read logic? Suppose you say that a man is as terrible as a tiger. That does not mean that he has a fearful tail or a tiger's pot-face!" (all laugh) – (p.639).
16. The Master said: "There is no collection plate here; therefore all come." (p. 363). He did not touch money and was very open. He did not stand on the high pedestal of a teacher. He said, "As long as I live so long do I learn", and we see him in the Gospel going to meet many learned people and saintly persons to compare notes and to see if he can learn something from them. "Three words – 'Master', 'Teacher'

and 'Father' – prick me like thorns. I am the son of God, His eternal child." (p. 600). "There is not a fellow under the sun who is my disciple. On the contrary, I am everybody's disciple. All are the children of God. All are His servants. I too am a child of God. I too am His servant. 'Uncle Moon' is every child's uncle!" (p. 855).

17. We can see at many places in the Gospel, the Master's concern and consideration for the devotees. "The Master lay down on the small couch. He seemed worried about Tarak. Suddenly he said to M., 'Why do I worry so much about these young boys?' (p. 698)." "The Master suddenly addressed Mohini's wife and said: 'By unnatural death one becomes an evil spirit. Beware... That will be all right (staying with the Holy Mother at the Nahabat). But you talk of dying. That frightens me. And the Ganges is so near!" (p. 698). Sri Ramakrishna said to M. tenderly, "Come early in the morning tomorrow. The hot sun of the rainy season is bad for health." (p. 824) "How strange! Tears also appeared in the Master's eyes. He wiped them away with his hands. Hriday had made him suffer endless agonies, yet the Master wept for him." (p. 612). See also pp. 495, 571, regarding Master's concern for Haripada and Narayana, and footnote 46.
18. When Vidyasagar asked M, what kind of Paramahamsa the Master was, saying, "Does he wear an ochre cloth?" M. replied: "No, Sir; he is an unusual person. He wears a red-bordered cloth and polished slippers. He lives in a room in Rani Rasmani's temple garden. In his room there is a couch with a mattress and mosquito net. He has no outer indication of holiness. But he doesn't know anything except God. Day and night he thinks of God alone." M. also records that the Master went to see Vidyasagar in a hackney carriage, and he did so whenever he went out to meet devotees. Ashwini Kumar Datta writes to M. (p. 1020) that when he visited the Master in the autumn of 1881: "He was sitting reclining against a bolster. He wore black-bordered cloth... Going nearer, I found him half leaning against the bolste r with his hands clasped around his drawn-up knees. Then I thought: 'Evidently he is not used to pillows as gentlemen are'..." Ashwini wrote his reminiscences probably in 1910, nearly thirty years after his visit and he has said he may have forgotten many things and confused the events. So it is likely, he may have confused a pillow for a bolster and the red-border of the Master's cloth for black border, for the Master has disapproved of both as rajasic. (Cf. pp. 145, 606 for bolster and pillow, and p. 101 for black border).
19. The Master was not always with the beard as seen in the usual photograph is clear from this. In the photograph taken at the studio (given opp. to p. 700), he seems to have a smaller beard and is also fully dressed. We can also see the slippers and the border.

20. Though the Master was mostly in a God-intoxicated state, he did not lack secular knowledge. "He sits in a tower, as it were, from which he gets all information and sees everything)". (p. 958), He had been to the Registry Office (p. 327); he had witnessed a balloon going up (p. 507; he knew Golap had to be approached for a job (p. 725); He had seen the human skeleton in the Asiatic Society Museum (p. 859); he knew how if one takes service, one has to suffer humiliation (p. 100); He says to Vijay Krishna Goswami:
"You yourself perceive how far you have gone down by being a servant of others. Again one finds that people with many university degrees, scholars with their vast English education accept service under their English masters and are daily trampled under their boots. The one cause of all this is woman. They have married and set up a gay fair with their wives and children. Now they cannot go back, much as they would like to. Hence all these insults and humiliations, all this suffering from slavery."
He knows a cheque and that it has to be passed (p. 241), and about the Bengal Bank (p. 300). The Master uses all this knowledge to give spiritual instructions in the course of his conversations.
21. We also find the other types of stern attitude of the Master: When M. who had a sense of duty and was worried about his wife, asked: "What shall one do if one's wife says: 'You are neglecting me. I shall commit suicide'?"
Master: (in a serious tone): "Give up such a wife if she proves an obstacle in the way of spiritual life, let her commit suicide or anything else she likes. The wife that hampers her husband's spiritual life is an ungodly wife."
Immersed in deep thought, M. stood leaning against the wall… Then, suddenly going to M., he whispered in his ear:
"But if a man has sincere love for God, then all come under his control – the king, wicked persons, and his wife. Sincere love of God on the husband's part may eventually help the wife to lead a spiritual life. if the husband is good, then through the grace of God the wife may also follow his example."
This had a most soothing effect on M.'s worried mind." (p. 54)
The Master tells Mani Mullick: "Don't hurry me please… I can't rush." (p. 411); he asks M. not to eat at the Kali temple guest house, but to cook his own food (p. 279); referring to Dr. Sarkar, the Master says, "He is a villain. He pressed my tongue as if I were a cow. (p. 831)"; When Dr. Sarkar was saying, "Listen to me–", the Master retorted: "Listen to you? You are greedy, lustful, and egoistic." (p. 900; see also p. 906); When the Pundit was arguing vehemently with Mani Mullick, the Master remarked smilingly, "This is the tamasic aspect of sattva, the attitude of a hero. This is necessary. One should not hold one's tongue at the sight

of injustice and untruth." (p. 441). "In that state of God-intoxication I used to speak out my mind to all. I was no respecter of persons. Even to men of position I was not afraid to speak the truth." (p. 46). "Surendra approached the Master with a garland and wanted to put it around his neck. But the Master took it in his hand and threw it aside. Surendra's pride was wounded and his eyes filled with tears... 'Now (Surendra) realized it was all his fault. God cannot be bought with money; He cannot be possessed by a vain person. He has really been vain.' " (p. 1011).

The Master also scolded the devotees when occasion called for it. We do not propose to give all the details in this short article. Please refer to pages 285, 321, 376, 387, 669 of the Gospel.

22. The Master told Keshab: "You don't look into people's nature before you make them your disciples, and so they break away from you. All men look alike, to be sure, but they have different nature. Some have an excess of sattva, others an excess of rajas, and still others an excess of tamas. You must have noticed that the cakes known as puli all look alike. But their contents are very different. Some contain condensed milk, some coconut kernel, and others mere boiled kalai pulse." (p. 71)

23. We find other instances in the Gospel regarding the Master's way of judging persons by bodily signs. He says: "When Narendra first came here he was dressed in dirty clothes, but his eyes and face betokened some inner stuff." (p. 494). "Sri Ramakrishna took Tarak's hand into his own and seemed to feel its weight. A few moments later he said: 'There is a little crookedness in your mind; but that will go.' " (p. 698).

See also Sri Ramakrishna the Great Master, pp. 768 for details of the Master's power of testing people by the bodily signs and how he tested Narendra in many ways.

The Master had the gift of judging persons in other ways too. He said: "Yes, I can see inside him (Pundit Samadhyayi) through his eyes, as one can see the objects in a room through the glass door." (p. 20) Regarding the young boys, Purna and younger Naren, the Master said: "A great soul! Or how could he (Purna) make me do japa for his welfare? But Purna doesn't know anything about it." ... "Look at him! How naive he (Naren) looks when he laughs, as if he knew nothing. He never thinks of these three things: land, wife and money." (p. 714). "Narendra belongs to a very high plane – the realm of the Absolute. He has a manly nature. So many devotees come here, but there is not one like him. Every now and then I take stock of the devotees. I find that some are like lotuses with ten petals, some like lotuses with sixteen petals, some like lotuses with a hundred petals. But among lotuses Narendra is a thousand-petaled lotus." (p. 793)

24. Though the Master was from a village, he knew the nature of Calcutta people. He says, "Don't you know how easily the people of Calcutta get excited? The milk in the kettle puffs up and boils as long as the fire burns underneath. Take away the fuel and all becomes quiet. The people of Calcutta love sensations." (p. 71)
25. "Do you know my attitude?", the Master queried and said, "As for myself, I eat, drink, and live happily. The rest the Divine Mother knows... There is only one Guru, and that is Satchidananda. He alone is the Teacher. My attitude towards God is that of a child toward its mother. One can get human gurus by the million. All want to be teachers. But who cares to be a disciple? ... Anyone and everyone cannot be a guru. A huge timber floats on the water and can carry animals as well. But a piece of worthless wood sinks, if a man sits on it, and drowns him. Therefore in every age God incarnates Himself as the guru, to teach humanity. Satchidananda alone is the guru." (p. 24. See also p. 71)
26. At other places in the Gospel, we find several other illustrations as well, such as of mud-fish living untainted in the mud; a loose woman doing all her work but with her mind on her paramour; a man with a carbuncle doing all his work while always aware of the pain; a dancing girl dancing with jars on the head; women talking and laughing while going with water-pitchers on their heads; etc.
27. The master was kind to the householders and often encouraged them and assured them. When a person asked: "Sir, is it ever possible to realize God while leading the life of a householder?" The master assured: "Certainly. But as I said just now, one must live in holy company and pray unceasingly. One should weep for God. When the impurities of the mind are thus washed away, one realizes God."(p. 23)
28. There are more than 70 parables mentioned in the Index to the Gospel. These do not include all the illustrations and similes, sayings and proverbs, analogies and anecdotes, allegories and mythological stories, etc., which the Master uses profusely.
29. "A hollow piece of drift-wood somehow manages to float; but it sinks if even a bird sits on it. But Narada and sages of his kind are like a huge log that not only can float across to the other shore but can carry many animals and other creatures as well. A steamship itself crosses the ocean and also carries people across," (p. 435). Sri Ramakrishna was a huge steamship.
30. See pages 71, 558, 581, 609, 692 etc.
31. The Master freely bestows praise and appreciation wherever he sees laudable qualities. See pages 341, 365, 546, 571, 605-6, 610, 793, 799, 835, 907, 908, etc.
32. Regarding appreciation of Narendra see also pages 219, 227, 705, 793, etc.

33. See pages 33, 212, 437, 639, 840 for the Master's ideas on faith and reasoning.
34. The master was full of wit and humour and often made the youngsters laugh heartily. See pages 70, 71, 146, 232, 408, 787, 788, 903 for witty remarks and page 692 for mimicry.
35. The Master said regarding Bhavanath: "Bhavanath is married; but he spends the whole night in spiritual conversation with his wife. The couple pass their time talking of God alone. I said to him, 'Have a little fun with your wife now and then.' (p. 690). cf. You see, he (Rakhal) has renounced his home and relatives and completely surrendered himself to me. It was I who sent him to his wife now and then. He still had a little desire for enjoyment." (p. 494).
36. The Master sometimes exhibited his spirit. He said to the other devotees: "Captain forbids me to go to see Keshab." Captain: "But, Sir, you act as you will. What shall I do?" Master (sharply): "Why shouldn't I go to see Keshab? You feel at ease when you go to the Governor General's house, and for money at that. Keshab thinks of God and chants His name. Isn't it you who are always saying that God Himself has become the universe and all its living beings? Doesn't God dwell in Keshab also?" (p. 218). The Master did not hesitate to scold the devotees when needed: Vijay (p. 100); M. (p. 285); Haladhari (p, 321); M. and Harish (p. 376); Adhar (p. 387); Niranjan (p. 402); Ishan (p. 577) etc.
37. Sri Ramakrishna's innate rational and scientific mind is evident in his going to several people to compare their realizations with his own. He had the scientist's humility. If someone cast doubts on any of his realizations, he would try to verify it. He laid emphasis on practical sadhana. He used to say, by mere saying 'siddhi, siddhi' you won't have intoxication; you must get some, make a paste of it and drink it mixed with water. (p. 547) He would also point out, though the almanac may forecast rain, if you squeeze it not a drop of water will come. Similar is the case with more theoretical knowledge of scriptures. He also declared that God can be seen and talked to by all if they undergo the necessary discipline and fulfill the conditions, and that he himself had seen God and talked to Him. (See pages 146, 175, 287, 357, 413, 600, 497, 780, 815, 818, 954, etc. for what the Master has said on himself and his experiences).

    We also see the Master had knowledge how a photograph was taken (p. 182); about telegraph (p. 578), medicine (pp. 23, 174, 826 – cf. Sri Ramakrishna's medical knowledge – a series of articles in Bhavan's Journal by a Doctor in 1979-80). We can see the Master's spirit of enquiry, when he enquires of M. about Pandit Shashadhar (p. 448); Narayana Shastri about Keshab (p. 835); and M. about Dr. Sarkar (p. 836) and the whole conversation with Dr. Sarkar (founder of the Science Association) is very illuminating (pp. 907-8). He also desired to visit the

Science Association (p. 895). His remarks on science as incapable of revealing God is also interesting: "And what does your 'science' say? This combined with this produces that; that combined with that produces this. One is more likely to lose consciousness by contemplating those things – by handling material things too much." (p. 907). He also recounts his experiences to Dr. Sarkar and others and allows himself to be tested (pp. 830-31).

38. The Master not only was fascinating, he also attracted devotees: "I found that the Doctor (Dr. Sarkar) will have spiritual awakening. But it will take some time. I won't have to tell him much. I saw another person while in that mood. My mind said to me, 'Attract him too'." (p. 902).
39. At another place M. says: "You are as infinite as He of whom we have been talking. Truly, no one can fathom your depth." (p. 56). (For the estimates of the Master's personality see also page 19.) "If you want to see a grog-shop, then come with me. You will see a huge jar of wine (bliss) there." (M. told Kali Krishna about the Master; 175; 254, 278, 306, 324, 387, 463, 836, 897, 958-9, etc.
40. This short pioneering article of its type cannot comprehend all the aspects of the Master' personality which a systematic and thorough analysis of the Gospel would yield. We have drawn attention to some salient aspects and tried to enrich some by way of footnotes. It has not been possible to give the details in all cases lest the article should become too long. We have contented ourselves by giving page references and seek the indulgence of interested readers to consult the Gospel for details as well as for further exploration.
41. The Master in his talks often made acknowledgement to persons from whom he learnt or heard certain ideas and facts; and he often encouraged others to recount while he listened. One may refer to pages 230, 341, 405, 522, 605-6, 835, 836, 838-9, 899.
42. See the large number of names of persons who were associated with Sri Ramakrishna from the Index to the Gospel as also the list given on pages 7 and 8 of the Condensed Gospel of Sri Ramakrishna (original English version in part by M.), published by Sri Ramakrishna Math, Madras.
43. A devotee asked the Master: "Sir, shall we hate women then?" The Master replied: "He who has realized God does not look upon a woman with the eye of lust; so he is not afraid of her. He perceives clearly that women are but so many aspects of the Divine Mother. He worships them all as the Mother Herself." (p. 100). However, he held that spiritual seekers, especially sannyasins, must keep aloof from women (p. 558). Naturally the opposite advice was given to women spiritual seekers, for the attraction between the sexes is very strong and brings down the mind to the physical level. Regarding the Master's attitude to women: He considered even

prostitutes as manifestations of the Divine Mother (p. 225); "I cannot bear to see women fast." (p. 384); "I look on women as my mother" (51); His love for his mother (pp. 535-6).; He scolds M. and Harish for neglecting their mothers (p. 376); etc.

44. Sri Ramakrishna was in the happiest mood with his young and pure devotees. He was seated on the small couch and was doing funny imitations of a kirtani. The devotees laughed heartily. The kirtani is dressed lavishly and covered with ornaments. She sings, standing on the floor, a coloured kerchief in her hand. Now and then she coughs to draw people's attention and blows her nose, raising her nose-ring. When a respectable gentleman enters the room, she welcomes him with appropriate words, still continuing her song. Now and then she pulls her sari from her arms to show her jewels.

    The devotees were convulsed with laughter at this mimicry by Sri Ramakrishna. Paltu rolled on the ground. Pointing to him, "The Master said to M.: 'Look at that child! He is rolling with laughter.' He said to Paltu with a smile: 'Don't report this to your father or he will lose the little respect he has for me. You see, he is an "Englishman". ' (p. 692). See also pp. 793, 824.

    Regarding the Master's habits, moods, simplicity, and humanness see pages 40, 146, 493, 608, 786, 788, 813, 841.

45. See, 'the description of the Master's extraordinary dance' (p. 697) and 'the dance in bhava-samadhi' (p. 824) by Swami Saradananda in his Sri Ramakrishna, the Great Master.

46. "On the morning of 23rd December (1885), Sri Ramakrishna gave unrestrained expression to his love for the devotees. He said to Niranjan, 'You are my father: I shall sit on your lap.' Touching Kalipada's chest, he said, 'May your inner spirit be awakened!' He stroked Kalipada's chin affectionately and said, 'Whoever has sincerely called on God or performed his daily religious devotions will certainly come here.' In the morning two ladies received his special blessing. In a state of samadhi he touched their hearts with his feet. They shed tears of joy. One of them said to him, weeping, 'You are so kind.' His love this day really broke all bounds. He wanted to bless Gopal of Sinthi and said to a devotee: 'Bring Gopal here." (p, 924)

    For the Master's concern and consideration for the devotees, see him doing japa for young Purna's welfare (p, 714); depressed about Hriday's illness (p. 214); worried about the grief of Mohini's wife on the death of her son (p. 696); worry about young boys (pp. 494, 698); concern for Hriday (p. 612); his heart writhed in pain at the death of devotees (p. 731); concern for the younger Naren (p.798) and Surendra (p. 411); for Girish Ghosh (p. 819); for the coachman (p. 828).

His compassion for all is also seen here: "In spite of his illness the Master keenly felt the sorrow and suffering of men. Day and night he thought about their welfare. The devotees wondered at his compassion. The assurance of Sri Ramakrishna that no sin can touch a man if he gives up his body while praying to God was deeply impressed on their minds." (p. 904).

The Master does not reject drunkard Surendra (p. 527); Master's illness is due to taking the sins of others (p. 897); "Don't take more people than your horse can draw", the Maste r says (p. 443); asks devotees to give alms to the beggar woman (p. 609).

47. For the Master's realization of and equal regard for different religions see pages 18, 497, 800, etc. For his breadth of outlook and spirit of equality see pages 225, 435, 571, 604, 837, 854, etc. For his universal vision see page 290, etc.

3

Sri Sri Ramakrishna Kathamrita The Gita of the grihasthas of all times

Basab Chaudhuri

Sri Mahendranath Gupta, popularly called Sri M and widely acclaimed for his compilation entitled Sri Sri Ramakrishna Kathamrita was born in Calcutta in the year 1854. He grew up to be a brilliant student and graduated third in his class from the University of Calcutta in 1875. He was teaching at the Metropolitan Institution founded by Pundit IswarchandraVidyasagar at the time when he first went to Dakhshineswar and met Sri Ramakrishna in 1882. Gradually he became very dear to his brother-devotees for his erudition, simplicity and saintly habits. Sri Ramakrishana used to say about Mahendranath: "He does not have pride." In fact, this quality in Mahendranath helped him compose the Kathamrita about which Swami Vivekananda had written in the year 1897, "I now understand why none of us attempted his life before. It has been reserved for you – this great work. Socratic dialogues are Plato all over. You are entirely hidden."

Sri Keshab Gupta wrote, "Restraint of a writer from hogging the limelight while describing the events happening before him is the major literary achievement of the Kathamrita. As if, an invisible flower at night is pushing its fragrance and this beauty is strewn all through the epic."

In the Indian Nation, Sri N. Ghose observed, "They take us straight to the truth and not through metaphysical maze. The Style is Biblical in simplicity. What a treasure it would have been to the world, if all the sayings of SreeKrishna, Buddha; Jesus; Mohammad; Nanak; Chaitanya could have been thus preserved."

Mahendranath completely surrendered himself to Sri Ramakrishna and his only objective in life was "to be as perfect as our Father in Heaven is Perfect." One day, he was asked by the Holy Mother Sarada Devi to read the Kathamrita for her. On hearing the contents of the compilation, Mother told Mahendranath that the descriptions were so vivid and enlivening that she got a feeling that Sri Ramakrishna was expressing himself. Emboldened Mahendranath went ahead as per the instructions of Sarada Devi and got the English version "Gospel of Sri Ramakrishna" (According to M, a Son of the Lord and disciple) published in the year 1897.

After the publication of Gospel in English language, Sri Ramchandra Datta, another devotee of Sri Ramakrishna, wrote in Tattwamanjari (published from Yogodyan in Agrahayan, Bengali year 1304): "Most revered Mahendranath Gupta has compiled Sri Ramakrishna's preaching with lucidity. They are already published in English language. It will be a great service to humanity if the preaching is published in the form of a book in Bengali language so that Sri Ramakrishna's ideas are made comprehensible to ordinary men and women." Gradually, Sri Sri Ramakrishna Kathamrita – as told by Sri M started being published in Bengali language in reputed monthly publications published in the-then Calcutta like Tattwamanjari, Bangadarshan, Udbodhan, The Hindu, etc. Later, in the year 1902, the First part of Sri Sri Ramakrishna Kathamrita was published by Swami Trigunatitananda from the Udbodhan Press. Then the Second, Third, Fourth and Fifth volumes were published in the years 1904, 1908, 1910 and 1932, respectively. All these volumes have been translated into many Indian and foreign languages to propagate the message of Sri Sri Ramakrishna.

Christopher Isherwood in his book "Ramakrishna and his disciples" writes, "The Gospel opens with an artless abruptness and incoherence which give an immediate impression of its authenticity. It is as if M, has been so moved by his experiences that he has not even paused to rehearse the sequence of events in his mind before starting to write ....."

What was the style of conversation of Sri Ramakrishna with his devotees and visitors? In simple language, Thakur used to talk about Philosophy and Religion and his stories on life's tribulations and keeping faith in the Supreme Power called "Ma" (Mother Kali) in the face of adversity were simply brilliant. In fact, they are peerless gems that broaden one's horizon and help develop a new perspective. Sri Ramakrishna was perhaps the greatest "LOK SHIKSHAK" who, without any formal education, could mesmerize highly educated people with his thought-provoking utterances. A few of such stories follow:

Consider mind that is like milk. Milk is so easily miscible with water; so is mind when it is immersed in worldly affairs. These worldly affairs taken together constitute what we called *sangsar*. Milk is quietly converted to curd and then butter may be extracted from it. Butter, a product from milk, when placed on water, remains just like that without mixing with water. Similarly, mind has to be prepared to give it a character of butter. Such a mind, even when deeply immersed in worldly affairs, remains unscathed and unperturbed. On November 26, 1883 – about one hundred thirty years ago - Sri Ramakrishna advises his devotees to create this mind through what is called *sadhana*. The simile used by Sri Ramakrishna is powerful, practical and apt. Through the example that is given in the Sri Ramakrishna *Kathamrita*, Thakur (as Sri Ramakrishna is popularly known) has charted the course of development in the mental and spiritual process of a devotee.

Sri Ramakrishna once said, "Advice of scholars having no faith in God is perplexing." This saying of Thakur is also given in the *Kathamrita*. In today's parlance, the advice means: scholarship bereft of wisdom is counterproductive. This powerful advice emanating from the mouth of an "illiterate priest" cuts all ages, boundaries and civilizations. Learning without wisdom is indeed dangerous, so said Sri Ramakrishna.

Thakur always advised his wealthy devotees not to be haughty. But the advice is given in a subtle form, creating a sense of universal greatness of mind. Thakur first talks about night-flies seen after dusk. Night-flies may have a feeling that they are giving light to the dark world. Soon after, stars start twinkling in the sky (and night-flies start feeling small and insignificant) and they feel they are the source of light. Then rises the beautiful moon and its beauty is so encompassing that stars lose their lustre. Finally darkness is completely removed with the rise of the sun in the sky and such is the brightness of the sun that the moon is not seen at all. Giving this example, Sri Ramakrishna says, "If wealthy men think about these, they will not feel unnecessarily proud of their acquisitions." The basic idea behind the example is basically putting things in perspectives. To Sri Ramakrishna, perspectives were extremely important; I sometimes feel, by perspectives, Sri Ramakrishana meant "chaitanya." Sri Ramakrishna was a strong proponent of a "free" mind instead of a "closed" mind. A closed mind is always immersed in worries and afflictions associated with living and cannot come out of them. Through a process that may be spiritual and to Sri Ramakrishana the path was spiritual, a mind in bondage is made free.

On October 19, 1884, Sri Ramakrishna was asked by Troilakya, a devotee, about the duties of ordinary men, so-called *grihasthas*. Thakur said, "You have lots of duties. Bring up your children, look after your wife, ensure that your wife can continue with her life when you will be no more, etc. If you do not perform such duties, you are a cruel person. A man without kindness is no man at all." From this simple advice, what does one make out of Sri Ramakrishna? In my opinion, he hammers the point: charity begins at home. One must be kind and compassionate to his near and dear ones first before venturing into the bigger responsibilities of the world. Thakur's advices thus centre around perspectives. The beauty of his teachings is that he is always eager to include and abhors any form of exclusion. The spirit of inclusion constituted Sri Ramakrishna's dharma or Sri Ramakrishna's doctrines that were established firmly by Swami Vivekananda. In his Chicago address, when Swamiji called the audience "Brothers and sisters of America", the audience were enthralled simply because they felt included in the universal concept of humanity. To Swamiji, there was sin, but no sinner and this idea is inherently an inclusive idea the founder of which was Sri Ramakrishna.

On June 25, 1884, Thakur utters a brilliant sentence: A learned man without conscience is not learned at all. This utterance comes out of an inconceivable depth of knowledge. This knowledge is not derived from books, but is produced within. There are so many learned men all around today, but the world is full of deceits and dissents. The prime reason behind it is the absence of conscience. Sri Ramakrishna taught his disciples the power of conscience. His dharma is not an idea imported from external sources; it is an idea of emancipation of self. Perhaps, this idea was given shape by Swami Vivekananda when he said, "Education is the manifestation of the perfection already in man," and "Religion is the manifestation of the divinity already in man."

Ordinary people in large number used to visit Dakhshineswar to get a glimpse of Sri Ramakrishna. Many used to ask him about God and how to get solace in the world of desires and their unfulfilment and the resulting tension. Sri Ramakrishna used to satisfy the queries with practical examples and small stories. In fact, he was one of the greatest story-tellers of all times and this aspect of Sri Ramakrishna has not been highlighted in necessary detail.

Prof. F. Max Muller in his book "Ramakrishna – His Life and Sayings" writes, "... when crowds of men and boys came to him to learn, he would select and point out some who, he said, would realize religion in his life, and of the rest he would say that they must enjoy life a little longer before they would have a sincere desire for religion. He used to say: 'That man who had been an emperor in his former birth, who had enjoyed the highest pleasures the world can give, and who had seen vanities of them all, would attain to perfection in this life on earth'."

Once M asked Sri Ramakrishna, "Sir, can one see God?"

Thakur said, "Most certainly you can! And this is what you must do in order to see him: Live in solitude from time to time. Chant the name of the Lord and his glories. And discriminate between the eternal and non-eternal."

M then asked Thakur what state of mind was necessary for seeing God.

Thakur: "Cry to him with a yearning heart, and you will see him. Men weep profusely for their wives and children. They cry endlessly for wealth and money. But who sheds tears for God? You must seek him with a loving heart."

Having said this, Thakur sang a devotional song:

> Seek Mother Shyama, O my mind,
> With a longing heart,
> With a yearning heart,
> She will not withhold herself.
> For how can the Mother withhold herself?
> How can Kali the Mother withhold her presence?
> Seek her, O my mind, seek her only.
> Gather the vilwa leaves,
> Gather hibiscus flowers,
> Then anoint them with sandal-paste,
> The sandal-paste of devotion,
> And lay them, as your offering, before her feet.

Sri Ramakrishna went on, "Yearning for God is like the coming of dawn. Dawn comes before the sun rises. When yearning for God comes, the vision of God himself must follow."

Sri Ramakrishna then explains what he means by the yearning. "The worldly man's attachment to his wealth, mother's love for her child, and the chaste wife's love for her husband: - when these three get together, you will see God."

"Call on God with a longing heart. The kitten cries, 'mew, mew'. The mother knows how to respond to the call. She runs to her rescue from far and wide."

Over the years, M's acquaintance with Thakur grew deeper and deeper.

One day Thakur asked M, "How do you feel about me? How many annas of knowledge of God do I have?" [the word anna is basically a smaller unit of a rupee that is called taka in Bengali.]

M said, "Sir, I do not know what you mean by annas. But this much I can say: Never before haveI come across such incontrovertible wisdom, such ecstatic love, such absolute faith, such complete dispassion and such broadmindedness." The answer brought delightful smile on the face of Sri Ramakrishna.

During his lifetime, Sri Ramakrishna met many distinguished men of his time and left them mesmerized with his ready wit and incomparable stories and anecdotes that related the external world as an ordinary man perceives, and the world beyond ordinary man's perception. One such reference is given below; the place being Shyampukurbati, a house in north Calcutta where Thakur stayed for some time for his treatment.

Says Sri Ramakrishna in the Gospel (to Dr.MahendralalSarkar, distinguished Homoeopath who had treated Thakur), "Many people think they cannot have knowledge or understanding of God without reading books. But hearing is better than reading, and seeing is better than hearing. Hearing about Benares is different from reading about it; but seeing Benares is different from either hearing or reading.

Those actually engaged in a game of chess do not always judge the moves on the board correctly. The onlookers often judge the moves better than players. Worldly people often think themselves very intelligent, but they are attached to the things in the world. They are the actual players and cannot understand their own moves correctly. But holy men, who have renounced everything, are unattached to the world; they are really more intelligent than worldly people. Since they do not take part in worldly life, their position is that of onlookers, and so they see things more clearly."

On hearing Sri Ramakrishna, Dr.Sarkar who was vastly educated in western science (and also founded the Indian Association for the Cultivation of Science) said to other devotees present, "If he (meaning Sri Ramakrishna) had studied books he could not have acquired so much knowledge. Faraday communed with nature; that is why he was able to discover many scientific truths. He could not have known so much from the mere study of books. Mathematical formulas only throw the brain into confusion and bar the path of original enquiry."

As such conversations went on, Girish Chandra Ghosh, a great Ramakrishna devotee and distinguished dramatist, reminded Dr. Sarkar, "You have already spent three or four hours here. What about your patients?"

Doctor said, "Well, my practice and patients! I shall lose everything on account of your Paramahansa!" As the doctor spoke, all the devotees present in the room laughed.

Thakur then said, "There is a river called the 'Karmanasha' (literally, 'destroyer of duties'). It is dangerous to dive into the river. If a man plunges into its waters he cannot perform any more action. It puts an end to his duties."

Dr.Sarkar then said to Girish, M and the other devotees, "My friends, consider me as one of you. I am not saying this as a physician. But if you think of me as your own, then I am yours."

Interjected Sri Ramakrishna, "There is such a thing as love for love's sake. It is very good if one can grow such love. Prahlada loved God for the sake of love. Says he, - O God, I do not want wealth, fame, creature comforts, or any such thing. Please grant me the boon that I may have genuine love for Thy Lotus Feet."

The argumentative Dr.Mahendralal is quick to point out, "You are right, Sir. I have seen people bowing down before the image of Kali. They seek worldly objects from the Goddess, such as, a job, the healing of disease, and so forth.

The illness you (meaning Sri Ramakrishna) are suffering from does not permit the patient to talk with people. But my case is an exception. You may talk with me when I am here."

Thakur then said, "Please cure my illness. I cannot chant the name and glories of God."

Dr.Sarkar said, "Meditation is enough."

Sri Ramakrishna: "What do you mean? Why should I lead a monotonous life? I enjoy my fish in a variety of dishes: curried fish, fried fish, pickled fish, and so forth! Sometimes I worship God with rituals, sometimes I repeat His name, sometimes I meditate on Him, sometimes I sing His name and glories, sometimes I dance in His name."

Thus, as one goes through the Kathamrita, one can't but refrain himself/herself from admiring Sri Ramakrishna's skill and ability to understand and convince others of his point of view through examples and anecdotes. M has gone on describing such incidents page after page in the Kathamritawith remarkable detachment that is rare and unworldly. Perhaps, M's absolute devotion to Sri Ramakrishna could make him so detached. He was inside the conversations, but was successful in keeping himself outside. But being outside, he was all the time inside the entire Kathamrita, giving a running commentary of the divine life of Sri Ramakrishna with ease and facility.

This article will be incomplete if the writer does not add a few points here and there, knowing fully well that many a great men have given their commentary on Sri Ramakrishna Kathamrita. So far as my understanding goes, Sri Ramakrishna was an Idea and Swami Vivekananda was the executor of his ideas. The relationship here was similar to that existing between Sri Krishna and the third Pandava Arjuna. In the battle of Kurukshetra, when Arjuna had left his bow and arrow and was determined not to fight against his near and dear ones, Sri Krishna had to make the oral composition called the Gita. I doubt whether one knows with a great deal of certainty the name of the composer who, for the first time in the history of civilization, put the Gita in the printed form. In the modern world, between Sri Ramakrishna and Swamiji, between the idea and its execution, however, it was certainly M who acted as the composer of the modern-day Gita.

Let's go back to the conversation between Thakur and Dr.Sarkar.

Thakur said, "Your son Amrita does not believe in the incarnation of God. What is the harm in that? One realizes God even if one believes Him to be formless. One also realizes God if one believes that God has form. Two things are necessary for the realization of God: faith and self-surrender. Man is ignorant by nature. Errors are natural to him. Can a one-seer pot hold four seers of milk? Whatever path you may follow, you must pray to God with a restless heart. He is the Ruler of the soul within. He will surely listen to your prayer if it is sincere. Whether you follow the ideal of the Personal God or that of the Impersonal Truth, you will realize God alone, provided you are restless for Him. A cake with icing tastes sweet whether you eat it straight or sidewise."

When Thakur said that Dr.Sarkar's son Amrita was a nice boy, Dr.Sarkar informed him that Amrita was Thakur disciple.

Thakur then said with a smile, "There is not a fellow under the sun who is my disciple. On the contrary, I am everybody's disciple. All are the children of God. All are His servants. I too am a child of God. I too am His servant. 'Uncle Moon' is every child's uncle!"

"LOK SIKSHAK" Sri Ramakrishna is at his brilliant best when he says that 'Uncle Moon' is every child's uncle. Here he compares God with the moon. Indeed, right from our childhood, the moon becomes our maternal uncle through an age-old and all-pervading relationship the genesis of which is not known to us and not even questioned. Sri Ramakrishna has taught his disciples the power of faith through the example and M has described that so well.

Max Muller writes about Sri Ramakrishna, "He was a wonderful mixture of God and man. In his ordinary state he would talk of himself as servant of all men and women. He looked upon them all as God. He himself would never be addressed as Guru, or teacher. Never would he claim for himself any high position. He would touch the ground reverently where his disciples had trodden. But every now and then strange fits of God-consciousness came upon him. He then became changed into a different being altogether. He then spoke of himself as being able to do and know everything. He spoke as if he had the power of giving anything to anybody. He would speak of himself as the same soul that had been born before as Rama, as Krishna, as Jesus, or as Buddha, born again as Ramakrishna. .... He said that he was free from all eternity, and the practices and struggles after religion which he went through were only meant to show people the way to salvation. He had done all for them alone. He would say he was a Nitya-mukta, or eternally free, and an incarnation of God Himself." In his long description, M tried to show this Ramakrishna who was Lord Narayan in the form of a man, and who was born on earth to teach people how to lead "human life" in the best possible way.

As one goes through the Kathamrita, one may find that Sri Ramakrishna's speech at times was abominably filthy. Many a time, Sri Ramakrishna told his followers to become "one in mouth and mind". So-called educated men commonly known as gentlemen know how to express their opinions on various issues articulately and in the process, they mask or hide their real feelings. This was not to be with Sri Ramakrishna who said what he thought and meant much more than what he said or expressed. It was for the follower to decode Sri Ramakrishna in its entirety. In my opinion, he could read peoples' minds so well that their inner desires and contradictions were revealed as soon as they appeared before him. Sri Ramakrishna's spiritual wisdom was the result of genius and practical observation, as described by M. In fact, M took days together to put down on paper what he heard or gathered from a single visit to Sri Ramakrishna. His modus operandi was to take "copious notes immediately after each of his meetings with Ramakrishna. It is said that he was often busy for three days writing down the sayings and events of a single visit. Nevertheless, when the time came for publication, he worked over all of his material, during the last thirty-five years of his life."

In his appreciation of M for the Gospel, Christopher Isherwood writes, "If I had to use one single word to describe the atmosphere of the Gospel narrative, it would be the word *Now*. The majority of us spend the greater part of our lives in the future or the past – fearing or desiring what is to come, regretting what is over. M shows us a being who lives in continuous contact with that which is eternally present. God's existence has no relation to past or future; it is always as of *now*. To be with Ramakrishna was to be in the presence of that Now. Not everybody who visited Dakshineswar was aware of this. M was aware, from the first; and he never ceased to be thankful for the privilege he was enjoying. He describes every scene of his narrative with a thankful wonder that he – the ordinary unworthy schoolmaster – should have been permitted to take part in it. M's sense of the greatness of each and every such occasion gives even his simplest descriptive passages a quality of excitement and magic:"

The above passage from Isherwood reminds me of Arjuna in the battlefield of Kurukshetra. He was unwilling to fight simply because he dwelt in the past or in the future. It was Sri Krishna who brought him back to the present, to *Now* of the above passage, through His sayings in the Gita, and Arjuna was thus transformed into a completely different being.

"M would have been overwhelmed, no doubt, if he could have known that Aldous Huxley would one day compare him to Boswell and call his Gospel 'unique in the literature of hagiography'. Yet Huxley's praise is no more than a statement of fact. The service M has rendered us and future generations can hardly be exaggerated. Even the vainest of authors might well have been humbled, finding himself entrusted with such a task. M was the least vain.

M embodies Ramakrishna's ideal of the household devotee. He was a distinguished teacher and scholar, vested with authority and held in honour. Yet he thought of himself always as a servant and the least of men. The world could never win him, even with its love; and everyone who met him loved him. It is said that he would often take his bedroll at night and lie down to sleep in the open porch of a public building, among the homeless boys of the city – to remind himself that, like the maid in Ramakrishna's parable, his real home was elsewhere."

To conclude this article (more apt will be the word nibedan instead of article), I raise a question to myself: what does a household devotee feel with Sri Sri Ramakrishna Kathamrita in his hands? I could not get a very clear answer. All on a sudden, however, the following lines from William Blake's poem – Auguries of Innocence – came to my mind:

"To see a world in a grain of sand
And a Heaven in a wild flower,
Hold Infinity in the palm of your hand
And Eternity in an hour."

I ask myself a direct question now: do I understand Kathamrita? I get an instantaneous answer that is negative. I then touch Kathamrita; I get a feeling of having Infinity in the palm of my hand. Where does this eternal bliss, this great feeling that soothes my mind, come from? I don't know. I really don't know.

REFERENCES

1. Sri Sri Ramakrishna Kathamrita as told by M.
2. Ramakrishna and his disciples, by Christopher Isherwood, AdvaitaAshrama, March 1965; ISBN 81 – 85301 – 18 – 2.
3. Ramakrishna His Life and Sayings, by Prof. F. Max Muller, AdvaitaAshrama, ISBN 978 – 81 – 7505 – 060 – 0.

4

Management skills of Sri Ramakrishna

Swami Vedatitananda

The topic of our deliberation is the management skills of Sri Ramakrishna. Sri Ramakrishna was found to be constantly in a god-intoxicated mood, hardly ever aware of the world around him. More often than not, he would be in Samadhi or in a deeply indrawn mood. So, are we stretching our imagination a bit too far in trying to expound on this topic?

Our justification however is that an Avatara establishes a new order of things. That work of establishing a new order of things calls for certain skills that are not different from the skills of management in kind, but there is a significant difference in degree. It is this aspect that we will be exploring in this article.

We will be studying this aspect of Sri Ramakrishna, the paragon of Incarnations, under six sub-sections which are:

1. Managing the Dakshineswar Temple
2. Searching for a reliable deputy – Narayan Shastri/Keshab Sen/ Narendranath
3. Grooming his deputies & a core group: Training of Sri Sarada Devi, Naren, Rakhal & Sharat
4. Closed door meetings with Naren – setting up an organization
5. Core-values indoctrination & rites of passage
6. Fruits of his management skills – Ramakrishna movement

A. Managing in the Dakshineswar Temple

Sri Ramakrishna entered into the Dakshineswar Temple with some inner resistance. His elder brother was the main priest of the Temple. He joined as an assistant to his elder brother. In due course, he got promoted to the main priest of the Temple. Then unfolded an unprecedented spiritual saga culminating in Sri Ramakrishna becoming the paragon of incarnations. From the time he entered service in the Temple, he was noticed by Mathurbabu and Rani Rashmoni. They noticed that his devotion was something unique. Gradually, Sri Ramakrishna rose to be the central figure of the Temple complex. His rectitude and moral strength cast its spell on others working there. For all practical purposes, he himself was just another employee there. But, his moral power, his utter dedication to the Goddess Kali of the Temple, exerted a subtle but perceptible pressure on every other employee to work and contribute. The Temple Trust was established with some clear objectives by Rani Rashmoni. The daily worship of the deities was to be ensured, as if they were living entities. Wandering monks and spiritual aspirants would be supplied food and lodging for a few days. Genuine spiritual aspirants would be given facilities to stay and perform their practices. Sri Ramakrishna would ensure that these objectives were met scrupulously even after Rani Rashmoni and Mathurnath Biswas passed away.

There is an interesting incident recorded in the Gospel of Sri Ramakrishna.

Sri Ramakrishna meets Trailokyanath Biswas, Mathurbabu's son. Trailokya had taken charge of the Temple Trust after his father passed away. Sri Ramakrishna tells Trailokya that a particular service in the Temple was not done properly and that was bad. This service had been instituted right from the inception of the Temple and the founding members Rani Rashmoni and Mathurnath Biswas had conscientiously conducted the service all their life. Now, with a change of guard, there was some laxity seen and Sri Ramakrishna was quick to point it out. Here we see a glimpse of how Sri Ramakrishna acted as the conscience keeper of the Temple. This is a vital aspect of management. From this one incident, we can infer that Sri Ramakrishna was quite active in this role of overlooking the activities of the Temple complex on a daily basis, although we lack written records of the same. There are however recorded instances of how he, despite his constant state of divine inebriation, was quick to point out any discrepancy in the daily food offering of the Divine Mother reaching his room, or any anomaly in his monthly payment.

Apart from this, we see another aspect of Sri Ramakrishna during his Sadhana period. One day around 2am, Hriday saw Sri Ramakrishna cutting fruits that were meant for offering early next morning in the Temple. He asked Sri Ramakrishna why he was cutting fruits in the midnight. Sri Ramakrishna replied that he had a habit of meditating from 3am every morning. When he sat for meditation, he used to get disturbed by the fact that he had to come out of meditation in time to cut the fruits meant for offering. This thought was becoming a hindrance to his smooth meditation. Hence, he had started cutting the fruits before he sat for meditation, so that, the offerings would be kept ready and his meditation would go on without any disturbance. We see here how Sri Ramakrishna was able to manage himself with great efficiency.

B. Searching for a Reliable Deputy–Narayan Shastri/Keshab Sen/ Narendranath

Sri Ramakrishna completed his spiritual practices and had achieved unprecedented success. He had some unique revelations. He came to realize that he was not an ordinary spiritual aspirant who had achieved success by dint of his own Sadhana. He was an Incarnation of God who had a mission to accomplish in this world. That mission was nothing short of the spiritual regeneration of entire humanity.

Let me quote *in extenso* from the authoritative book 'Sri Ramakrishna and his divine play' written by Swami Saradananda.

After he had attained perfection in various sadhanas, the Master had many unique intuitive perceptions. Some of them were related to the Master himself and other to spirituality in general. We present the most important ones here. We think that the Master realized the true meaning of those experiences when he was in Bhavamukha at the end of his sadhana, united with the Divine Mother. Although these revelations resulted from his yogic insight, we will try to express them in terms of human reasoning.

1. **The Master realized he was an incarnation of God**, a person commissioned by God to do good to the world, and that he sadhanas he undertook were practiced for the sake of others. When he compared his spiritual life with the lives of other aspirants, he realized that there was a significant difference between them from a general point of view. He observed that an ordinary aspirant attains peace by realizing God though lifelong practice of a single spiritual discipline; whereas he himself could not rest until he had practiced the sadhanaas of all paths. Moreover, it took very little time for him to attain perfection in each sadhana. There cannot be an effect without a cause: his sincere search to discover why that was so led him to deep meditation and revealed the cause to him. This inquiry revealed that such things happened to him because he was by nature pure, awakened, and free, and a special

incarnation of Almighty God. He also understood that his extraordinary sadhanas would shed new light in the realm of spirituality and that they had been undertaken for the good of humanity, rather than to remove any personal deficiency of his own.

2. The master realized that he would **not attain liberation like other beings.**
3. Absorbed in Yoga, the **Master knew the time of his death** long before it occurred. At Dakshineswar he once told the Holy Mother, in an ecstatic mood, "When you find me accepting food from anyone and everyone, spending nights in Calcutta, and feeding a portion of food first to someone else, then eating what is left – then know that the day I will leave this body is near." On another occasion at Dakshineswar, when he was in an exalted mood, he told the Holy Mother, "Towards the end I shall eat rice pudding only and nothing else." All these words were literally true.
4. **After attaining perfection through different religious paths, the Master was firmly convinced: "All religions are true. As many faiths, so many paths."** He understood this both intuitively and intellectually. He realized the ultimate goal of each of those paths. The purpose of the Master's advent in this present age was to stop religious conflict and degradation in this world by propagating the aforesaid truth. No other divine incarnation has fully realized this universality of truth through Sadhana ad has taught it to the world. If the greatness of an Avatara is to be determined on the basis of the catholicity of his spiritual views, undoubtedly the foremost place should be accorded to the Master for preaching this.
5. **The ideas of Dvaita, *Vishistadvaita* and *Advaita* emerge spontaneously according to one's spiritual growth.** The Master said that they were not contradictory but depended on the stages of one's spiritual progress. The sages recorded those three philosophical views in the Vedas, Upanishads and other scriptures. Consequently those ideas created unending confusion and made spiritual paths complicated. Unable to find any harmony in the experiences and statements of the sages, each philosophical school tortured the texts and tried to interpret them from its own point of view. This fear has engendered disbelief in the scriptures, which has led to the religious degradation of India. So the Master, the Avatara of this age, experienced for himself those three philosophical paths as different stages of the same truth and propagated their wonderful harmony. The only way to enter

into the study of the scriptures is to always remember this conclusion of the Master.

6. **The Master indicated the limits of action** when he said, "The action of a sattvic person drops off automatically. He cannot work even if he tries to; the Lord does not allow him to work. It is just as when a young wife advances in pregnancy. She is given less and less work to do; and when the child is born, she gives up household work altogether and is busied exclusively with the infant. But an ordinary person must try to do his duties with detachment, depending on the Lord, like the maidservant who does everything for her master, knowing in her heart that her home is elsewhere. This is known as Karma Yoga. As far as possible, one should take the name of the Lord and meditate on Him while discharging one's everyday duties in an unattached way."
7. **The Master realized that as an instrument of the Divine Mother, he would have to establish a new religious order based on the universal truths revealed in his life.** The Master first saw this through a vision he had during Mathur's lifetime. He then told Mathur that the Divine Mother had revealed to him that many devotees would come to him to attain spirituality. Later, this literally came true. At the Cossipore garden house the Master looked at his own photograph (Seated in meditation) and told us, 'This represents a high yogic state. This image will be worshipped in many homes as time goes by.'[1]

It is important for us to understand that these revelations are vital in our study of Sri Ramakrishna's Management skills. It is these revelations that acted as the touchstone with which he regulated his later actions, be it choosing his deputies, or training his disciples, or giving shape to the organization itself.

Soon as he received these revelations about his mission in life, he began looking for a deputy who would assist him in this mission. One of the first persons to come to him during this period was a sincere aspirant called Narayan Shastri. The way Sri Ramakrishna trained him, we get the clear feeling that he was exploring the possibility of his becoming Sri Ramakrishna's deputy in his grand mission. However, Narayan Shastri turned out otherwise. Once he had experienced the bliss of Samadhi under Sri Ramakrishna's training, he no longer had any wish to continue living in society. He bade goodbye to Sri Ramakrishna and went away to live a wandering life and enjoy the bliss of Samadhi. Nobody heard about him anymore after that. Undaunted, Sri Ramakrishna continued his search.

When he came in contact with Keshab Sen, the way he interacted with him, we again get the feeling that he was trying to see if Keshab could turn out to be a good deputy. However, in due course, Sri Ramakrishna found that Keshab had his own agenda, what with his Brahmo Samaj's innumerable activities. But, Sri Ramakrishna's contact with Keshab did turn out profitable for Sri Ramakrishna because, through Keshab, Sri Ramakrishna came in touch with some spirited young men from whom came Sri Ramakrishna's inner group of disciples.

Basically, Sri Ramakrishna was on a recruitment drive for an able deputy. From each case where he failed to develop his protégé (as in the case of Narayan Shastri or Keshab Chandra Sen), he learned some valuable lessons on how exactly to train his deputy. All those lessons, he was able to put into good use when he did come across a potential candidate in the form of Narendranath.

One of the members of Keshab Chandra Sen's Brahmo Samaj was a young man called Narendranath. Sri Ramakrishna and Naren met in Kolkata and the chemistry was instant. After this began a systematic training of the young Naren in the hands of Sri Ramakrishna. We shall discuss in a subsequent sub-section.

What we wish to highlight here is the special care that Sri Ramakrishna took to ensure and confirm that Naren would indeed be the deputy he was searching for, the one who would carry forward his mission after he was gone.

It may be argued here that Sri Ramakrishna did not indeed have to struggle too hard for choosing his deputy. He had in fact received some definite spiritual visions about Naren and Rakhal and his other inner group disciples. True. But we must always remember one important feature of an Avatara. An incarnation of God is no doubt divine, but is also utterly human. The visions he received were all symbolic in nature. There was a need to match those visions to reality. We find Sri Ramakrishna constantly testing in each case whether the person he saw in those visions was indeed the same person in reality or not.

C. Grooming his Deputies & a Core Group: Training of Sri Sarada Devi, Naren, Rakhal, Sarat & Hariprasanna

It is interesting to note that Sri Ramakrishna married a girl who was almost twenty years younger than him! Although this seemed absurd when he did it, it makes very sound sense when we see that she had a vital role to play in nurturing the fledgling organization that he initiated and left behind him when he passed away in his 50th year. She had very strong common sense, an excellent sense of proportion and a very strong will that helped sustain the budding Ramakrishna Math. In fact, when we see her later life, we find that the present form that the Ramakrishna Math and the Ramakrishna Mission has is entirely owing to her vision and guidance.

We see the following wonderful incident in her life: In 1890, Holy Mother visited Bodh Gaya. There she noticed how comfortably the members of a local monastery lived with all their physical needs supplied. She later recalled: "*Ah, how much I wept, how often I prayed to the Master! That is why you see all these monasteries established by his grace. Immediately after his passing away, the children renounced the world and sought out a temporary shelter. But soon after, they began to wander about independently. I felt very sad and prayed to the Master, 'O Master, you came down to earth, had fun with a few companions, and then departed in a happy mood. Was that he end of everything? If so, what was the need of assuming a human body and going through all this suffering? I have seen many sadhus at Varanasi and Vrindavan who live on alms and seek shelter under trees. There is no dearth of sadhus like them. I cannot bear the sight of my children, who have renounced everything in your name, going from door to door for a morsel of food. I fervently pray to you that those who give up the world in your name may not lack simple food and clothing. Let them live together with you and your teachings as their center. Those who are afflicted with the sorrows of the world will come to them and obtain peace by listening to your teachings. That is the purpose of your advent, isn't it so? I cannot control myself when I see them drifting about helplessly.' Afterwards, Naren slowly organized all this.*"[2]

He had groomed her for this job very well when he was alive. He groomed her to be a spiritual leader in her own right in later life. With this end in view, he taught her about the insubstantial nature of the world and warned her about its sorrows and pitfalls. He trained her to cultivate detachment from transitory objects and develop devotion to God, who alone is real and eternal. Lakshmi (Sri Ramakrishna's niece) later recalled the following incident, which she witnessed in Kamarpukur: "*One day the Master pointed to Aunt Sarada and said, 'What good is there in giving birth like dogs and jackals to a whole brood of children? You raised your young brothers and sisters tenderly; you witnessed how deeply your parents lamented when two of them died, and you also grieved for them. How miserable life in the world is! Why should you bother with it? Without any such trouble, you like a goddess now and will always remain a goddess.' One morning the Master was brushing his teeth with a twig and Aunt was mopping the mud floor, mixing mud with cow dung with water. Pointing to Aunt, the Master jokingly said, 'Bedecked with jewelry, you may dance and sing at the rice-eating ceremony for your son, but you will fall on the ground crying when he dies.' Hearing the Master harping on death, Aunt Sharada asked gently, 'But do they all die?' Perhaps the Master felt that Aunt had the innate longing for motherhood that is present in all women. At once he loudly called out to the other ladies, 'See, I have stepped on the tail of a cobra. Goodness gracious! I often said to myself: 'She is such a simple soul, unaware of the ways of the world.' But see how much she keeps inside her. Did you hear what she said? 'Do they all die?" Aunt ran away.*"[3]

When she came to Dakshineswar, he wrote a mantra on her tongue and initiated her. He asked her to offer the previous mantra she had received from Swami Purnananda at the feet of her Ishta.[4] He also taught her mantras for different gods and goddesses and transmitted his spiritual experiences to her so that she could conduct her spiritual ministry later on. She said later on, "*The mantras I give were taught to me by the Master. These are siddha-mantras.*"[5] Whenever an opportunity arose, the Master would give spiritual instructions to the Holy Mother. On another occasion the Master drew a diagram of the six centers of the kundalini on a piece of paper and gave it to Holy Mother. Unfortunately it was lost. She later lamented, "*Ah, how could I have known then that so many things would happen in connection with the Master? I lost that diagram of the six centers of the Kundalini and could not trace it anywhere.*"[6]

He had even given her certain specific advices on how to live in the world after he was gone. He was that thorough in his training! Holy Mother later recalled his advice, "*Look, don't extend your hand to anyone for a penny. You will never lack ordinary food and plain clothing. If you ask for money from anyone, your head will be sold to that person. It is better to get food from someone than to live with that person. Some devotees may lovingly offer their homes for you to live in, but never give up your cottage in Kamarpukur. Stay in Kamarpukur. Grow some spinach. Eat that spinach with rice and repeat Hari's name.*"[7]

A few days before the Master passed away, he sent for Holy Mother. He taught her eight mantras and then said, "*These are all siddha mantras. Please teach these mantras to those who come to you for initiation. Those who receive one of these mantras will have the vision of their Ishta during their lifetime or at least at the time of death. Later many people will come to you for initiation. Initiate them with these mantras.*"[8]

He had opened her Mother-heart and had shown her the necessity for the organization even when he was alive.

His training of Naren was equally wonderful. As mentioned earlier, Sri

Ramakrishna had indeed tried to make suitable deputies out of some other potential candidates such as Narayan Shastri, Keshab Chandra Sen, Vijay Krishna Goswami, etc. In each of those cases, he had failed. When he started working on Naren, he was careful to avoid all those pitfalls that the previous candidates had fallen into. In each of the earlier cases, Sri Ramakrishna had made some mistakes in training his disciple. He made corrections for all of them when he started training Naren. In Narayan Shastri's case, he taught him the path to attain Nirvikalpa Samadhi and that turned out to be his undoing. Having attained the pinnacle of spiritual practice in the form of Nirvikalpa Samadhi, Narayan Shastri was no longer interested in any Mission thereafter. He was an unfettered horse who simply left Dakshineswar, feeling utterly grateful to his Guru for having shown him the path. Later on, in Keshab & Vijay Krishna's case, Sri Ramakrishna found that these two extremely capable people, who could have been very able deputies for his work, already had organizations of their own. He found out that although both of them accepted the new ideal that he was revealing to the world, they found it impossible to officially endorse his views. The vital role of Mother Kali (or the vital role of the Divine Power as opposed to the Divine Existence) turned out to be too much for both these stalwarts to accept in public. We shall see how Sri Ramakrishna corrected these mistakes when he started his training of Narendranath.

D. Closed Door Meetings with Naren – Setting up an Organization

1. The Momentous Meeting

We have mentioned that Sri Ramakrishna had some very specific divine revelations about the mission he was to accomplish in his life. He planned to accomplish those things through a network of disciples which included his wife Sri Sarada Devi, and a handful of young spiritual aspirants, as noted above. During his last days at Cossipore, we find him plunging headlong into preparing this core team. He held several closed door meetings with Naren as recorded in the authentic biographies of Sri Ramakrishna and Swami Vivekananda. What happened during these closed door meetings? Unfortunately, we do not have any record of what transpired in those meetings. But by studying the later events in the life of Swami Vivekananda, we can sort of infer (safely, I guess!) that those meetings involved giving the young Naren some very specific instructions which he would later bring into fruition.

Time and again we find Swami Vivekananda saying that he was charged by his Master to keep the young spiritual aspirants together, not allow them to go back home, encourage them to practice the spiritual disciplines he had instructed them and also to do something for the spiritual regeneration of the land. We can safely infer that these repeated instructions to Naren were given by the Master during these closed door meetings, for, we do not find him giving these instructions during any other time in the authentic biographies.

We may also safely infer that Sri Ramakrishna never gave the young Naren any specific direction along which to work, just these broad directives. However, what is amazing to note is that these directives proved so powerful that in trying to work them out, the young Naren got transformed into the world famous Swami Vivekananda.

Let us look a bit more closely on how this amazing transformation took place. We must pay special attention to Sri Ramakrishna's style of working here. It is interesting to note that a lot of his own work of establishing his Mission, he got it done through his deputy Narendranath posthumously. I shall try to delineate how Sri Ramakrishna seems to reach out from beyond the grave, as it were, and guides every action of his trusted Deputy Narendranath. We will be describing some spiritual experiences that the young Narendranath had in the course of our explanation. These experiences will have to be understood as the handiwork of Sri Ramakrishna if we have to get a complete picture of his management style. This may sound like a bit far-fetched, but this happens to be the truth. Each of the spiritual experiences we describe herein under were orchestrated by Sri Ramakrishna, some while he was still alive on Earth, some after he left his human body.

It is worthy of special treatment because it is one of the rare instances where we find the power transmitted by a leader to his subordinate flowering in an amazing manner, creating a world leader in its course.[9]

A university student Narendranath came in contact with Sri Ramakrishna Paramahamsa sometime in Nov 1881. This meeting set in motion a series of transformations in the boy's life. Sri Ramakrishna had performed unprecedented spiritual practices for 12 years at a stretch and had received some specific instructions. This was about 10 years before Naren came to him. He received a specific command from the Divine Mother saying, '*Remain in Bhavamukha*[10].' As mentioned above, his biographer Swami Saradananda mentions the following as the summing up of his extraordinary spiritual experiences[11]: *The Master realized that as an instrument of the Divine Mother, he would have to* ***establish a new religious order based on the universal truths revealed in his life.*** This was the mission that Sri Ramakrishna entrusted Naren with during his last days at Cossipore.

Sri Ramakrishna found in Naren a fit instrument through whom he could fulfil this divine mandate that he had received. So, in Cossipore, during his last days, he instructed Naren that he would hold the young men together. He would also need to do something of a permanent nature that would help the common masses to get spiritual benefit. He also infused into Naren all the spiritual powers that he had obtained through his unprecedented Sadhana.

After Sri Ramakrishna attained Mahasamadhi, Naren and the group of young sadhakas took the vows of renunciation and became monks. During his stay at Cossipore with Sri Ramakrishna, Naren had experienced Nirvikalpa Samadhi. This experience convinced Naren once and for all that Reality was Impersonal and that he was non-distinct from the Impersonal Reality. He was in essence all that existed. In fact, apart from what he experienced during that Samadhi, nothing else existed. An unspeakable calm descended upon him. When he met his Guru after returning from the Samadhi at Cossipore, there was genuine gratitude to his Guru, just as it has been described in innumerable Hindu scriptures. However, there was still one nagging problem that Naren faced. When he returned back to perceiving duality, post Nirvikalpa Samadhi, he considered the return as a 'fall'[12] from the blessed state of Samadhi!

Not just that, he was also restless! This is something unheard of! Nirvikalpa Samadhi itself means that state which is devoid of all restlessness. A person who has attained Nirvikalpa Samadhi cannot become restless, ever. The memory of the experience is so overwhelming that never again does he lose his equanimity of mind. It has been traditionally believed that he who experiences Nirvikalpa Samadhi does not regain normal consciousness. He stays in that Samadhi for about three weeks and then leaves the body. Sri Ramakrishna used to say that only those rare few who had some Divine mission to fulfill would regain normal consciousness. But it was believed that under no circumstance does such a one experience restlessness! Why then was this happening? Swami Vivekananda himself stated that his mind was *burning*. It is quite natural that a Sadhaka who has attained to Nirvikalpa Samadhi feels he has 'fallen' from the blessed state when he returns to multiplicity, just as Tota Puri used to feel or any number of sadhakas in the Hindu lore have felt and recorded. But what is noteworthy here is the fact that Naren mentions specifically that his mind was agitated[13]! That is a new occurrence in the recorded spiritual history of mankind.

2. Raja Yoga as the Panacea

The only reason we can adduce to this peculiar state of things is – the responsibility that Sri Ramakrishna, his Guru, had burdened his young shoulders with, was weighing too heavily on him. That was the cause of his restlessness. Added to that, he was not physically very well, either. He was suffering from diabetes and lumbago and indigestion. Swamiji's mind was unique. That mind sought for integral solutions to problems. At the very least, he had three distinct problems at hand. [He was also trying to manage some issues related to his ancestral house, which we can discount at the moment.] Firstly, he had a weak physical constitution; second, he had to redeem his promise to his Guru of taking care of his brother disciples; third, he had to redeem his promise to his Guru about working out a scheme for spiritual development of the masses. He sought one solution that would take care of all these three problems simultaneously. What was that solution? He would learn Raja Yoga from Pavhari Baba. Using Hatha Yoga, a part of Raja Yoga, he would cure his ailments. Then, he would teach Raja Yoga to his brother disciples and form an Ashram where they would all live together and make disciples and preach Raja Yoga. His experience of the spiritual degradation of the region where he lived, Bengal, was that the people were too sentimental[14]. They attached too much importance to the external manifestations of *Bhava* rather than focus on the essential characteristic of spiritual development which is formation of a strong moral character, culminating in realization of one's true nature as Pure Consciousness. This he concluded was due to the inability of the Bengali people to see religion as a science. Thus, the masses would be benefitted as Raja Yoga is the most scientific method of spiritual development. He had almost decided to follow this path when the following incident occurred[15].

One day I reflected that I had not learnt any art for making this weak body strong, even though I had lived with Sri Ramakrishna for so many years. I had heard that Pavhari Baba knew the science of Hatha Yoga; so I thought that I would learn the practices of Hatha Yoga from him, and through them strengthen the body. You know, I have a dogged resolution, and whatever I set my heart on, I always carry out. On the eve of the day on which I was to take initiation, I was lying on a cot thinking; and just then I saw the form of Sri Ramakrishna standing on my right, looking steadfastly at me, as if very much grieved. I had dedicated myself to him, and at the thought that I was taking another Guru I felt much ashamed and kept looking at him. Thus perhaps two or three hours passed, but no words escaped my mouth: then he disappeared all on a sudden. Seeing Sri Ramakrishna that night my mind became upset, so I postponed the idea of initiation from Pavhari Baba for the day. After a day or two, again the idea of initiation from Pavhari Baba arose in the mind-and again at night Sri Ramakrishna appeared, as on the previous occasion. So when, for several nights in succession, I had the vision of Sri Ramakrishna, I gave up the idea of initiation altogether, thinking that since every time I resolved on it, I was having such a vision, no good, but only harm, would come of it."

Thus it was Sri Ramakrishna who in the end triumphed. Long afterwards, the Swami composed a song in Bengali entitled "A Song I Sing to Thee" in which one finds a glimpse of this experience.

As a result of this nerve-shattering experience, Naren concluded that his decision about Raja Yoga being the solution for all his problems was wrong. He must have somehow decided that Bengal was a prototype of mankind[16], which unfortunately wasn't the case. He needed more inputs before he could arrive at an informed decision. So now, he knew that Raja Yoga was not the solution, but again, Sri Ramakrishna did not specify what that solution would be in this vision, just as he hadn't specified it when he had ordered Naren with the onerous responsibility of working out a path for the new ideal that Sri Ramakrishna had revealed to mankind. He now needed to observe first-hand the condition of the masses elsewhere in India. So he started wandering around the whole country, all the while trying to grasp the root of the problem that ailed this wonderful nation, with a view to finding a suitable solution thereof.

3. Naren Establishes himself in Vijnana, the 'New Ideal'

During this wandering, he came to Almora, where he had yet another very intense spiritual experience. Let us see the description of this incident from 'Vivekananda-a biography'[17]:

After visiting one or two places, Naren and Akhandananda arrived at Nainital, their destination being the sacred Badrikashrama, in the heart of the Himalayas. They decided to travel the whole way on foot, and also not to touch money. Near Almora under an old peepal tree by the side of a stream, they spent many hours in meditation.

Naren had a deep spiritual experience, which he thus jotted down in his note-book:

In the beginning was the Word, etc. The microcosm and the macrocosm are built on the same plan. Just as the individual soul is encased in a living body, so is the Universal Soul, in the living Prakriti (nature), the objective universe. Kali is embracing Siva. This is not a fancy. This covering of the one (Soul) by the other (nature) is analogous to the relation between an idea and the word expressing it. They are one and the same, and it is only by a mental abstraction that one can distinguish them. Thought is impossible without words. Therefore in the beginning was the Word, etc.

This dual aspect of the Universal Soul is eternal. So what we perceive or feel is the combination of the Eternally Formed and the Eternally Formless.

Thus Naren realized, in the depths of meditation, the oneness of the universe and man, who is a universe in miniature. He realized that, all that exists in the universe also exists in the body, and further, that the whole universe exists in the atom.

This experience was *supremely vital* to the transformation that we are trying to analyze here in this article. Sri Ramakrishna had revealed a new spiritual ideal for mankind. He had a name for that ideal. He called it Vijnana. It is a post-Nirvikalpa state of existence[18]. While in the rich spiritual heritage of India, every previous case of post-Nirvikalpa perception of multiplicity was considered as a 'fall' from beatitude, Sri Ramakrishna said for the first time that there are valid states of existence beyond Nirvikalpa Samadhi, when multiplicity is perceived, although in a totally transformed way. It was possible for a sadhakas to return from Nirvikalpa Samadhi when the Divine Mother ordains that some special work of Her's needs to be done through that blessed soul. And this post-Nirvikalpa state was termed as Vijnana by him[19]. The particular point where the consciousness rests in such a person was termed as 'Bhavamukha' by him. It was this state of spiritual consciousness that he revealed to mankind as the 'new ideal'.

The important point to note here is that post-Nirvikalpa states of consciousness can be integrated into the Sadhaka's personality *only* when the sadhakas accepts the role of an active Divine Power as running this world. Reality will have to be conceptualized as ***Being-Will*** or the ***Personal-Impersonal.*** Traditional schools of thought in India had posited Reality to be either entirely Personal or entirely Impersonal. Traditionally, it has been considered that Nirvikalpa Samadhi requires that the Sadhaka mercilessly reject every object of perception. It was Sri Ramakrishna's discovery that if the Sadhaka takes the path of negating every perception in order to attain Nirvikalpa Samadhi, then, he will be constitutionally incapable of experiencing the Vijnana state. For, he will feel that his perception of multiplicity post-Nirvikalpa Samadhi is a 'fall' and he will exhibit a constant urge to regain that state of monistic experience. However, if the Sadhaka attains Nirvikalpa Samadhi through the path of devotion to a personal God, as a gift from his Ishta, in other words, when the Personal God reveals the Impersonal Reality as but another aspect of Oneself, then that Sadhaka will be able to experience his post-Nirvikalpa perception of multiplicity as an extremely rich spiritual experience which has been termed as Vijnana. We can recall the incident of Tota Puri and the young Sri Ramakrishna[20] here as an apt illustration of the point we are trying to make. It is in this light that we can make sense of the fact that Sri Ramakrishna was overjoyed when Naren had come to accept the Divine Mother while the latter lived at Dakshineswar. This incident is recorded in the Divine Play as follows[21]:

This acceptance of God with form was of course a most significant event in Narendra's life...This made the Master jubilant...The Master was seated alone in his room and Narendra was sleeping on the veranda outside. The Master was beaming with joy...he pointed to Narendra and said, 'Look at that boy – that boy is very good. His name is Narendra. He wouldn't accept the Divine Mother before, but last night he did. He was in need of money, so I advised him to ask Mother for it. But he couldn't; he said he felt ashamed. When he came back from the temple, he asked me to teach him a song in praise of Mother. So I taught him, "Mother, Thou are our sole Redeemer," and he sang it all night long. That's why he's sleeping now.' And then the Master smiled with joy and said, 'Narendra has accepted Mother Kali. That's very good, isn't it?' seeing that he was as happy as a child about this, I answered, 'Yes, sir, it is very good.' A little later he smiled and said again, 'Narendra has accepted the Mother. It's very good. What do you say?' And he kept smiling and saying that, over and over.

This experience at Almora helped Naren to completely integrate his Nirvikalpa Samadhi experience with the post-Nirvikalpa Samadhi perception of multiplicity as the blessed experience of Vijnana. Therefore this experience is by far the most important one when we consider the transformation of Naren into Swami Vivekananda. After this experience at Almora, the great responsibility that his Guru had kept on his shoulders no longer seemed to be a burden to be done with at the earliest, but as a ***divine play*** that he was participating in with great joy. No longer was there any conflict between monistic experience and the perception of multiplicity in him; it was rather a constant divine game of the One Real Existence appearing as the multiple, separate existences out of Its own sweet will. Armed with this unique vision of Unity behind multiplicity, Swamiji was able to clearly grasp the problem of India's decadence in its entirety during his subsequent wandering over the length & breadth of this vast country. No longer did there exist any distinction such as spiritual and mundane in Swamiji's eyes. It was all divine now. The problems were divine and the solution too would be a spiritual one. To deal with this world heroically was indeed as stern as a stance as the vow of renunciation & negation for him.

4. 'Condensed India'

With this unique set of eyes, he now sat at the last tip of Indian rock in Cape Comorin and had yet another nerve-shattering spiritual experience. Again, the '*Vivekananda-a biography*' records[22]:

At Cape Comorin the Swami became as excited as a child. He rushed to the temple to worship the Divine Mother. He prostrated himself before the Virgin Goddess. As he came out and looked at the sea his eyes fell on a rock. Swimming to the islet through shark-infested waters, he sat on a stone. His heart thumped with emotion. His great journey from the snow-capped Himalayas to the 'Land's End' was completed. He had travelled the whole length of the Indian subcontinent, his beloved motherland, which, together with his earthly mother, was 'superior to heaven itself.'

Sitting on the stone, he recalled what he had seen with his own eyes: the pitiable condition of the Indian masses, victims of the unscrupulous whims of their rulers, landlords, and priests. The tyranny of caste had sapped their last drop of blood. In most of the so-called leaders who shouted from the housetops for the liberation of the people, he had seen selfishness personified. And now he asked himself what his duty was in this situation. Should he regard the world as a dream and go into solitude to commune with God? He had tried this several times, but without success. He remembered that, as a sannyasin, he had taken the vow to dedicate himself to the service of God; but this God, he was convinced, was revealed through humanity. And his own service to this God must begin, therefore, with the humanity of India. 'May I be born again and again,' he exclaimed, 'and suffer a thousand miseries, if only I may worship the only God in whom I believe, the sum total of all souls, and above all, my God the wicked, my God the afflicted, my God the poor of all races! 'Through austerity and self-control the Swami had conserved great spiritual power. His mind had been filled with the wisdom of the East and the West. He had received in abundance Sri Ramakrishna's blessings. He also had had many spiritual experiences of his own. He must use all of these assets, he concluded, for the service of God in man.

But what was to be the way?

The clear-eyed prophet saw that religion was the backbone of the Indian nation. India would rise through a renewal and restoration of that highest spiritual consciousness which had made her, at all times, the cradle of nations and the cradle of faith. He totally disagreed with foreign critics and their Indian disciples who held that religion was the cause of India's downfall. The Swami blamed, rather, the falsehood, superstition, and hypocrisy that were practiced in the name of religion. He himself had discovered that the knowledge of God's presence in man was the source of man's strength and wisdom. He was determined to awaken this sleeping divinity. He knew that the Indian culture had been created and sustained by the twin ideals of renunciation and service, which formed the core of Hinduism. And he believed that if the national life could be intensified through these channels, everything else would take care of itself. The workers for India's regeneration must renounce selfishness, jealousy, greed, and lust for power, and they must dedicate themselves to the service of the poor, the illiterate, the hungry, and the sick, seeing in them the tangible manifestations of the Godhead. People required education, food, health, and the knowledge of science and technology to raise their standard of living. The attempt to teach metaphysics to empty stomachs was sheer madness. The masses everywhere were leading the life of animals on account of ignorance and poverty; therefore these conditions should be removed. But where would the Swami find the fellow workers to help him in this gigantic task?

He wanted whole-time servants of God; workers without worldly ties or vested interests. And he wanted them by thousands. His eyes fell upon the numerous monks who had renounced the world in search of God. But alas, in present-day India most of these led unproductive lives. He would have to infuse a new spirit into them, and they in their turn would have to dedicate themselves to the service of the people. He hit upon a plan, which he revealed later in a letter to a friend. 'Suppose,' the Swami wrote, 'some disinterested sannyasins, bent on doing good to others, went from village to village, disseminating education and seeking in various ways to better the condition of all, down to the untouchable, through oral teaching and by means of maps, magic lanterns, globes, and other accessories — would that not bring forth good in time? All these plans I cannot write out in this brief letter. The long and short of it is that if the mountain does not come to Mahomet, Mahomet must go to the mountain. The poor are too poor to go to schools; they will gain nothing by reading poetry and all that sort of thing. We, as a nation, have lost our individuality. We have to give back to the nation its lost individuality and raise the masses.' Verily, the Swami, at Kanyakumari, was the patriot and prophet in one. There he became, as he declared later to a Western disciple, 'a condensed India.'

But where were the resources to come from, to help him realize his great vision?

He himself was a sannyasin, a penniless beggar. The rich of the country talked big and did nothing. His admirers were poor. Suddenly a heroic thought entered his mind: he must approach the outside world and appeal to its conscience. But he was too proud to act like a beggar. He wanted to tell the West that the health of India and the sickness of India were the concern of the whole world. If India sank, the whole world would sink with her. For the outside world, in turn, needed India, her knowledge of the Soul and of God, her spiritual heritage, her ideal of genuine freedom through detachment and renunciation; it needed these in order to extricate itself from the sharp claws of the monster of materialism.

Then to the Swami, brooding alone and in silence on that point of rock off the tip of India, the vision came; there flashed before his mind the new continent of America, a land of optimism, great wealth, and unstinted generosity. He saw America as a country of unlimited opportunities, where people's minds were free from the encumbrance of castes or classes. He would give the receptive Americans the ancient wisdom of India and bring back to his motherland, in exchange, the knowledge of science and technology. If he succeeded in his mission to America, he would not only enhance India's prestige in the Occident, but create a new confidence among his own people. He recalled the earnest requests of his friends to represent India in the forthcoming Parliament of Religions in Chicago. And in particular, he remembered the words of the friends in Kathiawar who had been the first to encourage him to go to the West: 'Go and take it by storm, and then return!'

He swam back to the continent of India and started northwards again, by the eastern coast.

Thus, the nascent Vivekananda was now born! Naren had finally transformed into Vivekananda! But this Vivekananda was yet to bloom completely, for, he was to bring man *everywhere* to the 'new ideal', not just in Bengal or in India. He was yet to observe at first-hand the living condition of the man in the West. Moreover, there was one more vital experience that he lacked for giving his mission its full and final form. And that experience he got during his visit to the West.[23]

5. A Self-adjusting Organization

Although the recorded biographies of Swamiji do not categorize the following experience as a spiritual experience, this experience was no less vital than the Nirvikalpa Samadhi he experienced at Cossipore or the experience he had at Almora or again the experience he had at Cape Comorin. We understand this from the impact this experience had on giving a final shape to his plans.

While in the West, he was wonderstruck at the achievements that man had accomplished in this life. There was no known force of nature that the man in the West hadn't tamed. Every aspect of human life was studied as an end in itself and truths were discovered. These truths were then put into practical use by designing processes and gadgets and principles that enriched the experience of living in this world. His vision of Vijnana through which he now perceived all these enabled him to see each of these achievements as *manifestations of the Divine Power* that is lodged in man. He delved deeper into those wonderful achievements and then came face to face with the grandest achievement of them all – the one achievement that had made possible all other achievements that made the world modern – the '***Organization***'. Individuals can *conceive* of infinite power. But groups of men can *harness* infinite power to do their bidding. It was this revelation that gave the final touch to the sculpture of the 'new doctrine' that was taking shape in his magnificent brain.

He was now able to integrate all the experiences that he had had till then and found that forming an organization would redeem him of all his responsibilities. He would form an organization of monks. The nucleus would be formed by the jewels that his own Guru had hand-crafted over a period of 6 years. This organization would engage in every sort of activity that society needed to further its own journey to manifesting the truth that Man is divine. As he expressed it so clearly[24], "A *self-adjusting organization* is the great need of our time."

It was by an equally compelling series of incidents that one of his brother disciples, Swami Brahmananda, was being prepared by the Divine Mother to complement Swamiji when he would arrive at this incredible solution of forming an organization; [although I will go into that here.]

Thus, while he was still shuttling between America and Europe, he started giving a concrete shape to the unique organization that was to become

Ramakrishna Math in India. What was this organization meant to achieve[25]? His Master had discovered some universal truths regarding spiritual life. His Master had commanded Swamiji to form a group of dedicated monks who would 'live' the life and not just philosophize or ratiocinate about it. In fact, during his Cossipore days, Sri Ramakrishna himself had laid the foundation for this group, although it was on a purely informal basis. Swamiji was now giving it a formal shape and legal status as an organization. This group was meant to safeguard the living traditions of the spiritual fire that had been kindled by Sri Ramakrishna. At any given time, this organization would testify that the 'new ideal' was indeed realizable by means of practicing the 'new doctrine', which would result in the 'new life'. Apart from serving this vital need, this organization would also be creating a much needed space wherein the age-old, time-tested spiritual modes of life would be practiced and preserved in this modern age. Once this organization was set up, a big load was off Swamiji's chest. However, that would not be all.

6. The 'New Doctrine'

There was one more dimension of his Master's command that Swamiji was yet to fulfil, as we have mentioned before. And for that, he felt that his presence in India was necessary. But before he could do that, there was still the important work of *giving shape* to the 'new doctrine' that would lead man to manifesting the 'new life' by realizing the 'new ideal'.

By now, he had now studied the modern man in depth. He was now in a position to configure *praxis*, a 'doctrine', which could be as vast and all-inclusive as the ideal it was meant to achieve. His unprecedented personal experience of man enabled him to generalize that man, anywhere, could be categorized under one of four types – the emotional, the rational, the mystic and the practical. What this means is this – the entire personality of man is generally seen to be dominated by one or more of these faculties in him. There are people who are predominantly governed by their emotions. There are again those who are predominantly governed by reason, and so on. Swamiji now started giving a series of lectures that delineated one path for each of these faculties, namely Bhakti Yoga, Jnana Yoga, Raja Yoga and Karma Yoga. Further, he specified that the modern man would have to practice all these four yogas together, '*crowd all sail, put on all head of steam*'[26], to use his own words, since one of the chief characteristics of the modern man was his multi-sided-ness. He gave a new name to this doctrine – '***Practical Vedanta***'.

One interesting point may be highlighted here, though. While he delineated the four major paths of spiritual practice, his original contribution has been in delineating Karma Yoga[27]. He had learnt from his Master that sincere practice of one's allotted duties, with a selfless attitude, as an offering to God, was a safe and sure way of spiritual growth. The duties may involve activities as mundane as running a household as well as extend to large-scale socially beneficial activities such as disaster relief and national education. In short, spiritual growth does not need any new kind of activity. Any activity that you are already involved in is sufficiently potent to lead you to the 'new ideal', provided you are selfless. To put it in more concrete terms, one would need to practice *brahmacharya* and perform one's duties. The root of all selfishness is sex-consciousness. So, a person, irrespective of his being a monk or a married man, will have to practice complete continence, and then go on performing all duties that devolve upon him in his station of life. That was more than sufficient to lead him to a complete realization of Vijnana, the 'new ideal' in this very life. The practice of continence involved elements of the other three yogas, thus ensuring that a synthesis of all the four yogas was put into play.

This was indeed a stroke of genius on the part of Swamiji. A 'new ideal' called for a new set of rituals; else, the masses wouldn't get a hold of the doctrine that would lead to the realization of the 'new ideal'. Instead of creating yet another set of rituals in a world already riddled with innumerable rituals that were lifeless, [for all rituals lose their potency after a certain period of time, getting disconnected from the underlying thought that should accompany them] he apotheosized the *entire life of man* into a ritual that would lead him to the 'new ideal'! Thus, he was able to hew out a path from multiplicity to Vijnana directly, without negating this world in Nirvikalpa Samadhi!

7. 'Rejuvenation of the Motherland'

Swamiji then returned to India and created one more organization named Ramakrishna Mission apart from Ramakrishna Math. Through this organization, he opened up avenues for monks and married people to work out the 'new doctrine' and achieve the 'new ideal'. The aim and objective of this organization were to achieve the fullest manifestation of divinity everywhere on earth. This organization would enable the newbie to put the 'new doctrine' into practice and achieve the 'new ideal' while at the same time allowing the person who had already realized the 'new ideal' to live the 'new life'! But the immediate objective of this organization was 'nothing short of a rejuvenation of my motherland'!

Having set this mammoth machinery in motion, he was to move away from the scene, because the growth of the organization needed steady, soft and silent work, the kind of work his other brother-disciples could perform. While Swamiji was like the rock-cutter who places dynamite sticks and blasts huge chunks of marble from the hills at the quarry, his brother-disciples, especially Swami Brahmananda, Swami Saradananda, Swami Premananda & Swami Ramakrishnananda were like the sculptors who chisel out delicate figurines from those blocks of marble.

8. Divine Mother Validates his Decisions

His work was to end with yet another nerve-shattering spiritual experience that he was to have at Kshir-Bhavani, which is recorded in the 'Life of Swami Vivekananda' as follows[28]:

> ...The Swami retired abruptly on September 30th to the Colored Springs of Kshir- Bhavani (or Kheer Bhavani), leaving strict instructions that no one was to follow him. It was not until October 6th that he returned. Before this famous shrine of the Mother he daily performed Homa, and worshipped Her with offerings of Kshira or Kheer (thickened milk) made from one maund of milk, rice, and almonds. He told his beads like any humble pilgrim; and, as a special Sadhana, every morning he worshipped a Brahmin pundit's little daughter as Uma Kumari, the Divine Virgin. He began to practise the sternest austerities. It seemed as though he would tear off all the veils that had come upon his soul through years of work and thought, and again be a child before the Divine Mother. Even though Her caresses might give pain to the body they would give illumination and freedom to the soul. All thought of Leader, Worker, or Teacher was gone. He was now only the monk, in all the nakedness of pure Sannyasa.

When he returned to Srinagar, he appeared before his disciples a transfigured presence, writes Nivedita. He entered their houseboat, his hands raised in benediction; then he placed some marigolds that he had offered to the Mother, on the head of each of them. "No more 'Hari Om!' It is all 'Mother' now!" he said, sitting down. "All my patriotism is gone. Everything is gone. Now it is only 'Mother! Mother!' I have been very wrong. Mother said to me: 'What, even if unbelievers should enter my temples, and defile My images! What is that to you? Do you protect Me? Or do I protect you?' So there is no more patriotism. I am only a little child!"

One day at Kshir-Bhavani he had been pondering over the ruination and desecration of the temple wrought by the Muslim invaders. Distressed at heart he thought: "How could the people have permitted such sacrilege without offering strenuous resistance! If I were here then, I would never have allowed such things. I would have laid down my life to protect the Mother." It was then that he had heard the Mother speaking as above. The disciples sat silent, awe-inspired. They could not speak, "so tense was the spot with something that stilled thought". "I may not tell you more now; it is not in order", he said gently, adding, before he left, " — but spiritually, spiritually, I was not bound down!" In his meditation on the Terrible, in the dark hours of the nights at Kshir-Bhavani, there were other visions that he confided only to one or two of his brother-disciples. They were too sacred to make known to anyone else.

At this same shrine, in the course of worship one day, the Swami was brooding with pain on the dilapidated condition of the temple. He wished in his heart that he were able to build a new one there in its place, just as he wished to build monasteries and temples elsewhere, especially a temple to Sri Ramakrishna in the new Math at Belur. He was startled in his ruminations by the voice of the Mother Herself, saying to him, "My child! If I so wish I can have innumerable temples and magnificent monastic centres. I can even this moment raise a seven-storied golden temple on this very spot." "Since I heard that Divine Voice," said the Swami to a disciple in Calcutta much later, "**I have ceased making any more plans.** Let these things be as Mother wills!"

Sister Nivedita writes[29]: *He spoke of the future. There was nothing to be desired, but the life of the wanderer, in silence and nudity, on the banks of the Ganges. He would have nothing. 'Swamiji' was dead and gone. Who was he, that he should feel responsible for teaching the world? It was all fuss and vanity. The Mother had no need of him, but only he of Her. Even work, when one had seen this, was nothing but illusion.*

Swamiji was wracked by conflicts about the correctness of the measures he had taken for fulfilling the command of his Master. Almost every decision he had taken was unprecedented – organizing Hindu monks, asking all-renouncing monks to take up responsibility for socially productive activities on a national scale, re-introducing Karma Yoga back into Hinduism a thousand years after it was completely rooted out by Shankara [although the two versions were very different]. This experience he had at Kshir-Bhavani set at rest all those inner conflicts. Although, once in a while, these conflicts were to raise their head again in his super-sensitive mind as recorded by Sister Nivedita[30], he was able to conclude that the decisions he had taken in each case was indeed the handiwork of the Great Power that runs this world and holds itself responsible for its sustenance, the same Power that had incarnated as his Master Sri Ramakrishna.

Thus, we have seen how Naren became transformed into Swami Vivekananda. That transformation was the personal aspect of the impersonal manifestation of the 'new ideal and the new doctrine' that we mentioned in the beginning of this article.

It is amazing to study the details that Sri Ramakrishna worked into his mission. He developed his own wife to be an amazing tower of strength, training her adequately to take care of the spiritual ministry after he would be gone. Simultaneously he developed the young Naren to study the world afresh and diagnose what ails the world and what remedy needs to be administered for its spiritual well-being. Again, along with this, he guided and molded a handful of other young men like Rakhal, Baburam, Sharat, Shashi, etc to be loyal to Naren until death, while being absolutely sincere regarding their own spiritual life. He told unequivocally that they had to pledge allegiance to Naren no matter what. He would say repeatedly, "*Narendra belongs to a very high place- the realm of the Absolute. He has a manly nature. So many devotees come here, but there is no one like him. Every now and then I take stock of the devotees. I find that some are like lotuses with ten petals, some like lotuses with a hundred petals. But among lotuses Narendra is a thousand-petalled one. Other devotees may be like pots or pitchers; but Narendra is a huge water barrel. Others may be like pools or tanks; but Narendra is a huge reservoir like the Hadalpukur. Among fish, Narendra is a huge red-eyed carp; others are like minnows, or smelts, or sardines. Narendra is a very big receptacle, one that can hold many things. He is like a bamboo with a big hollow space inside. Narendra is not under the control of anything. He is not under the control of attachment or sense pleasures. He is like a male pigeon. If you hold a male pigeon by its beak, it breaks away from you; but the female pigeon keeps still. I feel great strength when Narendra is with me in a gathering.*"[31]

Apart from instilling in the minds of his young disciples the unshakeable conception of Naren being their leader, he also prepared each of them for distinct roles in his future organization. We find that he uttered time and again that Rakhal had the intelligence of a King, thereby readying the path for his being anointed as the President of his future organization. He went to great lengths to forge a deep friendship between Naren, Rakhal and Sharat. This deep friendship would later fructify as the core team of Founder, President and the Chief Functionary of his future organization.

Later on we find this action of Sri Ramakrishna developing in a most beautiful manner. Many times, some of the disciples like Yogananda and

Premananda would not accept Vivekananda's views of the details of the work of Ramakrishna Math and Mission. In fact, in some instances, they even verbalized their non-acceptance. But not once did they ever challenge their leader or act in defiance. This is the secret of any successful organization. Implicit obedience to the leadership is vital for growth of any organization. In fact, Swami Vivekananda himself knew this strength he had. He himself said once, "I know that even if the whole world should say that I have become the very devil tomorrow, there are a handful of people who will stand by me. It is friendship like that which brings God in our midst."

It is interesting to note that while he taught the Holy Mother different sacred mantras, he did nothing of the kind to Naren. It was very clear to Sri Ramakrishna the distinct roles each of them would play in later life. While Naren would busy himself in creating the infrastructure of the organizational edifice, his wife would have to cater to the spiritual needs of the thousands that would come to her.

E. Core-Values Indoctrination & Rites of Passage

In the middle of 1885 Sri Ramakrishna contracted throat cancer. For the convenience of his treatment he was first taken to Calcutta and then to Cossipore, a suburb of Calcutta. Without concern for his body, he continued to train his disciples. When they begged him not to strain himself, he replied, "I do not care. I will give up twenty thousand such bodies to help one person."

One day he distributed ochre monastic robes to Narendra and some of his young disciples and thus formed his own monastic order. He later told Narendra, "I leave them all to your care. See that they practice spiritual disciplines even after my passing away and that they do not return home." Another day he wrote on a piece of paper, "*Naren will teach people.*" When Narendra expressed opposition the Master said, "*But you must. Your very bones will do it.*"

Narendra once narrated how the Master had transmitted his power into him, "*Two or three days before Sri Ramakrishna's passing away, he called me to his side and looked steadily at me and went into Samadhi. Then I felt that a subtle force like an electric shock was entering my body! In a little while I also lost outward consciousness and sat motionless. How long I stayed in that condition I do not remember. When consciousness returned I found Sri Ramakrishna shedding tears. On questioning him, he answered me affectionately, 'Today, giving you my all, I have become a beggar. With this power, you are to do much work for the good of the world before you return.' I feel that that power is constantly directing me to this or that work. This body has not been made for remaining idle.*"

A couple of days before Sri Ramakrishna's passing away, when the Master was in excruciating pain, a thought flashed across Narendra's mind: "*Well, now if you can declare that you are God, then only will I believe you are really God Himself.*" Immediately the Master looked up towards Narendra and said distinctly, *"O my Naren, are you still not convinced? He who in the past was born as Rama and Krishna is now living in this very body as Ramakrishna – but not from the standpoint of your Vedanta, but actually so."*[32]

Long ago, when Sri Ramakrishna was a temple priest in the Dakshineswar Kali temple, one day, his cousin Hriday Ram committed a great blunder by worshipping the daughter of Mathurnath Biswas as Goddess Kumari. Hriday being a Brahmin should not have worshipped the girl who belonged to a low caste, for that could bring great misfortune to the girl. Naturally the girl's father (and the owner of the Temple) was livid with rage and ordered that Hriday should vacate the Temple Campus immediately. Someone came to Sri Ramakrishna and conveyed to him the wrong information that Trailokyanath Biswas had ordered that both Sri Ramakrishna and Hriday Ram should vacate the Temple Campus. Immediately, Sri Ramakrishna stood up and walked away. Trailokyanath saw this and fell at Sri Ramakrishna's feet and begged his pardon and pleaded with him to stay and that he had wanted only Hriday Ram to leave. Immediately Sri Ramakrishna returned. This must have happened sometime in the 1870s.

Much later on, in 1886, in Cossipore, when he was suffering from excruciating pain from throat cancer, some of his disciples approached him and asked him to cure himself of the disease. He said that his last days had come and said, "*I am ready to leave this body now. However, if you all permit me, I shall leave this body.*"

Notice the difference in approach. The Avatara of the age had bound himself to an organization of his own disciples and devotees, and organization which was still informal but a distinct entity nonetheless, and one of which he himself was an integral part now!

F. Fruits of his Management Skills – Ramakrishna Movement

The management skills of Sri Ramakrishna that we have attempted to study thus far have today found fructification in the form of a formal Ramakrishna Movement. The heart of this movement is the twin organizations – Ramakrishna Math and Ramakrishna Mission. What began in the form of divine revelations in Dakshineswar in Sri Ramakrishna has today taken the shape of about 1800 monks living together in about 180 Ashrams, devoted to the Vijnana Ideal of serious contemplation coupled with service of God in man. This takes the form of about 15 hospitals, 129 out-patient dispensaries, 49 mobile dispensaries, 12 colleges, 22 HS Schools, 41 Secondary Schools, 135 schools of other grades, 161 non-formal education centers, 78 night schools & adult education centers, 2 schools of languages, 1 school of Vedic education, 4 polytechnics, 6 junior technical & industrial schools, 119 hostels, 7 orphanages, 214 libraries, 10 major publication centers, 2 centers for the disabled, 3 institutes of agriculture, 4 rural development training institutes and several other institutions, dedicated to philanthropic, cultural and spiritual services. The twin organizations have also been ever vigilant and intensely active in rendering relief to the victims of earthquakes, floods, famines, epidemics, cyclones, riots and such calamities.[33]

REFERENCES

1. Cf: *Sri Ramakrishna & His Divine Play* by Swami Saradananda; Tr-Swami Chetanananda; pg: 359-362
2. Cf: *Sri Sarada Devi & Her Divine Play* by Swami Chetanananda; pg: 396
3. Cf: *ibid*; pg: 46
4. Cf: *ibid*; pg: 109
5. Cf: *ibid*; pg: 109
6. Cf: *ibid*; pg: 110
7. Cf: *ibid*; pg: 163
8. Cf: *ibid*; pg: 147
9. This portion is drawn extensively from '*The New Ideal, the New Doctrine, the New Life*' by Swami Vedatitananda: https://www.scribd.com/doc/246968262/The-New-Ideal-The-New-Doctrine-The-New-Life
10. Cf: *Sri Ramakrishna & His Divine Play* by Swami Saradananda; Tr-Swami Chetanananda; pg: 447
11. Cf: *ibid*; pg: 362.
12. This fall is termed as '*Anavastitattva*'; inability to hold on to a blessed state of spiritual experience. The urge then comes to constantly regain that blessed state and remain in that state of Nirvikalpa Samadhi.
13. Cf: *Gospel of Sri Ramakrishna*: pg: 988; Entry on 7th May 1887: Narendra says, '...but I still have no peace.' See also: *Letters of Swami Vivekananda*; pg-24; 26th May 1890 to Pramadadas Mitra :"I write this...in great agitation of mind"; See also: *Life of Swami Vivekananda by Eastern & Western Disciples-I*; pg 236; "What shall I say to you about the condition of my mind! Oh, it is as if hell-fire were burning there day & night!"

14. Cf: *Gospel of Sri Ramakrishna*: pg: 982; Entry on 25th Mar 1887: Narendra says, 'Does mere emotion make a man spiritually great?' See also: *Letters of Swami Vivekananda*: pg: 26; 26th May 1890 to Pramadadas Mitra; "The condition of Bengal is pitiable. The people here cannot even dream what renunciation truly means..."; See also: *Life of Swami Vivekananda by Eastern & Western Disciples-I*; pg: 236; "Our Bengal is the land of Bhakti & Jnana. Yoga is scarcely mentioned there. What little there is, is but the queer breathing exercise of the Hatha Yoga – which is nothing but a kind of gymnastics. Therefore I am staying with this wonderful Raja Yogi..."
15. Cf: *Life of Swami Vivekananda by Eastern & Western Disciples-I*; pp: 233-34.
16. We say 'prototype' because right from the beginning, Naren had the clarity that his Master's mission was nothing short of the spiritual regeneration of the *entire country*. See for instance: *Life of Swami Vivekananda-I;* pg: 221; "My son, I have a great mission to fulfil and I am in despair at the smallness of my capacity. I have an injunction from my Guru to carry out this mission. *It is nothing less than the regeneration of my motherland.* Spirituality has fallen to a ebb and starvation stalks the land. India must become dynamic and effect the conquest of the world through her spirituality." Swamiji said this to Swami Sadananda as early as 1888.
17. Cf: *Vivekananda, a biography* by Swami Nikhilananda; pg: 98.
18. For details, please refer to *Meditation & Spiritual Life*: pp: 542-551; Explanation of chart on Spiritual Unfoldment.
19. For details of this term & the term Bhavamukha, please see: *Sri Ramakrishna's thoughts on Man, World & God* by Swami Tapasyananda; pp: 26-30; 159-163; See also: *Sri Ramakrishna-Life & Teachings (an interpretative study)* by Swami Tapasyananda; pp: 57-71
20. Cf: *Sri Ramakrishna & His Divine Play*: pg: 538;
21. Cf: *ibid*; pg: 843-44
22. Cf: *Vivekananda-a biography*; pp: 110-114
23. It is really amazing the way Sri Ramakrishna micro-managed Swamiji's life even after he had passed away in 1886. Just before going to the West, Swamiji had a symbolic dream. He saw Sri Ramakrishna walking into the water of the acean and beckoning him to follow. He also heard the command, "Go!" It was after this dream that he started working seriously on attending the Parliament of World Religions in Chicago. Cf: *God lived with them*; Swami Chetanananda; pg: 42
24. Cf: *Inspired Talks*: Entry on July 1st, 1895
25. Sister Nivedita says 'Long ago, he had defined the mission of the Order of Ramakrishna as that of realizing and exchanging the highest ideals of the East and of the West.': *Complete Works of Sister Nivedita-I; Master as I saw him*; pg: 42.

26. Cf: Inspired Talks: Entry on 27th July 1895: "The ignorant will leads to bondage, the knowing will can free us. The will can be made strong in thousands of ways; every way is a kind of Yoga, but the systematized Yoga accomplishes the work more quickly. Bhakti, Karma, Raja, and Jnana-Yoga get over the ground more effectively. Put on all powers, philosophy, work, prayer, meditation — *crowd all sail, put on all head of steam* — reach the goal. The sooner, the better
27. Some say that his '*Raja Yoga*' too was quite original. But it will be seen that he just combined the existing schools of Patanjala Yoga with Tantra and Advaita Vedanta. This trend of seamlessly combining two or more schools of thought to produce a new path has been always present in India. For instance, one of the later Shankaracharyas combined Patanjala Yoga with Advaita Vedanta in the treatise '*Aparokshanubhutihi*'.
28. Cf: *Life of Swami Vivekananda-II*; pp: 381-83;
29. Cf: *Complete works of Sister Nivedita-I; Master as I saw him*; pp: 99-100.
30. Cf: *ibid*: Ch-Conflict of Ideals.
31. Cf: *God lived with them*; Swami Chetanananda; pg: 36
32. Cf: *God lived with them*; Swami Chetanananda; pg: 37
33. Cf: http://www.belurmath.org/

5

Sri Ramakrishna and Kathamrita: An analytic assessment

Subhas Chandra Saha

Sri Sri Ramakrishnakathamrita by Sri 'M' (Sri Mahandra Nath Gupta) is like an endless epic, epical in scope and dimensions, a splendid amalgam of poetry, conversations, facts, discourses, narratives, similes, metaphors, songs, and references to scriptures, all rolled into one saga of epical magnitude. One may call it a religious book, a narrative, a diary, a biography in snatches, an inspiring document, an account of a holy man's life that never fails to teach us every moment. The vastness of *Kathamrita's* significance is to be perceived slowly, bit by bit, day by day, so that no part of its significance is lost due to hurry. Each and every part of *Kathamrita* is holy and ennobling.

However, for our discussion and analysis, for our immersion and probing, we have chosen a miniscule part of *Kathamrita*, which Sri M has called an 'Appendix'. Though added as an appendix, the part under discussion is replete with facts, revelations and teachings. The appendix deals with Sri Ramakrishna and Swami Vivekananda. Swami Vivekananda's discourses in the West are all reflections of Sri Ramakrishna's teachings. The inner relation and connection between Sri Ramakrishna and Swami Vivekananda is presented and analysed with great keenness of insight and depth of understanding by Sri 'M'. While in the main body of *Kathamrita*, Sri 'M' is mostly a presenter, a presenter who keeps his own opinion withdrawn, in this appendix we find Sri 'M' as a careful and analytic writer who sheds light on the vast exchange or rather transmission of ideas and realizations from Sri Ramakrishna into Swami Vivekananda who eloquently articulated Ramakrishna's ideas before the Western devotees. It is because Vivekananda was presenting Ramakrishna's ideas, it became easy and possible for Vivekananda to present India's spiritual ideas more convincingly before the Western audience.

There are ten chapters in the appendix. Though called an appendix, its importance is too great and cannot be underestimated and diminished on any ground. Sri 'M''s treatment of the subject is no less excellent than that in the main book of *Kathamrita*. The appendix is also closely related to the main topic of the main book: only the mode of narration is different. But even the difference in the mode of presentation and treatment is very appropriate. Hence the appendix, as it is presented just after the main book is finished, and is, therefore, numbered 1, is highly relevant. We are immensely grateful to Sri 'M' for this superb appendix.

Since the appendix is not a chronological account but an analytic presentation, Sri 'M' shuttles back and forth in time, arranging events and statements in a shuffled manner, so that the illumination on the subject is at its brightest. The capacity of Sri 'M' as the writer with diverse capabilities reveals itself with a magnificent impact on the devotees as well as the readers of devotional literature.

Sri 'M' presents Ramakrishna's assessment of Narendra in an unmistakable manner. He always starts with a setting that becomes vivid and picturesque, at the same time authentic, as the writer mentions the date and venue of each event and conversation.

It was 15th July 1885, the day after the *Rathajatra*. Sri Sri Bhagawan Sri Ramakrishna is sitting along with the devotees in *Balaram Mandir* in the morning. He is speaking about the nobility of Narendra (Swami Vivekananda):

> Narendra's level is very high - his level is that of the formless level. His soul is the soul of manliness. So many devotees are coming; there is no one like him.
>
> Sometimes I sit back and ponder and compare... Then I see some lotus has ten petals, some lotus sixteen petals, some lotus hundred petals but among all the lotuses, Narendra's lotus is thousand-petalled.
>
> Others are earthen jars, or brass jars; but Narendra is a very large drum.
>
> Among the small water bodies and ponds, Narendra is a large lake, like Haldarpukur.
>
> Among the fish, Narendra is a large rohu with red eyes; others are various small fishes...
>
> A large receptacle he is – it can contain a large number of things.
>
> Narendra is not bound to anything. He is not bound to attachments

> and sensual pleasures. He is a male pigeon. If the female pigeon holds its beak, it snatches away its beak – the female pigeon keep quiet. (p. 1063)

The very beginning presents in a vivid manner through a series of similes and metaphors Sri Ramakrishna's keen perception of Narendra's greatness and uniqueness. The credit of Sri 'M' as a writer is that he is able to evoke the spirit of Ramakrishna's utterances about Vivekananda. The reading of the passage, though more than hundred years have passed since the writing of Kathamrita, is still inspiring and makes the readers and devotees tuned to a high level of spirituality. Sri Ramakrishna and Swami Vivekananda become a unique pair of spiritual educators for all of us.

This beginning part of the first chapter presents the theme and sets the tone. Since Sri 'M' has quoted Ramakrishna's sayings, we cannot but acknowledge the tremendous imaginative power of Sri Ramakrishna in graphically portraying his inmost perception of the greatness and magnificence of Narendra who later on, after the death of Ramakrishna, emerged as Swami Vivekananda who thundered forth the teachings of Ramakrishna throughout the world. Nobody has excelled Sri Ramakrishna in the assessment of Vivekananda's greatness. Hats off to Sri 'M' for his superb narration and presentation. Without Sri 'M' we would have lost this precious treasure - Sri Ramakrishna's assessment of Vivekananda.

Later on we encounter another important presentation. Sri 'M' goes back to 1882 in Dakshineswar when and where Sri Ramakrishna advised Vivekananda:

> First you purify your mind. When mind is purified then God comes and takes his holy seat (in the mind of the devotee). (p. 1064)
>
> First you dip yourself. You dip and then pick up gems; after that, other works. Let God be established (in your mind), then if you desire, give lectures. (p. 1064)
>
> In 1884, Sri Ramakrishna said: "Unless God orders, you cannot give lectures to the public." (p. 1064)

In 1886, when extremely ill, Sri Ramakrishna wrote on a piece of paper: "Naren will give lectures".

When he returned to India after staying for about three years in the Western countries, Swami Vivekananda whole-heartedly acknowledged his debt to Sri Ramakrishna, and publicly declared him as his guru who deserved the respect and reverence from people not only of India but of the whole world.

In reply to the ovation given to him in Madras, Vivekananda responded by paying sincerest homage to Sri Ramakrishna:

> It was your generous appreciation of Him whose message to India and to the whole world, I, the most unworthy of His servants, had the privilege to bear, it was your innate spiritual instinct which saw in Him and His message the first murmurs of that tidal wave of spirituality which is destined at no distant future to break upon India in all its irresistible powers ...(p. 1065).

In his third lecture in Madras, Vivekananda said:

> Let me conclude by saying that if in my life I have told one word of truth it was his and his alone; and if I have told you many things which were not true, correct and beneficial to the human race, it was all mine and on me is the responsibility. (p. 1065)

Sri 'M' very appropriately quoted from Vivekananda's reply to his ovation in Calcutta as under:

> If the nation wants to rise, it will have to come enthusiastically round his name. It does not matter who preaches Ramakrishna, whether I or you or anybody. But him I place before you and it is for you to judge, and for the good of our race, for the good of our nation, to judge now what you shall do with this great ideal life. ... ...Within ten years of his passing away this power has encircled the globe. Judge him not through me... I am only a weak instrument. His character was so great that I or any of his disciples, if we spent hundreds of lives, could do no justice to a millionth part of what he really was. (p. 1065)

Sri 'M' shows through apt quotations that not only Sri Ramakrishna found Narendra to be a disciple of great devotion and capability, but also Vivekananda realised the greatness of Sri Ramakrishna, and so prepared himself in every possible manner to truthfully and accurately disseminate Sri Ramakrishna's message to humanity with great convincing eloquence round the globe. Thus the first chapter of the Appendix presents two spiritual colossuses in their human form with abiding messages for the good of the entire humanity. Thus the first chapter of the Appendix is a fitting preamble to an epic of spiritual messages to humanity.

In Chapter II, Sri 'M' shows how Ramakrishna placed more emphasis on God within oneself than reading books about God. He refers to the conversation between Sri Ramakrishna and Mahimacharan Chakraborty that took place on 26 October 1884. Sri Ramakrishna says :

> How many Shastras will you study? How much will you gain by examining and judging? First you try to realize Him (God)...
>
> You labour for it. You meditate to realize God. You cannot realize Him just by sitting idle. Alone, you pray to Him. Call Him...(p. 1066)

Sri 'M' shows that Swami Vivekananda delivered lectures on Hinduism at the Parliament of Religions in Chicago, and repeated Ramakrishna's idea:

> The Hindu does not want to live upon words and theories. He must see God and that alone can destroy all doubts. So the best proof of a Hindu sage gives about the soul, about God, is I have seen the soul; I have seen God.... The whole struggle in their system is a constant struggle to become perfect, to become divine, to reach God and see God; and their reaching God, seeing God, becoming perfect even 'as the Father in Heaven is perfect' constitutes the religion of the Hindus. (pp. 1066-67)

Because the realization of God within oneself is the fundamental concept in Sri Ramakrishna's notion of spirituality, Swami Vivekananda repeats the idea in lecture after lecture in the West. Sri "M' quotes from Vivekananda's lecture delivered at Hartford:

> The next idea that I want to bring to you is that religion does not consist in doctrines or dogmas.... The end of all religions is the realisation of God in the soul. Ideals and methods may differ but that is the central point. That is the realisation of God, something behind that world of sense – this world of eternal eating and drinking and talking nonsense - this world of shadows and selfishness. There is that beyond all books, beyond all creeds, beyond the vanities of this world, and that is the realisation of God within yourself. (p. 1067)

Sri 'M' quotes from Vivekananda's lecture entitled 'Ideal of a Universal Religion' delivered in New York on 9th January 1896, to demonstrate how Vivekananda taught the Westerners Ramakrishna's concept of realization of God:

> Then again all these various yogas (work or worship, psychic control or philosophy) have to be carried out into practice; theories will not do. We have to meditate upon it, realise it until it becomes our whole life. Religion is realisation, not talk nor doctrine nor theories, however beautiful they may be. It is being and becoming, not hearing or acknowledging. It is not an intellectual assent. By intellectual assent

> we can come to a hundred sorts of foolish things and change them next day, but this being and becoming is what is Religion. (p. 1068)

In Chapter III, Sri 'M" shows that Ramakrishna taught his disciples the truth that one can reach God through all religions. This is a unique outlook that Ramakrishna emphasized again and again through various images, metaphors and similes. Sri 'M' quotes Ramakrishna as saying:

> All religions are true. One can reach Kalighat by various roads and lanes. However, religions are not God. One can reach God through various religions. For example, one can reach to the terrace by various means, by concrete staircase, or by wooden staircase, or round staircase or even by a rope. However, when reaching the terrace, one should climb by one type of staircase only; otherwise if one uses many types of staircase, one may not be able to reach the terrace. If one has reached the terrace he can climb down and go up by various means. (p. 1069)

Swami Vivekananda upheld the generosity and universality of the religion to which he belongs in his speech at the Parliament of Religions in Chicago:

> I am proud to belong to a religion which taught the world both tolerance and universal acceptance. We believe not only in universal toleration, but we accept all Religions as true. (p. 1071)

Thus Vivekananda's speeches became an eloquent embodiment of Ramakrishna's teachings. Thus Vivekananda internationalized the religion of Sri Ramakrishna which he taught in Dakshinewar, Shyampukur Bati and Cassipore Udyanbati.

In Chapter IV, Sri 'M' analyses various teachings of Sri Ramakrishna and Vivekananda's speeches and shows that Vivekananda reflects Ramakrishna's messages and teachings in his speeches. Sri 'M' quotes Ramakrishna as saying:

> I love only my countrymen; this is Maya (delusion). I love all people of all countries. I love all people of all religions: this comes from kindness, this comes from devotion or *bhakti.* Maya binds a man, he/she is turned away from God. From kindness and devotion only arises the realisation of God. (p. 1072)

Sri 'M" pays his glowing tribute to Vivekananda in the last paragraph of the chapter:

> Blessed are you, the all-renouncing personality. You have truly followed in the footsteps of your guru; you have truly practiced the great mantra of your gurudeva: first attain God, and then anything else. You understood that if you don't believe in God, this world is only a dreamlike magic show. That is why you renounced everything and devoted yourself to spiritual practice. When you saw that He is the life of all, when you saw that there is nothing but Him, then you put your mind on the world, O Mahayogin! You entered again the region of work for the service of Hari imminent in all. Thus all Hindus, Muslims, Christians, foreigners, wealthy, poor, all men and women became a part of your limitless love – you gave them all the embrace of ecstatic love.... (p. 1076)

In Chapters V, VI, VII, VIII, IX and X, Sri 'M' presents analytic expositions of Sri Ramakrishna's main tenets, and proves, by quoting extensively from Swami Vivekananda's speeches, that Ramakrishna's nectar of messages (*Kathamrita*) was spread throughout the world by Swami Vivekananda in a style that is understood by the Westerners. Ramakrishna is the true modern prophet of India whose messages are all important and relevant for the entire mankind. Vivekananda is brought up theoretically and spiritually by Sri Ramakrishna. Vivekananda grew up as an irresistible orator in English language to preach what he learnt from his Master. In gratitude, Vivekananda paid Ramakrishna the highest tribute in a Sanskrit prayer. I quote the same in English translation done by Dharm Pal Gupta:

> Om, Salutations to you, Ramakrishna, the foundation of virtue and embodiment of all religions, the most universal of incarnations. (p. 533)

Sri 'M' book is replete with spiritual significance. Each of its words and sentences breathe spirituality. Trying to expound the entire text will lead to a compendium and dissertation larger in size than the original text. Hence I desist from doing the same. Rather I have tried to suggest and pinpoint certain areas of ideas transmitted by Sri Ramakrishna through Swami Vivekananda. Sri 'M' displays excellent skill in exposing the process of transmission which is of a very high order, being spiritual as well as ethereal. The appendix is as important as the original book, since through it, Sri 'M' exposes the international and universal dimensions of Sri Ramakrishna's messages and teaching and Sri 'M' also highlights impressively Swami Vivekananda's superb depth of understanding of his Master as well as his development of a literary style in English capable of presenting the true spirit of Sri Ramakrishna's message of universal religion of love and brotherhood to the entire spectrum of humanity.

NOTES

1. *Sri Sri Ramakrishna Kathamrita* by Sri 'M' . Kolkata: Udbodhan, 2000 (the page numbers of this book are mentioned in the text against the quotations. Translated from Bengali by the writer of the article
2. *Sri Sri Ramakrishna Kathamrita*, tr. by Dharm Pal Gupta. Chandigarh: Sri Ma Trust , 2011 (the page numbers of this translation are mentioned when they are taken from this English Text)

6 The evolution of Swami Vivekananda's thought process as depicted in the Gospel of Sri Ramakrishna

Ratnabali Banerjee

In 1894, Swami Vivekananda wrote from U. S. A. to Swami Shivananda, his brother-disciple, that while he did not have the least doubt that Ramakrishna Paramahamsa was God incarnate, people had to find out for themselves what He used to teach. Those things could not be thrust upon them. This is from one of the letters in *Letters of Swami Vivekananda* (Advaita Ashrama, 1970: 180) where he further wrote, "Without studying Ramakrishna Paramahamsa first, one can never understand the real import of the Vedas, the Vedanta, of the *Bhâgavata* and the other Purânas. His life is a searchlight of infinite power thrown upon the whole mass of Indian religious thought. He was the living commentary to the Vedas and to their aim. He had lived in one life the whole cycle of the national religious existence in India." (ibid. : 180).

In 1894, Swami Vivekananda had reached a stage where he did not have any doubt that Sri Ramakrishna was God incarnate. But, how was it like for Narendranath Dutta – Naren, when he met Sri Ramakrishna? The first meeting was in 1881 at the house of Surendra Nath Mitra, who had asked him to play and sing to entertain his guests at a party and one of the guests was Sri Ramakrishna (Isherwood, 2007: 193). Sri Ramakrishna invited Narendra to visit him at Dakshineswar.

The evolution in the thought process of Narendra unfolds in the conversations recorded by Mahendranath Gupta, who wrote the book *Sri Sri Ramakrishna Kathamrita* under the pseudonym "M.". *The Gospel of Sri Ramakrishna* is the English translation of this pen picture of Sri Ramakrishna's life from March, 1882 to April, 1886 (Nikhilananda, 1981). Narendra figures in the record right from the beginning.

On his third visit to Sri Ramakrishna at Dakshineswar, M. met Narendra for the first time (Nikhilananda, 1981: 84). He was a college student who frequented the Sâdhâran Brâhmo Samâj. M. recorded, "His eyes were bright, his words were full of spirit, and he had the look of a lover of God." (ibid. :84). Sri Ramakrishna asked him what would he think of the people if they spoke ill of him. Narendra's reply was that he would think that dogs were barking at him. Sri Ramakrishna told him not to go that far since God dwelt in all beings.

Later, as Swami Vivekananda, he did have to face criticisms; people did speak ill of him. In a letter to Mr. E. T. Sturdy, an English devotee of Swami Vivekananda, he wrote in November, 1899 from New York, "For the last few months I have been hearing so much of the luxuries I was given to enjoy by the people of the West – luxuries which the hypocrite myself has been enjoying, although preaching renunciation all the while; .... ." This is from one of the many letters in *Letters of Swami Vivekananda*, where we read about the disparagement he had to continually encounter (Advaita Ashrama, 1970: 398)

We go back to March, 1882. M. recorded Sri Ramakrishna's comments about Narendra. "Narendra and people of his type belong to the class of the ever-free. They are never entangled in the world. When they grow a little older they feel the awakening of inner consciousness and go directly toward God. They come to the world only to teach others." (Nikhilananda, 1981: 88). Sri Ramakrishna praised Narendra, saying that he excelled in singing, playing on instruments, study and everything. He was appreciative of Narendra's reasoning – how he tore the Master's householder devotee, Kedarnath Chatterji's arguments to shreds.

On the same day, M. heard Narendra sing and recorded that he had never heard anyone except the Master (Sri Ramakrishna) sing so sweetly. This was also the first time that M. saw the Master in samâdhi (Nikhilananda, 1981: 89). On the next day also M. went to Sri Ramakrishna, at Dakshineswar. The Master was having fun with some young men of nineteen or twenty, Narendra being among them (ibid.: 90). The Master was treating them as if they were His most intimate friends and M. was left wondering if He was the same person who had, only a day before, been intoxicated with God!

The Master asked Narendra and M. to speak and argue in English. They laughed but did not oblige. Sri Ramakrishna asked Narendra to come a little more often. To Sri Ramakrishna, Narendra was still a new-comer and He said that on first acquaintance people visited each other quite often. He gave the example of a lover and his sweetheart. Narendra, being very particular about his promises, said that he would try.

Later, to M., the Master likened Narendra to a bullock that frisked about and showed spirit when his tail was touched. At dusk, the Master asked M. to talk to Narendra and then report to Him what he thought of Narendra. M. met Narendra on the bank of the Ganges. Narendra told M. that he was a college student, was a member of the Brâhmo Samâj and so on (ibid.: 92).

The next time we meet Narendra is on 16th October, 1882 (ibid.: 117). As recorded by M., Sri Ramakrishna was in a very happy mood because Narendra was with him. Narendra had his midday meal with the Master. Sri Ramakrishna sat near Narendra on the bed, like a child. With great joy He talked with the devotees, giving them spiritual teachings, but His eyes remained fixed on Narendra. Late in the afternoon, Narendra started singing (ibid. :119 – 120). Later, Narendra and the devotees began to sing kirtan and in the end Narendra, himself started playing on the drums. As recorded by M., Sri Ramakrishna was so happy that He could hardly contain Himself for joy (ibid. :121).

Narendra and M. were discussing about the attitude of the young men – many of them formed bad habits. However, when Sri Ramakrishna heard about their topic of conversation, He said that it was not desirable to talk on any subject but God (ibid. :122). Narendra stayed the night at Dakshineswar.

The next day we see Narendra asking the Master about spiritual discipline. He asked the Master about the Tantra and if it was true that the Tantra prescribed spiritual discipline in the company of women. Sri Ramakrishna said that it was not desirable and often caused the aspirant's downfall (ibid. : 123). Years later, in 1896, Swami Vivekananda wrote to the members of the Alambazar Math, "None of you are fit for Vâmâchâra form of practice. Therefore this should on no account be practised at the Math." This is documented in *Letters of Swami Vivekananda* (Advaita Ashrama, 1970: 290). He further wrote that if any woman came to have a talk with a Sannyasin, she had to meet him in the Visitors' Hall. No woman was to be allowed to enter any other room – except the Worship-room (ibid.: 290).

Going back to 1882, in *The Gospel of Sri Ramakrishna*, we see that the Master had sent Narendra and his friends to meditate in the Panchavati (Nikhilananda, 1981: 124). Later He, Himself went to the Panchavati and told the devotees that in meditation one must be absorbed in God. He returned to His room with them and instructed them about discrimination and renunciation. He gave them the example of alligators – they did not touch one if the body was smeared with turmeric. Similarly, one had to protect oneself from the alligators within oneself, like lust, anger, avarice, and so on, with the turmeric of discrimination and renunciation (ibid. :125).

Narendra is mentioned next on 22nd October, 1882. It was Vijaya Dashami. Sri Ramakrishna clearly told M. that Narendra was amongst his intimate disciples. He also mentioned Rakhal (later to be known as Swami Brahmananda) and Bhavanath Chatterji. The Master asked M. what he thought of Narendra and then went on to describe his many virtues (ibid.:127).

We meet Narendra again on 27th October, 1882 (ibid. : 144). Sri Ramakrishna had gone to Suresh Mitra's house after a boat trip with Keshab Chandra Sen, the Brâhmo leader. Narendra, who lived nearby, was sent for. The Master was happy to see His disciple. We meet him again on 16th November, 1882 at the house of Rajmohan, a member of the Brâhmo Samâj, where Narendra used to meet some of his young friends and worship, following Brâhmo ceremonies. Sri Ramakrishna watched the young men at their worship.

On 25th February , 1883, we see the Master conversing with His devotees. He said that Narendra, Rakhal and Bhavanath could be called nityasiddha. Their spiritual consciousness was awake from birth and they assumed human bodies only to impart spiritual illumination to others (ibid. : 182). Sri Ramakrishna, in His last year, had predicted that Narendra would shake the world with his intellect and spiritual power. The Master had prayed to the Mother so that she would keep the knowledge of the Absolute away from Narendra and cover his eyes with a veil of maya, because he had so much work to do. At the same time, the Master was apprehensive that the veil was too thin and it could be torn at any moment (Isherwood, 2007: 301).

On 29th March, 1883, M. recorded what the Master told some devotees; Sri Ramakrishna said that youngsters like Narendra and Rakhal were ever-perfect. They were devoted to God every time they were born. They had love of God from the very moment of their birth. He further went on to explain that the ever-perfect were like bees which lighted only on flowers and sipped the honey. They were never inclined to worldly pleasures (Nikhilananda, 1981: 196).

We meet Narendra again on 7th April, 1883 when Sri Ramakrishna was visiting Balaram Bose in Calcutta (ibid. :198-200). We learn that the Master had earlier been to the house of Keshab Sen with Narendra and Rakhal to see the performance of a play, Nava-Vrindâvan, where Narendra had also taken part. At Balaram Bose's house, Sri Ramakrishna wanted to hear Narendra sing.

Narendra sang, although he was not feeling well. Bhavanath also sang. Narendra told the Master that Bhavanath had given up fish and betel leaf (considered as luxuries). However, Sri Ramakrishna said that true renunciation was the renunciation of 'woman and gold'.

On 14th April, 1883, the Master told the devotees present that when He first met Narendra, He found him completely indifferent to his body. When He touched Narendra's chest, he lost consciousness of the outer world. When he regained consciousness, he was anxious about his father and mother at home. Apparently, he was not yet ready to renounce everything (ibid.: 230-231). The next day, the Master again spoke about Narendra (ibid.: 238). He asked M. to bring Narendra with him in a carriage and also bring some sweets. He also said that Bhavanath was devoted to Narendra. On 15th June (ibid. :249), the Master referred to Narendra's big, protruding eyes while saying that there were certain signs of a jnâni.

Narendra is mentioned again on 19th August, 1883. The Master requested him to sing. After hearing a few words of the song, the Master went into samâdhi. After coming down from samâdhi, Sri Ramakrishna could not find Narendra. He said that Narendra had lighted the fire and it did not matter if he stayed in the room or went out. Later, the Master found Narendra and Pratap Hazra, who was from a village near Kamarpukur, busy in discussion. The Master knew that Hazra loved to argue and indulge in dry philosophical discussions. Narendra told the Master that they were discussing about many things, too deep for others to understand. However, Sri Ramakrishna said that Pure Knowledge and Pure Love were one and the same and the path of Love was much easier (ibid.: 276-278). We learn from M.'s record (ibid.: 278) that Narendra was reading a book by Hamilton where the author had written, "A learned ignorance is the end of philosophy and the beginning of religion." During the 1830s, the notion that learned ignorance was the highest philosophical achievement began to be reasserted and the reassertion was pre-eminently made by Sir William Hamilton, the logician and metaphysician. This was part of an attempt to counter destruction of long-established ideas and practices, such as the idea that true wisdom consisted in knowing the extent of one's own ignorance (Jessop, 2012, Web 04.12.2013).

On 9th September, 1883, the Master was once again asking M. what he thought of Narendra. The Master went on to say that Narendra's intelligence was as great as his learning. He was gifted in music. He had control over his passions and had said that he would never marry (Nikhilananda, 1981: 286).

On the same day, Sri Ramakrishna told M. about His own state of mind. He did not go to the Kali temple during those days. He told M. that at one time Narendra used to express his surprise about His still going to the Kali temple (ibid.: 288). According to M.'s record of 26th September, 1883 (ibid. :296), Sri Ramakrishna told M. that Narendra had said of the Master, "He still goes to the Kali temple. But he will not when he truly understands." (ibid.:296). He, himself was yet to understand the Master. Later, Narendra's realisation that the Divine Mother was actually alive and his acceptance of the worship of God with form was a very important event in his life (Isherwood, 2007: 214-215).

We see from M.'s record that Sri Ramakrishna would often praise Narendra while conversing with the devotees. On 23rd September, 1883, the Master said of him that Narendra was versatile-gifted in singing, playing on instruments and in studies (Nikhilananda, 1981:294). He was independent and did not care about anybody. In His instruction to people, the Master would even quote Narendra. Narendra had once said that as the "I" of man recedes, the "I" of God approaches (ibid. :308) and Sri Ramakrishna quoted him when speaking about the Truth being covered by the feeling of ego. On 9th December, 1883, He told M. that Narendra belonged to a very high level (ibid. :331). On 24th December, 1883, He related to M. how Narendra, at first, would abuse Mother Kali. One day Sri Ramakrishna scolded him and told him not to come any more. But Narendra was His own and those who were His own would come to Him even if He scolded them. Sri Ramakrishna said that Narendra was perfect from his very birth and that he was devoted to the ideal of the formless God (ibid.: 363-364). This was before Narendra's acceptance of the worship of God with form.

We meet Narendra again on 2nd March, 1884. His father had passed away suddenly and the family was faced with serious financial difficulties (ibid. :394). The Master was conversing with the devotees. He explained about the three classes of devotees. The lowest one pointed to heaven as the abode of God. The mediocre devotee pointed to the heart. However, the highest devotee said that all that one perceived were so many forms of God. The Master said that Narendra would make fun of Him and say that a pot was God, a cup was God! (ibid. :396). We also learn from M.'s record that the Master spoke as if vexed at Narendra's suffering and piqued because God had not shown kindness to him, as yet (ibid.: 397). We learn that Narendra was then studying the views of the atheists.

On 23rd March, 1884, Ramchandra Dutta, a relative of Narendra, reported to the Master that there was talk of Narendra's marrying and that he had been offered a sizeable dowry (ibid.: 406). However, as recorded by M., the Master did not encourage further conversation about Narendra.

On 15th June, 1884, Sri Ramakrishna was conversing with Pratap Chandra Mazumdar of the Brâhmo Samâj at Suresh Mitra's house. He referred to Narendra (ibid.: 456). Pratap did not know Narendra and asked the Master who he was. Sri Ramakrishna did not elaborate. Instead He talked about the conversation with Narendra regarding the Ocean of Bliss. God was the Ocean of Bliss. The Master had asked Narendra that if there was a cup of syrup and he was a fly, where would he sit to sip the syrup. Narendra had replied that he would sit on the edge so as not to get drowned. However, the Master explained to him that in the Ocean of Satchidânanda there was no such fear. It was the Ocean of Immortality (ibid.: 456). Years later, in 1893, both Pratap and Narendra would be at the Parliament of Religions. Unfortunately, as recorded in *Letters of Swami Vivekananda* (Advaita Ashrama, 1970: 79, 83), Pratap did not take Swami Vivekananda's popularity very kindly.

We meet Narendra once again on 25th June, 1884, at the house of Ishan, a devotee of Sri Ramakrishna (Nikhilananda, 1981: 462-463). We learn that Narendra's troubles were not yet over. The Master was speaking to M. about how Narendra had been trying to get a job but had not yet been successful. The Master could feel that his mind was unsettled. The Master left for the house of Pundit Shashadhar, one of the renowned Sanskrit scholars of his time. Narendra, Rakhal, Ram, Hazra and M. went with Sri Ramakrishna (ibid.: 464). However, even while discussing about jnânayoga, bhaktiyoga and karmayoga with Pundit Shashadhar (ibid.: 467), the Master did not forget to admonish Narendra about his singing at Ishan's house, which had sounded dull since Narendra's mind was set on seeking a job (ibid. :470).

We meet Narendra again on 6th September, 1884 in Adhar's parlour (ibid. :508-510). Narendra sang after tuning the drums since one of the strings of the tânpura had snapped. Pundit Shashadhar's host had wanted to invite the Master for dinner. However, the Master had heard that he was immoral and did not drink the water he had touched. Had the Master heard or did He know? Hazra referred to a Vaishnava who had once come to see Sri Ramakrishna and the Master had turned His back on him. Narendra, at first, used to say that these were all hallucinations. But gradually he found that the Master was always right (ibid.: 511). He did admit the same to the Master. The Master asked him to come to Dakshineswar on the next day. However, on 7th September, 1884,

M. informed the Master that Narendra could not come (ibid. :512). He was going through a difficult time because of his father's death. Adhar, who was a Deputy Magistrate, asked the Master if Narendra would accept a job and the Master replied in the affirmative (ibid. :519). Sri Ramakrishna told Adhar that he loved Narendra, Rakhal and others, not for His personal gain but because He saw in them Narâyana Himself (ibid. :520).

On 14th September, 1884, Narendra was with the Master (ibid. :522). He was preparing for the forthcoming Law examination. Hearing Narendra in discussion with Hazra, Sri Ramakrishna referred to him as the chatterbox! He was still worried about his family (ibid. :524). The Master also told M. that once Narendra had said that he would look upon adversity as his good fortune (ibid. :524). He did have to face adversity. However, as he wrote to his dear Rakhal, Swami Brahmananda, on 11th October, 1897, "This life is not, in my view, such a sweet thing that I would long to live through so much care and caution and fear." In the same letter, documented in *Letters of Swami Vivekananda* (Advaita Ashrama, 1970 :369-371), he wrote, "This I have seen in life – he who is over-cautious about himself falls into dangers at every step; he who is afraid of losing honour and respect, gets only disgrace; he who is always afraid of loss always loses."

Going back to 14th September, 1884, we see Narendra engaged in furious discussion with a singer. He sang and Sri Ramakrishna also sang (Nikhilananda, 1981 :525-527). Later, Narendra specially sang the âgamani-songs invoking Durga, the Divine Mother (ibid. :529). Sri Ramakrishna went into samâdhi (ibid. :530).

On 19th September, 1884, as recorded by M., Sri Ramakrishna was speaking about Narendra (ibid. 535). When Narendra had first come, his clothes were dirty but his eyes and face manifested some "inner stuff" (ibid. :535). Whenever Narendra went to Him, Sri Ramakrishna would talk only with him, although the room was filled with people. The Master would actually weep for him. He said Narendra and Bhavanath belonged to the realm of the Formless Reality.

On 21st September, 1884, there is a reference to Narendra – his financial condition. Actually Hazra had blamed Sri Ramakrishna, saying that He loved those who had great wealth, name and fame (ibid. :549). How could Sri Ramakrishna agree when He loved Narendra, who could not even afford salt to season his roast banana?

28th September, 1884 – it was the day of Mahâshtami. Sri Ramakrishna was in Calcutta to visit Adhar's house where Durga Puja was being conducted.

Before going to Adhar's house, the Master went to the house of Ramchandra Dutta, where Narendra was present (ibid. :562). The Master saw his beloved disciple. He stood up and went into samâdhi. He placed one foot on Narendra's knee. Later, He discussed about food with Narendra (ibid. :564). Narendra said that one ought to take whatever came. However, the Master said that this applied only to a jnâni but not to a bhakta. To Narendra He clarified that he could eat everything.

The next day, Narendra visited the Master at Dakshineswar (ibid. :569) which made the Master very happy. M. recorded that Narendra lay on the mat, flat on his stomach. The Master looked at him and went into samâdhi. He even sat on Narendra's back. Later, he asked Narendra to have his lunch in His room. M. and other devotees went to the guest house (ibid. :570). When Bhavanath appeared in the garb of a brahmachâri, Narendra said that he would dress as a Tântrik worshipper. When Hazra pointed out that in that case he would have to follow the Tântrik rituals, with women, wine and so on, Sri Ramakrishna did not encourage the conversation (ibid. :570-571). When Narendra referred to various religious sects (Ghoshpâra, Panchanâmi, and others), Sri Ramakrishna condemned their immoral practices. He discouraged Narendra from listening to those things. He, himself, regarded woman as mother (ibid. :571-572). He told Narendra to remind Hazra about going home. Hazra had told the Master that he would go home but had subsequently forgotten about it (ibid. :574). Since there had been discussion on filthy topics, Sri Ramakrishna wanted the name of Hari to be chanted. Narendra sang and the Master danced in a circle, with the devotees joining Him. It was pure bliss! (ibid. :574-575)

There is a reference to Narendra on 5th October, 1884. The Master was telling M. that since his father's death, Narendra had been worried about his worldly affairs. The Master also remarked that Narendra had a slightly calculating mind (ibid. :595). Perhaps it was the will of the Lord. He had to lead, he had a mission to fulfil and for that a certain mental calibre was necessary. As documented in *God Lived with Them* (Chetanananda, 2006: 53), Swami Vivekananda was in a dilemma about the establishment of a monastic order that would carry the message of Vedanta across the world. If he went for organized religion, the spirit would diminish; if he did not, the message would not spread. Perhaps the calculating mind decided in favour of organized religion and on 1st May, 1897, the Ramakrishna Mission Association came into existence.

It was the day of Kalipuja – 18th October, 1884. Sri Ramakrishna suddenly went into samâdhi. After coming down from the ecstatic state, He told the devotees that He had seen everything – how far the devotees had advanced. He mentioned Rakhal, M., Surendra, Baburam, and many others. Hazra asked the Master if He had seen him. The Master replied in the affirmative. Then Hazra asked about Narendra. The Master said that He had not seen him. But He could tell about him. Narendra was a little entangled. But the Master had seen that everyone would succeed (Nikhilananda, 1981 :621). We see at many places, as recorded by M., how Sri Ramakrishna used to praise Narendra. However, when he was entangled, the Master openly said so. Earlier also, he had openly spoken about Narendra's slightly calculating mind (ibid. :595).

On 6th December, 1884, Bankim Chandra Chatterji, the famous writer, was introduced to Sri Ramakrishna at Adhar's house. To Bankim Chandra also, Sri Ramakrishna spoke about the Ocean of Bliss and repeated his conversation with Narendra, which He had earlier narrated to Pratap Chandra Mazumdar (ibid. :456); He said that by diving deep in God one became immortal (ibid. :675). Narendra had told the Master that if there was a cup of syrup and he was a fly, he would sit on the edge and drink the syrup. If he plunged into the middle of the cup he would die. But Sri Ramakrishna had explained to him that if the syrup was the Nectar of Satchidânanda, that would not happen. Man would become immortal by diving into It (ibid. :675).

We meet Narendra again on 22nd February, 1885 at Dakshineswar. Devotees were celebrating the Master's birthday, which had fallen on the previous Monday (ibid. :691). The Master's glance fell on Narendra, who was sitting close to Him. The Master stood up and went into samâdhi, touching Narendra's knee with His foot. After regaining consciousness, he whispered to Baburam, later to be known as Swami Premananda, to give some kshir, which was in the room, to Narendra. M. recorded, "Did the Master see Narendra as embodiment of God?"(ibid. :691). The Master Himself fed Narendra with sweets. Later, he asked Narendra to sing (ibid. :692). We learn from M.'s record that Narendra's financial worries were not yet over. Girish Chandra Ghosh, the famous Bengali dramatist, had come. The Master said to Girish Ghosh that He looked upon Narendra as Âtman and obeyed him (ibid. :693). Narendra had a manly nature and He had the nature of a woman. Narendra was a noble soul and belonged to the realm of the Indivisible Brahman. M. recorded the instruction He gave to Narendra (ibid. :695). The Master being aware of his financial difficulties, told him that although undoubtedly he was 'Kha' (the âkâsa), he had to worry about 'taxes' (pecuniary troubles). Sri Ramakrishna advised him to go beyond knowledge and ignorance. He gave the example of Sage Vasishtha, who was grief-stricken at the death of his sons. This was a surprise to Lakshmana. But Sri Rama explained to him that a person who had knowledge had ignorance as well. He, who was aware of light was also aware of darkness. He, who knew the good also knew the bad. He, who knew happiness had to be aware of misery. So Sri Rama asked Lakshmana to go beyond duality, beyond pleasure and pain, beyond knowledge and ignorance. The Master, after giving this example, asked Narendra to go beyond both knowledge and ignorance. After Narendra had left, the Master suddenly expressed to M.his appreciation for the sweetness of Narendra's music (ibid. :697).

The Master and Narendra met at the Star Theatre on 25th February, 1885. As recorded by M., the Master stood near Narendra and said to him, "I have come." The Master appreciated Girish Ghosh when he said that the theatre belonged to them (the entire group) and not to him. People who said "I" and "mine" were egotistic, small-minded (ibid. :704). Narendra said that the whole world was a theatre. When the Master said that in some places one saw the play of vidyâ and in some places that of avidyâ, Narendra replied that everything was the play of vidyâ. Sri Ramakrishna said that it was true but a man realized that when he had the knowledge of Brahman. For a bhakta, both vidyâmaya and avidyâmaya existed (ibid. :704 -705).

We meet Narendra again on Dolayâtrâ, 1st March, 1885. As recorded by M., the Master was discouraging Narendra from visiting Girish Ghosh frequently (ibid. :709). He knew that Narendra would renounce the world, that he would shun 'woman and gold' (ibid. :709). Girish was a householder after all. Sri Ramakrishna, Himself did not look down upon worldly people. When He met them, He applied the knowledge of Brahman, Oneness of Existence (ibid. :710). However, he told Narendra that to attain God, 'woman and gold' had to be renounced. We learn from *The Gospel of Sri Ramakrishna* that Narendra was passing through a critical period when he had a revelation and decided to become a monk immediately. He did not tell the Master about this. But nothing was hidden from Sri Ramakrishna and He was afraid lest Narendra should leave Him (ibid. :711-712). He told M. that Narendra was utterly guileless. Due to his family problems his spiritual progress was a little obstructed but that would not last long (ibid. :713).

Narendra was arguing with a Vedântist. Sri Ramakrishna, as recorded by M., did not like these discussions. He revealed to M. that He used to weep and pray to the Divine Mother to tell Him what the truth really was since He was troubled with arguments – one person saying it was this while another saying it was that (ibid. :715). Years later, as documented in *Letters of Swami Vivekananda,* we see that Swami Vivekananda had reached a stage beyond arguments and discussions. He wrote to Joe (Miss Josephine MacLeod) on 18th April, 1900, "Oh, it is so calm! My thoughts seem to come from a great, great distance in the interior of my own heart. They seem like faint, distant whispers, and peace is upon everything, sweet, sweet peace – like that one feels a few moments just before falling into sleep, when things are seen and felt like shadows – without fear, without love, without emotion." (Advaita Ashrama, 1970 :423). As recorded in his letter to Sister Christine, written on 14th October, 1900, he had found the pearl for which he had dived into the Ocean of life (ibid. :440). Sri Ramakrishna had assured him that he would not die if he plunged into the syrup which was the Nectar of Satchidânanda (Nikhilananda, 1981 : 456, 675).

However, going back to 1885, we find Narendra still arguing – arguing with Girish Ghosh, who spoke of Sri Ramakrishna as an Incarnation of God (Nikhilananda, 1981 :716). When He was told by Haripada, a devotee, that Narendra had been defeated in the argument, the Master corrected him saying that Narendra had said that Girish Ghosh was having such strong faith and he did not like to contradict him. But, we see that he was still not agreeing with Girish Ghosh; he was only stopping himself from contradicting Girish Ghosh, giving due regard to Girish Ghosh's strong faith.

On 11th March, 1885 (ibid. :725 – 726), we find Girish Ghosh in conversation with Sri Ramakrishna at the house of Balaram Bose. Girish told Sri Ramakrishna that Narendra had said God was infinite and had questioned the possibility of knowing all of God. Sri Ramakrishna, in His inimitable way, said that it was not possible to comprehend everything about God. It was enough to realize Him. He further added that one saw God Himself if he saw His Incarnation. It was enough to touch the water of the Ganges. It was not necessary to touch the whole lengh of the river from Hârdwâr to Gangâsâgar. Girish told the Master that according to Narendra, God was beyond words and thought. Sri Ramakrishna did not fully agree. Although God was beyond the ordinary mind, He could be realized by the pure mind, free from attachment. When Girish said that he had defeated Narendra in the argument, Sri Ramakrishna repeated what Narendra had told Him. Narendra had not meddled with Girish Ghosh's faith on God's Incarnation.

The Master started for Girish Ghosh's house late in the evening. Narendra was seen coming from a distance. Surprisingly, at first He ignored Narendra (ibid. :731). Later, He said, looking at him, "I want to tell you something. 'This' is one and 'that' is another." Did Narendra understand what was going on through His innermost soul? (ibid. :732).

On the same day, we see that there was a lot of discussion between Narendra and Girish (ibid. :732-733). Narendra, at that time, did not believe that God could manifest Himself through one person. God was beyond word and thought. The Master told him that God could be known by pure buddhi. Girish was of the opinion that unless God Himself taught men through His Human Incarnation, there would be none to teach them the spiritual mysteries. But Narendra believed that God dwelt in the heart of man and He would teach from within the heart. The Master seemed to agree, saying that God would teach as the Inner Guide. The argument continued between Girish Ghosh and Narendra. If God was Infinity, how could He have parts? What did the Western philosophers say? Besides Hamilton, we find that Spencer, Tyndall and Huxley were mentioned. Herbert Spencer, John Tyndall and Thomas Henry Huxley belonged to the X Club and were united by a devotion to science, free from religious dogmas. The members of the group became prominent in the scientific community during the 1870s and 1880s (Wikipedia, Web. 25.11.2013). However, we see that Sri Ramakrishna did not enjoy the discussions. He said that He would not argue at all since He clearly saw that God was everything. He said that at the sight of Narendra His mind lost itself in the consciousness of the Absolute (Nikhilananda, 1981 :733). As recorded by M., He went on to explain Qualified Non-Dualism to Narendra (ibid. :733-734). Brahman, according to Râmânuja, was qualified by the universe and the living beings.

On the same day, as recorded by M., we find that Narendra had meditated on Kali for three or four days, but nothing had come out of it (ibid. :734). Sri Ramakrishna explained to him that Kali was the same as Brahman. She was the Primal Energy. When the energy remained inactive, It was Brahman and when It created, preserved or destroyed, It was Kali.

The Master told Narendra that as long as a person argued about God, he had not realized Him (ibid.:735). The nearer one approached Him, the less one reasoned and argued. When one attained Him, all reasoning and disputing came to an end. Then, one went into samâdhi-sleep, communion with God in silence. In his letter to Joe, dated 18th April, 1900, Swami Vivekananda expressed his state of mind (Advaita Ashrama, 1970 :423). The signs were similar to those described by the Master for a person who had attained Him (Nikhilananda, 1981 :735).

On 24th April, 1885, we meet Narendra with other devotees at the house of Balaram Bose and then Girish Ghosh (ibid. :762). Sri Ramakrishna had a sore throat and the ladies at Balaram Bose's house sent a plate of hâluâ for him. We see the Master urging Narendra to eat some of the delicious hâluâ. We also see how Sri Ramakrishna was trying to alert Narendra about people (here Hazra). Narendra thought that he understood people. While Sri Ramakrishna, Himself knew that just as God took the form of holy men, He also took the form of cheats and rogues, He had to protect His disciple (ibid. :765-766). The argument (about Hazra) continued on 19th May, 1885, at Balaram Bose's drawing room (ibid. :768-769). The topic turned to God's Human Incarnation. Narendra was not the man to believe, without proof. Again, about the immortality of the Gods, he needed proof (ibid. :771). The Master recounted how Narendra used to tease Him. He would point out bats to the Master but would say that those were châtak birds (ibid. :772). He would say that the forms of God the Master saw were actually the fiction of His mind. Finally, we see Narendra enunciating that it was enough to have faith in God. According to him, infinite was the universe and infinite were the Incarnations (ibid. :773).

Narendra was there at Ramchandra Dutta's house on 23rd May, 1885 (ibid. :778). Sri Ramakrishna was surrounded by devotees. We meet him again on 13th June, 1885 at Dakshineswar. Sri Ramakrishna was to go to Calcutta in the evening from Dakshineswar. But He postponed His visit since Narendra arrived at Dakshineswar (ibid. :795). Seeing Narendra, His love overflowed. Narendra had come. How could Sri Ramakrishna leave for Calcutta?

On 13th July, 1885, Sri Ramakrishna was sitting in Balaram Bose's drawing room. For the first time we read about a change in Narendra's attitude. Sri Ramakrishna was telling the story of Aghoremani Devi, the brâhmani of Kamarhati, and her experiences with Gopâla – Baby Krishna – how he walked with her, talked with her. He also said that when Narendra heard the story, he wept (ibid. :798). Perhaps, he no longer thought that it was all imagination. On the next day too, Sri Ramakrishna told M. that at first Narendra used to say that these (the Master's visions) were figments of His imagination; but this had changed and he had started to accept everything (ibid. :803). Narendra arrived. It was the day of the Car Festival. Sri Ramakrishna was very happy to see him (ibid. :804). We see from M.'s record that Narendra was in a spiritual mood, with tears in his eyes – so different from the person who would argue and get involved in heated discussions (ibid. :808).

On 15th July, 1885, as recorded by M., the Master said that Narendra belonged to a very high plane – the realm of the Absolute. Some devotees were like lotuses with ten petals, some like those with sixteen petals, some like those with a hundred petals. Narendra was a thousand petalled one. If some devotees were like pots or pitchers, Narendra was a huge water barrel. Others would be like pools or tanks; but Narendra was a huge reservoir. Others could be like minnows, smelts and sardines but Narendra was a huge red-eyed carp. Narendra had the capacity to hold many things. He was not under the control of anything – attachments or sense pleasures. Sri Ramakrishna, Himself said that He felt great strength when Narendra was with Him in a gathering (ibid. :810-811).

On 9th August, 1885, Sri Ramakrishna was speaking about His amazing visions. He said that once He had a vision of the Indivisible Satchidânanda. Inside It He saw two groups with a fence between them. On one side were devotees who believed in the Personal God. On the other side, inside a luminous space like a heap of red brick-dust, sat Narendra, absorbed in meditation. Sri Ramakrishna recalled that He had called his name aloud and he had opened his eyes a little. The Master came to realize that he had been born, in another form, in Simlâ (North Calcutta), in a kâyastha family. At once, Sri Ramakrishna prayed to the Divine Mother to entangle him in maya or else he would give up his body in samâdhi (ibid. :831). The future leader of the Ramakrishna Movement had been identified. Narendra could not be allowed to give up his body in samâdhi because, as Swami Vivekananda, he had a mission to fulfil. The next day, when the Master was told of a devotee who had divine visions even while he was awake, He said that He was not surprised. Narendra too had started seeing forms of God (ibid. :834). The evolution of the thought process had got under way.

Then we come to the most heart-rending portion of *The Gospel of Sri Ramakrishna.* The first signs of the Master's illness was recorded on 11th August, 1885 (ibid. :834). On 1st September, 1885, the Master was unwell. Still He conversed with the devotees (ibid. :841). He said that it was very difficult to gather the dispersed mind when it was attached to 'woman and gold'. The minds of Narendra and other youngsters were not scattered. They were not yet touched by 'woman and gold'.

We see that Narendra was present in the house at Syâmpukur on 18th October and then again on 24th October, 1885, as recorded by M. (ibid. 848 and 876). The doctors had diagnosed Sri Ramakrishna's illness as cancer. The

Master had been shifted to the house at Syâmpukur in North Calcutta for better treatment and nursing. As desired by the Master, Narendra sang (ibid. :877-878). The Master pointed out to the devotees how Narendra's whole mind was being drawn towards Him (Sri Ramakrishna).

On 25th October, 1885, the Master was in deep samâdhi. After a long time he regained consciousness of the world. The Master said that while coming down from samâdhi He could not count correctly. He would say, 'One, seven, eight' or some such thing. Narendra attributed it to the fact that everything was one. However, the Master said that it was beyond one and two, where reason withered away (ibid. :881-882). Vijaykrishna Goswami, who had cut off his connection with the Brâhmo Samâj, was conversing with the devotees. He said that he had seen the Master in Dacca and even touched His body. While Sri Ramakrishna said with a smile that it must have been someone else, Narendra said that he too had seen Him many a time (ibid. :885).

On 26th October, 1885, M. recorded that the Master's illness had been declared as incurable. He also recorded that a band of young disciples, led by Narendra, was preparing to renounce the world and dedicate their lives to the realization of God and the service to humanity (ibid. :886). Their decision regarding service to humanity in addition to God realization was very important – it was the seed of the Ramakrishna Mission. On 15th May, 1897, Swami Akhandananda, a brother disciple of Swami Vivekananda, started famine relief work at Murshidabad. That was the first organized relief work of the Ramakrishna Mission which had been started by Swami Vivekananda on 1st May, 1897 (Chetanananda, 2006 :578-579). On 15th June, 1897, Swami Vivekananda wrote to his Gurubhai from Almora, "Books and learning, Yoga and meditation and illumination – all are but dust compared with love. It is love that gives you the supernatural powers, love that gives you Bhakti, love that gives illumination, and love, again, that leads to emancipation. This indeed is worship, worship of the Lord in the human tabernacle ... ." This is documented in *Letters of Swami Vivekananda* (Advaita Ashrama, 1970 :342).

On 27th October, 1885, we learn from M.'s record that Narendra was with the Master (Nikhilananda, 1981 :896). Since his father's death he had been worried about the financial condition of his family. He had to support his mother and brothers. He was preparing himself for his Law examination. Lately, he had served as a teacher in Vidyasagar School. The Master said that God certainly provided everything for the man who totally surrendered himself to Him. Narendra belonged to a high plane. Yet he was in difficulty. A man who felt intense renunciation within would not wait to make some arrangement for his family and then practise sâdhana. Sri Ramakrishna always explained with examples. A woman had been stricken with intense grief. She first tied her nose-ring in the corner of her cloth and then dropped to the ground wailing. But all the time she took care so that the nose-ring would not be broken! As recorded by M., while all laughed, Narendra felt as if struck by an arrow. He had wanted to make some arrangement for his family and get rid of all his worries. The Master had said that if a man felt intense renunciation within he would not calculate that way (ibid. :896). Afterwards, Narendra sang, pouring his heart and soul into the songs (ibid. :898-899).

Later, as recorded by M., Narendra told Dr. Mahendra Sarkar, who was treating the Master, that he did not say that the Master was God; Sri Ramakrishna was a godlike man (ibid. :904). He further said to Dr. Sarkar that one could devote one's life to scientific research without giving a thought to health or comfort. But the Science of God was the grandest of all sciences. So it was natural for the Master to risk His health to realize God (ibid. :905). The Master had earlier said that He sometimes thought that His illness could be due to samâdhi. However, He could not help His divine madness. According to M.'s record (ibid.:906), Narendra said to the doctor, "We offer worship to him bordering on divine worship.". We see in Syâmpukur, Narendra was at a stage when Sri Ramakrishna was not God but like God. The worship was not divine worship but bordering on divine worship.

On 31st October, 1885, the devotees were worried to see the Master's repeated ecstasies, although He was ill. He said that He would be quiet if someone sang a particular song. Narendra was sent for. He was in another room; from there he came and sang (ibid. :923-924).

The day was 23rd December, 1885. We learn from M.'s record that on 11th December, Sri Ramakrishna had been shifted to a beautiful house at Cossipore (ibid. :931). Here, the Master predicted that a band of young disciples, with Narendra as their leader, would in due course renounce the world and devote themselves to the realization of God and the service of humanity (ibid. :931). Their intention to do so had already been recorded by M. on 26th October, 1885 (ibid. :886).

On 4th January, 1886, as recorded by M., Narendra had cried all the way from home. The Master indicated the same to M. when Narendra arrived (ibid. :935). The Master asked Narendra if he would continue with his studies. Narendra replied that he would feel greatly relieved if he found a medicine that would make him forget all that he had studied. He spoke of his intention of going to Dakshineswar and meditating.

In the evening, on the same day, Narendra was describing to M. about some of his experiences while meditating. He told M. what he had said to Sri Ramakrishna. All others had had their realization. He entreated the Master to give him some also. The Master told him to settle his family affairs first. Then he would get everything. The Master had asked him what he wanted. When Narendra told him that he desired to remain absorbed in samâdhi, Sri Ramakrishna said that there was a state higher than that. He assured Narendra that he would attain a state higher than samâdhi. We can feel the struggle within Narendra, as depicted by M.; his soul was restless for the vision of God (ibid. :935-936). Later, the Master spoke about Narendra – how wonderful was his state of mind. This was the same Narendra who did not believe in the forms of God (ibid. :937).

On 5th January, 1886, Sri Ramakrishna was talking with M.; no one else was in the room. He spoke of Narendra. The Master said that when a man was seized with the spirit of intense renunciation, he would regard the world as a deep well and his relatives as venomous cobras. Narendra entered the room. He was going home; a friend would lend him a hundred rupees which would take care of his family for three months. He was passing through the state of intense renunciation and could not appear for his Law examination (ibid. :937-938).

The next record is dated 11th March, 1886. Sri Ramakrishna was giving instruction to the devotees. He was explaining about jnânis and bhaktas. As recorded by M., Sri Ramakrishna affectionately stroked Narendra's face and hands and told him that his face and hands showed that Narendra was a bhakta. The features of a jnâni were dry (ibid. :939).

The record of 14th March, 1886 is heart-rending. Sri Ramakrishna was very ill. Narendra and other young disciples were staying with Him at Cossipore. The Master, with great difficulty, said to M. that if the devotees would say that there was so much suffering and so the body be allowed to die, then He would give up the body (ibid. :940-941).

The next day, He felt a little better. As recorded by M., like a mother showing her tenderness to her children, He touched the faces and chins of Rakhal and Narendra (ibid. :942). Rakhal requested Him to speak to God so that God would preserve His body for some more time. When the Master replied that it depended on God's will, Narendra said that the Master's will and God's will had become one (ibid. :904). Had the thought process evolved from the stage at Syâmpukur, where Narendra had said that Sri Ramakrishna was not God but a godlike man? (ibid. :904).

As recorded by M., Narendra said that some people got angry with him when he spoke of renunciation. The Master said that renunciation was necessary. If one thing was placed upon another, one had to be removed to get to the other. When one saw everything filled with God alone, one did not see anything else. The Master further said that He saw how preparations were going on for a grand renunciation (ibid.:944). The Master asked Narendra what he thought of Him. Narendra replied, "You are a hero, a handmaid of God, and everything else." This was in continuation of the earlier conversation where Narendra was referred to as one with the attitude of a hero and M., that of a handmaid of God (ibid. :944). M. recorded that Sri Ramakrishna said to Narendra and the other devotees that He saw that all things – everything that existed – had come from "this". He had placed His hand on His heart. He asked Narendra by a sign, what he had understood. Narendra said, "All created objects have come from you." The Master's face beamed with joy (ibid. :945). As recorded by M., Narendra sang, intoxicated with the love of the Gopis of Braja for Sri Krishna (ibid. :945).

We meet Narendra again on 9th April, 1886. He was just back from a visit to Bodh-Gayâ. The conversation was on Buddha. Narendra said that Buddha could not express in words what he had realized by tapasyâ. So people said that he was an atheist. The Master explained what 'Buddha' meant. It was to become one with Bodha, Pure Intelligence, by meditating on That which was of the nature of Pure Intelligence; it was to become Pure Intelligence Itself (ibid. :947). Narendra spoke about Buddha's renunciation (ibid. :948). Sri Ramakrishna then revealed Himself. He said that He had seen that God and the one who dwelt in Sri Ramakrishna's heart were one and the same Person. Narendra said, "Yes, yes! *Soham* – I am He." (ibid. :949).

On 12th April, 1886, Narendra and Tarak, later to be known as Swami Shivananda, returned from Calcutta, where they had been to Girish Ghosh's house and other places. They had eaten meat and other heavy stuff. Narendra said that their minds had come down a great deal. So tapasyâ had to be practised. He likened themselves to coolies – as if the body and mind belonged not to them but to someone else (ibid. :950). They were carrying the weight of someone else's body and mind.

On 13th April, 1886, M., recorded that, in the afternoon, he and a few other devotees were seated near the Master. Narendra came in and he looked, as the Master used to say, like an unsheathed sword. Narendra expressed his utter annoyance with women. They were obstacles in the path of God realization (ibid. :953). He further said that he wanted peace. He did not care even for God. Sri Ramakrishna did not utter a word. As recorded by M. (ibid. :953-954), now and then Narendra chanted, "Brahman is Truth, Knowledge, the Infinite."

On 16th April, 1886, M. recorded that Narendra, Kali (later Swami Abhedananda) and Tarak had gone to Dakshineswar to spend the night in the Panchavati, meditating on God (ibid. :955). On 17th April, 1886, M. recorded that for some time Narendra had been going to Dakshineswar daily and spending time in the Panchavati, in meditation and contemplation. On the 17th, he returned from Dakshineswar in the evening. Many of the devotees were meditating in the room downstairs, at Cossipore. Referring to them, Narendra said to M. that they were shedding their upâdhis one by one (ibid. :959). How many upâdhis had he shed since first meeting the Master in 1881?

On the next day, Narendra and M. had a serious discussion in the Master's presence. Narendra raised the question about the existence of God. He referred to Berkeley. M. said that according to Berkeley, the existence of external objects depended on perception. The world existed as long as the sense organs perceived it. Sri Ramakrishna referred to Totapuri, His Guru, who used to say that the world existed in mind alone and disappeared in mind alone. However, as long as 'I-conciousness' existed, the servant-and-master relationship with God had to be assumed. Narendra questioned (to M.), how could one prove by reasoning that God existed. He went on to say that if one depended on faith, then one had to accept the relationship of servant and Master. If one accepted that, then one had also to say that God was kind. Narendra pointed out the three great things given to them by God. Those were, human birth, the yearning to know God, and the companionship of a great soul (ibid. :960). Later, Narendra said to M. (ibid. :961) that if one followed the path of bhakti, then the mind came down a little to the body. "Otherwise, who am I? Neither man nor God. I have neither pleasure nor pain."

On 21st April, 1886, as recorded by M., Narendra had not yet been able to solve the financial problems of his family. He told M. that there was no such thing as God. M. replied that Scepticism was a stage in the path of God-realization. One had to pass through stages like that and go much farther; only thus could one realize God. That was what the Master had said. Narendra argued, "Has anybody seen God as I see that tree?" When M. replied that Sri Ramakrishna had seen that way, Narendra said that it could be hallucination. He wanted to know the truth. He told M. that he had an argument with Sri Ramakrishna, Himself. The Master had said that some people called Him God. However, Narendra had replied that even if a thousand people called Him God, he would certainly not call Him God as long as he, himself did not know it to be true. Even when Sri Ramakrishna told him that whatever many people proclaimed was indeed the truth, he was not convinced. He, himself had to realize it as the truth (ibid. :962).

On 22nd April, 1886, we find from M.'s record that Bhavanath had married and the Master was worried about Bhavanath's being entangled in worldly life. He asked Narendra to give him a lot of courage (ibid. :965). Hirananda, a native of Sindh, came to see the Master. He had met the Master when he was studying in Calcutta. On hearing of the Master's illness, he had come to Calcutta, all the way from Sindh. Narendra entered and the Master wanted him and Hirananda to talk. When Hirananda asked, why a devotee of God suffered, Narendra replied that the plan of the universe was devilish. He, himself, could have created a better world. Hirananda asked if one could feel happiness without misery. Narendra said that he was not making a plan for the universe but simply giving his opinion of the existing plan. He added that all the problems would be solved if there was faith in one thing, and that was pantheism. All doubts would disappear if one believed that everything was God. God alone was responsible for all that took place (ibid. :966).

Narendra went on to sing Sankaracharya's Six Stanzas on Nirvana and then the Five Stanzas of Kaupin (the loin-cloth of the sannyâsi, an emblem of renunciation). He sang some more songs. Sri Ramakrishna said to Hirananda, pointing to Narendra, that Narendra seemed to be walking with an unsheathed sword in his hand (ibid. :967-969). Hirananda asked the Master, the question he had earlier asked Narendra. He wanted to know why a devotee of God suffered. The Master's reply was that it was the body that suffered. The body suffered for the purpose of teaching men. His life had to be like a book of reference. He had to show that in spite of so much physical suffering, his mind was one hundred per cent united with God. That was Sri Ramakrishna's reply to Hirananda (ibid. :969-970). We may compare this with the reply Narendra had given to the same question (ibid. :966).

On 23rd April, 1886, M. recorded that Narendra, Sarat (later to be known as Swami Saradananda) and M. were talking. Narendra said that it was amazing that one hardly learnt anything even after reading books for many years. How could a man realize God by practising sâdhanâ for two or three days? Was it so easy to realize God? Then he added that Sarat had obtained peace, M. too had obtained peace. But he had no peace. One feels the agony, the suffering, from his words (ibid. :971-972).

On the same day, Kedar Chatterji came to see Sri Ramakrishna, from Dacca. M. recorded that the Master drew Kedar's attention to Narendra and told him that Narendra had renounced everything. He further said to the devotees that Kedar had predicted that Narendra, in spite of all arguments and reasoning, would, in the end, roll on the ground, chanting the name of Hari. The Master asked Narendra to take the dust of Kedar's feet. Kedar, however, told Narendra to take the dust of Sri Ramakrishna's feet (ibid. :972). M. also recorded what Surendra said to Kedar. He told Kedar that a few days back, some of them – specially referring to Narendra – had put on the ochre robe of the sannyâsi and gone on a pilgrimage to Buddha-Gayâ. They wanted to see bigger sadhus there. The Master said that Surendra was right. They (including Narendra) were mere children and did not know what was good (ibid. :972).

M. made his last record during the Master's lifetime on 23rd April, 1886. Narendra was yet to find peace. Perhaps, that was the will of the Lord. Sri Ramakrishna had requested the Divine Mother to entangle him in maya or else he would give up his body in samâdhi (ibid. :831). From his letters, documented in *Letters of Swami Vivekananda* (Advaita Ashrama, 1970), we see the extent of agony and suffering he had to undergo for the fulfilment of his mission. Yet, his letters bear testimony to the evolution of his thought process. On 6th July, 1896, he wrote to Mr. Francis Legget, his disciple, "At twenty years of age I was the most unsympathetic, uncompromising fanatic; I would not walk on the footpath on the theatre side of the streets in Calcutta. At thirty-three, I can live in the same house with prostitutes and never would think of saying a word of reproach to them. Is it degenerate? Or is it that I am broadening out into the Universal Love which is the Lord Himself?" (Advaita Ashrama, 1970 :296).

In *The Gospel of Sri Ramakrishna*, we find that Narendra had said that the plan of the universe was devilish and he could have created a better world (Nikhilananda, 1981 :966). That was on 22nd April, 1886. On 12th April, 1900, as documented in *Letters of Swami Vivekananda,* he wrote to an American friend, "I am free. I am Mother's child. She works, She plays. Why should I plan? What should I plan? Things came and Things went, just as She liked, without my planning. We are Her automata. She is the wirepuller." (Advaita Ashrama, 1970 :421).

However, according to M.'s record during the lifetime of Sri Ramakrishna, even the last entry on 23rd April, 1886 shows that Narendra was far from surrendering to the Divine Mother. Sarat had obtained peace, M. had obtained peace. Narendra had no peace (Nikhilananda, 1981 :972). He would have none till the Ramakrishna–Vivekananda Movement had been set in motion and had gained momentum. This was his mission and it had to be fulfilled.

REFERENCES

1. Letters Of Swami Vivekananda, Advaita Ashrama (1970): Published by the President, Advaita Ashrama, Third (New) Edition, October 1970.
2. Isherwood, Christopher (2007): Ramakrishna And His Disciples, Published by the President, Advaita Ashrama, Tenth Impression, April 2007.
3. Nikhilananda, Swami (1981): The Gospel Of Sri Ramakrishna, Published by the President, Sri Ramakrishna Math, Madras, First Impression, January 1981.
4. Jessop, Ralph (2012): "On the activity of learned ignorance: Pope, Hamilton, Carlyle and Dickens's Hard Times for These Times" in Philosophy of Education Society of Great Britain, Annual Conference, 30 March–1 April, 2012, www. philosophy-of-education.org/uploads/papers2012/Jessop_R.pdf (Web. 04.12.2013)
5. Chetanananda, Swami (2006): God Lived With Them, Published by the President, Advaita Ashrama, Third Reprint, May 2006.
6. Wikipedia (2013): John Tyndall – Wikipedia, the free encyclopedia, en.wikipedia.org/wiki/John_Tyndall (Web. 25.11.2013).

7 Sri Ramakrishna Kathamrita : Sri M's unique contribution to Bengali Literature

Pranab Ranjan Ghosh

Great literature is always the creation of a great mind. To understand the greatness of that mind, his life and reminiscences may be of much help, but the depth of his soul must be ascertained from the writing itself. In world literature the Kathamrita stands unparalleled in its unfathomable spiritual quality. From the life force of rural Bengal came a serene and sublime form of expression, in the spoken words of Sri Ramakrishna. Following Srimad-Bhagavata, Sri M. named them 'Nectar of Words' (Kathamrita); in English he named them 'The Gospel of Sri Ramakrishna'. Both in Vaishnava and Christian sense these words signify eternal truth and love. Rarely human words have acquired such spiritual height; also it is rare to find a more competent recorder of such sayings. Sri Ramakrishna found in Mahendranath Gupta (Sri M.), the best ever scribe the world has ever found.

That his talks were being recorded by Sri M., Sri Ramakrishna was aware of. But that awareness did not make him self-conscious as is evident from the records. Sometimes well aware of the surrounding and his listeners, sometimes fully ignoring them and being immersed in his trance (samadhi); sometimes talking with the Mother Kali Herself, or to himself, he spoke in various moods which was impossible for a novice to note down. It was Sri M.'s deep and rich religious training, which made him a fit carrier of Sri Ramakrishna's words and ideas.

Sri M. could publish only a part of his immense treasures of Sri Ramakrishna's words. But in his private conversations he distributed this holy water of his language, (Gangajal i.e. water of the Ganges) to all who yearned for it. In later years, some of his associates published their memories of Sri M.[1] Those are actually reminiscences of Sri Ramakrishna, for Sri M. after coming in touch with Sri Ramakrishna, lost himself in that embodiment of blessedness. He was the incarnation of Sri Ramakrishna's sayings – as a Hindu would like to describe him.

One must be prepared to accept the world of Ramakrishna, before one can really appreciate the mastery of Sri M.'s art of writing. It was in the seventies of the nineteenth century Bengal, in India, where the East and the West met and struggled with their wide difference and inner unity. Of the difference we can talk a lot, but over the unity we rarely ponder. Man, everywhere is distinguished from the level of other animals, because he can think of the Eternal. There is no country in this world, where someone or other is not struggling to realize the Truth – truth in divine sense. Outward patterns of this search may be different, but the inner urge is everywhere the same.

Through Sri Ramakrishna India spoke to the world about this unity in the diverse ways of man's search for Truth. Much before Vivekananda started preaching, an English newspaper of Calcutta announced on 28 March 1875 –

"A Hindu Saint: – We met one (a sincere Hindu devotee) not long ago and were charmed by the depth, penetration and simplicity of his spirit. The never-ceasing metaphors and analogies in which he indulged, are most of them as apt as they are beautiful."[2] In these few lines we find the essence of literary appreciation of Sri Ramakrishna, as a litterateur of spoken words. More appreciations were to follow.

But the art of Sri M. was properly appreciated by Swami Vivekananda, perhaps for the first time in literary history, in a note dated 7 February 1889 – after reading the Gospel of Sri Ramakrishna in English: "Thanks! 100000 times Master. You have hit Ramkristo in the right point."

Later in a letter dated 24 November 1897, he wrote:

> "My dear 'M.', Many many, many, many thanks for your second leaflet. It is indeed wonderful. The move is quite original and never was the life of a great Teacher brought before the public untarnished by the writer's mind as you are doing. The language also is beyond all praise – so fresh, so pointed and withal so plain and easy, I cannot express in adequate terms how I have enjoyed them. I am really in transport when I read them. Strange, isn't it? ... I now understand why none of us attempted his life before. It has been reserved for you – this great work. He is with you, evidently ...

"(P.S.) Socratic dialogues are Plato all over – you are entirely hidden. Moreover, the dramatic part is infinitely beautiful. Everybody likes it, here or in the West."[3]

It is interesting to note that Swami Vivekananda saw the first volume of Bengali 'Kathamrita', which was published in March 1902. We can easily surmise that his opinion on the Bengali version was equally full of praise.

Mr. N. Ghosh wrote in "The Indian Nation" on 19 May 1902 – "Ramakrishna Kathamrita by M. (part I) is a work of singular value and interest. He has done a kind of work, which no Bengalee had ever done before, which so far as we are aware no native of India had ever done. It has been done only once in history namely by Boswell. But then the immortal biography is only the life of a scholar and a kind-hearted man. This Kathamrita on the other hand, is the record of the sayings of a saint. What is the wit or even the worldly wisdom of the great Doctor by the side of the divine teaching of a genuine devotee? Its value is immense. We say nothing of the sayings themselves for the character of the Teacher and teaching is wel-known."[4]

Compared to Swami Vivekananda's comments, Sri Ghosh's remarks are more on Sri Ramakrishna's sayings than on Sri M.'s literary skill. Still in the latter's comparison of Sri M. with Boswell there is a real insight of literary understanding. In recent times, Aldous Huxley referred to Eckerman also in this context.

In his foreword to the Gospel of Sri Ramakrishna, translated by Swami Nikhilananda, Huxley wrote – "The world has had many hundreds of admirable poets and philosophers; but of these hundreds, only a few have had the fortune to attract a Boswell or an Eckerman ...

"M., as the author modestly styles himself, was peculiarly qualified for his task. To a reverent love of his Master, to a deep and experiential knowledge of that Master's teaching, he added a prodigious memory for the small happenings of each day and a happy gift for recording them in an interesting and realistic way. Making good use of his natural gifts and of the circumstances in which he found himself, M. produced a book unique, so far as my knowledge goes, in the literature of hagiography. No other saint has had so able and so indefatigable a Boswell."[5]

From Plato to Boswell we have the world's best recorders of the sayings of great men in different periods of history. Along with this we may remember the Bible (King James' Version) by which Sri M. and all his contemporaries were more or less influenced. The sayings of Sri Ramakrishna are comparable to Christ's sayings in their utter simplicity, art in artlessness and direct spiritual quality. Naturally an English educated Brahmo-minded thinker like Sri M. took the sayings of Ramakrishna, as the Gospel of the modern age and tried to render them in somewhat Biblical language in his English leaflets of the Gospel of Sri Ramakrishna. Even in the English version, these sayings had a tremendous effect. But by publishing the sayings in the original Bengali, the real Ramakrishna was established once for all before the contemporary and future readers. We shall humbly make an attempt in this article to evaluate, as far as it is given to us, the merit of the Kathamrita as a piece of literature.

As a reader of Bengali literature, one is first struck by the creation of atmosphere in Kathamrita – the contemporary world of Sri Ramakrishna comes out in its minutest details in and around Calcutta. It would have been more interesting if we could find Ramakrishna in his native village among the common people. But as we have it, the first and foremost attraction is in the Dakshineshwar temple. In this temple and within its vicinity at the Panchavati, Sri Ramakrishna realized the Supreme Truth in its various phases. Mother Kali and various other deities of Hindu conception were revealed to him within the arena of Dakshineshwar temple. Later he referred to his visions time and again while discussing his religious experiences. Some of these narrations are full of poetry.

But when Sri M. first met Sri Ramakrishna in the month of February 1882, he did not believe in gods and goddesses with forms. His description of the second meeting (very soon after his first brief meeting) is so sincere, so revealing and full of humanity that the reader is at once taken in the fold of spiritual brotherhood of Sri Ramakrishna's apostles. The victory of Ramakrishna over this highly educated young man of his contemporary learned society reveals equally the greatness of these two minds – of the Master, as well as of the disciple:

"Master: Well, do you believe in God with form or without form?

M. (rather surprised said to himself): How can one believe in God without form

when one believes in God with Form? ...

M.: Sir, I like to think of God as formless.

Master: Very good. It is very good to have faith in either aspect. You believe in God without form. That is quite all right. But never for a moment think that this alone is true and all else false. Remember that God with form is just, as true as God without form. But hold fast to your own conviction...

M.: Sir, suppose one believes in God with form, certainly He is not the clay image!

Master (interrupting): But why clay? It is an image of Spirit.

M. could not quite understand the significance of this 'image of Spirit'. "But, sir," he said to the Master, "One should explain to those who worship the clay image that it is not God, and that, while worshipping it, they should have God in view and not the clay image. One should not worship clay."

Master (sharply): That's the one hobby of you Calcutta people – giving lectures and bringing light to others! Nobody ever stops to consider how to get the light himself! Who are you to teach others?

He who is the Lord of the Universe will teach everyone... If they need teaching, then He will be the Teacher. He is our Inner Guide...

This was M.'s first argument with the Master, and happily his last.[6]"

Thus from the very beginning the Kathamrita brings out a great drama of the inner soul. On the one hand there is a man (or God), whose every inch of being is nothing but spirituality, on the other there is a devotee who would not drink anything but divine nectar. May be, he is not a monk, a sannyasi. To us it is a divine grace that he remained in the so-called worldly life, and made this our worldly life full of his reminiscences of the Master. Thus he connected our limited world with the eternal divine world. His whole life became a constant worship through remembrance and meditation.

A product of the then modern English education, Sri M. was fondly referred to as an 'Englishman' by Sri Ramakrishna. In his characteristic coinage, Sri Ramakrishna meant by the word 'Englishman', both a man with knowledge of English and a man westernised by that knowledge. Of course, Sri M. was not like those young Bengalis who became drunk with western ideals. In reality, his western education made him a seeker of Truth. So when the real occasion came he shunned all complex of superiority, and offered himself at the feet of Sri Ramakrishna, as a true disciple in search of Truth. But this metamorphosis of Sri M.'s personality has been recorded by himself with such humility and devotion that he wins the hearts of his readers from the very beginning of the Kathamrita.

Regarding the dramatic quality of the Kathamrita, we may remember that Sri M. has recorded Sri Ramakrishna's many meetings with different personalities.

These meetings are full of intellectual and spiritual action-reactions, always dissolving in the great ocean of godliness. Vidyasagar, Keshab Chandra Sen, Bankim Chandra Chattopadhyay, Mahendranath Sarkar, young Narendranath (Vivekananda) – the great luminaries of the 19th century intellectual world are represented in the Kathamrita in various moments, and Sri Ramakrishna always comes out in these meetings as the hero of a great drama of bhakti and jnana (devotion and knowledge). For a future biographical dramatist of Sri Ramakrishna there are scores of scenes in the Kathamrita which can be compared with the scenes of any great drama of the world.

We are presenting here one such scene. Vidyasagar and Sri Ramakrishna met in the former's house on 5 August 1892. Sri M., at that time, a teacher in Vidyasagar's school, was instrumental in arranging this meeting. As a true dramatist, Sri M. put these two unique characters the world has ever produced in their own light and although he himself was present all the time, rarely came in front:

"Master: Ah! Today, at last, I have come to the ocean. Up till now I have seen only canals, marshes, or a river at the most. But today I am face to face with the sagar (the ocean). (All laugh).

Vidyasagar (smiling): Then please take home some salt water. (Laughter).

Master: Oh, no! Why salt water? You aren't the ocean of ignorance. You are the ocean of Vidya, knowledge. You are the ocean of Khsira (condensed milk). (All laugh)

Vidyasagar: Well, you may put it that way.

Vidyasagar became silent. Sri Ramakrishna said, "Your activities are inspired by sattva. Though they are rajasik, they are influenced by sattva. Compassion springs from sattva. Though work for the good of others belongs to rajas, yet this rajas has sattva for its basis and is not harmful. Suka and other sages cherished compassion in their minds to give people religious instruction, to teach them about God. You are distributing food and learning. That is good too. If these activities are done in a selfless spirit they lead to God. But most people work for fame or to acquire merit (punya). Their activities are not selfless. Besides, you are already a siddha (one perfected by religious practice or who is mellowed by devotion just as rice becomes soft after boiling.)

Vidyasagar: How is that, Sir?

Master (laughing): When potatoes and other vegetables are well cooked, they become soft and tender. And you possess such a tender nature! You are so compassionate! (Laughter)

Vidyasagar (laughing): But when the paste of Kalai pulse is boiled, it becomes all the harder.

Master: But you don't belong to this class. Mere pandits are like a diseased fruit that becomes hard and will not ripen at all. Such a fruit has neither the freshness of a green fruit nor the flavour of a ripe one ... Compassion, love of God, and renunciation are the glories of true knowledge.

Vidyasagar listened to these words in silence.[7]

Both in humour and wit these two masters of conversation gave ample evidence of their wealth of language. Through the pen of Sri M., the world has found this wealth forever recorded. In fact, Sri Ramakrishna's literary genius has found its widest expression in Sri M.'s records. But there was no such Boswell for Vidyasagar.

We can give another example of Sri M.'s capacity of capturing dramatic moments from Sri Ramakrishna's life. This is one of the earliest meetings of Narendranath (at that time a young man of nineteen) and Sri Ramakrishna. Time: 5 March, 1882. It was the day of Sri M.'s third visit. Place: small north verandah of Ramakrishna's room at Dakshineshwar.

"Sri Ramakrishna was standing still, surrounded by a few devotees, and Narendra was singing. M. had never heard anyone except the Master sing so sweetly. When he looked at Sri Ramakrishna he was struck with wonder for the Master stood motionless, with eyes transfixed. He seemed not even to breathe. A devotee told M. that the Master was in samadhi. M. had never before seen or heard of such a thing. Silent with wonder, he thought: "Is it possible for a man to be so oblivious of the outer world in the consciousness of God? How deep his faith and devotion must be to bring about such a state!

Narendra was singing –

> Meditate, O my mind, on the Lord Hari ...
> Ever more beauteous in fresh blossoming love
> That shames the splendour of a million moons,
> Like lightning gleams the glory of His form,
> Raising erect the hair for very joy.'

The Master shuddered when this last line was sung. His hair stood on end, and tears of joy streamed down his cheeks. Now and then his lips parted in a smile. Was he seeing the peerless beauty of God, "that shames the splendour of a million moons"? Was this the vision of God, true Essence of Spirit? How much austerity and discipline, how much faith and devotion, must be necessary for such a vision!

The song went on –

> Worship His feet in the lotus of your heart;
> With mind serene and eyes made radiant
> With heavenly love, behold that matchless sight.

Again that bewitching smile. The body motionless as before, the eyes half shut, as if beholding a strange inner vision."[8]

Thus by a few strokes, Sri M. brought out the inner sublimity of Sri Ramakrishna. The picture is so vivid, almost photographic The readers of this book will find so many instances of this kind and realize that the disciple M. had a rare gift of creating the atmosphere from his prodigious memory. In the above mentioned first quotation we saw Sri Ramakrishna in conversation, in the second quotation we find him all in trance and Sri M. recording the various finer shades of feelings on his face. With minimum words Sri M. brought out maximum expression. Here is one of his best pen-pictures.

The Kathamrita is a great drama in which Sri M.'s conversations are more in soliloquy. On the one side he described the occasion of Sri Ramakrishna's sayings, with minutest details, on the other he has recorded his own reactions to those occasions. In world literature there are other biographies where talks of the central figures are recorded, but rarely do we find such accuracy of atmospheric details. With such atmospheric details the words or moods of Sri Ramakrishna had a total dimension which is essential for a real biography.

We are quoting here one such example in English translation from the original Kathamrita (second part) – "Brother, let us visit Sri Ramakrishna in the Dakshineshwar temple. How he is playing with his disciples, how deeply he is in divine ecstasy! Sometimes in trance, sometimes merged in the joy of singing kirtana, again sometimes conversing with the devotees just like an ordinary man. There is nothing but God's name in his holy mouth; he is always drawn into his inner self; his behaviour is like a child of five. With every breath he is uttering the name of the Divine Mother. A child of five has no ego, always full of joy, simple and large-hearted.

Sri Ramakrishna says only this – 'God alone is permanent, all else is temporary. Let us visit that God-intoxicated young boy! A great yogi! Moving alone beside the endless Sea of Satchidananda!..."[9]

To a modern reader of Bengali literature the language of Sri Ramakrishna is as fresh as ever. Even today his conversations as recorded in the Kathamrita put us in an immediate rapport with him. Sri M.'s language in the Kathamrita has a touch of embellishment, which reminds the reader, more or less of the 19th century prose-style. Still Sri M.'s expression is absorbing, lucid, and picturesque, with a melody of its own. Throughout the Kathamrita, in Sri M.'s observation and presentation of Sri Ramakrishna's personality and sayings there is something like a mood of constant worship. We can feel the man, with his deep meditation, devotion and submission to God. To Sri M. nothing is more important than Sri Ramakrishna. So his personality and his pen both are steeped in that great ocean of spirituality, and thus the Kathamrita came out in five volumes.

The Kathamrita no doubt is a hagiography, instead of a modern biography in scientific sense. But how can one distinguish between biography and hagiography when one wants to write on a divine personality? One who seeks and realizes God, lives in a world of his own where visions are more true than ordinary seeing. But these visions became the foundation of Truth, Love and Sacrifice on the lines of Buddha, Christ or Ramakrishna. While reading the Kathamrita the reader feels that supreme sense of direct spiritual realization, for which both the Master and the disciple can deserve almost equal credit.

Sri M. was a poet who wrote poems in prose in the Kathamrita. Throughout the Kathamrita we find him as a lover of nature, preferring the quiet of Dakshineshwar more than the din and bustle of city life. His short descriptions of nature's beauty have enriched the Kathamrita time and again and these descriptions became a grand background for the words of the highest realisation uttered by his Master.

We are presenting before our readers one such example, where Sri M.'s love of nature's beauty became a wonderful background for the meditation of his dearest Master Sri Ramakrishna –

"It was night. The moon rose, flooding all the quarters with its silvery light. M. was walking alone in the garden of the temple. On one side of the path stood the Panchavati, the bakul-grove, the nahabat, and the Master's room; and on the other side flowed the Ganges, reflecting millions of broken moons on its rippling surface.

M. said to himself: Can one really see God? The Master says it is possible. He says that if one makes a little effort, then someone comes forward and shows the way. Well, I am married. I have children. Can one realize God in spite of all that?

M. reflected awhile and continued his soliloquy. Surely one can. Otherwise why should the Master say so?"[10]

This intermingling of nature's beauty and Sri M.'s soliloquy has enriched the Kathamrita time and again. But although a bhakta (devotee), Sri M. showed a fine balance between bhakti and jnana. Whenever he tried, in a few words, to explain the impact of Sri Ramakrishna's sayings, we find him a genuine teacher, always ready to help his followers with sympathetic understanding. But such occasions are rare. Sri M.'s greatest style is in effacing himself as much as possible, and focusing all attention on Sri Ramakrishna. Still he is always present with his Master, like the refrain of a song announcing the advent of God.

Little did the world know that a silent revolution was going on in and around the Dakshineshwar Temple – a revolution both in the field of religion and in the field of literature. Since Sri Ramakrishna's time, Bengali language has become the medium of the highest realisation, the language of the common man, and the ideal form of expression in literature. Vivekananda became the forerunner of modern Bengali prose, Girish Chandra gave a new impetus to Bengali drama, Saradananda wrote one of the best biographies of Ramakrishna;[11] in modern times Achintya Kumar Sengupta wrote two very popular books on Ramakrishna.[12] Swami Nityatmananda continued with the tradition of Sri M.'s Kathamrita with his sixteen-volume 'Sri Ma Darshan' which is based on his association with Sri M.

With Sri Ramakrishna's growing influence on Bengali literature, Sri M.'s impact is also being felt day by day. He is the modern Garuda, carrying the message of Sri Ramakrishna for all those who are weary and thirsty at present or in future.

REFERENCES

1. 'Sri Ma Darshan' by Swami Nityatmananda, in 16 volumes, is the most exhaustive record in this respect.
2. The Indian Mirror, 28 March 1875: This paper was run by the renowned preacher Keshab Chandra Sen of Brahmo Samaj (Nava Vidhan Group). Incidentally Keshab Sen may be reckoned as the first preacher to write about Sri Ramakrishna in newspapers. (Quoted from 'Samasamayik Dristite Sri Ramakrishna': Bengali: Edited by Brajendranath Bandyopadhyay and Sajani Kanta Das, Publisher: General Printers).

3. Kathamrita: Part V. Bengali edition.
4. Kathamrita. Part V: Bengali edition.
5. The Gospel of Sri Ramakrishna published by Ramakrishna Math, Madras.
6. Ibid.
7. Adapted from the translation of Swami Nikhilananda in the Gospel of Sri Ramakrishna; p. 27; Fifth Madras R.K. Math edition. [Vide the original Bengali version of Kathamrita; Part III.]
8. The Gospel of Sri Ramakrishna: Sri Ramakrishna Math, Madras: 5th ed.: pp. 13-14.
9. Adapted from the Kathamrita:. Part II. Place: Dakshineshwar. Date: 8 April 1883. This portion has been omitted in the English Gospel.
10. Vide Kathamrita (Part II): dt. 14-12-1883. Place: Dakshineshwar. Gospel of Sri Ramakrishna: p. 278.
11. ' Sri Sri Ramakrishna Lilaprasanga' (in 5 volumes).
12. 'Parampurusha Sri Ramakrishna' and 'Kavi Sri Ramakrishna'

8

The Gospel of Sri Ramakrishna and Ecology – A study

Swami Kamalasthananda

Nowadays the term 'ecology' is an important topic for the present day world. Newer invention of man makes more concern about environment and environmental issue in present day compare to the past with a knowledge of its different components and their relation with surrounding animate and inanimate world. Here comes the use of ecology. Haeckel first time in 1969 used this term and defined ecology as *the total relations of animal to both its organic and inorganic environment*[1] . Modern time the term ecology defines not only the relation between the organism and environment, but assigns it to the ecosystem in a proper position so that it is an integrated component in the whole ecosystem structure. According to the modern ecologist Smith (1977) the ecology is – *a multidisciplinary science which deals with organism and its place to live and focuses on the ecosystem* [2].

Throughout the human civilization all section of people believes the nature as an important entity and its relation with the human beings. The two main issues are being addressed again and again in all groups of people – a) the effect of environment on the man, b) the effect of man on environment. These two never-meeting parallel debates give the concept environmentalism in course of time. So before dealing the present sate of affairs, we have to go back the ancient culture of all groups of people. Aristotle and other Greek philosophers believed that the nature is ordered, balanced, harmonious and the divine purpose of nature is for human benefit. Hinduism gives ample stress on environmental issue. The old scriptures repeatedly lay emphasis on the importance of environment. In its rituals and daily practices for human beings environment and its both animate and inanimate entities are treated as venerable object of meditation and prayer. The Hindu philosophers no only attach importance to environment but attach divinity to it. In the prayer of Durga, Hindu says ....*So long as the earth has mountains, forests and trees, human race will survive (Chandi).* The sustainable development which is a hot issue in modern world and the issue is so appealing in the Vedic prayer to earth ....*The core of the concept of sustainable development, now being advocated at international flora, is contained in the vedic payers to the earth. It says : What of thee I dig out, let that quickly grow over, / Let me not hit thy vitals, or thy heart. (Atharva veda)*[3] In the Islamic tradition the earth and environment are treated as most sacred thing. Islamic religion again and again gives stress upon the preservation of earth and ecosystem. The Prophet Mohammed said – *Whoever plants a tree and diligently looks after it until it matures and bears fruits is rewarded.* Buddha through His teaching preaches ecological integration to all mankind to develop a civilization in holistic line. According to the Sikh scripture Guru Grantha Sahib the human being like all is composed five elements which are the vital matter of physical, mental and spiritual body of human being. .....***Earth*** *teaches us patience, love; /* ***Air*** *teaches us mobility and liberty; /* ***Fire*** *teaches us warmth and courage; /* ***Sky*** *teaches us equality and broad mindedness; / Water teaches us purity and cleanliness* (Guru Grantha Sahib). Ecology deals in one side the balance between individual freedom and social freedom for formation a well-trained society in vanguard of civilization. *Ecological ethics limit social as well as individual freedom of action in the struggle for existence* [4]. But on other side human beings are interconnected to plants, animals, soils, atmosphere and generally whole environment. We deny this law and dictum. ....*Concepts that refer to the "unity of life" and our "rootedness in nature" may invoke a historical premise, namely, that all life-forms are descended from a common source, or at least that human beings are related to other life-forms through the long historical processes of evolution. Ironically, however, the results of genomic research suggest that humans are related to the rest of life—or rooted in nature—in unexpected ways*[5] .

Environmentalism is an interdisciplinary subject which deals the activities of human beings with the environment fruitfully eliminating its probable hazards. The concept of environmentalism grows in different countries in different circumstances. The root behind all movements is to protect the environment from ever growing pollution and calamities........... *In Victorian Britain, an early "Back-to-Nature" movement that anticipated modern environmentalism was advocated by intellectuals such as John Ruskin, William Morris and Edward Carpenter, who were all against consumerism, pollution and other activities that were harmful to the natural world. Their ideas also inspired various proto-environmental groups in the UK, such as the Commons Preservation Society, the*

Kyrle Society, the Royal Society for the Protection of Birds and the Garden city movement, as well as encouraging the Socialist League and The Clarion movement to advocate measures of nature conservation.

In the United States, the beginnings of an environmental movement can be traced as far back as 1739, though it was not called environmentalism and was still considered conservation until the 1950s. Benjamin Franklin and other Philadelphia residents, citing "public rights," petitioned the Pennsylvania Assembly to stop waste dumping and remove tanneries from Philadelphia's commercial district. The US movement expanded in the 1800s, out of concerns for protecting the natural resources of the West, with individuals such as John Muir and Henry David Thoreau making key philosophical contributions. Thoreau was interested in peoples' relationship with nature and studied this by living close to nature in a simple life. He published his experiences in the book Walden, which argues that people should become intimately close with nature. Muir came to believe in nature's inherent right, especially after spending time hiking in Yosemite Valley and studying both the ecology and geology. He successfully lobbied congress to form Yosemite National Park and went on to set up the Sierra Club. The conservationist principles as well as the belief in an inherent right of nature were to become the bedrock of modern environmentalism.

In the 20th century, environmental ideas continued to grow in popularity and recognition. Efforts were starting to be made to save some wildlife, particularly the American Bison. The death of the last Passenger Pigeon as well as the endangerment of the American Bison helped to focus the minds of conservationists and popularize their concerns. In 1916 the National Park Service was founded by US President Woodrow Wilson [6]. Later Chipko Movement in India and the observation of Earth Day in USA give new dimension in the environment issue. Nowadays this issue is entering the schools and colleges to think the students properly from their very teen age. All students are sincerely thinking the future of earth and ecosystem. ....*The division between anthropocentric and biocentric approaches played a central role in the development of environmental thought in the late 20th century. Whereas some earlier schools, such as apocalyptic (survivalist) environmentalism and emancipatory environmentalism—as well as its offshoot, human-welfare ecology—were animated primarily by a concern for human well-being, later movements, including social ecology, deep ecology, the animal-rights and animal-liberation movements, and ecofeminism, were centrally concerned with the moral worth of nonhuman nature* [7].

We carefully observe that environmentalism is guided following laws or principles. Solving these are important task for any environmentalist. These laws are the basis of all debates and their solution leads to permanent basis for future progress and development. These laws are —-

1. Man can change environment and modify it according to the need.
2. Man has moral and ethical duty to protect and preserve the environment.
3. Environment or nature is beautiful, magnificent, powerful and not properly known.
4. A life supported integrated system is required for survival of human being.

The Gospel of Sri Ramakrishna is the drops of divine nectar oozing out from the mouth of Sri Ramakrishna in form of an unadulterated preservation and presentation to humanity. Sri Ramakrishna is the divine son of earth with full expression of human qualities blended with all sorts of ethical and moral expression perfectly matching with day to day affairs without hindering the progress of every individual supporting the full expression of individual self and all other centering Him everyday. His sayings are ample source for incidents and affairs which are so natural and nature oriented that all groups of people from Illiterate person to University graduate are awe-stricken to feel His expression. Our effort is to locate these expressions in a systematic manner in support to different principles which are classified above. As we have discussed man and nature are interconnected, it gives us clue to think the reason behind the all captivated words of Sri Ramakrishna helping all in their individual paths and simultaneously solving the problems of everybody.

Man Can Change Environment and Modify it according to the Need

................At Kamarpukur I have seen the farmers cutting channels to irrigate their fields. Sometimes the water rushes in with such force that the ridges around the fields are washed away and the crops destroyed. For this reason the farmers make holes here and there in the ridges. Since the water escapes through the holes, the ridges are not destroyed by the rush of the water. Furthermore, the escaping water deposits soft clay in the fields, which increases their fertility and gives a richer crop. He who gives away in charity achieves great results. He achieves the four fruits: dharma, artha, kama, and moksha[8]. Here through this story Sri Ramakrishna depicts that man can change the environment and to modify it according to their need. Here the need should be justified. Otherwise, it will

lead to selfish demand from the environment to fulfill it. The modification will be always helpful in all respect to give ultimate wellbeing to nature.

..........*There is another class of devotees, known as Kripasiddha, that is to say, those on whom the grace of God descends all of a sudden and who at once attain His vision and Knowledge. Such people may be likened to a room that has been dark a thousand years, which, when a lamp is brought into it, becomes light immediately, not little by little* [9]. The dark room remains dark for thousand years. So only way is to bring a lamp in this room the darkness will dispel immediately. We change the surrounding nature for shake of more fruitful purpose.

First rub your hands with oil and then break open the jack-fruit; otherwise they will be smeared with its sticky milk. First secure the oil of divine love, and then set your hands to the duties of the world[10]. It helps us to change the external environment in such a way that we can properly encounter with the external without affecting its basis. Smearing oil in hand helps us to remove the sticky substance present in the jack-fruit. Sticky milk is the hindrance for getting the fleshy fruit of jack-fruit. The effective technique by which we get the fruit is the modification of the environment i.e. applying oil in the hands.

..............................*Speaking of householders entangled in worldliness, the Master said: "They are like the silk-worm. They can come out of the cocoon of their worldly life if they wish. But they can't bear to; for they themselves have built the cocoon with great love and care. So they die there. Or they are like the fish in a trap. They can come out of it by the way they entered, but they sport inside the trap with other fish and hear the sweet sound of the murmuring water and forget everything else. They don't even make an effort to free themselves from the trap*[11]. Man for silk purpose kills the silk-worm inside the cocoon before coming out of it. It is essential for man's civilization and progress. So the case of trap the fish enter into it for getting bait, but they are caught inside the trap. So man can modify the nature for better living standard of ownself.

Man has Moral and Ethical Duty to Protect and Preserve the Environment

.......................*You don't have to be afraid of walking on thorns if you are wearing shoes. You needn't be afraid of 'woman and gold' if you know that God alone is real and all else illusory* [12]. The world is full of all types of creature. Best way to preserve the environment is protecting one from external thorn. So we need not remove all thorn. But using shoe can solve the purpose.

......*One may enter the world after attaining discrimination and dispassion. In the ocean of the world there are six alligators: lust, anger, and so forth. But you need not fear the alligators if you smear your body with turmeric before you go into the water. Discrimination and dispassion are the turmeric. Discrimination is the knowledge of what is real and what is unreal. It is the realization that God alone is the real and eternal Substance and that all else is unreal, transitory, impermanent*[13]. Ocean has all types of dreadful animals like alligators. But we could not exterminate all for shake of our life. We protect us in such a way that all will live together without disturbing one's existence in this environmental setup.

...............*Second, a dog. When it chases you or barks at you, you must stand still, talk to it gently, and pacify it. Third, a bull. If it runs after you with lowered horns, you must calm it with a gentle voice*[14]. Everyday life we all witness these types of incidents. All animals like dog, bull etc. will behave what are natural to the animals. But this world is a dwelling place for all living beings. We can not claim that it is a place for only human beings. Nowadays problems are coming from this idea that we always think only for protection and preservation of our species. But human being is a part of whole ecosystem where all varieties of flora and fauna are present. Sri Ramakrishna in His unique story-telling mood depicts the phase of style of living with all types of being without disturbing the normal eco-balance.

DOCTOR: "It has also been noticed that a vulture runs away for fear of a crow. In my opinion one should serve all creatures, not men alone. Often I feed the sparrows with flour. I throw small pellets of flour to them and they come in swarms. They love to eat them."

MASTER: Bravo! That's grand. Holy men should feed other creatures. They feed ants with sugar[15]." If we want to live in this earth peacefully, it is our moral duty to look after all beings, whatever possible, with supplying all kinds of living-staff necessary for growth and sustainable existence. In conversation with Doctor Sarkar Sri Ramakrishna appraise the manner and habit of Doctor Sarkar emphatically. Giving food to other living beings like small insects - ants is a holy work. This activity can also widen the heart and helps the human being to feel identity with the all present in the environment which is always pervading in and through the living body of human for growth and maintenance.

Once I heard a story. A man heard the command of God that he should see his Ideal Deity in a ram. He at once believed it. It is God who exists in all beings.

A guru said to his disciple, 'It is Râma alone who resides in all bodies.' The disciple was a man of great faith. One day a dog snatched a piece of bread from him and started to run away. He ran after the dog, with a jar of butter in his hand, and cried again and again: 'O Râma, stand still a minute. That bread hasn't been buttered.'

.... *Sometimes I too feel that way. The Mother reveals to me that She Herself has become everything. One day I was coming from the pine-grove toward the Panchavati. A dog followed me. I stood still for a while near the Panchavati. The thought came to my mind that the Mother might say something to me through that dog* [16]. Sri Ramakrishna is a God-intoxicated man. In his small life time he has realized the supreme reality and became identified with this reality. But his path of spiritual attainment is not an isolated journey in a smoggy stalk with the imaginary plan of execution, it is every time based with or related in the surrounding environment. So his words are so appealing to everybody who has come in contact anyhow to his magic spell of expression. So in his story ram and dog are also the means for God-realization of a devotee who is a seeker after truth. He has given importance the animals like dog, ram etc. In this world of self-interest the message of Sri Ramakrishna can help us to consider the interest of other being present in the eco-system.

.................*Living in the world and entangled in many of its duties, the aspirant, during the first stage of spiritual life, finds many obstacles in the path of concentration. While the trees on the foot-path are young, they must be fenced around; otherwise they will be destroyed by cattle. The fence is necessary when the tree is young, but it can be taken away when the trunk is thick and strong. Then the tree won't be hurt even if an elephant is tied to it* [17]. His another story - the growth of a plant in the footpath gives us the duty and obligation towards trees and creepers. His all stories are based on present day incidents and happenings but are meant for giving lesson to spiritual seekers. This story is also gives us another lesson towards the plant system present in the environment. In progress of human civilization the roads are expanded and simultaneously the footpath for use of human beings are increased. Not only man all animal systems are solely depend upon the existence of plant system. But with increased urbanization and road the great onslaught are being enforced upon the plant system. In this situation plantation in footpath is the one way to increase the plant population to a great extent for our survival and growth. Sri Ramakrishna has shown us the way how we can plant a seedling in a busy footpath like common place. The hedging is the way we can protect the little scavenger of earth from all sorts of odd. Let the massage of Sri Ramakrishna be the heading and hoarding of the all environmentalist in the world who are actively participated in the Green movement of protecting the Mother Earth and making it a happy abode for all.

Environment or Nature is Beautiful, Magnificent, Powerful and Not Properly Known

........But dogmatism is not good. You have no doubt heard the story of the chameleon. A man entered a wood and saw a chameleon on a tree. He reported to his friends, 'I have seen a red lizard.' He was firmly convinced that it was nothing but red. Another person, after visiting the tree, said, 'I have seen a green lizard.' He was firmly convinced that it was nothing but green. But the man who lived under the tree said: 'What both of you have said is true. But the fact is that the creature is sometimes red, sometimes green, sometimes yellow, and sometimes has no colour at all[18].' Environment is beautiful, magnificent, powerful and unknown to all. Its every erasure is unique and strange. So this nature is beautiful. In the story of chameleon Sri Ramakrishna is depicting the very nature of the animal i.e. it can change its body pigment according to the need. We are fascinated always by the one-side of nature and fighting each other to establish that we have understood the nature fully. But one who is always aware the all pervading environment can accept the idea of each regarding the environment.

.... *After the destruction of the universe, at the end of a great cycle, the Divine Mother garners the seeds for the next creation. She is like the elderly mistress of the house, who has a hotchpotch-pot in which she keeps different articles for household use. (All laugh.)*

Oh, yes! Housewives have pots like that, where they keep 'sea-foam', blue pills, small bundles of seeds of cucumber, pumpkin, and gourd, and so on. They take them out when they want them. In the same way, after the destruction of the universe, my Divine Mother, the Embodiment of Brahman, gathers together the seeds for the next creation. After the creation the Primal Power dwells in the universe itself. She brings forth this phenomenal world and then pervades it. In the Vedas creation is likened to the spider and its web. The spider brings the web out of itself and then remains in it. God is the container of the universe and also what is contained in It[19] . We do not know the creation fabric of the environment and also its dissolution. Sri Ramakrishna has explained His unique language. The seeds of all beings are manifested in time of creation and again these are gathered by supreme power for its next expression. The little spider creates the web and remains present in the web. Similarly the Supreme power of Universe creates this magnificent ecosystem with all varied entities.

In this creation of God there is a variety of things: men, animals, trees, plants. Among the animals some are good, some bad. There are ferocious animals like the tiger. Some trees bear fruit sweet as nectar, and others bear fruit that is poisonous.

Likewise, among human beings, there are the good and the wicked, the holy and the unholy. There are some who are devoted to God, and others who are attached to the world[20] . Sri Ramakrishna has described the whole environment with all its multifarious manifestation. It is full of many varies of species with different tendencies matched oppositely. In few words He describes the magnificent expression of the environment as a creation of Supreme Lord. This type of interconnectedness is not new in ecology. It is nowadays called DEEP ECOLOGY. The definition of Deep Ecology is given by *Arne Naess, who coined the phrase 'deep ecology' in 1972——Life is fundamentally one. ... The deep ecology movement is the ecology movement which questions deeper. ..The adjective 'deep' stresses that we ask why and how, where others do not.* Michael Zimmerman again clarified the Deep Ecology in his unique words of expression ——*Deep ecologists claim that before knowing what we ought to do, we must understand who we really are.* So this movement of the concept – 'larger self' emerges to protect this beautiful universe and its varied manifestation from all sorts of competitive attitude among human beings and between other beings. ....*What is wrong with our culture is that it offers us an inaccurate conception of the self. It depicts the personal self as existing in competition with and in opposition to nature. [We fail to realise that] if we destroy our environment, we are destroying what is in fact our larger self—Freya Matthew.* This unity of reality and its foundation lie with the ancient philosophers. For thousands of years, philosophers have gazed at the stars and known that One thing must exist that is common to and connects the Many things within the Universe. As Gottfried Wilhelm Leibniz profoundly says; ....*Reality cannot be found except in One single source, because of the interconnection of all things with one another. (Leibniz, 1670)*

.................*But he who has attained God knows that it is God who has become all this. Then he sees that God, maya, living beings, and the universe form one whole. God includes the universe and its living beings. Suppose you have separated the shell, flesh, and seeds of a bel-fruit and someone asks you the weight of the fruit. Will you leave aside the shell and the seeds, and weigh only the flesh? Not at all. To know the real weight of the fruit, you must weigh the whole of it-the shell, the flesh, and the seeds. Only then can you tell its real weight. The shell may be likened to the universe, and the seeds to living beings. While one is engaged in discrimination one says to oneself that the universe and the living beings are non-Self and unsubstantial. At that time one thinks of the flesh alone as the substance, and the shell and seeds as unsubstantial. But after discrimination is over, one feels that all three parts of the fruit together form a unity. Then one further realizes that the stuff that has produced the flesh of the fruit has also produced the shell and seeds. To know the real nature of the bel-fruit one must know all three*[21]. The Universe in form of environment, its living beings and the creator are described by Sri Ramakrishna as shell, seeds and flesh of the bel-fruits. But bel-fruit is an aggregate of all these three components. So the environment, the created all beings and the creator are one. We can not differentiate one from another. This oneness is the message from Sri Ramakrishna to all human beings for their proper understanding of environment.

A Life Supported Integrated System is Required for Survival of Human Being

The grain-dealer stores rice in huge bags in his warehouse. Near them he puts some puffed rice in a tray. This is to keep the rats away. The puffed rice tastes sweet to the rats and they nibble at it all night; they do not seek the rice itself. But just think! One seer of rice yields fourteen seers of puffed rice[22]. We always think that whole universe is trying to crash us and we are to protect us somehow from their engulfing paw. So we want to exterminate all ecosystem elements from the path of struggle. Sri Ramakrishna has described a model system where a grain-dealer saves his grain from the rat. He puts some puffed rice in a tray so that rat can easily attracted to the sweet tasted puffed rice and leaving untouched the grain bags. This is also very economical and eco-friendly. The large quantity of puffed rice is produced from a small amount of rice. So it is a simple model depicted by Sri Ramakrishna helps us to think an integrated environmental system for all.

Let me tell you a story. In a forest there lived a holy man who had many disciples. One day he taught them to see God in all beings and, knowing this, to bow low before them all. A disciple went to the forest to gather wood for the sacrificial fire. Suddenly he heard an outcry: 'Get out of the way! A mad elephant is coming!' All but the disciple of the holy man took to their heels. He reasoned that the elephant was also God in another form. Then why should he run away from it? He stood still, bowed before the animal, and began to sing its praises. The mahut of the elephant was shouting: 'Run away! Run away!' But the disciple didn't move. The animal seized him with its trunk, cast him to one side, and went on its way. Hurt and bruised, the disciple lay unconscious on the ground. Hearing what had happened, his teacher and his brother disciples came to him and carried him to the hermitage. With the help of some medicine he soon regained consciousness. Someone asked him, 'You knew the elephant was coming - why didn't you leave the place?' 'But', he said, 'our teacher has told us that God Himself has taken all these forms, of animals as well as men. Therefore, thinking it was only the elephant God that was coming, I didn't run away.' At this the teacher said: 'Yes, my child, it is true that the elephant God was coming; but the mahut God forbade you to stay there. Since all are manifestations of God, why didn't you trust the mahut's words? You should have heeded the words of the mahut God.' (Laughter)

"It is said in the scriptures that water is a form of God. But some water is fit to be used for worship, some water for washing the face, and some only for washing plates or dirty linen. This last sort cannot be used for drinking or for a holy purpose. In like manner, God undoubtedly dwells in the hearts of all - holy and unholy, righteous and unrighteous; but a man should not have dealings with the unholy, the wicked, the impure. He must not be intimate with them. With some of them he may exchange words, but with others he shouldn't go even that far. He should keep aloof from such people[23]*."* Previously we have sheen that oneness is the goal of all human beings in this ecosystem for betterment not only the cause of themselves but for the cause of all. Through this story Sri Ramakrishna has shown us a practical dealing with different beings in this ecosystem. Elephant always behaves according its nature. So in practical purpose we should be cautious regarding the nature of the all entities and behave accordingly. Good-bad like dual appearance what we put accordingly, is the main criteria of all beings in this ecosystem. We have to response one way to the good and acts differently to bad accepting their natural consequences.

A DEVOTEE: "*Sir, if a wicked man is about to do harm, or actually does so, should we keep quiet then?*"

MASTER: *"A man living in society should make a show of tamas to protect himself from evil-minded people. But he should not harm anybody in anticipation of harm likely to be done him.*

Parable of the snake :

Listen to a story. Some cowherd boys used to tend their cows in a meadow where a terrible poisonous snake lived. Everyone was on the alert for fear of it. One day a brahmachari was going along the meadow. The boys ran to him and said: 'Revered sir, please don't go that way. A venomous snake lives over there.' 'What of it, my good children?' said the brahmachari. 'I am not afraid of the snake. I know some mantras.' So saying, he continued on his way along the meadow. But the cowherd boys, being afraid, did not accompany him. In the mean time the snake moved swiftly toward him with upraised hood. As soon as it came near, he recited a mantra, and the snake lay at his feet like an earthworm. The brahmachari said: 'Look here. Why do you go about doing harm? Come, I will give you a holy word.

By repeating it you will learn to love God. Ultimately you will realize Him and so get rid of your violent nature.' Saying this, he taught the snake a holy word and initiated him into spiritual life. The snake bowed before the teacher and said, 'Revered sir, how shall I practise spiritual discipline?' 'Repeat that sacred word', said the teacher, 'and do no harm to anybody'. As he was about to depart, the brahmachari said, 'I shall see you again.'

Some days passed and the cowherd boys noticed that the snake would not bite. They threw stones at it. Still it showed no anger; it behaved as if it were an earthworm. One day one of the boys came close to it, caught it by the tail, and, whirling it round and round, dashed it again and again on the ground and threw it away. The snake vomited blood and became unconscious. It was stunned. It could not move. So, thinking it dead, the boys went their way.

Late at night the snake regained consciousness. Slowly and with great difficulty it dragged itself into its hole; its bones were broken and it could scarcely move. Many days passed. The snake became a mere skeleton covered with a skin. Now and then, at night, it would come out in search of food. For fear of the boys it would not leave its hole during the day-time. Since receiving the sacred word from the teacher, it had given up doing harm to others. It maintained its life on dirt, leaves, or the fruit that dropped from the trees.

About a year later the brahmachari came that way again and asked after the snake. The cowherd boys told him that it was dead. But he couldn't believe them. He knew that the snake would not die before attaining the fruit of the holy word with which it had been initiated. He found his way to the place and, searching here and there, called it by the name he had given it. Hearing the teacher's voice, it came out of its hole and bowed before him with great reverence. 'How are you?' asked the brahmachari. 'I am well, sir', replied the snake. 'But', the teacher asked, 'why are you so thin?' The snake replied: 'Revered sir, you ordered me not to harm any body. So I have been living only on leaves and fruit. Perhaps that has made me thinner.'

The snake had developed the quality of sattva; it could not be angry with anyone. It had totally forgotten that the cowherd boys had almost killed it.

The brahmachari said: 'It can't be mere want of food that has reduced you to this state. There must be some other reason. Think a little.' Then the snake remembered that the boys had dashed it against the ground. It said: 'Yes, revered sir, now I remember. The boys one day dashed me violently against the ground. They are ignorant, after all. They didn't realize what a great change had come over my mind. How could they know I wouldn't bite or harm anyone?' The brahmachari exclaimed: 'What a shame! You are such a fool! You don't know how to protect yourself. I asked you not to bite, but I didn't forbid you to hiss. Why didn't you scare them by hissing?'

So you must hiss at wicked people. You must frighten them lest they should do you harm. But never inject your venom into them. One must not injure others.

In this creation of God there is a variety of things: men, animals, trees, plants. Among the animals some are good, some bad. There are ferocious animals like the tiger. Some trees bear fruit sweet as nectar, and others bear fruit that is poisonous. Likewise, among human beings, there are the good and the wicked, the holy and the unholy. There are some who are devoted to God, and others who are attached to the world[24]. It is essay to behave or interact with the good person or being, but it is very difficult with evil. Sri Ramakrishna , on His answer to a question of a devotee describes a story. The essence of the whole story is the evil company which is ready to harm one every way, is to be scared when necessity arises. The scaring is not harming it but resisting the evil things from its normal activity. This is a practical solution by which we can change the eco-competitive world into the eco-friendly dwelling place for all beings.

Conclusion

Man is part and parcel of the whole universe. So we always think ourselves integrated with nature and its manifested different forms. So the unified attitude of reality must be nurtured for proper balanced state of existence in this Earth. Albert Einstein also had a good understanding of humans as an inseparable part of the One, as he writes—

> *A human being is part of the whole called by us universe ... We experience ourselves, our thoughts and feelings as something separate from the rest. A kind of optical delusion of consciousness. This delusion is a kind of prison for us, restricting us to our personal desires and to affection for a few persons nearest to us. Our task must be to free ourselves from the prison by widening our circle of compassion to embrace all living creatures and the whole of nature in its beauty. The true value of a human being is determined by the measure and the sense in which they have obtained liberation from the self. We shall require a substantially new manner of thinking if humanity is to survive. (Albert Einstein)*

Sri Ramakrishna in the end of nineteenth century has proclaimed this idea of sameness regarding the idea of universe. The same thing which is called by different group in different name is the manifestation of the Supreme Reality.

So people call in different names- Manifestation of Creator, Universe, Ecology, Environment etc. All indicate one and same thing. In this way Meta-physicist, Philosopher, Ecologist, Environmentalist, etc have expressed their views and ideas according to the terms suited for their subjects but all describe the same and one thing. So the sameness among all ideas gives moral and meaningful motive for sustainable growth and development of human beings which is essential for integration of human-self and proper balance with other beings existed in the Earth. So the words of Sri Ramakrishna are not only echoing the principles of Ecology, Deep Ecology etc. but are announcing the new dimension i.e. *Essential Ecology* of human life. Again we are focusing our mind to the simple and significant uttering of Sri Ramakrishna ———— "*It is like water, called in different languages by different names, such as 'jal', 'pani', and so forth. There are three or four ghats on a lake. The Hindus, who drink water at one place, call it 'jal'. The Mussalmans at another place call it 'pani'. And the English at a third place call it 'water'. All three denote one and the same thing, the difference being in the name only. In the same way, some address the Reality as 'Allah', some as 'God', some as 'Brahman', some as 'Kâli', and others by such names as 'Rama', 'Jesus', 'Durga', 'Hari.*'[25]

REFERENCES

1. Haeckel,E. (1869), Generelle Morphologie der Organismen, Vls I and II, Georg Remer, Berlin.
2. Smith, R. L. (1977), Elements of Ecology and Field biology, Harper and row, New York.
3. Rana, S.V.S.(2010), Essentials of Ecology and Environmental science (4th Ed.), PHI Learning Private Limited, New Delhi, p. 15
4. Nash, R. (1977), " Do rocks have rights?" Center Magazine, 10, pp 2-12.
5. Sagoff, Mark (2005), "Nature and Human Nature" Is Human Nature Obsolete? (Eds. Harold W. Baillie and Timothy K. Casey, The MIT Press, Cambridge)
6. http://en.wikipedia.org/wiki/Environmentalism
7. http://www.britannica.com/EBchecked/topic/189205/environmentalism
8. Gupta, Mahendranath, The Gospel of Sri Ramakrishna(Translated from the Bengali by Swami Nikhilananda), p. 762.
9. Ibid, p. 202
10. Ibid, p. 90
11. Ibid, p. 171
12. Ibid, p. 744
13. Ibid, p. 744
14. Ibid, p. 610

15. Ibid, p. 1001
16. Ibid, p. 324
17. Ibid, p. 152
18. Ibid, p. 628
19. Ibid, pp. 147-148
20. Ibid, p. 92
21. Ibid, p. 360
22. Ibid, p. 426
23. Ibid, pp. 90-91
24. Ibid, pp. 90-91
25. Ibid, p. 147

9

Echoes of 'Ecosophies' in the Gospel of Sri Ramakrishna

Br. Shrutichaitanya

Arne Naess, a Norwegian environmental philosopher, was watching a flea immolate itself in an acid bath under a microscope. Naess deeply empathized with the suffering flea, identified with it, and thereby felt deeply connected with the entire lifeworld.[1] This sort of experiences and ideas created an urge for formulating an ecological philosophy or '*ecosophy*' which would 'recognize the values that inhere objectively in nature independently of human wants, needs or desires.'[2] This came to be known as the *'Deep Ecology'* in the 1970s in contrast to the prevalent '*shallow*' version of ecology based on anthropocentrism which is concerned about conservation and preservation of biodiversity only because of the use-value of non-human nature for human welfare. According to Næss, every being, whether human, animal or vegetable has an equal right to live and to blossom.[3]

Apart from Naess the other major contributors towards analyzing the phenomenon of Deep Ecology are George Sessions and David Rothenberg from America and Warwick Fox from Australia. Diverse streams of ideas and inspirations have commingled into the present form of Deep Ecology. Authors have pointed out the connections between Deep Ecology and ecological science (Golley, 1987), religions from around the world (Barnhill and Gottlieb, 2001), New Age spirituality (La Chapelle , 1978), direct action / ecological sabotage (Foreman, 1991), the poetry of Robinson Jeffers (Sessions 1977), the land ethic of Aldo Leopold (Devall and Sessions, 1985), the monism of Baruch Spinoza (Sessions 1977, 1979, 1985; Naess 2005), and the phenomenology of Martin Heidegger (Zimmerman 1986).[4]

Another feature of the developing models of Deep Ecology is its openness to newer versions. Naess named his own environmental philosophy as 'ecosophy T'.The 'T' stands for Naess's secluded boreal hut, Tvergastein. He gives this just as a template for other personal ecosophies to emerge.

The Foundations of Deep Ecology

The two foundations of Deep Ecology consist of an axiology, the study of the criteria of value systems in ethics and an ontology, the study of existence.

(a) Axiology of 'Biocentric egalitarianism':

It proposes biocentric equality and states that biota have equal intrinsic value as against differential valuation of organisms. In this sense, Deep Ecology is not just non-anthropocentric but is anti-anthropocentric.

(b) Ontology of 'Metaphysical holism':

It emphasizes that biosphere is not just a collection of discrete entities but rather internally related ontologically *unbroken whole.*

Ontological Interconnectedness & 'Deep Ecological Consciousness'

Now one may wonder how this interconnectedness with the entire biosphere can be perceived. The Deep Ecologists prescribe nothing short of a 'self-realization' which breaks down all preconceived ontological boundaries and accommodates the entire life world into the self. Deep Ecologist Fox says "'It is the idea that we can make no firm ontological divide in reality between the human and the nonhuman realms. . . . [T]o the extent that we perceive boundaries, we fall short of deep ecological consciousness" (Fox 1984, p. 196).[5]This sort of enlightenment will convince us that there is only one big Self. Watts, in 1966 has developed a similar idea in his article named 'The World is Your Body'. Fox claims that the human and nonhuman entities are actually "aspects of a single unfolding reality"[6]

Welfare: No More an Individual Affair

Once this interrelatedness is revealed by the awakening of the Deep Ecological Consciousness, individual interests will be meaningless and the interests of the entire biosphere become one. While asserting this point Devall and Sessions say "'if we harm the rest of Nature then we are harming ourselves. There are no boundaries and everything is interrelated" (1985, p. 68). Environmental activist John Seed, notices the change in attitude: "I am protecting the rain forest" develops into "'I am part of the rain forest protecting myself.' I am that part of the rain forest recently emerged into thinking. . . . [T]he change is a spiritual one, thinking like a mountain, sometimes referred to as 'Deep Ecology'" (Devall and Sessions1985, p. 199). Because the rainforest is part of the activist Seed, he is inherently obliged to look after its welfare. The rainforest's well-being and needs are indistinguishable from Seed's.[7]

Emphasis is Not on Ethics but on Experience

What makes Deep Ecology scientific is its emphasis on experience of the biospheric whole and not just upon any dictum or ethics. Naess remarks "'I'm not much interested in ethics or morals. I'm interested in how we experience the world. . . . " (Fox 1995,p. 219). Sessions also emphasizes in the same vein, "The search . . . is not for environmental ethics but for ecological consciousness" (Fox 1995, p. 225).[8]

The Ultimate Derivations: The Eight Point Platform

Proponents of deep ecology believe that the world does not exist as a resource to be freely exploited by humans. The ethics of deep ecology hold that the survival of any part is dependent upon the well-being of the whole. Proponents of deep ecology offer an eight-tier platform to elucidate their claims. Naess and Sessions came up with the eight point program:

1. The well-being and flourishing of human and nonhuman life on Earth have value in themselves (synonyms: intrinsic value, inherent value). These values are independent of the usefulness of the nonhuman world for human purposes.
2. Richness and diversity of life forms contribute to the realization of these values and are also values in themselves.
3. Humans have no right to reduce this richness and diversity except to satisfy vital human needs.
4. The flourishing of human life and cultures is compatible with a substantial decrease of the human population. The flourishing of nonhuman life requires such a decrease.
5. Present human interference with the nonhuman world is excessive, and the situation is rapidly worsening.
6. Policies must therefore be changed. These policies affect basic economic, technological, and ideological structures. The resulting state of affairs will be deeply different from the present.
7. The ideological change is mainly that of appreciating life quality (dwelling in situations of inherent value) rather than adhering to an increasingly higher standard of living. There will be a profound awareness of the difference between big and great.
8. Those who subscribe to the foregoing points have an obligation directly or indirectly to try to implement the necessary changes.

The Apron Diagram

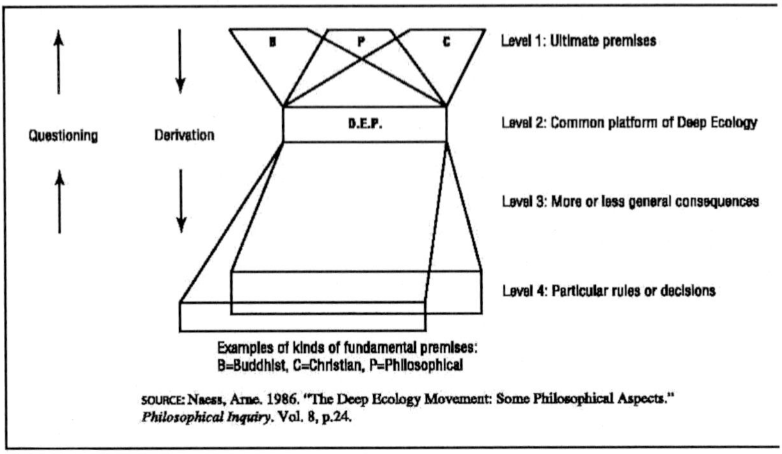

Figure 1*. Arne Naess's Apron Diagram.* CENGAGE LEARNING, GALE

'In the diagram Buddhist, secular philosophical,and Christian first principles (the bust) converge in the eight-point platform (the waist), which then justifies an array of activisms (the skirt [see Figure 1]). Buddhist metaphysics might channel through the waist of deep ecological principles calling for environmental action to Deep Ecology reduce consumption; secular metaphysics might channel through the waist of Deep Ecology calling for action to reduce human population growth; or Christian metaphysics might channel through the waist of Deep Ecology to call for action to preserve biodiversity. Both the eightpoint platform and the apron diagram imply that Deep Ecology is above all an ontology and incidentally an ethic.'[9]

'Ecological Wisdom' hidden in the Religious 'Niches'

The word 'ecosophy' literally means ecological wisdom. With the emergence of fields like Deep Ecology etc it is becoming clear that there is a paradigm shift from utilitarianism to a much more unselfish way of dealing with nature and her resources. Narrow human interests can no longer pass unscathed. The journey from mere 'human' self-centred environmentalism to a biospheric-whole 'self-realization' drew much of it's inspiration from various religions of the world. Taylor and Zimmerman remarks 'It is a common perception within the deep ecology movement that the religions of indigenous cultures, the world's remnant and newly revitalized or invented pagan religions, and religions originating in Asia (especially Taoism, Buddhism, and Hinduism), provide superior grounds for ecological ethics, and greater ecological wisdom, than do Occidental religions. Theologians such as Matthew Fox and Thomas Berry, however, have shown that Western religions such as Christianity may be interpreted in ways largely compatible with the deep ecology movement.'[10]

Overlaps between Deep Ecology and Sri Ramakrishna

It is quite interesting to note that much of the conclusions and experiences which the Deep Ecologists are talking about find similar reverberations in *The Gospel of Sri Ramakrishna* recorded by Mahendranath Gupta (Translated by Swami Nikhilananda into English from the Bengali original). *The Gospel of Sri Ramakrishna* is a first-hand record of Ramakrishna's words by Mahendranath Gupta. Some expressions made by Sri Ramakrishna are very similar to the ideas expressed by the Deep Ecologists like 'biocentric egalitarianism' , 'metaphysical holism', 'self-realization of the one single entity – 'biospheric whole' .However Sri Ramakrishna (1836-1886) precedes all attempts to formularize a 'Deep Ecology' by almost a century.

Why is *The Gospel of Sri Ramakrishna* important for Deep Ecologists?

Deep Ecology takes a gigantic leap from the traditional environmentalism based on experimental facts and observations and enters into the arena of 'experiencing' the wholeness and interconnectedness of the entire biosphere. This reliance on subjective experience as an essential criterion of Deep Ecology makes Sri Ramakrishna relevant. Sri Ramakrishna was always inclined towards direct realization of the subtle truths hidden behind the superficial layer of mere sense perception. Mere belief and dictums would not satisfy him unless he himself 'experienced' it. It may not be a very easy task for the Deep Ecologists to find out people gifted with such experiences of a one single 'self' pervading the human and non-human spheres of existence, which they emphasise. So, Sri Ramakrishna is a 'gift unopened' for the Deep Ecologists. Moreover, *The Gospel of Sri Ramakrishna*'s authenticity, being recorded by one who was present when the words were uttered, makes it a valid support for many of the ideas proposed by today's Deep Ecologists.

One more unique aspect is the naturalness with which this so called deep ecological consciousness seems to be manifest in Sri Ramakrishna without any preemption or preconception. This validates the veracity of the fact.

Though one may cite similar experiences from the lives of other seers, still such detailed, authentic and historic account as is the case with Sri Ramakrishna may be rare indeed.

Parallel Instances of Deep Ecological Consciousness from *The Gospel of Sri Ramakrishna*

Before beginning our discussion on *The Gospel of Sri Ramakrishna* we must remember a few aspects. Sri Ramakrishna's language of expression is mostly couched in devotional flavour .However this must not lead us to infer that his ideas have nothing to do with science or ecology as such. We must keenly observe the core of his expression, wherein lies a wonderful discovery about nature and about reality, much similar to what the Deep Ecologists claim. One need not become a theist to appreciate *The Gospel of Sri Ramakrishna* from a deep ecological point of view. Only what the Deep ecologists are calling as 'the one whole' etc is addressed by Sri Ramakrishna as God or Brahman or Divine Mother. So one should not be disappointed by such theistic expressions and lose the opportunity to read an account of true experience of the much emphasized holism in Deep Ecology.

'Biocentric Egalitarianism': Reflections in The Gospel of Sri Ramakrishna

The Deep Ecologists speak about the 'equal worth of the entire biota' and how human exploitation for anthropocentric uses is to be curbed. In *the Gospel of Sri Ramakrishna* , Saturday, December 27, 1884 entry we find Sri Ramakrishna saying about his natural biocentric egalitarianism born out of his experience of the *Virat,* the all-pervading One Consciousness:

'You see that bel-tree. I used to go there to pluck its leaves. One day, as I plucked a leaf, a bit of the bark came off. I found the tree full of Consciousness. I felt grieved because I had hurt the tree. One day I tried to pluck some Durva grass, but I found I couldn't do it very well....

"I cannot cut a lemon. The other day I managed to cut one only with great difficulty; ... One day I was about to gather some flowers.

They were everywhere on the trees. At once I had a vision of Virat; it appeared that His worship was just over. The flowers looked like a bouquet placed on the head of the Deity. I could not pluck them."[11]

In the biography of Sri Ramakrishna 'Sri Ramakrishna The Great Master' by Swami Saradananda (Translated into English by Swami Jagadananda) we come across few more similar experiences of Sri Ramakrishna established in this oneness with the entire nature. The author writes about Sri Ramakrishna's experiences of identifying himself with both human and non-human elements of the nature:

"At one time a particular spot of the garden of the Kali Temple was covered with newly grown Durva grass and was beautiful to look at. While he was looking at it, the Master transcended the normal consciousness and was feeling identified with that spot when a man just happened to walk across that field at which he became very restless, feeling unbearable pain in his chest. Mentioning that event, he said to us later, "I then felt just that kind of pain which is felt when anybody tramples on one's chest. That state of Bhavasamadhi is very painful. Although I had it for six hours only, it became quite unbearable.

One day the Master while in Bhavasamadhi was looking on the Ganga, standing at the spacious Ghat with the open portico. Two boats were at anchor at the Ghat and the boatmen were quarrelling over some matter. The quarrel became gradually bitter and the stronger man gave a severe slap on the back of the weaker. At that, the Master cried out suddenly with pain. Hriday heard it from the Kali Temple, went there quickly and saw that the Master's back had become red and swollen….." [12]

In the words of Sri Sarada Devi, another incident regarding Sri Ramakrishna's natural biocentric egalitarianism is evident.

Once, in Kamarpukur, the Master came across a big fish, which had come on the road from the nearby overflowing tank. He helped it back into the tank, saying, "Run, run for your life! If Hridu sees you, he will finish you off in no time." Returning home, he told Hriday, "O Hridu! Today I saw a very big fish of yellow hue, that had come on the road. I helped it back into the tank." "O Uncle! What have you done!" cried Hriday, "Alas! A big fish like that would have made a delicious dish!"[13]

Metaphysical Holism: A Vivid Reality in The Gospel of Sri Ramakrishna

The experiential metaphysical holism in Deep Ecology finds numerous evidences in *the Gospel of Sri Ramakrishna*. On various occasions Sri Ramakrishna tells about his experience of one indivisible phenomenon behind the apparently plural earthly manifestations. On Friday, September 7, 1883, Sri Ramakrishna relates one of such instances:

"One day I had the vision of Consciousness, non-dual and indivisible. At first it had been revealed to me that there were innumerable men, animals, and other creatures. Among them there were aristocrats, the English, the Mussalmans, myself, scavengers, dogs, and also a bearded Mussalman with an earthenware tray of rice in his hand……

"Another day I saw rice, vegetables, and other food-stuff, and filth and dirt as well, lying around…. It was revealed to me that all these are one Substance, the

non-dual and indivisible Consciousness.'[14]

On Saturday, July 21, 1883, Sri Ramakrishna cites further more examples in this regard:

"'The universe is conscious on account of the Consciousness of God. Sometimes I find that this Consciousness wriggles about, as it were, even in small fish."

... Sometimes I find that the universe is saturated with the Consciousness of God, as the earth is soaked with water in the rainy season.'[15]

The Divine Mother revealed to me in the Kâli temple that it was She who had become everything. She showed me that everything was full of Consciousness. The image was Consciousness, the altar was Consciousness, the water-vessels were Consciousness, the door-sill was Consciousness, the marble floor was Consciousness - all was Consciousness. I found everything inside the room soaked, as it were, in Bliss - the Bliss of God. I saw a wicked man in front of the Kâli temple; but in him also I saw the power of the Divine Mother vibrating. That was why I fed a cat with the food that was to be offered to the Divine Mother. I clearly perceived that all this was the Divine Mother - even the cat.'[16]

Anti-anthropocentric Features

Sri Ramakrishna tells a story in the Gospel in February, 1882:

"'Listen to a story. Some cowherd boys used to tend their cows in a meadow where a terrible poisonous snake lived. Everyone was on the alert for fear of it. One day a brahmachari was going along the meadow. The boys ran to him and said: 'Revered sir, please don't go that way. A venomous snake lives over there.' 'What of it, my good children?' said the brahmachari. 'I am not afraid of the snake. I know some mantras.' So saying, he continued on his way along the meadow. But the cowherd boys, being afraid, did not accompany him. In the mean time the snake moved swiftly toward him with upraised hood. As soon as it came near, he recited a mantra, and the snake lay at his feet like an earthworm. The brahmachari said: 'Look here. Why do you go about doing harm? Come, I will give you a holy word. By repeating it you will learn to love God. Ultimately you will realize Him and so get rid of your violent nature.' Saying this, he taught the snake a holy word and initiated him into spiritual life. The snake bowed before the teacher and said, 'Revered sir, how shall I practise spiritual discipline?' 'Repeat that sacred word', said the teacher, 'and do no harm to anybody'. As he was about to depart, the brahmachari said,

'I shall see you again.'

"Some days passed and the cowherd boys noticed that the snake would not bite. They threw stones at it. Still it showed no anger; it behaved as if it were an earthworm. One day one of the boys came close to it, caught it by the tail, and, whirling it round and round, dashed it again and again on the ground and threw it away. The snake vomited blood and became unconscious. It was stunned. It could not move. So, thinking it dead, the boys went their way.

"Late at night the snake regained consciousness. Slowly and with great difficulty it dragged itself into its hole; its bones were broken and it could scarcely move. Many days passed. The snake became a mere skeleton covered with a skin. Now and then, at night, it would come out in search of food. For fear of the boys it would not leave its hole during the day-time. Since receiving the sacred word from the teacher, it had given up doing harm to others. It maintained its life on dirt, leaves, or the fruit that dropped from the trees.

"About a year later the brahmachari came that way again and asked after the snake. The cowherd boys told him that it was dead. But he couldn't believe them. He knew that the snake would not die before attaining the fruit of the holy word with which it had been initiated. He found his way to the place and, searching here and there, called it by the name he had given it. Hearing the teacher's voice, it came out of its hole and bowed before him with great reverence. 'How are you?' asked the brahmachari. 'I am well, sir', replied the snake. 'But', the teacher asked, 'why are you so thin?' The snake replied: 'Revered sir, you ordered me not to harm any body. So I have been living only on leaves and fruit. Perhaps that has made me thinner.'

"The snake had developed the quality of sattva; it could not be angry with anyone. It had totally forgotten that the cowherd boys had almost killed it.

"The brahmachari said: 'It can't be mere want of food that has reduced you to this state. There must be some other reason. Think a little.' Then the snake remembered that the boys had dashed it against the ground. It said: 'Yes, revered sir, now I remember. The boys one day dashed me violently against the ground. They are ignorant, after all. They didn't realize what a great change had come over my mind. How could they know I wouldn't bite or harm anyone?' The brahmachari exclaimed: 'What a shame! You are

such a fool! You don't know how to protect yourself. I asked you not to bite, but I didn't forbid you to hiss. Why didn't you scare them by hissing?'

"So you must hiss at wicked people. You must frighten them lest they should do you harm. But never inject your venom into them. One must not injure others."[17]

The parable clearly gives an implication for anti-anthropocentrism. Mere fun and frolick at the cost of non-human creatures is admonished. On the other hand the snake's attitude of non-injury is nearer to what is expected from mankind by the deep ecologists.

On another occasion, July 22, 1883, Sri Ramakrishna makes his stand clear as far as far-fetched selfish anthropocentric motives are concerened:

"'Once Hriday brought a bull-calf here. I saw, one day, that he had tied it with a rope in the garden, so that it might graze there. I asked him, 'Hriday, why do you tie the calf there every day?' 'Uncle,' he said, 'I am going to send this calf to our village. When it grows strong I shall yoke it to the plough.' As soon as I heard these words I was stunned to think: 'How inscrutable is the play of the divine maya! Kamarpukur and Sihore are so far away from Calcutta! This poor calf must go all that way. Then it will grow, and at length it will be yoked to the plough. This is indeed the world! This is indeed maya!' I fell down unconscious. Only after a long time did I regain consciousness."[18]

Habitation Boundaries are Imaginary

Another very unconventional idea which is raised in the Gospel of Sri Ramakrishna is ,no particular portion on the earth can be called one's own. The entire earth is a single home with a single room! A similar Sanskrit saying goes as follows '*Yatra vishwam bhavati eka nidam*'. Sri Ramakrishna says in the Gospel on August 5, 1882:

'God laughs again when two brothers divide their land with a string, saying to each other, 'This side is mine and that side is your'. He laughs and says to Himself, 'The whole universe belongs to Me, but they say they own this portion or that portion."[19]

The Deep Ecological concept of 'equal right to flourish and bloom' irresepective of any reservation for human interference and domination even in terms of habitat runs in the similar vein. The 4th point in the Eight point programme, is 'The flourishing of human life and cultures is compatible with a substantial decrease of the human population. The flourishing of nonhuman life requires such a decrease.' So the Programme goes even to the extent of decreasing the human population for non human nature to flourish freely with equal rights. We know very well how human dominance for more and more expansion over the earthly habitat is decreasing the natural habitats in the wild.

Deep Ecological Consciousness : A Special 'state' to be Attained

In the *Gospel*, Sri Ramakrishna mentions that this state of feeling of being identified with all creatures is a particular state of mind which is not ordinary but needs to be attained.On March 9, 1883 he says:

"I am now in such a state of mind that I cannot watch a sacrifice. Also I cannot eat meat ....

"Again, in a certain state of mind I see God in all beings, even in an ant. At that time, if I see a living being die, I find consolation in the thought that it is the death of the body, the soul being beyond life and death.[20]

The Comparative Analysis between *Maya* and *Daya* in the Gospel : a Parallel Concept of 'Shallow' and 'Deep' Ecology

In December, 1882, Sri Ramakrishna says in the *Gospel*:

"'Remember that daya, compassion, and maya, attachment, are two different things. Attachment means the feeling of 'my-ness' toward one's relatives. It is the love one feels for one's parents, one's brother, one's sister, one's wife and children. Compassion is the love one feels for all beings of the world. It is an attitude of equality. ... Through compassion one serves all beings. ... But one thing should be remembered: maya keeps us in ignorance and entangles us in the world, whereas daya makes our hearts pure and gradually unties our bonds.[21]

The idea of '*maya*' is similar to the anthropocentric environmentalism which focuses on human welfare only. Whereas, the idea of '*daya*' is similar to the theme of Deep ecology which is concerned about the entire biosphere to flourish and not just human beings.

In the *Gospel*, Sri Ramakrishna further illustrates this attempt to look upon non-human creatures as an object of supreme adoration with the same humane intensity with which an ordinary man takes care of himself and his human counterparts.

"Once I heard a story. A man heard the command of God that he should see his Ideal Deity in a ram. He at once believed it. It is God who exists in all beings."[22]

"A guru said to his disciple, 'It is Râma alone who resides in all bodies.' The

disciple was a man of great faith. One day a dog snatched a piece of bread from him and started to run away. He ran after the dog, with a jar of butter in his hand, and cried again and again: 'O Râma, stand still a minute. That bread hasn't been buttered.'"[23]

Mud Walls to Glass Walls: Essential for a Universal Outlook: Deep Ecological Consciousness

By the arousal of the deep ecological consciousness one can surpass the limitations of being inside a room with mud walls where only our selfish interests concern human prosperity alone and start living in a room with glass walls where both the inside and outside are visible where both the human and non-human concerns can be taken into account simultaneously. In the Gospel, Sri Ramakrishna says:

"'But some people live in the world even after attaining jnâna. They see both what is inside and what is outside the room. The light of God illumines the world. Therefore with that light they can discriminate between good and bad, permanent and impermanent. The ignorant, who lead a worldly life without knowing God, are like people living in a house with mud walls.

With the help of a dim light they can see the inside of the house but nothing more. But those who live in the world after having attained Knowledge and realized God, are like people living in a glass house. They see the inside of the room and also all that is outside. The light from the sun of Knowledge enters strongly into the room. They perceive everything inside the room very clearly. They know what is good and what is bad, what is permanent and what is impermanent.'[24]

Criticisms Against the Concept of 'Deep Ecology'

Various sections of the society like those who are adherents of social ecology, socialist ecology, liberalist democracy etc have criticized the concept of deep ecology. Some criticisms put forward by these people are as follows:

1. Given to mysticism and misanthropy
2. Ignorant of socio-economic factors
3. Promotes 'ecofascism' namely the sacrifice of individual humans for the benefit of the ecological whole.
4. The concept of 'ecological self' constitutes a totalizing view that obliterates legitimate distinctions between self and other.
5. It being a totalizing worldview threatens cultural diversity.

What the Deep Ecologists Say in Defence?

'Warwick Fox has replied that impartial and wider identification does not cancel out particular or personal attachments, but instead, puts them in the context of more encompassing concerns that are otherwise ignored, as when for example concern for one's family blinds one to concerns about concerns of the community. Fox adds that deep ecology criticizes the ideology—anthropocentrism—that has always been used to by social agents to legitimate oppression of groups regarded as sub- or non-human. While modern liberation movements have sought to include more and more people into the class of full humans, such movements have typically not criticized anthropocentrism as such. Even a fully egalitarian society, in other words, could continue to use anthropocentrism to justify exploiting the non-human realm.

In response to the claim that deep ecology is, or threatens to be, a totalizing worldview that excludes alternatives and that—ironically—threatens cultural diversity, Arne Naess responds that, to the contrary, deep ecology is constituted by multiple perspectives or "ecosophies" (ecological-philosophies) and is compatible with a wide range of religious perspectives and philosophical orientations.'[25]

How does the Gospel of Sri Ramakrishna Answer the Critics of Deep Ecology?

The ordinary sensory experience of the world gives us an impression of an infinitely fragmented world of living and non-living beings, human and non-human creatures.The experience of one whole consciousness pervading the entire phenomenal world is no doubt a mystical experience. Sri Ramakrishna terms his experience of this one manifested as many as '*Vijnana*'.He says in the Gospel:

'*The man coming down from samâdhi perceives that it is Brahman that has become the ego, the universe, and all living beings. This is known as vijnâna.*'[26]

But this sort of mystical experience may be extremely rare and requires a superlative degree in fineness of perception of a different order. So the critics of deep ecology are not in favour of giving any importance to such an experience in the arena of environmentalism. However we should remember that we start reading science in our schooldays just 'intellectually' and regard what the scientists say are true. One day we start 'understanding' the 'truth' behind the 'hypothesis' as we mature. Similarly by having intellectual conviction in the 'true experiences of the 'spiritual scientists' we may one day verify it for ourselves. Even if we don't reach that lofty a state even then following the trail of such scientists will lead us to a better earth undoubtedly. In the *Gospel of Sri Ramakrishna* we find the prescription of mere intellectual faith as an aid to this sort of a superior vision of the world:

> *"Faith! Faith! Faith! Once a guru said to his pupil, 'Râma alone has become everything.' When a dog began to eat the pupil's bread, he said to it: 'O Râma, wait a little. I shall butter Your bread.' Such was his faith in the words of his guru."*[27]

Therefore having conviction in the deep ecological experiences of few gifted individuals like Sri Ramakrishna one can alter one's way of life and simulate that state of seeing the world as one's own body or as one's Self.

It may not be out of the context to mention such an experience of Mahendranath Gupta the recorder of the *Gospel of Sri Ramakrishna* which must have resulted out of simple and profound faith that everything is associated with the Supreme Indivisible Spirit percolating through nature :

> *"By the grace of the Master, he saw the entire Kamarpukur as a holy place bathed in an effulgent Light. Trees and creepers, beasts and birds and men all were made of effulgence. So he prostrated to all on the road. He saw a torn cat, which appeared to him luminous with the Light of Consciousness. Immediately he fell to the ground and saluted it."*[28]

Has the Gospel Anything more to say? Does it have a Message for the Deep Ecologists?

Till now we have mentioned how *The Gospel of Sri Ramakrishna* supports the views expressed by the Deep Ecologists in many ways. But we must be aware that the *Gospel* has its unique way of proceeding along environmentalism which may coincide with or run parallel to or may even differ with the till date version of Deep Ecology. The points of coincidence have already been discussed. Now let us look at the features of the Gospel which may be exclusively its own and may also help the Deep Ecologists to dive deeper:

1. The experience of 'biocentric egalitarianism' and 'metaphysical holism' may sound very appealing to some and to some bit poetic. But according to Sri Ramakrishna, the genuine realization of this ontological interconnectedness demands intense practice of self-control and self-sacrifice which the deep ecologists have not emphasized. The *Gospel of Sri Ramakrishna* prescribes discrimination regarding one real nature as separate from the body,

mind and intellect and one with pure consciousness. It is only after this disidentification with one's own body-mind complex that one can feel identified with every body-mind complex as one's own. For most of the deep ecologists it must have been just a 'stumbling upon' a deep ecological experience which must have been momentary. For many ecologists it must have been entirely an imagination and an intellectual idea. But for Sri Ramakrishna it was a 'constant reality' derived from 'actual experience' of the deep ecological consciousness pervading the entire nature.

2. Another aspect which is unique for the Gospel is the inclusion of inanimate, inert matter within the realm of Sri Ramakrishna's experience of 'One whole' expressing as the manifold universe.Let us note his experience recorded in the *Gospel* :"*The Divine Mother revealed to me in the Kâli temple that it was She who had become everything. She showed me that everything was full of Consciousness. The image was Consciousness, the altar was Consciousness, the water-vessels were Consciousness, the door-sill was Consciousness, the marble floor was Consciousness - all was Consciousness. I found everything inside the room soaked, as it were, in Bliss - the Bliss of God. I saw a wicked man in front of the Kâli temple; but in him also I saw the power of the Divine Mother vibrating. That was why I fed a cat with the food that was to be offered to the Divine Mother. I clearly perceived that all this was the Divine Mother - even the cat.*"[29]

   Therefore we find that Sri Ramakrishna's 'one whole' reality manifesting through nature includes water vessels, door-sill, marble floor along with the wicked man and the cat. Thus it is not just related with the 'biotic whole' but also the abiotic fraction.

3. The conflict between the concept of 'equal intrinsic value' of the deep ecologists and the objection put forth by the anthropocentric sections are renconciled by the concepts of *'vibhu'* and *'shaktivishesh'* in *The Gospel of Sri Ramakrishna.* The practical application of these principles find an extra-ordinary expression in the allegory of the 'Elephant-Narayana' and the 'Mahout-Narayana'. This on one hand honours the intrinsic value of the elephant as a veritable expression of the Godhead and at the same time does not profess ecofascism where men simply embrace death without any sort of intelligent escape.

4. Let us take into account two apparently opposing accounts in the *Gospel.* Sri Ramakrishna on one hand is feeding the cat as the Divine Mother in an exalted state [30]. On the other hand there is a record of his advice to

M:

M: "At meal-time, sometimes a cat stretches out its paw to take the fish from my plate. But I cannot show any resentment."

MASTER: "Why? You may even beat it once in a while. What's the harm? A worldly man should hiss, but he shouldn't pour out his venom. He mustn't actually injure others. But he should make a show of anger to protect himself from enemies. Otherwise they will injure him. But a sannyasi need not even hiss."[31]

This illustrates Sri Ramakrishna's stand for a sannyasi, a person who has realized the one reality pervading everything and on the contrary for the common man. However we must not be mistaken by this utterance of Sri Ramakrishna as something ordinary and against deep ecology since he prescribes hissing but not pouring venom or going for mindless atrocities on non-human creatures.

5. One very unique conclusion of The Gospel of Sri Ramakrishna is : Nature as pure consciousness manifested in varied forms is eternally free from any danger of extinction and damage. Death, disease and killing may harm the physical bodies of the individuals but as Consciousness it is unperturbed forever.

   In the Gospel we find Sri Ramakrishna relating his experience:

   "Do you know what I see? I see that God alone has become everything. Men and animals are only frameworks covered with skin, and it is He who is moving through their heads and limbs. I see that it is God Himself who has become the block, the executioner, and the victim for the sacrifice."[32]

   In 'Sri Ramakrishna The Great Master' by Swami Saradananda we find a similar experience:

   "One day at Dakshineswar the Master saw a butterfly flying with a tiny stick stuck to its tail. He was at first pained to think that some naughty urchin had done it, but the next moment he was inspired and burst into laughter saying, "O Rama, Thou hast brought Thyself to this plight!"[33]

Thus we see that to Sri Ramakrishna the entire spectrum consisting of the block, the executioner and the victim is a playful manifestation of One single Reality untouched by destruction.

One may ask then what is the use of such an idea in Deep Ecology where death, and destruction mean no danger at all? The answer to this paradox is, one who realizes this entire creation as manifestation of that eternally invulnerable consciousness can do no harm to the creation himself. Sri Ramakrishna gives the example of the sword which when touched by the touchstone turns to gold and can no longer be used for killing. So non-injury to the nature comes as a strange corollary to the experience of nature as pure consciousness untouched by death, disease and damage with only outer physical forms changing through death, disease and killing. So unlike the deep ecologists who are worried to save the nature with all her components, *The Gospel of Sri Ramakrishna* goes for a natural non-injury proceeding from a vision of one's own Indestructible Self manifesting in every corner of the physical universe.

Therefore to such a man of realization, like Sri Ramakrishna in the Gospel, the world appears to be built upon an unperturbed screen of pure Consciousness on which the fleeting scenes of pleasures and pains rise and fall in an eternal drama born out of the sportive aspect of that very Consciousness. On the other hand there often comes moments when that very man of realization feels identified with the physical sheath of this all pervading Consciousness and rejoices with the slightest joys of the ordinary creatures and experiences excruciating pain at any sort of agony at the level of the body and the mind experienced by even a blade of grass!

Conclusion

Deep Ecology is undoubtedly the cry of the day rising from the depths of creation. However the practicable model is yet to be formulated. *The Gospel of Sri Ramakrishna* can serve as a handbook for the deep ecologists who are interested to find the varied shades of the experience of 'the ecological whole' and ways to reach it since they claim that they are not satisfied with mere ecological 'ethics' but seek ecological 'experience'. But as long as that search remains within the realm of intellect and senses this is indeed a difficult proposition. *The Gospel of Sri Ramakrishna* however offers a simple path of faith in the words of men who have realized that state of oneness with the entire universe. Poised in that child-like faith one may move sooner towards reaching the goal. Today's imagination will become tomorrow's realization. What is required is an urge to step out of our older identity of a separate individual and jump into the ocean of a universal identity. What is required is to go beyond our selfish concerns and seek that state where we can smile and weep with the entire creation with a background knowledge of the unmoved Consciousness vibrating through every movement. *The Gospel of Sri Ramakrishna* thus offers a deeper ecology free from fears and anxieties to protect the nature but is naturally non-injurious and all-inclusive.

REFERENCES

1. Encyclopedia of Environmental Ethics and Philosophy – 2nd/ 7/18/2008 18:08 Page 207
2. Ibid,p.206
3. Næss, Arne (1989). *Ecology, community and lifestyle.* Cambridge University Press. pp. 164-65
4. Encyclopedia of Environmental Ethics and Philosophy – 2nd/ 7/18/2008 18:08 Page 206
5. Ibid, p.207
6. Fox, Warwick, (1990) *Towards a Transpersonal Ecology* (Shambhala Books)
7. Encyclopedia of Environmental Ethics and Philosophy – 2nd/ 7/18/2008 18:08 Page 207
8. Ibid, p.207
9. Ibid pp.207-08
10. Taylor Bron & Zimmerman Michael, The Encyclopedia of Religion and Nature (London: Continuum , 2005),*Deep Ecology,*p.2
11. M, *The Gospel of Sri Ramakrishna*, trans. Swami Nikhilananda (Chennai: Ramakrishna Math,2002),p.752
12. Saradananda Swami, Sri Ramakrishna , The Great Master, trans.Swami Jagadananda (Chennai: Ramakrishna Math, 1952)pp.261-262
13. The Gospel of the Holy Mother Sri Sarada Devi,p.234
14. M, *The Gospel of Sri Ramakrishna*, trans. Swami Nikhilananda (Chennai: Ramakrishna Math,2002), p.312
15. Ibid, p.287
16. Ibid, pp.28-29
17. Ibid, pp.93-94
18. Ibid, p.298
19. Ibid, p.117
20. Ibid, p.205
21. Ibid,p.177
22. Ibid,p.324
23. Ibid,p. 324
24. Ibid,p.877
25. Taylor Bron & Zimmerman Michael, The Encyclopedia of Religion and Nature (London: Continuum , 2005),*Deep Ecology,*pp.6-7
26. M, *The Gospel of Sri Ramakrishna*, trans. Swami Nikhilananda (Chennai: Ramakrishna Math,2002), p.115
27. Ibid,p.278

28. Nityatmananda Swami, M *The Apostle and the Evangelist* vol. I., p. 40
29. M, *The Gospel of Sri Ramakrishna*, trans. Swami Nikhilananda (Chennai: Ramakrishna Math,2002), pp. 28-29
30. Ibid. p.28
31. Ibid,pp. 272-273
32. Ibid,p.80
33. Saradananda Swami, Sri Ramakrishna , The Great Master, trans.Swami Jagadananda (Chennai: Ramakrishna Math, 1952) pp.261

10

A Play of two Masters

Somnath Bhattacharya

The word 'Master' has various meanings, including 'a male teacher, schoolmaster, or tutor'. The author of Shri Shri RamakrishnaKathamrita (translated as 'Gospel' in English), Mahendranath Gupta—better known by the pseudonym 'M', was a teacher by profession. Ramakrishna often used to lovingly call him as 'Master' or 'Mahendra Master'. When he started going to Ramakrishna in 1882, he was the headmaster of a renowned school. The pseudonym used most by 'M' in the Kathamrita is 'Master'. The English translation, however, refers to Ramakrishna as 'Master' (originally 'Thakur' in Bengali) in the sense of God or the Lord. This article will use the word 'Master' to mean 'a teacher'. That way one finds not one, but two 'Master's in the Gospel (henceforth the word 'Gospel' will be applicable to the Kathamrita or any of its translations)—Ramakrishna himself, and M. The Gospel, by the way, is not a piece of fiction, nor a biography or a mere narrative. It is more like a play. M himself looked at it that way. Often he used to tell the devotees that it would suffice to meditate upon some particular 'scene's of the Gospel. Truly, the Gospel looks like a play with a series of animated scenes, depicting an incessant array of multifarious moods of Ramakrishna, devoutly noted and honestly projected by M. The Gospel, then, is a play of two 'Master's.

The First 'Master'

Ramakrishna, the central figure of the Gospel, is a 'Master'—though not by profession. He is a teacher of mankind (an *acharya*). He is a world-teacher (*jagadguru*). He came to teach humanity the essence of life and its goal. A competent teacher teaches keeping in view the time, place and the taught. The Gospel bears ample examples. Sitting in Calcutta, the then capital of India, Ramakrishna talks in the language loved by his mostly urban audience, citing objects and places from the city of Calcutta, such as 'gas connection' and 'Asiatic Society'. Picturing the typical 'babu' or middle class fashionable gentleman, he illustrates the lack of seriousness in the apparently pious expressions of an otherwise worldly person (19 Oct 1884):

> Do you know how the god of worldly people is? It's like children, having heard quarrels of elderly aunts, telling among themselves while at play, 'I swear by god.' Again, it's like a well-groomed 'Babu', chewing a betel leaf and strolling in the garden with a stick in hand, picking up a flower and telling his friend, 'See, what a fantastic flower god has created.'

Ramakrishna uses the same 'babu' to portray the dawning of divine quality in human beings (8 April 1883):

> There are certain signs of God-realisation. One in whom the treasure of God-ward love is being manifested is not far off from God realisation. What are the treasures of God-ward love? Discrimination, detachment, compassion for living beings, serving the holy, companion of the holy, chanting the name and glory of God, telling the truth, and the like. If these signs of God-ward love be found in someone, it can be definitely said that God realisation is not far off from him. If it has been planned that the 'Babu' will visit the house of a servant, then it can be told unmistakably from the state of the servant's house. First the jungle and weeds are cut off, then the soot and dirt are removed from the rooms, and all places are swept clean. Then the Babu himself sends various items like the carpet, hubble-bubble for smoking, and the like. Seeing all these coming, men make no mistake in understanding that the Babu will arrive in no time.

Persons with single-pointed commitment often mentally relate their varied day-to-day experiences to their subject of interest. A committed teacher goes one step further, and explains in detail such connections to clarify the subject matter to his or her students. The Gospel has Ramakrishna alluding now and then to many commonplace objects and incidents to illustrate sublime topics. He uses the ordinary to bring home the extra-ordinary. For example, he talks about the power of a genuine *guru* (or *sad-guru*) (14 December 1882):

> Once while going to the pine-grove… I heard a bullfrog croaking terribly. I thought it must have been caught by a snake. On my way back after a long time, I could still hear its moaning. I looked to see what the matter was, and found that it had been caught by a water-snake which could neither swallow nor give it up. And the frog's suffering was also un-ending. I thought that had it been seized by a

cobra it would have been silenced after three cries. As it was only a water-snake, so it was the suffering of both the snake and the frog. If it is a genuine *guru* (*sad-guru*), then man's ego vanishes in three cries. If the *guru* is unripe, then it is the suffering of both the *guru* and his disciple! Whatever be the effort, the disciple's ego doesn't die; his worldly ties don't sever. If the disciple falls under the clutches of an unripe *guru*, he doesn't attain liberation.

Ramakrishna also shows sharp alertness about the nature and mindset of his audience. He talks to Naren and Rakhal in one way, while to Dr Mahendralal Sarkar in some other way. Once he made a point to Dr Sarkar, and the latter said satisfactorily, "These are very good ideas." Ramakrishna said, smilingly, "Yes! How are the ideas?" The doctor said, "Quite good." Immediately came the unexpected yet apt repartee of Ramakrishna: "Give a 'thank you' "! Undoubtedly, he knew how to address the urban intelligentsia.

Another important characteristic of a true teacher is that he does not impose; he suggests. Ramakrishna shows mastery here also. The Gospel records a number of instances where he waits for the listener's nod before proceeding. Once (22 April 1883) he was talking to Shri Becharam, a preacher (*acharya*) of Adi Brahma Samaj about the supreme truth expressing itself both as with form and without form. In the process of trying to drive home a point somewhat alien to the *acharya*, Ramakrishna said, "See, the formless is true, and so is the one with a form; what do you say?" Ramakrishna does not impose here; but suggests higher possibilities of thoughts or realisation.

His suggestive style would manifest at its best sometimes in moods of humour. A noted modern biographer of Ramakrishna says, "At Dakshineswar, one could occasionally hear Ramakrishna's followers break out in uproarious laughter at something that he had said. However, when the fun had subsided, at least a few would pause to reflect on the wisdom that lay hidden in the peals of laughter."

In fact, this was the characteristic style of Ramakrishna. He talked with ease. The Gospel is replete with episodes where the Master speaks elevated things effortlessly, creating a very cool and congenial atmosphere. At the same time, he used to turn grave if required, uttering the needful without mixing words. Once (11 March 1883) alerting a young aspirant he said, "Be on your guards, O monk!" M noted that the words of the Master sounded like the solemn rumble of clouds.

The Second 'Master'

As already noted, M was a teacher by profession. This second 'Master' in the Gospel taught in different schools and colleges. At one time he had been working as the Headmaster of three schools, moving from one to another in a palanquin. He taught in Rippon, City and Metropolitan colleges; his subjects being English, Psychology and Economics. It has already been mentioned that Ramakrishna would often call him as 'Master'. Like, on 15 June 1884, Ramakrishna told his disciple Niranjan, referring to M: "He's a Headmaster. He went to see you. I sent him." M was reverentially called 'Master Mahashay' by many. In fact, the recorded history of those who came in contact with Ramakrishna reveals that the two most scholarly were M and Adharlal Sen.

What M has written in the form of the 'Gospel' is unique. It verily reads like a 'play' with one scene unfolding after another. Once referring to an absorbing episode from the Gospel, M himself said to someone: "You meditate on this scene for twenty-four hours. This will serve the purpose of meditation—and will evoke his (i.e., Ramakrishna's) memory." (ShriMa Darshan, Swami Nityatmananda, Part 2, page 246). M's using the word 'scene' is conspicuous. The Gospel is a play by the 'Master' called Mahendranath Gupta.

In the Gospel M has evinced his 'mastery' over language too. In fact it was Ramakrishna who very well knew the art of 'playing' with language. Giving unexpected twists and turns here and there (like what happens if the word Gita in Bengali is spelt in the reverse order) he brought fresh flavour and power out of words. Effectively did he use a beautiful blend of Bengali and English. M also used his language 'masterly', as if 'playing' with it. The Gospel is full of extraordinary literary styles of M, including brevity of expression, art of natural flashbacking and imaginative suggestions. The unique description of the Ganga is one such, where M writes:

> The devotees are seated on the floor—some on the mat, some on their own seats. Everyone is gazing at the blissful figure of the great saint with unblinking eyes. The holy river Ganga was flowing due south, past the western side of the strand lying close to the room. It was monsoon; tremendous was the current of the river—as if she was so very eager to reach and unite with the sea! Only, on the way she just flows past the temple of meditation of the great soul, visiting and touching it piously.

The Master of the Master

Ramakrishna is the teacher of the teacher—the Master of the Master. And that gets established as early as during the very second visit of M to Ramakrishna. When M replied to Ramakrishna's query—'what kind of person is your wife…', saying that 'she is good, but unwise…', instant came Ramakrishna's displeased remark: "And you are wise?" One wonders if M, a Master by profession, ever faced such an attack even in his student life! However, in course of the further description of that day's conversations, M unhesitatingly declares that at one point "his (i.e., M's) ego got crushed totally", and that "this was his first and last argument with the Master (i.e., Ramakrishna)." Evidently, this portrays the absolute surrender of one Master to another.

Another definite proof of such surrender and self-effacement of M is his happy and candid descriptions of the admonitions he received from Ramakrishna! For instance, the account of 16 October 1882, where M is found chit-chatting with Narendranath near the Eastern door of Ramakrishna's room, with the latter coming out of his room and smilingly asking what the two were talking about. The moment he heard that the subject matter was the moral degradation of the school students etc., he told M gravely, "Such talks are not good. You are elder than these, you have grown intelligence; you should not have consented to the raising of such issues." Curiously, M has not only narrated the incident, but also added: "Master (meaning he) felt embarrassed".

Again, on some occasions it was the modern men that Ramakrishna pulled up through M, like when he came down (during the said second visit itself) critically on their tendency of tutoring others before self, and told M: "That is one peculiarity of you the people of Calcutta! Only lecturing and explaining others! Nobody ever stops to think who will teach himself! Who are you to explain? He who is the Lord of this universe will explain."

Not Two, but One

However, a careful journey through the Gospel reveals that there are not two, but only one 'Master'. And it is Ramakrishna. It was he who worked through M. He had spotted and ordained M for the writing of the Gospel. Swami Shivananda, a monastic disciple of Ramakrishna, said that he was so fond of the words of Ramakrishna that once he started noting them down. But Ramakrishna forbade him, saying that he had already kept someone selected for the purpose.

That being the matter of fact, it would not be inappropriate to conclude that what would be recorded in the Gospel was also decided by Ramakrishna himself. That is why M did not say that the Gospel was 'written' by him, but 'told' ('*ShriMa kathita*'). In other words, he has only 'told' what he had heard. Hence the Gospel is a work of Ramakrishna himself. This is yet another 'play' of the real 'Master'—to lie hidden behind the apparent 'Master'—M. The hidden 'Master' made the apparent 'Master' capable of comprehending his message, putting it down in black and white in codified form, holding the details in memory, and decoding it much later to produce the Gospel in printed form. Ramakrishna remained seated as the powers of comprehension, memory and expression in the head and heart of M. Incidentally, Ramakrishna occasionally used to check if M was getting things properly. For example, the Gospel records the interactions of the night of 9 November 1884. M was gently massaging the feet of Ramakrishna, seated on the small cot at his room in Dakshineswar. A lamp was burning on a stand near the wall. Ramakrishna smilingly asked M what were the things talked about that day, and what he said about Emperor Akbar etc. M was replying as much as he could. About 'dependence' he said, "I heard another thing: at a feast a small boy cannot by himself find a place to eat the meal; someone finds it out for him." Immediately Ramakrishna said, "No, not quite. If the father holds his son while walking, the boy doesn't fall." After that Ramakrishna wanted to know what further talks had there been that day. M narrated a few. Lastly he referred to a point, saying that Ramakrishna had told that to Pandit Padmalochan. Immediately Ramakrishna corrected him, saying, "No, (I told it) to Bamandas of Ulo."

The Gospel has another day's (28 July 1885) proceedings thus:

M: The other day you were nicely explaining this subject matter of 'incarnation'.

Ramakrishna: Please tell me what it was.

M: As if there a boundless field! Its vast expanse extends to the horizon and beyond! I can't see it on account of a boundary wall in front; there is only a round hole in that wall! Through that hole a part of the infinite field can be seen!

Ramakrishna: Now tell, what that hole is?

M: You are that hole! Through you everything can be seen; that infinite expanse of the field can be seen through you!

Ramakrishna, highly pleased, started patting M, and said, "You have been able to get the meaning… it's so nice."

When M was preparing to publish the Gospel, the Holy Mother blessed him by writing: "His (Ramakrishna's) words that you have with you are all true…. Hearing those from you one day, I felt like he himself was speaking."

Seen in this light, it is obvious that the Gospel is a play written by none other than Ramakrishna himself. However, it is Ramakrishna's 'play' in another sense also.

'Play' with a Difference

Another meaning of the word 'play' is sport. The Gospel is verily Ramakrishna's play, his *leela* or divine sport. What M has penned is a play in the sense of drama, and what Ramakrishna has done through it is a play in the sense of *leela*. It is said of *Shri-Chaitanya-Charitamrita* that it is Chaitanya himself who speaks through Vrindabandas, the author. Similarly it is Ramakrishna himself who speaks through M. Swami Vivekananda praised M by saying that he is 'entirely hidden' in the Gospel. Truly, this is an unparalleled real-life drama, a divine sport, where the playwright, director and lead role are one and the same. Gospel, thus, is the *leela* or grand play of the one and only one 'Master', Shri Ramakrishna.

REFERENCES

1. ShriShriRamakrishnaKathamrita, ShriMa
2. ShriMa Darshan, Swami Nityatmananda, Sri Ma Trust, Chandigarh
3. Ramakrishna Paramahamsa: The Sadhaka of Dakshineswar, Amiya P Sen, Penguin-Viking

11 Sri Ramakrishna and scientific humanism in the light of Kathamrita

Tarit Kumar Bandyopadhyay

Despite being an epitome of the spiritual world, Sri Ramakrishna believed in logic and possessed a scientific temper. This scientific consciousness was reflected in his manners, speeches and religious rigour. He was against narrow religious rituals. He never encouraged religious fanaticism. Anyone who is a blind follower of any religion was called a fool by him. Despite being a priest in Hindu Temple, he was equally attracted towards others faiths like Islam, Christianity, Buddhism and others. He used to patronize other religions and mixed with the believers of other faiths in a free uninhibited manner. If we follow his words as explicated in "KATHAMRITA", we can come to the conclusion that he believed in truthfulness, logicality, and empathy of a human being more than the religion. He wanted to saw the seeds of social consciousness in the young mind. Anybody acquainted with the life of Sri Ramakrishna must be aware of his iconic uttering "Human and Human consciousness: any human with human consciousness knows the truth of God, everything else is temporal". To him, God is the symbol supreme consciousness. He wanted to create individuals- one who will be ideologically firm in the belief of ultimate truth. He wanted normal citizens to raise themselves so that they become enlighten citizens. In order to achieve that he sought the growth of scientific consciousness which can be expressed in modern time as Scientific Humanism or the Path to be an Enlighten Citizen.

We believe that normal citizens can become enlighten citizens if they rigorously undertake scientific education. Our earnest prayer to Sri Ramakrishna is that we need the strength to imbibe his scientific spirit in order to achieve that supreme state.

We find various scientific aspects of Sri Ramakrishna in his attitude and sayings. He had rational conviction in various branches of material science and the scientific facts. It shows his belief and earnestness for scientific truths.

Scientific inquiry was a part of his mental setup. Albert Einstein once said, "I do not consider anybody as a scientist who just uses the scientific instruments. To me the main thing is the scientific mind"[1]. Jawaharlal Nehru termed it as 'Scientific Humanism'[2]. Swami Vivekananda called it the 'Scientific Outlook'. It means that there should be proper observation, impartial and full evaluation of the fact, deep thinking and verification before acceptance, discriminating intelligence, rationality, unbiased outlook and accepting the truth arrived at by scientific experimentation. Julian Huxley laid down similar rational basis for this 'Scientific Humanism'[3]. Let us now investigate the attitude or Sri Ramakrishna towards this Scientific Humanism.

Truth

The goal of science is to find the truth, to discover the reality behind the apparent fact. The practice of science is a journey towards this reality. Bertrand Russell said (Introduction to Mathematical Philosophy), "Every proposition having a communicate significance must be true "[4].

Sri Ramakrishna had this devotion to truth. He was keen on finding the truth just as a scientist. Searching for the truth becomes a habit with him. Swami Someswarananda impeccably described it : "He wanted to free himself from all kind of small ego to arrive at the truth. He offered flowers at the feet of his deity and told her, "Mother, take back your virtue and vice, your purity and impurity, your propriety and impropriety." But he could tell Her to take back the truth. He told the devotees, "Where shall I be without the truth ?" He challenged the commonplace beliefs about virtue and vice, purity and impurity, propriety and impropriety. He questioned them, experimented with them only to get to the essence or the truth"[5].

Rationality

Rationality is another sign of scientific attitude. The life of Sri Ramakrishna is resplendent with rationality. Not only did he evaluate everything on a rational basis, but inspired his devotees to do the same. Once he told Swamiji, "As the cashier counts the money to the last penny, so you do the same with me. Do not accept me till you are completely above any suspicion" [6]. When Mathur Babu and Jogin wanted to verify his control over lust, he said without any irritation, "Very well. You observe the holy man during the day and observe him during the night. Then only you trust him"[7].

His rationality made him a practical man. We hear him saying, "Why should you be a fool even if you are devotee"[8]? He advised against unnecessary pity towards bedbugs[9] or cockroaches[10]. His saying include : "Do not be a coward in the name of civility,"[11] "Do not be spineless even if you see God in every being"[12], Do not be sloppy even if you are busy,"[13] "Do not be prudish about lust"[14]. He conquered lust in his personal life, still he said to young Harinath that it was an inevitable vital force that cannot be avoided, ignored or destroyed. This force must be turned towards God[15]. His advice to the young disciples was to turn the force of anger or lust towards God[16].

No Superstition

From his boyhood he fought against many social injunctions. The extent of his freethinking is surprising. In the nineteenth century setup of superstitious rural society, he boldly declared that he would not learn the priesthood that would earn the pittance of life[17]. He was a Brahmin by caste who wears the sacred thread. He threw it away as a symbol of vanity. During the initiation ceremony of sacred thread he was supposed to beg for his daily rice. Against the prevalent social norm he begged first from Dhani Kamarni who was inferior in caste. Again, in spite of the opposition by the Bahmins he accepted a job in the temple established by Rani Rasmani who was way below in caste hierarchy. His guru was woman (Vairabi Brahmani). He was always against the religious rites. He told Ishan to throw away the outside equipment of worship (Kosha Kushi, used for offering water during the ceremonial worship). Instead, he advised him to be mad in the love of God[18].

Nothing was indispensable to him in the journey towards God – scholarship, erudition, worldly affairs, Tantra, Mantra, rituals, yajnas, scriptural injunctions, austerity, japas, cleanliness, etc. To him 'It is all in the mind. In mind the man is free, and in mind he is bound'[19]. In his free mind he declared that in the Kali Yuga, the Karma-Kanda and the Jnana-Kanda of the Vedas are hard to follow. The life now is hand to mouth [20].

He never supported the hypocrisy of untouchability. He admitted the necessity of the guru in the life of the seeker. But he was vocal against all kinds of blind practices in the name of relation that were rampant during his time. He accepted Islam and Christianity without any qualm, going against the social restrictions. Everybody had an open door to him – the low castes, the outcastes, the drunkards, the ruffians, and the prostitutes. About caste, his unequivocal declaration " "The devotee has no caste"[21].

Unbiased Attitude

Julian Huxley said that 'the Scientific Humanism is a protest against bias and blind faith. The spread of human intellect in various fields cannot be suppressed by any dogma of blind faith[22].' He was against limiting man's thoughts and understanding to a single idea. To him nobody had a monopoly over the truth. Once during a discussion someone told him that he knows all about the subject. He corrected him and said that one should not pose to be all knowing. 'We learn everyday in our life'[23]. There is no end to the realization of the truth – it manifests in various ways. Sri Ramakrishna applied it in life and said, "As many views, so many paths," Swami Someswarananda explained, "This saying of Sri Ramakrishna is a respectful acceptance of the various forms of man's realization. Truth is not exclusive, never exhausted. Time and time again Sri Ramakrishna cautioned against dogmatism, against any kind of bias[24]. Dogmatism is blind faith, a tunnel vision. He condemned this mentality and said that 'everybody thinks that only his watch is correct.' This is the mentality that breeds hatred towards others of different faith. This mentality was unscientific to him. The final truth is not limited to a single conclusion. There is no final truth in science. Everything is relative. The object seen under a compound microscope would look different under an electron microscope. Science has concluded that an incident is dependent on its current state and environment. Swamiji said that 'the whole of truth cannot lie inside a man or book'[25]. A scientific mentality is flexible and liberal.

Diligence

A scientific mentality required diligence. Scientific research is gathering of date and analysis of the experimental results. It calls for diligence with faith. The Scientists show an untiring zeal in arriving at the right justification of a theory. The lives of Pasteur and Galilio are glaring examples. We see the same diligence, effort and earnestness in the life of Sri Ramakrishna. His pursuit of various religions spread over a long period of twelve year (1856 – 1867). The author of 'Sri Ramakrishna the Great Master' mentioned his single-mindedness in this endeavour. 'During mediations his body would remain still with no sign of movement. The uncombed hair became matted. At times he would be so overwhelmed with emotion that he would rub his face hard on the ground and blood would ooze out of the skin. The day passed by and he would not stop. When darkness feel his sad voice would cry out that another day passed and still the Mother did not appear before him[26].

Sense of Organization

The efforts of scientific mentality are based on organizing skill. Organization is man's natural trait. The success of any scientific discovery is measured by its application on the human society. The valuation of any truth is its significance in man's needs. That leads to organization. The religious pursuit of Sri Ramakrishna was a great help in preserving the endangered culture of India under the aggressive colonial domination of the nineteenth century. His teaching helped the educated class to discipline itself against rootless, wanton, licentious behaviour. He also provides the inspiration for nationalism.

He wanted his beliefs to be fully utilized in the society. He became eager to gather a group of young people for this purpose. Standing on the roof of the Dakshineswar temple he would shout, 'Oh you there ! Come, come here.' He brought together a group of educated young men for the service of humanity through his teachings, compassion and love. He entrusted Swamiji even under his vehement protest, and said, "Naren will teach the people"[27].

Methods of Valuation

The aim of scientific research is to identify the reality behind the particular facts and arrive at a general theory[28]. The teachings of Sri Ramakrishna draw similes from the worldly facts. He referred to may scientific facts to direct one's life towards the ultimate truth.

He was a seeker in the path of religion, but never neglected the practical side of life. He referred to many subjects of material science. His teachings are spiritual as well as practical. They lead to social revolution and provide answeers to life's enquiries.

His spiritual pursuit and teachings can be explained in scientific context that leads from the known to the unknown, from the particular to the general, and from the concrete to the abstract.

There was a constant flow of visitors to him, both men and women, irrespective of their caste, creed or religion. Romain Rolland said of Sri Ramakrishna that due to his irresistible force of attraction a multitude of people, men and women, of all castes, creeds and faith always crowded around him[29]. He was really 'Sri Ramakrishna of the people'[30].

Sense of Value

There is a change of the sense of value in the social life due to the advent of technology. Science is intimately connected with this change. There is a terminal value of the goal of any scientific research. There is also an instrumental value in the field of scientific research. Robert Nisbet said, "Contemporary social problems is thought to be reduced as the result of spread of knowledge and of the humanitarian ethics. Other problems will undoubtedly take their place given the nature of human dependence upon social norms and the differential responses of individuals to these norms" [31].

Referring to the basis of the sense of value Journalist Pranabesh Chakraborty said, "There is a search for value in the material world. It goes in the spiritual world as well. The values identified in the spiritual world are truthfulness, beauty, love, respect, feelings, honestly, etc. These values are both individual and social. They may be relative or they may be of eternal value. Knowingly we accept these eternal values, and at times we leave them out. The sense of value is the sense of the absolute One. This sense is reflected in the ideal of service, it indicates the path for a healthy social life. The individual sense of value becomes social when it spreads in all branches of social life – culture, education, history, behavior, etc. – and leads towards a desired goal. The journey towards that goal is progress" [32].

Through his religious teachings and conduct Sri Ramakrishna awakened in the whole society a sense of respect towards the Indian culture. Respect the respectful irrespective of the caste or creed – this is science and its application. Sri Ramakrishna said without any hesitation, "I bow down to the feet of the seekers of knowledge (jnani), the devotees, the devotees of deities, and also the members of the modern Brahmo-samaj" [33].

Sri Ramakrishna believed that the inner qualities of man were 'the manifestation of the infinite power'[34]. So he was ever ready to 'respect the respectful'[35], 'give up pride'[36], 'bow down to everyone'[37]. Mahendranath Dutta, brother of Swami Vivekananda, said, "We discarded the social norm of bowing down to others as a superstition. Coming in contact of the Paramhansa we learnt to greet others with our folded hands. He taught us to do so by doing it himself"[38].

To Sri Ramakrishna individual pride had no scientific basis. He said, "He can never have wisdom who is proud of his knowledge or wealth"[39]. Ego does not let the individual to be social. He taught to discard it. He said, "There are two signs of knowledge : first there is no self-conceit, and then a gentle behaviors"[40]. He strongly advised everybody to give up the ego and to be simple and liberal. He said, "If you are simple, you reach God soon"[41].

Love and compassion are indispensable for individual development and social harmony. The Indian Mirror published an account showing the love of Sri Ramakrishna to all irrespective of their social status[42]. Swami Vivekananda said, "He was love personified"[43]. He advised everybody, "Love one another. That would bring the Good"[44], He firmly believed that without love and compassion, social stabilization was impossible.

The human mind was a very important subject for Sri Ramakrishna. He said, "The mind is the most important thing. Man is free in mind, bound in mind. The mind will take to any colour that you soak it in"[45]. He wanted the mind to have constant good thoughts. It must be cultivated. He taught bow the mind could be elevated to pure intelligence [46].

This sense of value is a special requirement for scientific humanism. Julian Huxley said, "This new humanism – a task which demands a combination of altruism and tolerance – it must attempt to do justice to our incompleteness and the constant change in knowledge and outlook which we must hope for"[47].

Scientific Motive behind Religious Investigation of Sri Ramakrishna

During his time Sri Ramakrishna was known as a religious person. Deep investigation would reveal that even if he talked in religious terms, his conclusions were expressed very scientifically.

He experimented for a long period of twelve years that can be categorized into sequences of different practices – Devotion (1856 – 57), Hata Yoga (1857), Worship as a servant of God (1857-58), Worship with parental affection (1863), Worship as a lover (1864), Practice of Advaita (1865), Islam (1866), and Christianity (1873).

Now we shall see how through scientific analysis he applied the realized truths to practical life.

Practice	**Observation**	**Conclusion**
Devotion	The Mother of the Universe. An infinite ocean of light approaching with roaring waves all around.	Discard sacred thread. Offering the flower for the deity to own feet. Said : "Get rid of the discriminating intelligence"[48]. Concept : Unbiased free mind.
Hatha Yoga	Restriction of food. Excessive cleanliness. Constant attention to body.	Said : "Not fit for this age. No time or this. People now have shorter life depending on food"[49].

Practice	**Observation**	**Conclusion**
Servant of God	Visualized luminous figure of Mother Sita, an image of love, compassion and forbearance.	Said : "Only love and devotion are real, all else are unreal"[50]. "If you utter 'Gita' ten times, you will be a renouncer" [51]. "He survives who forbears. He who doesn't is destroyed"[52]. Concept : The essential element for healthy social life love, devotion and renunciation [53].
Parental affection	Seeing life in the image of Ramlala given by Jatadhari. Eager for his nursing.	Said : "I love young people, because they are to pure"[54]. "When I see the young people, I find solace"[55] Concept : To awaken youth power.
Lover	Feeling himself as Srimati, eager to see Sri Krishna. Saw a special light that came out of the image of Sri Krishna and touched him and the book, Bhagavat.	Said : "The scripture, the devotee and God all three are one, the One is three"[56]. "Man is God"[57]. Concept : The center of worship – the spark of man.
Advaita	Nirbikalpa Samadhi Realized Brahman, the sameness of individual self and the self. Felt pain in picking up grass. Felt the pain of beating of someone else.	Said "Brahman and Shakti are identical"[58]. "He has become the universe and all its constituents"[59]. "I do not see the difference between a chaste woman and a prostitute"[60]. Concept: Vision of equality, no division.
Islam	Japa of Allah. Regular namaz. Vision of luminous personality with log beard.	Said : "All faiths are true. All are paths. As may faiths, so many paths"[61]. "The Hindus call water jal, the Muslims pani, the Christians water"[62]. "Dogmatism about faith is not good." Concept: Social beha-viour excludes religious fanati-cism, tolerates other's views, takes a non-communal attitude.

Practice	Observation	Conclusion
Christianity	In the living room of Jadunath Mullick saw the picture of young Jesus in his mother's lap and went into a trance. Realized the sayings of Jesus.	Said : "Thou art me, I am Thee"[63]. "Compassion is love for all beings"[64]. "Service to living beings as God"[65] Concept : Service to humanity is the Religion.

We can safely conclude that the center of religious practice of Sri Ramakrishna was Man. He spoke in religious terms, but never accepted anything as presumptive truth. He experimented, investigated and observed, and then only drew his conclusion. And his conclusions were not limited to religious precepts, but were meant or a practical guide for life's application. His teachings are not 'religion', but a spiritual social science, a scheme to 'bring the Vedanta from the forest to the home'[66], to make man conscious of his humanity'[67].

Sri Ramakrishna's Scientific Religion

The readers of the life of Sri Ramakrishna know that he made the religious concepts simple and illustrative, free from any prejudice. The modern life is overwhelmed with materialism. The science has become our daily life through the dynamics of industrialization and urban living. Sri Ramakrishna was aware of it. One day he made a witty remark to a devotee, 'Perhaps your science does not say it.' Again the same Ramakrishna cited the example of water and ice, the change of state of matter, to explain God with forms and without forms. He was a critique of the material science, and its supporter as well.

'Science comes after knowledge' – that is how he described science. 'Science is the visualization that God has become all the universe and the living beings'[68]. He advocated 'practical science', rational and above blind faith, prudent in application for the higher journey towards 'religious science'. Swami Vivekananda raised a question in this context. The material sciences rationally justify their theories relating to the outside world by analyzing the discoveries. Should religion be doing the same thing? Should it follow the same investigation methods? Swamiji thought that it should be so[69].

To bolster our concept we further quote Swamiji (CW V, Conversations and Dialogues IX, p.368) : "What we need, you know, is to study, independent of foreign control, different branches of the knowledge that is our own, and with it the English language and Western science. We need technical education and all else that may develop industries so that men, instead of seeking for service, may earn enough to provide for themselves, and save something against a rainy day"[70].

Sri Ramakrishna made religion practical. It is his conclusion : "If the clay image can be worshiped, why cannot man be worshiped "[71]? At another time he said, "Man is not insignificant"[72]. He did not find religion merely contained in the scriptures or in the images, but found it in Man. Religion to him was 'the realization of the inner divinity.' It is a confluence of modern education, science and wisdom that would develop man to blossom into true humanity. Sri Ramakrishna's religion is both 'religious humanism' and scientific humanism.'

We believe that normal citizens can become enlighten citizens if they rigorously undertake scientific education. Our earnest prayer to Sri Ramakrishna is that we need the strength to imbibe his scientific spirit in order to achieve that supreme state.

REFERENCES

1. Albert Einstein (Selections from and on Einstein) composed by M.G.V. Murthy, Indian National Science Academy and Council of Scientific and Industrial Research, New Delhi, 1984, P.32
2. Eminent Scientist said that he got the term "Scientific Humanism" from Pandit JawarLal Nehru. Swami Vivekananda liked to say the same as "Scientific Judgement", Udhbodon, Vol . 88. No. 3, P. 160.
3. What Dare I think – Julian Huxley, Chatto and Windus, London, 1933, P. 149-77.
4. Introduction to Mathematical Philosophy, Bertrand Russell, Blackie & Sons (India) Limited, Bombay,1954, P.61.
5. Lok Jivane Sri Ramakrishna – Swami Someswarananda, Sujon Publication, Calcutta,1983, P. 55
6. Sri Ramakrishna and His Disciples – Christopher Isherwood (Bengali Version by Rabi Sekhar Sengupta), Mondal Book House, Calcutta, Bengali Calendar 1388, P. 179.
7. Sri Ramakrishna Bhakta Malika – (Vol -I), Swami Gambhirananda, Udbodhon Office, Kolkata, 3rd Edition, Bengali Calendar 1370, P. 471 (In brief Bhakta Malika).
8. Sri Sri Ramakrishna Leelaprasanga Unit Volume (Sw. Saradananda), Riflect Publication, Calcutta 1984, P. 564 (In brief Leelaprasanga).
9. Bhakta Malika (Vol - I), P. 257.

10. Ibid, P.185
11. Sri Ramakrishna and His Disciples - P. 181
12. Sri Sri Ramakrishna Kathamrita.- (Unit Volume)- M, Udbodhon, Office1407, P. (In brief Kathamrita)
13. Leelaprasanga , P. 662-63.
14. Ibid, P. 377
15. Sri Ramakrishna and his Disciples. P.195
16. Kthamrita. P. 128
17. Leelaprasanga. P.179
18. Kthamrita. P. 647
19. Ibid, P.87
20. Ibid, P. 269
21. Ibid, P. 110
22. What Dare I think. P. 174
23. Viswa Chetanaya Sri Ramakrishna – Edited by Swami Prameyananda, Nalini Ranjan Chattopadhyay & Swami Chaitanyananda, Udbodhon office, 1987, P. 168
24. Lokjivane Sri Ramakrishna. P.60
25. Swamiji –O- Netajir Bhabnaya Juba Samaj – Mitra Koutilya, Samata Prakashan, 1987, P.77
26. Lilaprasanga. P.218-22
27. Yuga Nayak Vivekananda (Vol –I), Swami Gambhirananda, Udbodhon Office, 1384, P. 194
28. Education Psychology – Shusil Roy, Soma Book Agency, Kolkata, 1985, P.150
29. Ramakrishner Jivan – Romain Rolland (Bengali- Rishi Das)- Orient Book Company, Kolkata, 1949, P-157-58
30. Souvenir Sri Ramakrishna Ashram, Batanagar, 24 Pargana, 1988
31. Contemporary Social Problems -Robert K Meston and Robert Nisbet, Barcourt Brace Jovanovich Inc, USA, 4th Edition,1976. P- 756
32. Souvenir , (Batanagar), 1988
33. Kthamrita, P-105
34. Kathamitra, P-345
35. Lilaprasanga, P-614
36. Ibid, P-614
37. Ibid, P-616
38. Sri Sri Ramakrishna Annudhyan- Mahendra Nath Dutta, Mahendra Publishing Committee, Kolkata 1386, P- 67
39. Kathamrita. P-930

40. Ibid, P- 938
41. Ibid, P-738
42. Samasamayik Dristite Sri Ramkrishna -Bengali- Brajendra Nath Bandoppadhyay –O- Sajanikanta Das, General Printers and Publishers Pvt. Ltd. Kolkata 1375, P-26.
43. Bhakta Malika, P-473.
44. Kathamrita , P- 441.
45. Ibid, P-87.
46. Ibid, P- 919.
47. What Dare I think, P-161
48. Kathamrita , P-372
49. Ibid , P-50
50. Ibid, P-755
51. Ibid, P- 233
52. Sri Sri Ramkrishna Kathasar (Bengali)- Sri Kumar Krishna Nandi, Student's Library, Calcutta, 1345, P- 21-22
53. Lilaprasanga, P-605
54. Kathamrita, P-744
55. Ibid, P-893
56. Ibid, P-105
57. Ibid, P-403
58. Ibid,P-55
59. Ibid, P-99
60. Ibid, P-751
61. Lilaprasanga, P-601
62. Kathamrita , P-60
63. Ibid, P-269
64. Ibid, P-242
65. Yuganayak Vivekananda (Vol- I), P-141
66. Swamiji –o- Netajir Bhabanaya Yuba Samaj, P-42
67. Kathamrita, P-919
68. Ibid, P-266
69. Swamijir Bani –O- Rachana, (Vol- 3), Udbodhan Office, 1387, P-132
70. Ibid, (Vol-7), Udbodhan Office, 1384, P-403
71. Kathamrita, P-413
72. Ibid, P-433

12

Sri Sri Ramakrishna Kathamrita in Comparison with the Jaina and Samkhya thought : An Analysis

Anupam Jash

Sri Ramakrishna was not a Philosopher in the academic sense of the term. But we may try to derive a philosophy of Sri Ramakrishna from the great book '*Sri Sri Ramakrishna Kathamrita*' and tried to make an in-depth study of different aspects of Sri Ramakrishna's philosophical thought and to make a systematic presentation of it. As Aldous Huxley has says in his foreword of '*The Gospels of Sri Ramakrishna*' that the book contains 'the casual and unstudied utterances of a great religious teacher'[1], it may be useful to present in a systematic form what Sri Ramakrishna's utterances mean as far as we can make it out. In the publishers note of the book '*Sri Ramakrishna's thoughts on Man, World and God*' written by Swami Tapasyananda, the President of Sri Ramakrishna Math, Mylapore, also says in the same strain that, "there is an urgent need today to make an in-depth study of Sri Ramakrishna's ideas, to discover his philosophy, and to present it in a systematic format"[2]. An attempt has been made here to focus on Sri Ramakrishna's philosophical thought at least some main strands of it, as evidenced in his utterances in the '*Gospel*', by relating it to the concepts of Jaina systems of Philosophy.

I

Jainism is among the oldest and the most influential system of classical Indian thought and religious practice. In its classical form it constitute one of the major systems of Hindu philosophy, and its influence has been pervasive throughout Indian culture.

When we say that the Jaina is a system of Indian philosophy, we use the term 'system' in this way: the Sanskrit term that we have chiefly in mind is *darsana*. A *darsana* is literally a 'vision', an event of 'seeing'; but, more figuratively, it has traditionally been used to mean a worldview or systematic attempt to represent how reality is. Thus a *darsana* can be said to be a philosophy, or a philosophical viewpoint or system. The Jaina philosopher Haribhadra Suri first uses the term '*darsana*' in this technical sense[3]. In philosophical discussion in India this term '*darsana*' has come to be used in this sense since then.

The Indian philosophical tradition known as Jaina has attracted less attention from scholars than other systems of thought, such as Vedanta.

II

Bimal Krishna Matilal, in his book *Logic, Language and Reality* says, 'the unique contribution of Jainism to the philosophic tradition of India consists in its doctrine of *anekântavâda*'[4]. According to some distinguished Jaina scholars the propounders of different systems of philosophy being dogmatic in their assertions produced bitterness among themselves. The age-old theoretical disputes and controversies between these various philosophical schools were on account of their conditional assertion in regard to philosophical propositions. On account of their unbending attitude, no school really tried to realize the viewpoints of others, which gave rise to hatred and enmity towards other systems of thought. This was also a kind of intellectual intolerance and violence in the realm of thought. To avoid such kind of intellectual violence Jaina thinkers evolved a unique, synthetic, philosophical methodology, which is technically known as *anekântavâda* i.e., doctrine of many-sidedness of reality.

The *anekânta* philosophy, in fact, is a *philosophy of synthesis*, a philosophy of integrated approach to different ontological standpoints. Conflicting philosophical theories are treated by the Jaina philosophers as viewing the same reality from different points of view. Reality has infinite characters, and it can be viewed from different standpoints. According to the Jaina thinkers, truth can be grasped only by affirming, integrating and synthesizing all the opposite viewpoints in regard to the same real. 'Truth is one and there are various ways of approaching it' -this is really a great truth propounded by the doctrine of *anekântavâda* which leads us to understand the truth comprehensively and at the same time shows the liberal and all –compromising spirit of Jainism.

Anekântavâda is regarded as the central philosophy of Jainism. This is a theory of many-sidedness of reality and truth. The law of *anekântavâda* affirms that there is no opposition between the unity of being and plurality of aspects. The identity of real is not contradicted by the possession of varying attributes.

The synoptic presentation of reality by *anekântavâda* gives a true picture of reality in all its aspects and that is the essence of the Jaina outlook, which helps to remove the intellectual cobwebs arising out of *ekânta*. H. M. Bhattacharyya in his article *The Anekântavâda of the Jainism* says[5], *anekântavâda* is a fundamental doctrine, which forms the keynote to the philosophy of the Jainas. *Anekântavâda* or the doctrine of many-sidedness of reality of the Jainas is a distinctive contribution to Indian thought in so far as realistic metaphysics and epistemology are concerned.

The *anekânta* theory is the heart of Jaina ontology, epistemology and logic. It claims the many-sidedness of reality, its knowledge and its verbal expression. If reality is infinitely manifold logically there must be infinite ways of intellectually cognizing it and verbally expressing its infinite aspects. This presupposition enables one to harmonize various apparently contradictory descriptions of reality into one.

The approach of *anekânta* theory is based on the acceptance of the manifoldness of reality or in other words, acceptance of the fact that every proposition or thesis has many aspects - all of which have some element of truth from different standpoints. As such a philosophical proposition or metaphysical thesis can be true if it is viewed from a particular standpoint. Therefore, the doctrine of non-one-sidedness not only tolerates the view point of the opposite side, but also tries to understand the basis or standpoints of the divergent propositions with a view to reconcile the apparent contradictions.

Anekântavâda is an attempt to reconcile the so called different and opposite points of view by understanding them and as such it is rightly called a doctrine of synthesis and assimilation as well as toleration and understanding. This takes us to the philosophic source or origin of this doctrine which lies in the concept of non-violence of Jainism and which was responsible to a great extent for the development of non-one-sided approach — *anekânta* attitude in Jaina Philosophy'.

The doctrine of *anekântavâda* finds the most important place in Jainism. It is the foundation-stone of other theories of the Jaina philosophy.

III

Among the Jaina philosophers of this period of transition, *Âcârya* Umâsvâti (1-85 AD) stands as the first and foremost figure. His *Tattvârtha Sûtra* with *Svopajña Bhâsya* is a compendium of the *âgamas*, which leaves nothing of philosophical importance out of consideration. Nathmal Tatia says[6], Umâsvâti gives a critical shape to the *anekântavâda* through his exposition of the *nayas*, *nik?epas* and the nature of the '*sat*' (a real), and *dravya* (substance). He also introduces the elements of *saptabha?gî* in his own way.

Umâsvâti's definition of the '*sat*' (a real) as consisting of origination, cessation and permanence (*utpâda-vyâyadhrauvya-yukta? sat*[7]) gives the fundamentals of *anekântavâda* in a nutshell.

Siddhasena Divakara (5th Cent.), the author of *Sanmatitarka-prakara?a*, and *Nyâyâvatâra*. The application of the *anekânta* principle to ontological problems raised most probably, for the first time by Siddhasena Divâkara in his book *Nyâyâvatâra* and *Sanmatitarka prakarana.*

Siddhasena in his book *Nyâyâvatâra* says:

> *Anekântâtmâkam vastu gocarah sarvasamvidam*
> *Ekadesavisistohartho nayasya visayo matah*[8]

'Since a thing has infinite characters, it is a comprehended only by the omniscient. But a thing becomes the subject matter of a *naya,* when it is conceived from one particular standpoint '. Interesting is his following statement of *Sanmatitarka* :

> *jâvaiya vayanavaha tavaiya ceva homti nayavaya*
> *jâvaiya nayavaya tavaiya cevâ parasamaya.*[9]

'there are as many views of the form of *nayas* as there are the ways of speaking, while there are as many non-Jaina rival philosophical tenets as there are views of the form of *nayas*'. Again he declares :

> *niyayavayanijjasacca savvanaya paraviyalane moha*
> *Te una na ditthasamayo vibhayai sacce vâ aliya vâ*[10]

'All the standpoints (*nayas*) are right in their own respective spheres – but if they are taken to be refutations, each of the other, then they are wrong. But a man who knows the 'non-onesided' (*anekânta*) nature of reality never says that a particular view is absolutely wrong'.

Jainism through its philosophy of *anekânta*, inculcates in its followers the spirit of tolerance for all religions. Haribhadra, the great Jaina *âcâryya*, has tried to show that there is no essential difference between one religion and another. As there is no controversy regarding the highest goal of all religions, there should be none regarding the path leading to that goal. He says that the same truth is expressed by different terms in different religions. Thus the self-same principle of consciousness is known as *purusa* in the Vedanta, *paramâtman* in the Jaina system, *ksetravit* in the Sâmkhya discipline, *jñâna* in the Buddhist school. Similarly, the fundamental ground of worldly existence is known as *avidyâ* in the Vedanta and the Buddhist system. Moreover, the relation between matter and spirit is known as *bhrânti* in the Vedanta and Buddhist system, *pravrtti* in the Sâmkhya School, and *bandhana* in the Jaina system. There is thus fundamental unity among all the apparently conflicting systems of thought. Nathamal Tatia says, there ought to be no real controversy among them about the fundamental things[11]. Truth is truth. It is our different ways of looking at it that is responsible for the building up of different systems. For a spiritual aspirant it is necessary to avoid controversy and strive for self-realization.

IV

Following the method of *anekânta*, the mystic saint Œri Ramakrishna Paramahamsa (1836-1886), fought against all sectarian doctrines and dogmas; yet at the same time, he showed that all sects and creeds were but the paths which lead sincere and earnest souls to the one universal goal of all religions[12]. For the first time it was absolutely demonstrated by Sri Ramakrishna that all religions are like so many paths leading to the same goal, that the realization of the same Almighty Being is the highest Ideal of Cristianity, Mohammedanism, Judaism, Zoroastrianism, Hinduism, as well as of all other religions of the world. He had tried successively Hindu, Muslim and Christian symbols as means of his *sâdhanâ*, and compared in a parable the various religions to the *ghâts* (banks or bathing places) around the same tank[13]. The Muslims take water from one *ghât* and call it *'pâni'*, while the Hindus taking water from another *ghât*, call it *'jal'*, and the Christians use a third *ghât* and take what they call 'water'. Though names are different, it is the same water. Sri ramakrishna's mission was to proclaim the eternal Truth that God is one but has many aspects, and that the same one God is worshipped by different nations under various names and forms; that He is personal, impersonal and beyond both; that He is with name and form and yet nameless and formless[14].

The idea of universal religion is not something new in Sri Ramakrishna's thought. We may see how ancient Indian thought took a great step towards religious harmony when it discovered the One God of whom all other gods are but manifestations. This is the great idea embodied in the famous verse of the RgVeda: "*Ekam sat vipra bahudha vadanti*" —Truth is one; sages call it by various names. The oneness of all existence is the message which also teaches by the Vedanta philosophy.

Swami Vivekananda also spreads this doctrine of the equality of all religions and expected a universal religion all-over the world. Religions are like various rivers all leading to the sea. He said: 'there never was my religion or yours, my national religion or your national religion; there never existed many religions, there is only the one. One infinite religion existed all through eternity and will ever exist, and this religion is expressing itself in various ways'[15]. like 'so many rivers, having their source in different mountains, roll down, crooked or straight, and at last come to the ocean – so all these various creeds and religions, taking their start from different standpoints at last come unto thee'[16]. This is the concept of tolerance embodied in Indian culture. Jaina doctrine of non-onesidedness (*anekânta*) provides a strong philosophical support to the concept of tolerance.

V

Sri Ramakrishna's Philosophy and Samkhya Philosophy

Samkhya is among the oldest and the most influential system of classical Indian thought and religious practice. In its classical form it constitute one of the six major systems of Hindu philosophy, and its influence has been pervasive throughout Indian culture.

When we say that the Samkhya is a system of Indian philosophy, we use the term 'system' in this way: the Sanskrit term that we have chiefly in mind is *darsana*. A *darsana* is literally a 'vision', an event of 'seeing'; but, more figuratively, it has traditionally been used to mean a worldview or systematic attempt to represent how reality is. Thus a *darsana* can be said to be a philosophy, or a philosophical viewpoint or system. The Jaina philosopher Haribhadra Suri first use the term '*darsana*' in this technical sense[17]. In philosophical discussion in India this term '*darsana*' has come to be used in this sense since then.

The Indian philosophical tradition known as Samkhya has attracted less attention from scholars than other systems of thought, such as Vedanta.

Mikel burley says, 'the prototypical Indian philosophy is often taken in the West to be some kind of monism, yet Samkhya is an uncompromisingly dualist system that upholds an ontological distinction between self and 'matter' or 'nature'. Furthermore, it is one of the earliest traditions to offer a description of human experience; how contact with the world through the senses occurs, and how this contact is processed through our mental apparatus'[18].

Samkhya system is metaphysically dualist. it hold that reality comprises two mutually irreducible entities (or 'substances' or 'principles'). One of them being what Samkhya generally calls the 'self' (*Purusa*) and Yoga calls the 'seer' (*drastr*), and the other being what Samkhya generally calls *Prakrti* and Yoga calls the 'seeable' (*drsya*).

Purusa is the principle of subjectivity or consciousness. Only in its presence can experience take place. There is a multiplicity – indeed, an infinity – of *Purusas*, which in themselves are numerically distinct despite being qualitatively indistinguishable from one another. *Prakrti* is the principle of objectivity and materiality. It comprises three co-essential constituents or, more literally, 'strands' (*gunas*).When these are undisturbed and in equal tension with one another, *Prakrti* remains unmanifest (*avyakta*). When they are disturbed and out of equilibrium, *Prakrti* becomes manifest (*vyakta*). It is normally assumed that *Prakrti* is singular[19].

To explain the concept of Ultimate Reality, Sri Ramakrishna uses the concepts of *Purusa* and *Prakrti* but these concepts do not seem, on the face of it, to be exactly like the concepts of *Purusa* and *Prakrti* of Samkhya Philosophy. According to Sri Ramakrishna the reality is one and only one. According to him, the Brahma and its primal energy, both are the two aspects of the same reality. The same reality assumes different forms and performs different functions. He says: "nothing exists except the one. That one is the supreme Brahman. That which is Brahman is also the primal energy. Brahman and the primal energy at first appear to be two. But after attaining the knowledge of *Brahman* one does not see the two. Then there are no differentiations. It is one, without a second"[20].

In Samkhya philosophy the *Purusa* is inactive and the *Prakrti* is active, is energy. While in Sri Ramakrishna's thought, there is no two, but only one the ultimate reality. He expresses it in this way: "when the reality appears as the creator, preserver and the destroyer, we call it *Sakti*; when it is inactive, we call it Brahman. But reality is one and the same thing indivisible"[21]. Through using the philosophical terms of Samkhya tradition, he explains: "he who is Brahman is the *Adyasakti*, the primordial energy. When inactive he is called Brahman the *Purusa*. He is called *Sakti* or *Prakrti* when he is in creation, preservation or destruction. There are the two aspects of reality: *Purusa* and *Prakrti*. He who is the *Purusa* is also the *Prakrti*. Both are the embodiment of bliss"[22].

Thus it is seen that the concepts of *Purusa* and the *Prakrti* are different from those Samkhya philosophy in Sri Ramakrishna's thinking. In Samkhya the *Purusa* indicates the self, while in Sri Ramakrishna's thought, *Purusa* is one aspect of the ultimate reality. In the same way, In Samkhya philosophy, the *Prakrti* is inert, while in Sri Ramakrishna's thought *Prakrti* is one aspect of the ultimate reality. And that itself becomes the world. As Sri Ramakrishna says: "the *Citsakti, Mahamaya* has become the twenty-four cosmic principle[23]" and that "it is the primordial power that has become the world and all living beings[24]".

There is a surreptitious push of monism or some kind of concealed monism in samkhya,.

Samkhya *Satkâryavâda* and Sri Ramakrishna

Sri Ramakrishna explained the nature of God as the metaphysical ground of the universe. He says "It is a case of involution and evolution". Though this universe exist in and through God, it is not true to say from the point of view of Sri Ramakrishna that, it has been brought into existence 'ex nihilo' at a particular time. Like Samkhya philosophy Sri Ramakrishna accepts *Satkâryavâda* and emphasizes the ultimate identity of cause and effect. It follows from this that there is no absolute beginning of anything. What is called creation is really evolution, actualization of the potential. Thus According to Sri Ramakrishna the universe is not created but 'evolved from *Mahâmâyâ'* or *Sakti.* Thus Sri Ramakrishna believes in the theory of *Satkâryavâdâ* in respect of the creation of the world. The theory of *Satkâryavâdâ* in the Samkhya the evolution is possible through the existence of *Prakrti*, what is different from *Purusa*. While in Sri Ramakrishna's philosophy the *Purusa* (Brahman) and *Prakrti* (*Sakti*) are identical. To explain the process of evolution, Sri Ramakrishna said "all elements finally merge in *Akâsa*. Again at the time of creation *Akâsa* evolves into *Mahat* and *Mahat* into *Ahamkâra*. In this way the whole world system is evolved. It is process of the involution and evolution"[25].

Thus according to Sri Ramakrishna, "*Kâli* is none other than *Brahman*, that which is called *Brahman* is really *Kâli*. She is the primal energy. When that energy remains inactive, I call it *Brahman* and when it creates or preserves or destroys, I call it *Sakti* or *Kâli*. What you call *Brahman* I call *Kâli*. *Brahman* and *Kâli* are not different"[26].

In this way, when we try to describe the philosophical position of Sri Ramakrishna, and if we carefully analyze the Gospel we will find that he accepts Monism whether qualified or absolute. The dualism between God or *Brahman* and the World exist for man at a lower level of his consciousness, but the dualism is superseded, when man attempts the highest level of consciousness or *Samadhi*.

REFERENCES

1. Huxley, Aldous. *The Gospels of Sri Ramakrishna*, foreword, page. v-vi.
2. Tapasyananda, Swami. *Sri Ramakrishna's Thoughts on Man, World and God*, Sri Ramakrishna Math, Mylapore, Madras, 1981, page. Vi.
3. Bhattacharyya, Sibajiban.

4. Matilal, B. K. *Logic, Language and Reality*, Motilal Banarasidass, Delhi, 1997, p. 301.
5. Bhattacharyya, H. M. '*The Anekântavâda of the Jainas*', in *Encyclopedia of Jainism*, Vol.1, Anmol Pub., New Delhi, 2001, p. 162.
6. Tatia. Dr. Nathmal, *Anekânta,* In Sancheti Asoo Lal & Bhandari manak Lal,(ed.) *First steps to Jainism* (part II), Sumcheti Trust, Jodhpur, 1994, p. 110.
7. Tatia, Nathamal, *Umâsvâti's Tattvârthasûtra That which is,* Motilal Banarasidass, Delhi, 2007, verse 5.29.
8. *Nyâyavatâra of Siddhasena Divâkara,* ed. by Satis Chandra Vidyabhusana, reprinted, Sanskrit Book Dipot, Calcutta, 1981, Verse. 29, p. 23.
9. Sanghvi Pandit Sukhalalji & Doshi, Bechardas. (edited) *Sanmati Tarka of Siddhasena Divâkara,* tr. by A. S. Gopani, Sri Jain Swetambara Education Board, Bombay, 1939. Reprinted in L. D. Institute of Indology, Ahmedabad, 2000. Verse 3..47, p.120-121.
10. Sanghvi Pandit Sukhalalji & Doshi, Bechardas. (edited) *Sanmati Tarka of Siddhasena Divâkara,* tr. by A. S. Gopani, Sri Jain Swetambara Education Board, Bombay, 1939. Reprinted in L. D. Institute of Indology, Ahmedabad, 2000. Verse 1.28, p.22-23.
11. Tatia, Nathmal. *Lectures on Jainism*, University of Madras, Madras, 1988, P. 9.
12. Abhedananda, Swami. "*Sri Ramakrishna: the Great Saint of Modern India*", in *Studies on Sri Ramakrishna*, The Ramakrishna Mission Institute of Culture, Calcutta, 1988, P. 13.
13. Gupta, Mahendra Nath. *The Gospels of Sri Ramakrishna*, tr. by Swami Nikhilananda, Sri Ramakrishna Math, Mylapore, Madras, 1981, p. 151.
14. Abhedananda, Swami. "*Sri Ramakrishna: the Great Saint of Modern India*", in *Studies on Sri Ramakrishna*, The Ramakrishna Mission Institute of Culture, Calcutta, 1988, P. 15.
15. Vivekananda, Swami. *The Complete Works*, Vol. IV, Advaita Ashrama, Kolkata, 1973, p. 180.
16. Vivekananda, Swami. *The Complete Works,* Vol. I, Advaita Ashrama, Kolkata, 1973, p. 390.
17. Bhattacharyya, Sibajiban.
18. Burley, Mikel. *Classical Samkhya And Yoga An Indian Metaphysics Of Experience*, Routledge, New York, 2007, preface.
19. Burley, Mikel. *Classical Samkhya And Yoga An Indian Metaphysics Of Experience*, Routledge, New York, 2007, p. 74
20. Gupta, Mahendra Nath. *The Gospels of Sri Ramakrishna*, tr. by Swami Nikhilananda, Sri Ramakrishna Math, Mylapore, Madras, 1981, page. 242

21. Gupta, Mahendra Nath. *The Gospels of Sri Ramakrishna*, tr. by Swami Nikhilananda, Sri Ramakrishna Math, Mylapore, Madras, 1981, page. 567.
22. Gupta, Mahendra Nath. *The Gospels of Sri Ramakrishna*, tr. by Swami Nikhilananda, Sri Ramakrishna Math, Mylapore, Madras, 1981, page. 321
23. Gupta, Mahendra Nath. *The Gospels of Sri Ramakrishna*, tr. by Swami Nikhilananda, Sri Ramakrishna Math, Mylapore, Madras, 1981, page. 291
24. Gupta, Mahendra Nath. *The Gospels of Sri Ramakrishna*, tr. by Swami Nikhilananda, Sri Ramakrishna Math, Mylapore, Madras, 1981, page. 343
25. Gupta, Mahendra Nath. *The Gospels of Sri Ramakrishna*, tr. by Swami Nikhilananda, Sri Ramakrishna Math, Mylapore, Madras, 1981, page. 395
26. Gupta, Mahendra Nath. *The Gospels of Sri Ramakrishna*, tr. by Swami Nikhilananda, Sri Ramakrishna Math, Mylapore, Madras, 1981, page 733.

13

Philosophical treasures in Kathamrita

Mamata Kundu

I

In the quiet temple of Dakshineswar near Kolkata, on the banks of the sacred river Ganga, Sri Ramakrishna lived all the major religions one by one and tasted the truth through all of them. By the year 1875, he had finished the experiments and very soon, he came in to intimate contact with the thought currents and aspirations of Renascent India through Keshab Chandra Sen and the Brahmo samaj. For the next eleven years, till his entering in to mahasamadhi or final passing away in 1886, he was constantly pouring forth in simple words and rich eloquence, with the aid of stories and parables, the great truths he had realized, and hundreds of men and women, educated and unlettered, young and old, were his listeners. All these teachings were recorded by Sri Mohendra nath Gupta (Sri 'M'), the direct disciple of Sri Ramakrishna and Saradamani which ultimately were published in the book form 'The Gospel of Ramakrishna' in English and 'Kathamrita ' in Bengali. Kathamrita literally means those types of stories and words which are good as well as amrita (nectar).It is highly accepted by the readers all over the world for its colloquial language and for its techniques of expressing eternal truths of profound philosophy in a very simple manner through analogies and metaphors. Sri Ramakrishna is an ocean of knowledge where devotion and truth are mingled. The truth he realized was spontaneously expressed through his words, the words of all morals of our lives and our spiritual path for the attainment of God. The world has heard this teaching before, but his teaching made a vast difference; for 'he spoke as one with authority and not as the scribes.'

In this age of very critical situation we often question ourselves, 'do we survive?' or 'do we continue as species?' as the diminishing culture of our moral and spiritual life causes our destruction from all concerns and we find no more ways of coming out of this crisis. But if we go ahead we may be hopeful about the fact that life enhancing concepts will guide our world and a new world culture will be established on earth. Character and virtue are the essential means by which humanity will build its sustainable, synergetic society on truthful education for adults and youths alike. Kathamrita is an eternal source of a new world culture based on ethics and philosophy of value and harmony. A tree is to be judged by its best fruits, the fruit of Kathamrita is sainthood which is character and character which is sainthood. Judged by this standard, we shall find that all religions have produced men and women of the most exalted character and saintliness. To be religious , therefore, according to Sri Ramkrishna , is to struggle to realize God; nothing more and nothing less. All his teachings lead us to grow to be more human and perfect being.

II

'The Gospel of Sri Ramkrishna' by Sri 'M' has the mighty power to lead the religious movement in India in 19th century in more advanced stage with the help of spiritual awakening of people due to which they realized the need of one universal religion humanistic in character. Ramakrishna Paramahansa appeared as a unique personality in India for his simplicity, broadmindedness and his vision of truth. His teachings paved the way for universal religion what India needed at that time to abolish the conflicts regarding disharmony in religions. Values and harmony in all phases of lives are pointed out as the pivotal point of progress of the nation, of the world which ultimately leads to peace. The words of the 'Gospel' reflect the truths where we find the spirit of our traditional religion of the past has been nicely combined with the modern new out look. The scientific temper, rationalistic out look, humanistic approach and belief in secularism of the west have been associated with the spiritualistic temper, intuitive approach, divine humanism and belief in sacredness of the East. The need of the synthesis of the east and the West has been realized by Ramakrishna in his direct experience and it was declared by Vivekananda in the world meeting.[1] Here synthesis of all religions and all thoughts of both old and new, east and west and sacred and secular has been proved and established in a spontaneous way. It is the result of living experience of truth by the seer, the great thinker in modern India. In the words of Sri Nemai Sadhan Bose, "Before Ramakrishna, Rammohan, Devendranath and Keshab Chandra Sen had striven to build up a unity. But the synthesis of Ramakrishna was spontaneous and the direct result of the light of knowledge and vivid realization."[2]

The blending of ancient and modern, spirit and matter, sacred and secular becomes a new construction of some living principles which points out one reality to realize in our actual life. Thus the Advaita Vedanta of Sankaracharya which was so long purely theoretical possessing negative attitude to the world became enriched with some new ideals highly significant for man's life and became converted in to practical Vedanta. In this great work of re-interpreting Vedanta in a practical way and convincing people what religion is, "Ramakrishna was the spirit and Vivekananda his voice. Ramakrishna was the realization and Vivekananda the actualization. Ramakrishna was the messiah and Vivekananda was his messenger."[3]

Ramakrishna's experiment with forms of religious life according to Hinduism, Islam and Christianity is a great challenge against the camouflage of religion in dogmas, rituals and ceremonies. He points out the essence regarding which all religions are true. One may be a Christian, a Mohammedan, or a Hindu but all will meet at a point of perfection. In his words, "There are several bathing ghats in a large tank. Who ever goes to whichever ghat he pleases to take a bath or to fill his vessel riches the water, and it is useless to quarrel with one another claiming one's ghat to be better than another's. Similarly there are many ghats that lead to the water of the fountain of Eternal Bliss. Every religion of the world is one ghat. Go direct with a sincere and earnest heart through any one of these ghats, and you shall reach the water of Eternal Bliss. But say not that your religion is better than that of another."[4] From these words it is very clearly seen that Ramakrishna revitalized all religions, respected each for its uniqueness and found out harmony of all religions. He not only says that all religions are ways of attaining truth but emphasizes on the point that all religions are true; neither of them is false. Religious harmony as realized by Ramakrishna is somehow different from that of others. There are several types of religious harmony. There is synergetic harmony in which all religions are united by ignoring differences, a harmony epitomized in the new, common slogan 'all religions reach the same thing' etc. There is eclectic harmony in which best parts of each religion are taken and combined into a new system. Ramakrishna was neither of these.[5] He did not teach the sameness of religions, but the uniqueness of each path was realized by him, he gave equal respect to all religions. Universality lies in his regard of oneness of truth.' Truth is one though its facets are many' has been echoed by him several times. Each religion with its particular name has its own distinctive value which may not be ignored. Harmony of religions is based on the experience of oneness of truth and for this reason it is an experimental fact more than a logical deduction.

But unique individuality of each religion does not indicate that it should be exclusive in character. Rather all religions are intimately related to each other to share all growth and all learning though they have their own independent existence. For this reason they all should be equally respected .It shows that each religion by itself if followed sincerely respects the vision of the one God of many faces. [6]

It is evident that religious tolerance as we find in Asia is different from that of Europe. In this concern Europe is not founded upon the belief that all religions are true but rather founded on a growing indifference to all religious doctrines. [7] The advantages of Asian thought are that here theology and the symbolic peculiarities of each faith are not suppressed. Tolerance if sought through suppression of theology leads to construct a new faith, a secular and worldly one, but it affords no genuine religious satisfaction. Religious tolerance should be spontaneous and be based on the living experience of oneness of truth. Because Truth has no geographical boundary, has no frontier. The great contribution of Ramakrishna high lights on this point that all religions as ways to reach the goal are neither false nor inferior to others. In his words, "God is Infinite……. Infinite are the ways."[8] Religions differ from each other regarding non essentials but in essentials they are all one. Religion does not mean the doctrine, dogmas or creeds. They are of no avail in the pursuit of truth. Truth is itself inexpressible in nature. Dogmas are superficial aspects of religion and hence should be regarded as non essentials of religion while the manifestation of truth is the essential core of religion. This we find in Ramakrishna's teaching, " Do not care for the doctrines, do not care for dogmas or sects or churches or temples. They can not for little be compared with the essence of existence in each man, which is spirituality and the more this is developed in a man the more powerful is he for good. Earn that first, acquire that and criticize no one; for all doctrines and creeds have some good in them. Show by your lives that religion does not mean words or names or sects, but that it means spiritual realization."[9]

III

The whole of the Upanishadic philosophy has been substantiated by Ramakrishna without having studied them. Even he did not learn them from any teacher. Ramakrishna's thoughts are the living representation of truth based on his direct realization. Regarding the nature of Brahman whether it is saguna or nirguna controvery arises between Advaitavada of Sankara and Visistadvaitavada of Ramanuja as we often meet with the Vedic texts which are indicatives to Brahman both as having qualification and without qualification. Once it is said, "Sarva karma sarva kamah sarva gandhah"(Chan, 3.14.2) and in another place it has been stated, " atha asthulam ananu" (Brh. 3.8.8). "He is the doer of all good tastes" (Chan,3. 14.2) indicates that Brahman has attributes and texts; " it is neither gross, nor minute, neither short nor long" (Brhd, 3.8.8) and others indicate that it is devoid of attributes.

In order to avoid the contradiction Sankara upholds the view that Brahyman as Ultimate Reality is absolutely unqualified nirvisesa. Brahman can never be admitted as possessed of attributes and also to apprehend both with form and formless leads to a self contradiction. Sankara argues, "the supreme Brahman, considered in itself, can not logically have both the characteristics; for it can not be admitted that the very same thing is naturally possessed of attributes like form etc and it is also without these; for that is self-contradictory."[10] Again in a reply to the opponents, Sankara says that "........ it is Brahman that is absolute less and unchangeable that has to be accepted and not the opposite. For in all texts which aim at presenting the real nature of Brahman, as for instance, is "Soundless, touch less, colourless, undiminishing."[11] (asabdam, asparsam arupam avyayam). Brahman is presented as devoid of all distinguishing attributes.[12]

The Absolute is nirguna; It transcends the gunas or phenomenal being because it is the only principle without a second." Brahman satyam jaganmithya" is the basis of Advaita philosophy. Here the problem arises regarding the validity of the judgment about the false appearance of the world as being accustomed with the planned world we can not ignore its real existence. So there must be a creator of this world. In order to meet with a solution on the basis of Sruti Sankara offers a reconciliation between the negative and positive descriptions of Brahman. While Brahman is devoid of attributes, still those of being, consciousness and bliss may be said to be its essential features (svarupa laksana) and while this highest principle in relation to us be the creator and governor of the universe, the creatorship etc. are described as secondary ones (tatastha laksana). Thus from the lower stand point of view Brahman is determinate or saguna and from transcendental point of view It is nirguna.

Ramakrishna's approach to interpret the nature of ultimate reality is very similar to that of Ramanuja as he says that there is no contradiction between these two aspects of Brahman nirguna and saguna. Ramakrishna realizes that the Ultimate Reality can be comprehended both as nirguna and as saguna, the two aspects of the same Reality. The world, finite beings, mind, intellect, devotion, renunciation and knowledge all are nothing but have their real existence as the wealth of God. So God with qualities (saguna Brahman) is equally real as nirguna Brahman as both are one and same reality. God without any quality con never be known to any body.[13] Ramakriswhna supports Ramanuja for refutation of mayavada. In his words, "It is maya which reveals Brahman. Without Maya who could have known Brahman? Without knowing sakti, the manifested power of God, there is no means of knowing Him."[14] Maya in Ramakrishna's philosophy is the manifested power of God instead of being mere illusion. From his living experience Ramakrishna established the point that God has become every thing in the universe.[15] He was firmly convinced that the world can never be false; rather it is the manifestation of the supreme self on a real background. In his words, just as to find out the total weight of a bel fruit we have to put together its kernel, stones and skin, so to know Brahman or Absolute fully and comprehensively we will have to admit all the revelations.[16] The Absolute is not without phenomenal world but the latter is the manifestation of the former.

Ramakrishna says that maya is evil and entangles us in the world and keeps us in ignorance. Maya also comes from God. It is God's lila (Gospel, P. 161). God has the power of maya where with He creates and sustains the universe. But His maya is a twofold power; it is the power of ignorance as well as the power of knowledge. He on the one hand keeps men in ignorance and on the other the principle of light, i.e., knowledge, which is calculated to lift them out of sense life and lead them eventually to the life of the spirit.[17] It is very significant that good and bad, virtue and vice, real and unreal are only glories of God's maya. It is God who gives us evil as well as good tendencies. In creation there must be honest and dishonest persons, there is light as well as darkness. Evil causes suffering and unhappiness in life and society, but they can be over come through spiritual force of man and for the development of this force we are to follow Sri Ramakrishna's teaching and way of life. Evil in the world is manifested in war, in conflict and in clashes, in struggle and unhappiness; it is also expressed through physical and mental pain, moral sin and social crime. There is feeling of universal anxiety caused by the world affairs. It opposes good, beauty and delights and retards our progress. The way of attaining highest happiness and peace is to overcome ignorance and to reach to true knowledge and to live spiritual life. One lives spiritual life if one, unswayed by sensuous desires, ever aspires to realize God or self. It seems that spiritual life is apart and that it can not be lived in society and the state. One can not attain to life for God or spirit except by renouncing the world. According to Ramakrishna one's mind is covered with sex and wealth and without rejection of them one can not attain God. He adds at the same time that one need not be an ascetic for attaining spiritual life. However he points out that there is no short cut to the spiritual goal. Therefore, the aspirant should not be in a hurry or do any thing at haphazard. He can only proceed towards the realization of his ideal by some stages, which are to be worked out of worldly life itself. But how? Ramakrishna tells us there are infinite paths to God, yoga of knowledge, the yoga of action and the yoga of love and devotion.[18]

Society is a living whole and has its history. From a small beginning society has by stages come to its present state of existence. We are what we are today certainly because of society. It is little wonder that Ramakrishna emphasizes social life and insists on the strict performing of one's duties. He makes an approach to worldly life but on the condition that every one should perform his or her proper functions in life based on truth. The Upanishad says, " Truth shall triumph, not falsehood."[19] Humanity is going from evil to good and so we hear universal prayer from the Rishis—"Lead me from unreal to Real, lead me from darkness to light, and lead me from death to life Immortal."

IV

The humanistic philosophy of Advaita Vedanta is made lived and more practically applicable in the life of man by Ramakrishna whose teachings are not theoretical utterances but living experiments through out his life. From the time of Ramakrishna and Vivekananda many social changes have also been marked. Ramakrishna liberated Hinduism from sectarianism pointing out the basic unity underlying different sects of Hinduism. Asceticism in religious philosophy has been converted in to active service. His humanistic philosophy develops the feeling for the suffering humanity which grew from his unique realization of oneness with all. He had many instances in his life that he realized oneness with the cosmic world and consequently with all living beings. He could not walk on grass, could not pluck flowers from the plant realizing the manifestation of consciousness every where. Another unique feeling Ramakrishna had experienced. Once Sri Ramakrishna was standing on the Ganga near bathing ghat, Dakshineswar, in a high spiritual mood. There was a boat nearby on the river. Two boatmen were then quarreling and came to blows. Ramakrishna felt those blows on his person and cried out of agony. Having heard the cries, Hriday, his attendant, came to him running and clearly saw the scars of the blows on his back.[20]. The universe according to modern science is a manifestation of cosmic energy and the whole universe is dynamic or moving. According to Ramakrishna this energy is not blind or unconscious material energy as modern scientists consider. Rather it is a divine or spiritual energy which vibrates in the heart of every thing. The immanence of this spiritual energy as the soul of everything gives us a new conception of man interpreting the meaning and value of human life in a new light. The spirit which is dynamic in nature is also the essence of man is an inspiring message and sustains us with an inner strength for soul culture. On this basic point Ramakrishna established the Truth'Jiva is Shiva' and 'not mercy but service and service, for man must be regarded as God'. We find the conception in our tradition when the Upanishad said, "Srinvantu Visheve amtritasya Putra' Ramakrishna's realization of living oneness alone can furnish the world with the rationale behind the concept of equality, fraternity and provide it with the basis on which it may build up an edifice of universal brotherhood.

The philosophy of Sri Ramakrishna Paramahansa and his practical ideas relating to individual and society propounded a lot of solutions to safe guard the relations among the people of diverse mentalities. He not only synthesized various religious ideologies but his applied views founded a philosophical as well as ethical bases to uphold real nature of human beings. The real thoughts of Ramakrishna reflected not for time being but for awakening in all the means whatever and how for they are applicable to society in order to prove the nature of human beings. His precepts and practices inspired and enlightened the life and behavior of people and continued to be a beacon light to the humanity and enable them to march towards the real goal of perfection. His practical philosophy is a right, straight and bright route to fulfill the 'summum bonum' of life. His concept of the 'Unity of all Religions' emphasizes on religious tolerance. He preaches universal brotherhood, universal welfare, universal love, universal devotion and catholic and charitable humanistic attitude for the salvation of man and world peace. It denounces sinful activities sinning against religions. It helps to reduce foolish conflicts and confrontation, hatred and jealousy, selfishness and rituals. God manifests in different forms or in no forms to the individuals according to their aspirations. Creeds and paths may differ but spiritual experience is the same.

Sri Ramakrishna is an embodiment of spirituality. Spiritualism in India is not merely an intellectual exercise. It is the way for integral transformation. Spiritual realization does not come through learning grammar and reading books, it comes by total surrender and search for it. He teaches the intrinsic fundamentals of the eternal gospel inherent in the myriad religions. To enter in to spiritual life, one must ardently purify one's self through pure charity, complete devotion to the lord, and love of all creation. The pure and moral life removes all egoism and selfishness and affords the all embracing love of god. Divine life transforms 'human nature' in to 'Divine nature'. Spiritual life is impossible without total commitment to morality, morality means selfless without non attachment and renunciation. The spirit of renunciation is rooted in purity of character, devoted service and complete surrender to God. Through pure renunciation one can have the vision of the Divine. Sri Ramakrishna personifies in himself the highest values of our heritage. He exhorted that people should work for the good of the society without selfishness. The universal outlook of Ramakrishna and his philosophical thought based on spirituality with practical orientation enable people to endure within and expand their tolerance and understanding in the interest of social harmony and peace. The Gospel of Sri Ramakrishna was practical framework of religion which developed practical Vedanta aiming at the real transformation of people to experience social harmony and establish religious tolerance. A new society was visualized based on tolerance and love.

It may be said that the urge for the Supreme is the common factor of all ages. It was realized by the ancient Vedic Rishis as the essence of religion and with an open heart they vested this heritage to the human race. Even today, to our utter astonishment and bewilderment, we find the very urge in every human heart to illuminate the globe and to show a world of bliss over the human race by uniting them in to one and oneness. The attempt to established oneness of truth lies in the attunement of divine plan inspiring man to expand himself through out the world overcoming the limitations of ego is needed in the world as its unique and universal flame cleanses the mankind. Sacrifice, love, and brotherhood develop the inspiring spirit in human race to establish unity in diversity. Difference is there, variation of expression is there and this variation we shall appreciate. Love and hate, admiration and scorn, sympathy and antipathy, attraction and repulsion are various expressions of thoughts and feelings. But behind the variation we shall always see the complete and immutable who dwells within it and we shall feel, know the divine necessity of the particular manifestation whether it appears to our human standards harmonious and perfect or crude and unfinished or even false and evil. Harmony of all concern is the ground for divine manifestation. Musical instruments are the best examples of harmony. Different strings are previously adjusted to certain levels separately first, again they are adjusted together from which a melodious sound comes out. This is called harmony among sound waves vibrated and reflected on different planes. Similarly in human life variation is welcomed because principle of unity and oneness of all lies behind. Sri Aurobindo rightly says, "The quarrel between the individual and society or disastrous struggle between one community and another could not exist; the cosmic consciousness imbedded in embodied beings would assure a harmonious diversity in oneness." The ideal of human unity could not be achieved unless man was sacred to man. The hope of future rests on the evolution of a religion of humanity based on recognition that the inner spirit is one.

The harmony of devotion and reason is the main scientific pursuit of Rabindranath's creation. Rabindranath once said, "If all my creative works sink in to oblivion, my songs will survive." The poet's observation seems to be true. Like many other songs of Tagore, song no. 65 from Gitanjali reveals the greatest findings of modern science. It is harmony and important keynote in poet's creation. Modern Science, particularly modern Physics has proved beyond doubt the inherent harmony of nature. Harmony is not uniformity, it is not identity. It is not oneness without a second, but oneness with a second. Harmony between two entities gives continuums without losses of their identity, i.e., the two is distinguishable but inseparable. The two more successful theories of Physics developed in the last century. The Theory of Relativity and the Theory of Quantum Mechanics explained respectively the phenomenal world and sub-atomic world. Theory of Relativity proved conclusively the harmony of space and time, matter and energy whereas the harmony of particle and wave is the foundation of Quantum Mechanics. The two theories have also brought immense benefit to mankind. Harmony is a tested truth. It develops in human plane; the harmony will pave the way for peace in our strife-torn world today. The song " Seemar maje asim tumi bajao apan sur, amar modhay tomar prakash tai ato madhur". (Oh! Limitless play your tune in the midst of all limits. Your revelation within me is therefore is so sweet) displays the harmony between limit and limitless. The manifestation of God in man makes the harmony so sweet. Limit and limitless are distinguishable but inseparable. Man and his divinity within are inseparable. The nest and the sky are both indispensible for a bird. The two are inseparable in a true bird's life. [21]

Ramakrishna's whole life was a living embodiment of peace, love and harmony. So we can not be unmindful of this simple but extra ordinary man of faith, a man of God. He is a beacon light which can best guide humanity out of darkness caused by the forces of communalism, sectarianism, regionalism and above all fundamentalism. Our world at the present day faces some dangers and difficulties and we can get rid of them if we follow Ramakrishna's teachings of equality, tolerance and love. Teachings of Kathamrita are very appropriate to prevent the present situational crisis spread all over the world. Peaceful environment has to be created; it is essential for our progress, peace and happiness, which is our end. Indeed an international society is our goal to which we are moving. We cannot reverse the process of history. Our crisis is not only social, economic, political and other but it is moral and spiritual too. Science though greatly advanced cannot overcome the crisis as it has neglected spirituality and so can not enjoy peace. Sri Ramakrishna's lofty ideas of spiritual consciousness, unity of existence, love, tolerance and honor to all religions, cultures and Communities, if materialized, will save the world full of strife and conflicts. Sri Ramakrishna has given humanity a message of hope and vision which are too precious to be forgotten. He has a message of lasting values for the modern man. So his teachings have acquired a new relevance today and they will be relevant in the time to come. We will have to develop a cosmic consciousness and world view for our global peace. This can be affected by following Ramakrishna teaching, ethical, psychological, and spiritual. Prof. Arnold Toynbee says that "the art of contemplation is really another name for the art of living. This spiritual gift that makes man human is still alive in Indian souls. Nothing else can do so much to help mankind to save itself from self destruction." [22] Our motto is 'live and let live;' 'Vasudhaiva Kutumbakam' . Our highest good is ' let all be happy, let all be healthy'. Sarve Sukhinah bhavantu.

REFERENCES

1. Christopher Isherwood. Vedanta for modern man. George Allen and Unwin Ltd. Ruskin House, Museum Street, London. 1952. P-132
2. Nemai Sadhan Bose. Indian Awakening and Bengal. Firma K.L. Mukhopadhyaya, 257-B, B.B. Ganguly Street, Calcutta. 1976.P-180
3. Swami Siddhinathananda. " Sri Ramakrishna and Vivekananda." The Vedanta Kesari. Sri Ramakrishna Matha. Madras. July,1975. Vol. LXII No. 3, P-91.
4. Sayings of Sri Ramakrishna. Sri Ramakrishna Matha, Madras. 1975. PP-148-149.
5. Ramakrishna Matha and Mission Convention. 1980. PP-65-66.
6. Ibid.
7. Coomerswamy, Selected papers on Metaphysics. Ed. Roger Lipsy. Bollongn Series, LXXXIX. Princeton University Press. 1977. P-35.

8. S.C. Chatterjee. Classical Indian Philosophies. University of Calcutta. 1963. P-148.
9. What Religion is in the words of Swami Vivekananda. Ed. Swami Vidyatmananda. P-333
10. Brahmasutra Bhasya of Sri Sankaracharya. Tr. Swami Gambhirananda. Advaita Ashrama,5, Dehi Entally Road. Calcutta. 1965. P-609.
11. Katha Upanishad. 1.3.15
12. Brahmasutra Bhasya of Sri Sankaracharya, Tr. Swami Gambhirananda. Advaita Ashrama, Calcutta. 1965. PP-609-610.
13. Sri Sri Ramakrishna Kathamrita (Bengali) Ed. by Sri 'M', Guruprasad Chowdhury Lane, Calcutta. 1388 (Bengali). Vol. 3. P-10
14. Sayings of Sri Ramakrishna. Sri Ramakrishna Matha, Madras.1975.P-42.
15. Sri Sri Ramakrishna Kathamrita. Ed. Sri 'M'.(Bengali).Guru Prasad Chowdhury Lane,Calcutta.1388(Bengali). Vol. 3 P-249.
16. Ibid. Vol. 4. P-32.
17. A.C.Das. Studies in Philosophy. Firma K.L.Mukhopadhayay. Calcutta .1962. PP-96-97.
18. Sri Sri Ramakrishna Kathamrita. (Bengali). I,XI, 4.
19. Mundaka Upanishad. I:16
20. Swami Saradananda. Sri Sri Ramakrishna Lila Prasanga. Udbodhan Karyalaya. Calcutta. 1973. Part-I, P-312.
21. Gobinda Chandra Bandopadhayay. "In search of science awareness in Rabindranath Tagore." Culture and Quest on World Thinkers' and Poets' Peace Meet-2010. ISISAR, Kolkata. Ed. Dr. S.N.Chattopadhayay.
22. Arnold Toyenbee. One World and India, Indian Council for cultural Relations. New Delhi.

14

Sri Ramakrishna and Sri Aurobindo : Towards a new spirituality

Goutam Ghosal

The new spirituality breaks away from the older schools with its rejection of the priest cult, religionism, divisionism and needless superstitions. It accept the value of the individual as the most important factor in the growth of society, in a new nationalism in India as a condition for global development, the importance of the rise of the proletariat against the domination of the upper classes (which of course is no more relevant in 2015) and above all in Mother-worship, which alone has the power to lift humanity to the supreme heights.

Sri Aurobindo, then Aurobindo Ghose, the revolutionary leader of Bengal since he took over the editorship of Bandemataran in 1906, was more devoted to Sri Ramakrishna than to Vivekananda. He had a profound respect for the great Swami, but Sri Ramakrishna was his ultimate choice because of his integral acceptance of life and the spirit. All the three were mother-worshippers, but Sri Ramakrishna was an epitome of complete life, complete experience, a person of supreme realisation, which connects Matter and the Spirit. And it was this completeness, which drew Aurobindo Ghose to the priest of Dakhsineswar. 1893 was a significant year. Aurobindo Ghose was returning from the West and Vivekananda was going to the West. The country was bubbling over with the spirit of new nationalism mixed up with the element of Mother-Worship. Sri Ramakrishna had passed away in 1889 leaving in the native air a strong essence of Mother-Worship. Bankim Chandra Chatterjee died in 1894. Both Sri Ramakrishna and Bankim Chandra insisted on integral living, leaving no corner of life untouched.

Aurobindo Ghose who was frantically trying to re-Indianise himself in 1893, embraced the culture created by the joint influence of Sri Ramakrishna and Bankim Chandra. In all the three, and four if we include the great Swami, there was a strong stress on a re-discovery of the native tradition, a stress on the value of native tradition, a memory of the ancient Indian scriptures and literatures. And all of them was seeking to find a contemporary relevance of the old texts. It is a mistake to believe that Sri Ramakrishna was uneducated. He learnt texts through his ears, and he had an uncanny memory of what he had heard from the speakers in the temples and the playhouses. His was a very perceptive mind, a creative consciousness, which could relate with a remarkable accuracy. His eyes on life and nature were almost Shakespearean, *Virat* and *Hiranyagarbha,* the gross exterior and the luminous inside. He spoke literature and his speech style recorded in the *Gospel* is densely allusive, indicating an Emersonian scholarship, which comes through an observation of life and Nature, the great panorama of life and its inner signification. He reached the Essence through all paths, leaving the impression of his versatility on the spiritual tracks to the Infinite. His experience made him tolerant and he could absorb the whole world in his single breast. Unlike Vivekananda, he was a happy soul because nothing was unknown to him. His happiness was the happiness of a complete mastery of the Matter and the Spirit. Aurobindo found in him the perfect predecessor of his philosophy of integral life, a life that embraces all life, from every angle. He was attracted to his purity of life, his *knowledge by identity*, his basic path of knowledge, which moves through the World Mother to the Divine. Not many have noticed that apart from the fact of re-indianising himself, Aurobindo was learning to be strongly anti-intellectual in his personal life, a kind of un-learning or an effort to learn to be simple despite the mad rush of revolutionary activities in Calcutta (1906-1910). One suspects, Sri Ramakrishna was the living example before him of a stark simplicity, as he kept the soil of Dakshineswar close to his head while sleeping on the floor. For Aurobindo, in Calcutta, Dakshineswar was a living image of a sacred life, a flame of aspiration, an ideal of new spirituality. Let us listen to him in the pages of Bandemataram :

> Of all these souls Sri Ramakrishna was the last and greatest, for while others felt God in a single or limited aspect, he felt Him in His illimitable unity as the sum of an illimitable variety. In him the spiritual experiences of the millions of saints who had gone before were renewed and united. Sri Ramakrishna gave to India the final message of Hinduism to the world. A new era dates from his birth, an era in which the peoples of the earth will be lifted for a while into communion with God and spirituality become the dominant note of human life. (SABCL-1:801: 1972)

What is this new spirituality ? One may well ask. Sri Aurobindo has explained it is various ways and at various places. It may be called the 'modernism' or 'postmodernism' in the field of spirituality. An awakened eye looks upon every material aspect with a true attitude. All life becomes the field of yoga and realization. It is a reversal of consciousness. Here is Sri Aurobindo's masterful definition of spirituality in *The Future Poetry* :

> The meaning of spirituality is a new and greater inner life of man founded in the consciousness of his true, his inmost, highest and largest self and spirit by which he receives the whole of existence as a progressive manifestation of the self in the universe and his own life as a field of possible transformation in which its divine sense will be found, its potentialities highly evolved, the now imperfect forms changed into an image of the divine perfection, and an effort not only to see but to live out these greater possibilities of his being. (SABCL9: 251: 1972)

Sri Ramakrishna's life and preachings illustrate this definition. He touched every aspect of life and matter, but he was not attached to anything. *The Gospel* is a living record of his realization. He preaches what he practises :

> Live with all – with wife and children, father and mother – and serve them. Treat them as if they were very dear to you, but know in your heart of hearts that they do not belong to you (*Gospel*: Vol 1: 81: 1985)

The phrase "heart of hearts" stands for what Sri Aurobindo calls the psychic being, the *Purusha Antaratma* of the Upanishads. Both stress on an inner rejection instead of the outward gestures of a monk. The rejection of the lower nature must be integral. All parts of the being should be placed before God for the act of purification. This purification cannot be achieved without the aid of the Divine Shakti, the Divine Mother, who initiates the opening of the *Purusha Antaratma* and remains with the individual to guide him to Superconsciousness. While Sri Ramakrishna metaphorically says, "stick to the pole of the Mother and encirde around it speedily", Sri Aurobindo sheds additional light on the action of the Divine Mother on earth in his great little book, *The Mother* :

> The power that mediates between the sanction and the call is the presence and power of the Divine Mother. The Mother's power and not any human endeavour and tapasya can alone rend the lid and tear the covering and shape the vessel and bring down into this world of obscurity and falsehood and death and suffering truth and light and life divine and the immortal's Ananda. (SABCL 25:41: 1972)

The fusion of the Tantrik cult and the vaishnav cult had first been done by Sri Ramakrishna. Sri Aurobindo carried this modern tradition further ahead. The Mother is the 'magnet' which pulls us up in the ladder of consciousness, towards the Supreme Divine Purushottama. For Sri Ramakrishna, the women must be worshipped as the Divine Mother. For Sri Aurobindo, the purest of Tantrik cult means to elevate woman as an object of profound respect and worship. (SABCL 15:4) Sri Ramakrishna uses "woman and gold" as a singular subject, *Kaminikanchan.*

> 'Woman and gold' alone is the obstacle to yoga. Always analyse what you see. What is there in the body of a woman? Only such things as blood, flesh, fat, entrails and the like. Why should one love such a body? (*Gospel*: 1: 113)

While Sri Aurobindo is as strict as Sri Ramakrishna regarding celibacy, he prescribes another method for the non-attachment to money and women. He simply calls it "attitude". A proper attitude to women, money and all mundane things is needed to practise yoga. But, both of these return to their basic lesson : to aspire to the Supreme Godhead through the World–Mother.

> God has created the world in play, as it were. This is called *Mahamaya* the great illusion. Therefore, one must take refuge in the Divine Mother, the Cosmic Power Itself. It is she who has bound us with shackles of illusion. The realization of God is possible only when those shackles are severed … one must propitiate the Divine Mother, the Primal Energy, in order to obtain God's grace". (*Gospel*: 1: 116)

The aspect of Mother-Worship is the one striking similarity between these two incarnations of the Divine. The next most important resemblance is the stress on surrender or devotion or love, which is the ultimate lesson of the *Gita*. The first and the last word in Sri Aurobindo's yoga is surrender. Sri Ramakrishna had stressed on this element in the *Gospel.*

> Bhakti, love of God, is the essence of all spiritual disciplines. Through love one acquires renunciation and discrimination naturally. (*Gospel*: 1: 123)

Apart from *Essays on the Gita*, *The Synthesis of yoga* is another text where Sri Aurobindo explains in detail the importance of total sacrifice, surrender or love to the Divine.

> It is the inner offering of the heart's adoration, the soul of it in the symbol, the spirit of it in the act, that is the very life of the sacrifice.

> If the offering is to be complete and universal, then a turning of all our emotions to the Divine is imperative. This is the intensest way of purification for the human heart, more powerful than any ethical or aesthetic catharsis could ever by its half-power and superficial pressure. A psychic fire within must be lit into which all is thrown with the Divine Name upon it. In that fire all the emotions are compelled to cast off their grosser elements and those that are undivine perversions are burned away and the others discard their insufficiencies, till a spirit of largest love and a stainless divine delight arises out of the flame and smoke and frankincense. (SABCL 20: 155: 1971)

The ultimate perfection and purification will come through this fire of love for the Divine. Sri Aurobindo's passage has a memory of the Vedic Agni, the purifying five, which comes along with the sacrifice of the baser instincts and an aspiration for true love or devotion. Both Sri Ramakrishna and Sri Aurobindo stress on this element of absolute surrender through love.

Finally, both Sri Ramakrishna and Sri Aurobindo wish to go beyond *Nirvana*, with a positive effort to return to earth for the change of human life. Sri Ramakrishna indicates that after the supreme realization one can do the household duties. The new spirituality is concerned with this earth and not with one's ascent into heaven. The change of an individual consciousness alone has the capacity to change the group, society and the world. The leaders of the future society will come out of an enlargement of human consciousness, an enfoldment of man's highest possibilities, a growth into a divine life on earth, for the benefit of the world. Let us conclude with Sri Aurobindo's masterful summary of Sri Ramakrishna's achievement, which lights up Sri Aurobindo's own efforts.

> … in the life of Ramakrishna Paramahansa, we see a colossal spiritual capacity, first driving straight to the divine realization, taking, as it were, the kingdom of heaven by violence, and then seining upon one yogic method after another and extracting the substance out of it with an incredible rapidity, always to return to the heart of the whole matter, the realization and possession of God by the power of love, by the extension of inborn spirituality into various experience and by the spontaneous play of an intuitive knowledge … its object was … to exemplify in the great and decisive experience of a master-soul the truth, now most necessary to humanity, towards which a world long divided into jarring sects and scholars is with difficulty labouring,

> that all sects are forms and fragments of single integral truth and all disciplines labour in their different ways towards one supreme experience. (on SV and SR: 5: 2003)

Sri Aurobindo has found his guru in the above passage, who had already spoken of integreal spirituality, excluding nothing of the past religious thinkers.

Works Cited and Consulted

1. Sri Aurobindo. *Sri Aurobindo Birth Centenary Library*, Vol-1, Pondicherry: Sri Aurobindo Ashram, 1972, Print.
2. Sri Aurobindo. SABCL, Vol-9, Pondicherry: Sri Aurobindo Ashram, 1972, Print.
3. Swami Nikhilaranda (Trans). *The Gospel of Sri Ramakrishna*, Vol-1, Madras: Sri Ramakrishna Halth, 1985.
4. Sri Aurobindo. SABCL, Vol-25 (*The Mother*) and Vol-15 (*Social Writings*).
5. Sri Aurobindo. SABCL, Vol-20 (*The Synthesis of Yoga*).
6. Swami Ghanananda. *Sri Ramakrishna and His Unique Message*, Kolkata: Advaita Ashrama, 2005. With a Foreword by DR. Arnold J. Toynbee.
7. K.C. Anand (ed). *Swami Vivekananda and Sri Ramakrishna in Sri Aurobindo's Writings*, Pondicherry: Sri Aurobindo Society, 2003.

15 Knowledge within and without: The Gospel of Sri Ramakrishna and the Life Divine

Sarani Ghosal Mondal

Sri Ramakrishna (1836-1886) and Sri Aurobindo (1872-1950) have been the two towering figures of Indian Spirituality. The only difference lies in their cultural background. Sri Ramakrishna hails from a village in West Bengal and his successor hails from a relatively rich family of Kolkata. Sri Ramakrishna did not receive any formal education and once he told his brother, "Brother, what shall I do with a mere bread-winning education?"[1] (*Gospel*, 6) On the other hand, Sri Aurobindo was sent to England for his formal education and he returned to India as an accomplished westerner.

Whatever may be the differences in their cultural background, they reached the summit of spirituality in their own ways. Both of them are intuitive in their approach and their knowledge is experiential. Time and again, Sri Ramakrishna claims his ignorance of scriptures and says, "...believe me, I know nothing about it".[2] (*Gospel*, 33) And he insists on devotion and sincerity towards the Divine.

Sri Aurobindo in *The Life Divine* says, "The sages of the Veda and Vedanta relied entirely upon intuition and spiritual experience. It is by an error that scholars sometimes speak of great debates or discussions in the Upanishad... nowhere in the Upanishads do we find any trace of logical reasoning urged in support of the truths of Vedanta. Intuition, the sages seem to have held, must be corrected by a more perfect intuition; logical reasoning cannot be its judge".[3] (L.D., 75)

Thus, as seekers of the Supreme Light, both of them stressed on intuitive knowledge. Religion and the elaborate rituals are not acceptable to both of them. In the introduction to the *Gospel* and so also in the first chapter entitled "Master and Disciple", Sri Ramakrishna says to M:

> When hearing the name of Hari or Rama once, you shed tears and your hair stands on end, then you may know for certain that you do not have to perform such devotions as the sandhya anymore. Then only will you have a right to renounce rituals; or rather, rituals will drop away themselves. Then it will be enough if you repeat only the name of Rama or Hari, or even simply Om....[4] (*Gospel*,77)

Then again in the same chapter the Master says that God is knowledge and not to know Him is ignorance.[5] (Gospel, 1942, 80) Realisation of the Supreme is all to these inspired sages. Degrees and formal education have nothing to do in their quest for the Supreme. Intellect is not the path towards the Divine. One must shed the baggage of ratiocination and ego to surrender to the feet of the Divine.

> But it is only when we cease to reason and to go deep into ourselves, into that secrecy where the activity of mind is stilled, that this other consciousness becomes really manifest to us— however imperfectly owing to our long habit of mental reaction and mental limitation. Then we can know surely in an increasing illumination that which we had uncertainly conceived by the pale and flickering light of Reason. Knowledge waits seated beyond mind and intellectual reasoning, throned in the luminous vast of illimitable self-vision.[6] (LD,129)

Sri Aurobindo like our Master speaks of the same thing in *The Life Divine* that intellect and reasoning create barriers in the path of realisation. Thus, Spiritual experiences cannot be explained in terms of reason.

The concept of detachment is also very dear to them. Time and again, Sri Ramakrishna speaks of it through different examples taken from every walk of life. Here I am citing two examples from the Gospel: "The tortoise moves about in the water. But you can guess where her thoughts are? There on the bank, where her eggs are lying. Do all your duties in the world, but keep your mind on God".[7] (Gospel, 81) In the second example, the Master says, "First rub your hand with oil and then break open the jack-fruit; otherwise they will be smeared with its sticky milk. First secure the oil of divine love, and set your hands to the duties of the world". [8] (*Gospel*, 82)

One has to be in the world without being involved in the family and the household duties. As these things keep us preoccupied and we cannot surrender ourselves to God. Therefore, the Master suggests his married devotees to remember God constantly amidst responsibilities and obligations. Whatever we do, we must remember the Divine like the tortoise or else we can smear ourselves with oil so that we cannot get stuck in the obligation of the mundane demands.

His spiritual successor, Sri Aurobindo in *Essays on the Gita,* emphasises on the abandonment of desire for things of the world. And at some places in the Gospel, Sri Ramakrishna specifically asks to reject "Gold" and "Women". Both Gold and Women symbolise worldly desire, attachment, lust and craving and common men find it difficult to reject these two things. Sri Aurobindo in *Essays on the Gita* says:

> Man is not now conscious of this self, because he is wrapped up in his outward-going mind, because he will not learn or has not learned to live within; he does not detach himself, draw back from his action and observe it as the work of Nature. Ego is the obstacle, the linch-pin of the wheel of delusion, the loss of the ego in the soul's self the first condition of freedom... Arjuna has been therefore called upon first to give up all desire of the fruits of his works and become simply the desireless impartial doer of whatever has to be done,—leaving the fruit to whatever power may be the master of the cosmic workings.[9] (L.D. The Secret of Secrets, 304-305)

Time and again, Sri Aurobindo says that action should not produce any subjective reaction on us and the result must not stain our ego or spirit's purity and peace. Detachment is the beginning of mastery. When Sri Ramakrishna preaches that meditation should be secretly done from inside and in a solitary place, he is hinting at Sri Aurobindo's idea of constant remembrance of the Divine everywhere, all the time, without showing off an external gesture of concentration. Faith, sincerity and surrender are the key words of both the giants of spirituality. Sri Aurobindo takes the cue from Sri Ramakrishna's stress on devotion and makes the word "surrender" the first and the last word of his yoga. Both of them demand from us a complete surrender, which will seize all the parts of our being. Sri Aurobindo expands the clues offered by Sri Ramakrishna and makes a whole map of the tiers of consciousness, the various layers of the physical, the vital and the mental and also what Sri Ramakrishna calls the hidden soul or the hidden gold buried inside with reference to Iswar Chandra Vidyasagar. This "hidden gold" is the "central being" in Sri Aurobindo's terminology or the "psychic being", of which he refers again and again in *The Life Divine:*

> ...this veiled psychic entity is the flame of the Godhead always alight within us, inextinguishable even by that dense unconsciousness of any

> spiritual self within which observes our outward nature. It is a flame born out of the Divine and, luminous inhabitants of the Ignorance, grows in it till it is able to turn it towards the knowledge. It is the Concealed Witness and Control, the hidden guide, the Daemon of Socrates, the inner light or inner voice of the mystic. It is that which endures and is imperishable in us from birth to birth, untouched by death, decay or corruption, an indestructible spark of the Divine. [10] (L.D., 238)

The flowing or the opening of the psychic being is the beginning of our Sadhana and it is that imprisoned gold in Vidyasagar that made Sri Ramakrishna so enthusiastic about the great Bengali scholar. The kindness of Vidyasagar has a close relation with this central self or psychic being. The psychic being is characterised by kindness and love, a kind of widening of the self, which made Vidyasagar so catholic. Apart from the psychic being, both of them highlight the role of the Divine Mother in our Sadhana. Sri Aurobindo is never tired of telling us that without the help of the Mother Divine, whom he calls "conscious force" or "Consciousness Force" in the *Life Divine.* It is impossible to climb to the Supernature or the Supermind. According to him, the Divine Mother is working as a mediatrix connecting the human individual with the Supreme Divine. Sri Ramakrishna had put the same stress on the role of the Divine Mother in the *Gospel.* Let us listen to him from the *Gospel*:

> One must propitiate the Divine Mother, the primal Energy, in order to obtain God's grace. God himself is Mahamaya, who demands the world with her illusion and conjures up the magic of creation, presentation, and destruction. She has spread this veil of ignorance before our eyes. We can go into the inner chamber only when she lets us pass through the door ... Sakti alone is the root of the universe. That Primal Energy has two aspects: Vidya and Avidya. Avidya deludes. Avidya conjures up "woman and gold", which casts the spell. Vidya begets devotion, kindness, wisdom, and Love, which lead one to God.[11] (*Gospel*, 116)

Sri Aurobindo takes from his predecessor the entire idea of Mother-Worship, which for him simply means to elevate profound respect and worship. The Divine Mother is sleeping Consciousness Force in us, which has to be aroused by constant prayer and invocation. In Sri Aurobindo's yoga, the Divine Mother helps the psychic being to come to the front so that it can take the lead of our being. Sri Aurobindo clarifies the idea in chapter entitled, "Brahma, Purusha , Ishwara":

> If we would realise a higher formation or status of being, then it is still through her, through the Divine Shakti, the Consciousness-Force of the Spirit that it has to be done; our surrender must be to the Divine Being through the Divine Mother: for it is towards or into the supreme Nature that our ascension has to take place and it can only be done by the supramental Shakti taking up our mentality and transforming it into her supramentality. [12] (L.D. 371-2)

Both Sri Ramakrishna and Sri Aurobindo believe that without the aid of this Linking Force, no human being can rise to the supreme consciousness. Taken the two Avatars together, we may conclude that their yoga is primarily based on the ideal of Mother-worship, through which one can ascend to the superconsciousness and finally to the supreme Satchidananda.

REFERENCES

1. Gupta, Mahendra. *The Gospel of Sri Ramakrishna,* Vol.1,trans Swami Nikhilananda, Madras: Sri Ramakrishna Math,1944 (all the quotes are from this edition)
2. Aurobindo, Sri. *The Life Divine,* Pondicherry: Sri Aurobindo Ashram, 1939-40. (For the present paper, I have used the Seventh Edition of *The Life Divine*, which came out in 2006)

16 Dvaita, Advaita and Vishistadvaita: Conflict and Reconciliation in Sri Sri Ramakrishna Kathamrita

Swami Chandrakantananda

Sri Sri Ramakrishna Kathamrita is text that stands out among the literatures of the world. It is a religious text in a sense that it speaks of spiritual attainment as the goal of human life. It is a text of literature since it deals with societal problems. It also a text with profound philosophical deliberations. Apparently, very lucid and simple and devoid of much philosophical jargons, *Sri Sri Ramakrishna Kathamrita* appeals to the heart of the simple readers. But as one delves deep into the text, it no less reveals its philosophical form with all its detail intricacies.

There is much debate in Indian academic circles since ages about the three principal schools of Vedanta Philosophy—the monist school (*advaita*), the qualified monists (*vishistadvaita*) and the dualists (*dvaita*). Questions also abound as regards to Kathamrita's allegiance to one of these schools of Vedanta. Pramadadas Mitra, a pundit of Varanasi and a staunch Advaitin, raised questions about Sri Ramakrishna's philosophy as represented in the Kathamrita. He believed that Sri Ramakrishna was a follower of Advaita and Kathamrita does not bring this fact out aptly. In reply 'M' or MahendranathGupta, the recorder of Kathamrita, wrote that he had recorded the words of the Master as he '*understood it*'. To 'M', Sri Ramakrishna was primarily a *Vishistadvaitin*. Some of the later critics, however, have insisted that Sri Ramakrishna was essentially a *dvaitin*—a worshipper of Kali and a devotee to the core.

This debate cannot be understood superficially. Let us delve deep into Kathamrita and Sri Ramakrishna's preaching to appreciate this.

Dvaita School and Kathamrita

Though most of the schools of the Indian Philosophy and so also other theistic philosophies of the world are basically dualistic, the term *dvaitavada* of the Vedanta school is more aptly denoted by the term *Svatantrasvatantra-vada* (the doctrine of the independent and dependents) and this school is traditionally called *Brahma sampradaya*. The most famous of its *acharyas* is Madhva.

Like all other dualist philosophies and theisms of the world, Madhvacharya very simply states that the world with its multiplicity is real and distinct from God and the individual souls. His philosophy has been paraphrased as :

श्रीमन्मध्वमते हरिः परतरः सत्यं जगत्तवती
भिन्नाजीवगणाः हरेरनुचरानीचोच्चभावं गताः।
मुक्तिर्नैजसुखानुभूतिरमला भक्तिश्चतत्साधनं
ह्यक्षादित्रयं प्रमाणखिलाम्नायैकवेद्यो हरिः।।

(B.N. Singh, History of Madhva School, p.7)

—According to the Madhva doctrine, Hari (Brahman) is the Supreme Reality and this creation is real too. The individual souls (*jiva*s) are all distinct and servant of the Lord. These souls are classified into different categories in hierarchal level. Experience of pure bliss is called Mukti which can be attained by devotion (*bhakti*). The epistemology acceptable to this school are three – direct perception (*pratyaksha*), inference (*anumana*) and scriptural authority (*shabda*) of which only the last is the proof for Supreme Lord and hence ultimate source of knowledge.

Sri Sri Ramakrishna Kathamrita to some extent agrees with this doctrine. The first and foremost principle as enunciated by *Dvaita* School is—God is the supreme element and He is to be attained by devotion. The Kathamrita seems to concede with this view. That Sri Ramakrishna emphasizes, 'God realization is the goal of human life' (Kathamrita, 18 Aug, 1893) is a tacit admission that God (Hari) is the Supreme Reality. Had it not been so, God realization could never have been called supreme or ultimate achievement.

Again Sri Ramakrishna says, 'Again sometimes God shows me that He has created the universe and all living beings (*jivajagat*). He is the Mater, and the universe His garden.

'He is the Master and the universe and all its living beings belong to Him—that is knowledge. And 'I am the doer', 'I am the guru', 'I am the father'—that is ignorance.' *(Kathamrita, 16/10/83)* This is in fact a support to the Creator God and multiplicity of existence, which is the basic pillar of the *dvaita* thought Madhva says that through scriptures, one can know about God and this is a unanimous conclusion reached by all schools of Indian Philosophy.

Even Sri Ramakrishna in Kathamrita says, 'In the scriptures you will find the way to realize God.' (*Kathamrita,11 March, 1885*)

The Madhvas do not accept jiva as inert elements. They believe that the individual souls are parts of God though this 'part' is not actual; they are rather part in the sense that reflections or shadows are the part of the man. (*Madhvasiddhantasara - 'jivaprakarana, 2/3/43-50, quoted in* Vedanta Darshanam(Bengali), Swami Viswarupananda, Vol., I, *p.xxxiv-xiv*) Naturally, the individuals have to be conscious elements as distinct from unconscious elements or *jadaprakriti*. That jiva is essentially divine in also admitted by Sri Ramakrishna. He says, 'There is manifestation of God is man.' (*Kathamrita, 26/12/83, p.423*)

This view of innumerable and conscious yet distinct individual souls (*jivatman)* is also supported by Vedic scriptures on which Madhva based his doctrine. In some point of his life as a spiritual seeker, Sri Ramakrishna too had this realization: Jiva is conscious, innumerable and separate from each other. This *dvaitic* realization was also taken up by BrahmoSamaj, especially Devendranath Tagore. In the *Sri Sri Ramakrishna Kathamrita*, Sri Ramakrishna narrates his expression of *dvaitic*jiva-view as follows: 'Once I visited Devendranath Tagore with Mathur Babu.....He said, "This world is like chandelier, and each living being (*jiva*) is a light in it". Once meditating in the Panchavati, I had a vision like that....I asked him to explain his words. He said, "God has created men to manifest His own glory. Otherwise who could have known this universe? Without the light of the chandelier, everything is dark, even the chandelier cannot be been."' (*Kathamrita, 26 October, 1884*)

Being a devotee, it was abhorrent to Madhva that someone could claim that his or her identity with Brahman. It was most blasphemous of all acts and greatest sin. In this, he did not differ from the Abrahamic religious traditions. He took a strong stand to this mode of thinking and declared, 'He who declares himself as "I am the king", the king slays him and he who eulogizes the king is rewarded.' (*Sarvadarshansamgraha, Purnaprajnadarshana*):

घातयन्ति हि राजानः राजाहमिति वादिनः।
ददत्यखिलमिष्टं च स्वगुणोत्कर्षवादिनाम्।।

Sri Ramakrishna cannot be said to have ascribed this view in toto to but it has been observed that at times he took to stand opposing the celebrated advaitic declaration 'I am the Supreme Brahman'. Once he admonished Girish Chandra Ghosh saying, 'Shame! Never say that again. I look myself upon as a devotee of Krishna, not Krishna himself (*bhaktavat na cha krishnavat*).' (*Kathamrita, September 1885, p.1018*)

On another occasion he instructed his devotees, 'As long as the covering of ignorance remains, the Vedantic formula 'I am He' that is man is Supreme Brahman does not rightly apply....If the servant comes forward of his own will to sit by the master, will not the master be angry!' (*Kathamrita, 22 September 1883, p.315*)

But Sri Ramakrishna expressed that it was his desire to sing praises of the Lord with an attitude of servant-master. He had warned people without sufficient purification of mind about the dangers of practising advaitic dictum of 'I am Brahman'. He said, 'It is not good to inculcate the ego of 'I am He'. He who takes up this attitude even when the idea of body-consciousness still lingering in him, come of grief; he cannot proceed, and gradually falls. He deceives others as well as himself, he cannot comprehend his own state.' (*Kathamrita, 14 December 1882, p.139*)

But there is a difference between Madhva and Sri Ramakrishna. Sri Ramakrishna never actually says that slave-master relationship always holds. He says that as long as ignorance persists, the advaitic standpoint should be avoided but not so when the veil of ignorance drops.

Though Sri Ramakrishna sparingly spoke of dvaita conception of *jivatman*, it was not altogether missing from his precepts. He had accepted the distinction between individual souls, like different qualities of human beings. He said that though men all appeared same from outside yet, they were actually different in their temperaments. On 4 June, 1883, Sri Ramakrishna comments to 'M', 'The fact is, all men look alike from the outside, but some of them have condensed milk or powdered black grams, but they all look alike from the outside.' (*Kathamrita, p.231, 4/6/1883*) But he never did accept that this difference was the essential element of human soul. He rather stressed that everyone will attain to that final state of illumination but in time. Whereas though Madhva does not say this explicitly, yet the impression is conveyed that the state of *jivas* is final and ultimate. The *nityabaddha* (eternally bound) state of an individual soul was something not endorsed by Sri Ramakrishna. Unlike Madhva, he did not accept *nityabaddha* (eternal bound) beings though he did mention that some people, however they may try, would never attain spiritual hankering in this present life. Swami Vivekananda testified the fact, as Swami Saradananda points out in *Sri Sri Ramakrishna Lilaprasanga*.

However, *dvaita* concept of *jiva* as servant of the Lord was encouraged by

Sri Ramakrishna to some of his disciples. Swami Saradananda, in his magnum opus, Sri *Sri Ramakrishna Lilaprasanga* writes that though Sri Ramakrishna usually spoke of the concepts of Vishistadvaita to common people, yet at times he would also speak of having devotion to God in the spirit of *dvaita*-concept. He writes, 'Not having likewise love for God and bereft of high spiritual attainments, yet arguing and declaring the lofty concepts of *Advaita* or *Vishistadvaita*, would irritate him and he used to admonish them with harsh words.' (*Lilaprasanga, Vol. II, p.42*) In this context, one of his parables may be quoted as recorded by Suresh Chandra Dutta.

Sri Ramakrishna narrates: 'Shankaracharya had a stout disciple. Shankara used to say "Shivo'ham", he too said "Shivo'ham". Whatever Shankara did, he emulated him....One day Shankara took him to a blacksmith and devoured a red-hot iron rod and gave a part of it to his disciple to eat. The disciple was stunned; how could he eat a red hot iron rod? He could not do it and from then on he understood that uttering "Shivo'ham" is not just repeating words.' (*Sri Sri Ramakrishner Upadesh, Suresh Dutta, No. 694, p. 194-95*)

The doctrine of differentiation (*bhedavada*) is central to Madhva philosophy. There are five kinds of differentiation accepted by Madhva School (a) between jiva and Ishwara (b) between jiva and jiva, (c) between inert matter and conscious principle God, (d) between inert matter and conscious principle jiva, (e) between two inert matters.

These apparent distinctions were sometimes spoken of by Sri Ramakrishna but he never accepted them as eternally separate or essentially distinct.

So far, we see that the dvaita school of Vedanta is to a certain extent represented in the Kathamrita.

Vishistadvaita and Kathamrita

Vishistadvaita claims to be an ancient school of thought, traditionally called *Shree sampradaya*, with sages like Dramida, Tanka and others among its followers who find mention in the *Brahmasutras*. However, it was strongly established as a coherent school of thought by Ramanuja in historical times. It seems that Sri Ramakrishna was familiar with both the tenets of this school of thought and also with Ramanuja's life. Swami Saradananda mentions in his *Sri Sri Ramakrishna Lilaprasanga*, 'Though he maintained that the Advaitic thought was ultimate, yet to common people engaged in enjoying the sense objects, he usually preached the principles of Vishistadvaita...' (*Lilaprasanga, Vol II, p.41*) In Kathamrita we find mention of the doctrine where Sri Ramakrishna explains to Narendra, 'Shankara's non-dualistic explanation of Vedanta is true, and so is the Qualified non-dualistic interpretation of Ramanuja.' (*Kathamrita, 11 March 1885, p.897*)

Even the life of Ramanuja was familiar to Sri Ramakrishna. The rivalry of Ramanuja with his guru Yadavaprakasha has also been pointed out by Sri Ramakrishna to Kesub Sen when he says, 'Ramanuja was a Vishistadvaitin. His guru was an Advaitin. So, they fell out with each other.' (*Kathamrita, p.102, 27 October, 1882*)

Ramanuja takes a unique position on philosophical viewpoints and ultimately harmonizing the divergent views of *dvaita* and *advaita*. His harmony is of course tossed on Vedic injuctions. The doctrine of Ramanuja has been paraphrased by himself in his *Vedarthasamgraha*:

अत्रेदं सर्वशास्त्रहृदयं–जीवात्मानः स्वयं असंकुचित–अपरिच्छिन्ननिर्मलज्ञानस्वरूपाः सन्तः कर्मारूपाऽविद्या–वेष्टितास्तत्तत् कर्मानुरूपज्ञानसंकोचमापन्नाः, ब्रह्मादिस्ताम्बपर्यन्त–विविध–विचित्र देहेषु प्रविष्टास्तत्तद्देहोचित–लब्धज्ञान–प्रसारास्तत्तद्देहात्माभिमानिन–स्तदुचितकर्मानि कुवीनास्तदनुगुणसुखदुःखभोगरूप–संसारप्रवाहं प्रतिपद्यन्ते। एतेषां संसारमोचनं भगवत्प्रतिपत्तिमन्तरेणनोपपद्यते इति तदर्थं प्रथममेषां देवादिभेदरहित–ज्ञानैककारतयासर्वेषां साम्यं प्रतिपाद्य, तस्यापि स्वरूपस्य भगवच्छेषतैकस्वरूपैकरसतया भगवदात्मकतामपि प्रतिपाद्य, भगवत्स्वरूपं च हेयप्रत्यनिक–कल्याणैकताननतयासकलेतरविषजातीय मनवध्किातिशयसांख्येय–कल्याणगुणगणालयं संकल्पप्रवृत्तसमस्तचिदचिद्वस्तुजाततया सर्वस्यात्मभूतं प्रतिपाद्य, तदुपासनं साङ्गं तत्प्रापकं प्रतिपादयति शास्त्राणीति।

—This is the gist of all scriptures: the individual souls are essentially unconstricted and of the nature of knowledge. Being constricted due to their ignorance and the works arising out of it, these souls enter the bodies from Brahma to the blades of grass. Having the idea of ego attached with these bodies these individual souls work according to their given body-mind and senses and thus enjoy the consequent happiness or sorrow—this constitutes transmigration. Nothing other than surrender to Lord is the way to get rid of this—to establish this knowledge first the idea of *atman* as conscious-principle and their sameness is being told and their all the *atmas* are the part of the Lord is being propagated. This is also being established—the nature of the Lord is free from all traces of blemish, full of only pure qualities distinct from all sentient and insentient objects, repository of all divine qualities and having created all sentient and insentient objects, enters into them. Then it has been stated that the way to attain the Lord is by performing one's duty with the idea of worship of the Lord along with pleasing the Lord with bhakti.

The *Yatindramatadeepika* says —

'श्रीमन्नारायण एव चिद्चिद्विशिष्टाद्वैततत्त्वं भक्तिप्रपत्तिभ्यां प्रसन्नः स उपायः, अप्राकृतिकदेशविशिष्टः स एव प्राप्य इति–' (श्लोक 2)

—Lord Narayana along with *Shree* (His Divine Power) alone, having sentience and insentience as his qualifications, is the sole Reality—one without a second. He alone, propitiated by devotion and surrender, is the means to salvation and He alone, qualified by his belonging to the non-material realm, is the goal to be attained.

Sri Ramakrishna wonderfully summarizes this doctrine in *Kathmrita*. On being asked by Narendra what Vishistadvaita doctrine is, Sri Ramakrishna replies, 'Vishistadvaita is the doctrine of Ramanuja. According to this doctrine, Brahman or Absolute, qualified by the universe and living beings (*jivajagat*). These three – Brahman, the world and the living beings together constitute One.

'Take the example of bel-fruit. A man wanted to know the weight of the fruit. He separated the shell, the flesh and the seeds. Now, can a man get the weight by weighing only the flesh? He must weigh the shell, the flesh and the seeds together. At first, it appears that the real thing in the fruit is the flesh and not the seeds or the shell. Then by reasoning you find that the shell, seeds and flesh all belong to the fruit. …First, you have to negate everything by reasoning 'Brahman is not the living beings (*jiva*)', 'Brahman is not the universe (*jagat*)', only Brahman and real and all else non-real. Then you realize...the Existence that you term Brahman is the source of the living beings and the universe.... That is why, Ramanuja used to say, Brahman qualified by living being (*jiva*) and universe (*jagat*). This is called Vishistadvaita.' (*Kathamrita, 11March, 1885, p.897-8*)

Many traces of Vishistadvaita doctrine is found in the Kathamrita. To some Sri Ramakrishna posits of God endowed with Divine Properties (*Aishvarya*): 'God is endowed with six divine powers (*shadaishvarya*). If He had no powers, who would respect Him?' According to Ramanuja, Narayana endowed with Shree (that is Supreme Brahman) possesses six divine powers (*shadaishvarya*) and can never be bereft of these.

Ramayana does not believe in Impersonal Godhead devoid of all attributes. But the Vedas also speak of Godhead without any attributes (*Nirguna Brahman*). So how do we reconcile these two contradictory standpoints? To this, Ramanuja replies that when the Supreme Godhead is spoken of as without attributes, it means that the Godhead is free from all defects (निरस्तनिखिलदोषा:) and without any undesirable attributes (हेयगुणरहित). Srimannarayana (Supreme Brahman) is entirely endowed with pure and blissful qualities. Hence in a way, God is with attributes and also without attributes.

Here Sri Ramakrishna seems significantly to differ with him. He does not dogmatically state that God is all good rather he makes an exception to that effect for the devotees. He says, 'But you can say this, for some devotees He is Eternally with Form. There are places, where ice never melts, it crystallizes.' But in the same breath he says, 'Yes, God is both with form and without form, and again beyond birth form and formless. There is no limiting Him.' (*Kathamrita, 11 March 1883*) In this context he uses the illustration of a chameleon which changes its colours from red to blue to grenn and likewise. This represents the infinite attribute of the Godhead (*anantagunamaya Ishwara*). However, there are times, when the chameleon is totally devoid of all colours thus representing the Impersonal Goghead (*nirguna Brahman*)

The impression conveyed by 'M', the recorder of the Kathamrita, is that Sri Ramakrishna speaks of Vishistadvaita only. In a soliloquy in the Kathamrita (26 October 1884), he muses, 'The Master does not speak of this world as a dream. He says, 'Then it would not be properly weighed.' Not Màyàvàda, but Vishishtadvaitavada. Since, he does not speak of the creation as unreal or imagination of the mind. God is real and man is real, again world too is real. Brahman qualified by world and living beings.'

One of the unique tenets of Ramanuja is that this entire creation is the actual extension of the Lord. The world is neither illusory, as the Advaitins claim, nor is entirely distinct from the Lord as the Dvaitins contend. In fact this world is a part of the Lord. The cosmic body of the Narayana (or Brahman) comprises two broad sections—insentient (achit) and sentient (chit). The *prakriti* resides within the Lord and therefore projects the creation like limbs of an organism. From the *Prakriti* (also called *avidya* or *ajnana*) ejects 'Mahat' and from Mahat comes 'ahamkara' and hence 'Manas' (or mind). This 'Manas' is the cause of all bondage and liberation of the individual soul which are a part of the sentient aspect of the Lord. During dissolution, the elements dissolve to their previous elements and finally all merge into 'Mahat' before becoming one with prakriti.

Though Sri Ramakrishna did not speak much about the process of creation and dissolution, yet on occasions he did he seem to corroborate this view. He says, 'All elements (*Tattvas*) ultimately merge in Akasha-tattva. Again during creation, from Akasha-tattva comes Mahat, from Mahat comes Ahamkara, and in this sequence creation continues.' (*Kathamrita, 2 March 1884*)

A question is often raised to a Ramanujin: if *avidya* or *maya* resides in the Lord as His part, does not the purity of the Lord get soiled or the attributes of Brahman vilified? To this they reply, take the example of a human body. Youth and old age are the attributes of the human body but the individual is not affected by those attributes of his body. Similarly, the Lord is not affected by the decay and ignorance residing in this body which is this entire creation. Sri Ramakrishna does not actually support this principle in toto, but he agrees with the Ramanujins as regards to the unadulterated nature of Brahman inspite of being associated with maya or avidya. He says, 'The poison resides within a snake, but it does not affect the snake....Similarly, Brahman is unattached itself.'

Another typical concept of the Vishishtadvaita is its concept of *Shree*, the compassionate consort of Brahman (Narayana). This Shree is the power of Brahman, imagined as a female form. She is like a mother to the devotees and always comes with the Lord. Her existence is same as that of the Lord (or according to some schools, just a notch below the Lord) and she represents the compassionate nature of the Lord. She intervenes with the Lord on behalf of the devotees like a loving mother and devotees are free of the transmigration due to her intervening role with the Lord. The Lord and Shree are inseparably related (*avinabhavena*) and hence the Lord is called *Srimannarayana*—Narayana endowed with Shree.

Sri Ramakrishna comes very close to this concept when he says, 'Brahman and Shakti are non-different.' To Sri Ramakrishna Brahman is inseparably associated with Shakti, like fire and its power to burn, or milk and its whiteness. Where Sri Ramakrishna differs from Ramanuja is that the Brahman of Sri Ramakrishna is not *endowed* with Shakti (like Narayana is endowed with Shree) but rather, Brahman *is* Shakti, in a different manifestation. He gives the example of a serpent. When a serpent remains coiled and static, it is Brahman and when it slithers, it is shakti with manifestation of powers like creation, dissolution etc. Though philosophically Sri Ramakrishna and Ramanuja slightly differs (*samvayisambandha* in case of Ramanuja and *anyonyasambandha* in case Sri Ramakrishna), for all practical purposes, they look upon the female aspect Godhead as Mother, the compassionate. Sri Ramakrishna, like Ramanuja, believed in the salvage power of the female aspect of God which actually coincides with Tantric doctrine. No doubt Ramanuja followed the *Pancharatra* school which is a Vaishnava-tantra while Sri Ramakrishna practiced and followed Shakta and Vaishnava Tantras.

There is another point of similarity between Ramanuja and Sri Ramakrishna's doctrine. Vishistadvaita classifies the individual souls (jivas) into three categories—*Nityajiva* or eternal beings like Gaduda, Ananta, Narada etc. For them the eternal knowledge never contracts and hence they never come under the sway of Màyà. The second category of individual souls are—*muktajiva* or liberated beings. These souls, by their supreme efforts and grace of the Lord, attain liberation which is unification with the Lord (*sayujya*). The third category of jivas is—*baddhajiva* or bound souls. These are the common souls tied down by ignorance and are subject to transmigration. But all these souls are parts of the Lord, like sparks of fire are parts of the bonfire.

In Kathamrita, we find Sri Ramakrishna accepts this classification in its entirety and adds one intermediary class of his own. He says, '*Jivas* are of four kinds—bound souls (*baddhajiva*), souls that desire liberation (*mumukshujiva*), liberated souls (*muktajiva*) and eternal souls (*nityajiva*).

'Nityajiva—Like Narada and others. They live in the world for the good of others—to teach other living beings.

Baddhajiva—Attached to sense-objects, and does not think of God—never thinks of the Lord, even by mistake.

Mumukshujiva—Those who aspire liberation. But among them some attain liberation, some cannot.

Muktajiva—Those who are not bound to this world and to women and gold—like the monks and saints. There is no trace of worldliness in them and they always think of the Lord.'

(Kathamrita,March, 1882, p.26)

In Sri Ramakrishna's opinion, Nityajivas are like 'estatemanagers', who ably manage one estate and then is sent to manage another; or like a big ship which can ferry a multitude to the shore. (*Kathamrita,19 October, 1884, p.779*)

Ramanuja, like all other Bhakti schools, could never accept the idea of identity of individual soul and Brahman. To him, liberation consists in residing in the same sphere as the Lord (*samipya*) and unifying with the Lord (*sayujya*), of which the last was the highest. Sri Ramakrishna does not deny these and yet accepts that nirvana-mukti (identity of Brahman and jiva) too. But to some, who would not be in a position to appreciate this advaitic tenet, he preferred to posit the Vishishtadvaita position that *jiva* is a part of the Divine Lord and serving him is the liberation to be desired. The points out, 'The devotees say, all these are the powers of the Lord....But seeing the devotion of the aspirant, when He says, 'You and me are one' that is a different thing altogether. Suppose, a king is seated in his court and his cook enters the hall, sits on the throne and says, "O King, you and I are the same". People will certainly call him a madman. But if, pleased with the cook's services to the king, one day, the king tells him, "Come, sit beside me. There is no difference between you and me". If then the cook sits on the throne, there is no harm. If ordinary souls say, 'I am He', that is not proper. The wave belongs to the sea, does sea belong to the wave?' (*Kathamrita, 15 June, 1883, p.253-4*)

Incidentally, the wave-sea analogy is a celebrated example of Vishishtadvaita concept of relationship between jiva and God, which has quoted by Madhusudana Saraswati—

सत्यपि भेदापगमे नाथ तवाहं न मामकीनस्त्वम्।
सामुद्रो कि तरङ्गं क्वचन समुद्रो न तारङ्गः।।

—Inspite of the dissolution of the difference between you and one, O Lord, I am thine, not thee mine. Since, it is the waves that belong to the sea and not sea to the waves.

Along with the 'part-nature' of *jiva* this illustration gives us two distinct impressions:

(a) Firstly, this liberation is akin to *sayujya* (sameness) since the distinction of Servant-Master sustains but the love unifies them on another level. There seems a concurrence between Ramanuja and Sri Ramakrishna on this.

(b) The second impression that we get from this illustration is that the liberation is attained with the grace of the Lord. In fact at other places too Sri Ramakrishna emphasizes the fact the liberation or God realization is possible with the grace of the Lord and the grace comes with practicing of austerities. (*Kathamrita, 24 May, 1884, p.515*) In Kathamrita, Narendra (later Swami Vivekananda) makes an exposition on this saying, 'Without God's grace nothing can help realize God.' (*Kathamrita, p.1242*)

This follows that grace must be attained. Ramanuja says, grace can be attained by two means—*bhakti* (devotion) and *prapatti* (surrender). Of these, the path of surrender to the Lord is the highest. Sri Ramakrishna agrees. His natural attitude was of surrender to the Divine Mother. He actually proposes that liberation comes through surrender (*Kathamrita, 15 November, 1882, p.121*). In fact when he defines the goal of the individual souls as 'God realization' or liberation, he categorically states that it is the duty of every individual to surrender to the Lord and pray in earnest for His vision. (*Kathamrita, 6 December 1884, p.1214*) This is another concept, where Sri Ramakrishna sides with Ramanuja and Madhva as against Shankara, who, from the standpoint of highest philosophy, does not accept the role grace of God.

There is another point of similarity between the Vishistadvaita School and Kathamrita. Though Sri Ramakrishna always placed the 'pure-devotion' or devotion in which all ideas of powers and greatness of God is obliterated and only the love aspect remains (*Shuddha bhakti*) on higher pedastal, yet he did not prescribe it for all and sundry. His prescription to common people was *Naradiya Bhakti* which has also been referred to as *Jnana-bhakti* in Kathamrita. Swami Saradananda points out that Sri Ramakrishna preferred the masses to follow this concept of devotion coupled with knowledge (of the divinity of the Lord). He urged people to follow the ideal of Hanuman who was a jnani-bhakta and had prayed to the Lord for not being entangled in world-enchanting Màyà of the Lord and having pure devotion at His feet. (*Kathamrita, 28 July, 1885, p.994*) Ramanuja too equates Bhakti with jnana saying—Bhakti is a particular type of jnana, in which apart from eternal bliss and adoration of the Lord, nothing else is craved for and in all other things a total dispassion occurs.'—भक्तिस्तु निरतिशयान्दप्रियानन्य प्रयोजनसकलेतरवैतृष्ण्यवज् ज्ञानविशेष एव। (*SarvadarshanSangraha, Ramanuja, p.62*). In effect this is same as craving the devotion of Lord and non-attachment to the world. In his *Bhaktiyoga*, Swami Vivekananda too presents the bhakti yoga to be practiced on these lines of bhakti coupled with jnana, though he too, like his Master, admits that the *suddhabhakti* of the Gopis is superior to this.

Advaita School of Vedanta and Kathamrita

The Advaita Vedanta is a unique system of philosophy in so far as no other philosophy or theology admits the complete identity of soul and God and illusoriness of the world at the same time. The Advaita system has been famously summarized as—

श्लोकार्धेन प्रवक्ष्यामि यदुक्तं ग्रन्थकोटिभिः।
ब्रह्मसत्य जगन्मिथ्याजीवो ब्रह्मैव नापरः।।

—What the millions of texts elucidate, can be proclaimed thus: Brahman alone is real world is illusory and individual Soul and Brahman are non-different.

On the basis of Kathamrita many a scholars have tried to prove that

Sri Ramakrishna was basically a Vishishtadvaitin; not only that he actually abhorred advaita philosophy. To substantiate their view, it would be suffice to supply just one instance whence Sri Ramakrishna remarks to the Divine Mother: 'Mere knowledge of advaita! Fie on it! As long as you have kept the 'I' so long 'you' remains. Paramahamsa is a child. Doesn't a child need his mother?' (*Kathamrita, 23 December 1883, p.412*) These scholars claim that this shows that Sri Ramakrishna despised the idea of advaita at worst or at best kept it at bay.

They have other contentions as well. By advaita, they of course mean the advaita doctrine propounded by Shankara. The critics point out that Sri Ramakrishna preferred to adopt an attitude of 'Master-Servant' attitude, and more importantly 'Mother-child' attitude which implies *dvaita* or at the most *vishistadvaita*. They further claim that advaita has no place for *Shakti* as a divine entity. Even if *Shakti* is accepted, it is equated with Maya, which has no actual existence in the ultimate level (*paramarthika*). However, in case Sri Ramakrishna, *Shakti* has been accepted as an aspect of Godhead or rather Brahman has been regarded identical with it, thus giving it a real and actual existence in the ultimate level (*paramarthika satta*).

Another fundamental difference, they point out, between Shankara and Sri Ramakrishna is that the later posits that the world with all its multiplicity is the sportive creative activity (lila) of Brahman, the Absolute. It is not an imaginary show conjured up by an illusion-producing màyà. (*Classical Indian Philosophies:* Their synthesis in the Philosophy of Sri Ramakrishna, Satis Chandra *Chatterji, 1985, Calcutta University, p.125*)

These critics even underline the fact that Sri Ramakrishna did not actually prescribe *shravana, manana* and *nididhyasana*, as the direct means to realization, like all traditional advaitins. He rather stresses on loving God and praying to Him, unlike the followers of Shankara.

These arguments are true to some extent, and a superficial reading of Kathamrita does give us these impressions. However, it must be pointed out that there are some points of similarities between Shankara School of thought and the Kathamrita's views.

First, about the nature of Brahman. Sri Ramakrishna feels that Brahman is beyond Maya—beyond *vidya* and *avidya*. (*Kathamrita, 5 August 182, p.51*) This is in perfect agreement with Shankara who point to Brahman as 'beyond existence and non existence' or beyond good and evil.

Regarding the identity of jiva and Brahman which is the carnial tenet of Advaita system, Sri Ramakrishna could not agree more. 'I and mine is ignorance. With reasoning you will find that the One you call 'I' is none other than Atman....Then you will see that you are nothing, you have no attributes. Then you know "I have done nothing, I have no blemish, no qualities; I have neither sin nor merit." ' (*Kathamrita,8 April, 1883, p.197-98*) Sri Ramakrishna does not only speak of atman as attribute-less entity he also reveals his realization of oneness with the Divine. His experience is narrated thus: 'Sometimes I say, "You are me, I am you". Again sometimes it occurs to me "You are you"! Then I cannot find the "I".' (*Kathamrita,18 August 1883, p.288*)

Sri Ramakrishna does not rule out traditional advaitic mode of practice but he insisted that only those who have overcome their senses organs are fit to practice those discipline. He then emphasizes on prayer and other rituals as modes of spiritual discipline for cleansing of mind (*chittashuddhi*). Even Shankara had conceded that for recipients of mediocre qualities must practice *upasana*, which is similar to that of Sri Ramakrishna's idea of prayer.

In case of the nature of world, Shankara calls it an illusory having no ultimate existence (*paramarthika satta*). The advaitins like to compare this world with dream state. In Sri Ramakrishna, we never find him hinting that the universe is a permanent existence. He rather says that, it is all transient; it is real so long as 'empirical ego' continues and beyond that state 'whatever is, is.' As long as the idea of body persists, the duality of world persists. To Sri Ramakrishna, the final realization lies in realizing the world as a dream. (*Kathamrita, June 1883, p.266*)In Kathamrita, he cites the example of a learned peasant who explained to his grieving wife that this world as a mere dream and hence the loss of his son was nothing but a dream. In fact, Sri Ramakrishna's idea of religion can also be traced back to his idea of advaita.

But the greatest support of advaita comes from Sri Ramakrishna in form of the statement: 'Tying the knot of knowledge of advaita on your cloth, do whatever you like.' This statement have been often quoted to show Sri Ramakrishna believed that advaitic realization was the highest of all.

Sri Ramakrishna's Philosophy: Standpoint of Vijnani

Swami Turiyananda, a direct monastic disciple of Sri Ramakrishna, was a great scholar and follower of advaita. Once he was asked whether Shankara's teachings differed from that of Sri Ramakrishna. In reply, he said, 'Yes, Shankara taught only one phase, how to get freedom, nirvana. Our Master first made one free and then taught how one should live in the world....Do away with name and form and the entire universe. Then see Mother in all, then be her playfellow.' (*God lived with them, Swami Chetanananda, Advaita Ashrama, p.327*)

Let us look into the sayings of Sri Ramakrishna which apprantly are non-advaitic in nature. He points state of *vijnana* which is higher than the state of *Brahmajnana*. He defined vijnana as, 'knowing God intimately. To know that fire is potential in wood is *jnana* (knowledge) and to cook food on that fire, and deriving nourishment from consuming the food is called *vijnana*. To realize that God exists is *jnana*; . . . to see that He has become this creation and universe is *vijnana*.' (*Kathamrita, 9 September, 1883, p.311*)

When an advaitin, as a knower of Brahman, tries to realize the Ultimate Reality, he negates everything saying 'not this, not this' and finally attaining illumination. But if the person then comes to the state of normal consciousness again, what will he see? Will see this duality of universe or the only one existence? Sri Ramakrishna's solution is simple. He often uses the analogy of a man climbing the stairs to reach the terrace. After having reached there, he cannot stay there forever; he has to come down. When he comes down, he sees that while climbing the stairs he had negated the steps as not terrace itself, but now he sees that the constituent elements of the terrace and the stairs, like the bricks, cement and other things, are the same. Similarly, when this man of highest advaitic realization comes down, he sees that same Brahman has become this world of manifoldness and all the created beings. He sees that the attribute-less God and the God with fullest attributes are the same. (*Kathamrita, 5 August 1882, p.54*)

To him the ultimate realization of the Impersonal Absolute is equally real as this Relative world. Sri Ramakrishna's very words : 'Therefore, I say, in the reasoning according to Vedanta, Brahman is without any attributes. His nature cannot be spoken of. But as long as you are real, so long this world is real too. The multiple forms of God are true, and Personal God also real.' (*Kathamrita, 28 October 1882, p.114*)

Sri Ramakrishna had a firm belief that dvaita, vishishtadvaita and advaita are the stages of realization which come to a spiritual aspirant as one progresses along the path. At a particular stage, one of these ideas actually seems real and the rest as false. As a result of his twelve-year long sàdhanà, Swami Saradananda points out, Sri Ramakrishna realized that the ideas of *dvaita*, *vishishtadvaita* and *advaita* emerge spontaneously according to one's spiritual growth which are not actually contradictory but depended on the stage of the aspirant's progress.

In this, he actually reconciled age-old animosity among these schools. To him, of course, the idea of oneness (i.e. *advaita*) was the highest point of realization for a common man. He used to say, 'Know that non duality is the last word in realization. It is beyond the mind and speech and a matter of experience.' Then about *vishishtadvaita* he used to say, 'Only the states upto vishishtadvaita can be understood through the mind and intellect expressed in words. There the Absolute and the Relative both are equally real. The Lord Himself, His name, and his abode—all are pure consciousness.' And finally about *dvaita* he commented, '*Dvaita* is meant for ordinary human beings who are attached to sense objects. An excellent practice for them is to chant the Lord's name loudly as prescribed in the *Narada Pancharatra*.' (*Cf, Sri Ramakrishna and his Divine Play, p.361*)

This is easily understandable as he illustrates in his one of stories in the Kathamrita. 'A king insisted that he must have the knowledge of Brahman in a word. The yogi said, "Well, you will have your realization with in a word only." After a while a magician came to the king. The king saw, the magician was only moving his two fingers and repeating "O King, look at this, look at this." The king was wonder struck. A little later he saw that the two fingers have become one. The magician was moving just one finger and muttering, "O King! Look at it, look at it." This means, initially Brahman and Shakti appear different but in the knowledge of Brahman duality cease to exist. Nondifferentiation! One! The one without a second! Advaitam.' (*Kathamrita, 10 June 1883, p.246*)

About Sri Ramakrishna's own experience—he calls it Bhavamukha. This is the state of vijnani who realizes the duality of this world, yet knows that all these are manifestations of the Lord. To some this might appear like dvaita. But the difference is, in *dvaita* the soul, God and the world are three distinct entities—always mutually separate, but in this state of bhavamukha there is no actual distinction. The same principle manifests Itself as God, all living beings and the world. This sometimes look akin to *vishishtadvaita*, which says all these are the parts of Brahman. But still there is a difference. The *vishishtadvaita* considers these parts of the Absolute but *vijnani* sees them as nothing but Brahman Itself. To a vijnani everything appears as Consciousness whereas *vishishtadvaita* sees this universe as insentience. Thus, in vijnani all these three states persist—he sees multiplicity, yet non-differentiated and totality of consciousness.

There is a shloka attributed to Madhusudana Saraswati, the famous advaitin:

द्वैतं मोहाय भवति बोधेः प्राक् मनीषिणः।
भवत्या कल्पते द्वैतं अद्वैतादपि सुन्दरम्।।

—Dualism is the cause of bondage before the rise of illumination. But after illumination, the dvaita that persists is even more beautiful than advaita.

This is the state of vijnani. To Sri Ramakrishna, God alone appears as the individuals, world and all constituent elements—'Anuloma and Viloma'. (*Kathamrita,19 September 1884, p.669*) He moved spontaneously between the Relative (lila) and the Absolute (Nitya). But he realized that nitya is the source of the lila (*Kathamrita,16 October 1883, p.341*); in that sense advaita is the basis of all realization.

To Sri Ramakrishna, the state of Bhavamukha or *vijnana* was even beyond the state of *Brahmajnana*. To Narendra he had said, 'You are mean minded. Go beyond samadhi. Samadhi is a mere trifle.' (*Kathamrita, 9 April 1887, p.1231*)

Sri Ramakrishna accepts Shakti as Brahma. Though the word *Shakti* in case of Sri Ramakrishna, is equal to that of Ishvara in advaita school. When one sees the creator, sustainer and destroyer aspect of Brahman, one sees Shakti which is equivalent Ishvara. But unlike the staunch Vedantins who deny the actual (*paramarthika*) existence of Ishvara, Sri Ramakrishna accepts Shakti even at *paramarthika* level but as identified with Brahman, not as a separate entity.

The undiluted Shankara doctrine, also called 'Mayavada' was not recommended by Sri Ramakrishna to everyone. He called it 'dry' (*Kathamrita, 11 March 1886, p.1121*) and he spat on mere dry reasoning. His attitude was: so long as 'I' remains, it is preferable to maintain the attitude of bhakta and not call everything an illusion. *(Kathamrita, 22 July 1883, p.287)*

Sri Ramakrishna's realization in a vijnani state appears similar to *vishishtadvaita* because the illustration he used to explain the doctrine of vijnana and vishishtadvaita is the same. He cites the example of a garden of wax in both cases. He believes that a devotee sees the oneness; he sees there is nothing but God. The devotee does not call the universe a 'dream-like' state, but says that God has become all, as in the garden of wax everything is made of wax but they have different forms. By constantly thinking of God, devotees become egoless and then eventually he sees "He is me", "I am He" after which comes liberation.' (*Kathamrita, 25 February 1885, p.862*)

Sri Ramakrishna has a district theory about liberation (*mukti*). The dvaita and some schools of vishishtadvaita maintain that the servitude of the Lord is the highest mukti while many vishistadvaitins believe, union and companionship of the Lord is mukti. Advaita Vedanta considers total identity with Brahman as liberation. Without negating the other two aspects, Sri Ramakrishna takes can advaitic standpoint regarding liberation but it is tempered with bhakti. He himself admits that he does not like total nirvana but prefers to have sport with Brahman. 'I don't want to the sugar, I like to eat sugar.' Was his motto. He said, 'I never desire that I say "I am Brahman". I say, "You are God, I am your servant." It is better to move between the fifth and sixth planes (of *Shatchakra*). I do not want to remain long in the seventh plane (of *samadhi*) after crossing the sixth.' (*Kathamrita, 14 December 1882, p.139*)

Again as to the means of liberation Sri Ramakrishna states a reconciliatory approach. While the bhakti schools of Madhva and Ramanuja declares bhakti to the supreme, and jnana as stepping stone to bhakti, advaitin Shankara proposes that bhakti is the lower form of jnana and jnana is the ultimate sàdhanà. Sri Ramakrishna equals jnana and bhakti saying—Pure devotion (*Shuddha bhakti*) and pure knowledge (*suddha jnana*) is one and the same. They lead to the same goal. (*Kathamrita, 11 August, 1883, p.296*) What he, in fact, means is that perfect devotion and perfect knowledge are the same and in vijnani, they can reconciled. (*Kathamrita,15 July 1885, p.943*)

So what is actual standpoint of Sri Ramakrishna? He accepts all these three schools and yet adds something of his own. Sri Ramakrishna's Vedanta has been called 'Synthetic Vedanta' or '*Samanvayi Vedanta*' by Prof. Satis Chandra Chatterjee. He believes that, precisely speaking, Sri Ramakrishna's philosophy is Neo-Advaita, neither Dvaita nor Vishishtadvaita. It is not Dvaita because it holds that there is only one ultimate reality, Brahman, neither two, nor more. It cannot be called Vishishtadvaita because, unlike Ramanuja, Sri Ramakrishna believed in Nirguna Brahman. It is a philosophy of Advaita 'like' Shankara. He reconciles Dvaita, Advaita, Vishishtadvaita, Shakti-advaita, Tantra and other types of Advaita while Shankara excluded them from him doctrine. Furthermore, Sri Ramakrishna somewhat accepts the reality of creation. (*Satish, p.149*)

Let us look into the interpretation of Swami Turiyananda on the philosophical idea of Sri Ramakrishna. On being asked about it, he wrote, 'It is not easy to speak of the Master's philosophical doctrine....The ultimate truth is one without second, which has been delineated as Brahman, Paramatman, Bhagavan etc. He who has realized that truth, tries to express it according to it his own taste and tendency.

'But nobody has been able to reveal 'Complete whole Truth'. 'He is that

He is'—this attitude is the final conclusion of all realized souls.

'The *Ajatavada* of Gaudapada, *Vivartavada* of Shankara, *Parinamavada* of Ramanuja or *Shivadvaitavada* are all true in particular states of mind.

'Again, these apart, He is beyond speech and mind. The proponents of these doctrines have undergone spiritual practices and having received special grace of God, have founded diverse and doctrines with instructions from Him.

'All 'isms' are about Him, but He Himself is beyond all debates. It seems this was the idea that Sri Ramakrishna wanted to preach.

देहबुद्ध्यादासोऽस्मि जीवबुद्ध्यात्वदंशकः।
आत्मबुद्ध्यात्वमेवाहं इति मे निश्चिता मतिः।।

—When I consider myself as body, I think I am your servant, when I think of myself as jiva, I think I am a part of you, when O consider myself as atman, I feel that you are me, this is my firm conviction.

'He used to call this a sound conclusion....' (*Swami Turiyanander Patrabali (Bengali), Udbodhan, Kolkata, p.255*)

REFERENCES

1. His Eastern and Western Disciples, The Life of Swami Vivekananda, 2 vols, Advaita Ashrama, Kolkata, 2008
2. Swami Turiyanander Patrabali (Bengali), Udbodhan, Kolkata
3. Nikhilananda, Swami(trans.) , M, The Gospel of Sri Ramakrishna, Ramakrishna Math, Chennai, 2002
4. Basu, Sankari Prasad, Vivekananda O Samakalin Bharatvarsha (Bengali), Mandal Book House, Calcutta, 1976.
5. Chetanananda, Swami, God Lived With Them, Advaita Ashrama, Kolkata, 1997.
6. Brihadaranyakopanishad, Advaita Ashrama, Kolkata, 1934.
7. Chandogyopanishad, Udbodhan Karyalaya, Kolkata, 1983.

17

Revisiting the aesthetic world of Shri Ramakrishna

Mohit Chakrabarti & Sobdo Chakrabarti

The world of aesthetics is the abode of human refinement in sense and sensibilities. It is the world that assures us with advancement of the self to be in perfect fusion with the Supreme Self by means of unending striving for excellence and ascent. Shri Ramakrishna, one of the greatest aesthetic visionaries for all time and all ages, has considered the life of every human being in association with the flora and fauna of this world a complete and worthwhile manifestation of Truth, Beauty and Goodness. At the same time, he upholds this aesthetic vision that the whole life and work of man in this world is the flowering of the inherent Divine Self through service and simplicity, poignance and catholicity in crystallised contemplation. His aesthetic frankness of vision is transparent, easily accessible, lucid, appealing, loving and down-to-earth to any one anywhere as we always recall his all-endearing and all-embracing opinion: "*Yata mat tata path*" (As there are opinions, so are avenues there). Such superb expressions through simple words with pregnant ideas spread like priceless aesthetic pearls in *Kathamrita.*

An aesthetic visionary of incomparable excellence, Shri Ramakrishna has proved that Bhakti stands for love to the All Love, and to be a lover of the All Love, to be blessed with the immortality as it genuinely becomes the identity of love, man must rise above desire, satisfaction, sorrow, loss, jealousy and so on that testify the true seeker of God. As Swami Vivekananda characteristically reminds us of the invaluable words of Shri Ramakrishna :

> This world is a huge lunatic asylum where all men are mad, some after money, some after women, some after name or fame, and a few after God. Prefer to be mad after God. God is the philosophers' stone that turns us to gold in an instant; the form remains, but the nature is changed— the human form remains, but no more can we hurt or sin.[1]

The essence of aesthetics of the Indian religious thought is best represented by Shri Ramakrishna. He has translated the kernel of the Vedas, the *Bhagavata* and the Vedanta in addition to the other Puranas in all simplicity and cadence, catholicity and poignance. What is more interesting is that the cultivation of aesthetics through religion has become an indivisible and loving part of his life – living, stimulating, easily accessible and pure in practice and perfection. This is why Vivekananda has revered his Master as Ramakrishna Paramahamsa, God incarnate.[2]

A new concept of religion in terms of aesthetics that Shri Ramakrishna has introduced is the religion that heightens the individual and honours him as the real exponent of God; his very existence represents the All Existent so that he declares: gI am That h. Vivekananda unfolds this aesthetic vision of Shri Ramakrishna, his Master, as follows:

> My Master taught that religion is one; all prophets teach the same; but they can only present the principle in a form; so they take it out of the old form and put it before us in a new one. When we free ourselves from name and form, especially from a body— when we need no body, good or bad— then only do we escape from bondage . Eternal progression is eternal bondage; annihilation of form is to be preferred. We must get free from any body, even a ggod-body h. God is the only real existence, there cannot be two. There is but One Soul, and I am That.[3]

Tat Sat, the only real existence through which Shri Ramakrishna identifies the All Love as the essence of religion is the real identity of the aesthetic man. That must be the end-in-view of our existence in the world. Otherwise, we cease to be truly religious. True religion is never different from true love and vice versa. Vivekananda envisions the All Love in the same way as his Master does. In a letter written to Professor John Henry Wright on 4th September, 1893 from Salem, he exposes his aesthetic vision of the All Love in the following lines of a poem:

> A flash illumined all my soul;
> The heart of my heart opened wide.
> O joy, O bliss, what do I find!
> My love, my love, you are here,
> And you are here, my love, my all!
> And I was searching thee!

From all eternity you were there
Enthroned in majesty!

From that day forth, where'er I roam,
I feel Him standing by
O'er hill and dale, high mount and vale,
Far far away and high.

The moon's soft light, the stars so bright,
The glorious orb of day,
He shines in them; His beauty— might—
Reflected lights are they.
The majestic morn, the melting eve,
The boundless billowy sea,
In nature's beauty, songs of birds,
I see through them— it is He.

When dire calamity seizes me,
The heart seems weak and faint,
All nature seems to crush me down,
With laws that never bend.

Meseems I hear Thee whispering sweet
My love, gI am near h, gI am near h.
My heart gets strong. With Thee, my love,
A thousand deaths no fear.
Thou speakest in the mother's lay
That shuts the baby's eye;
When innocent children laugh and play
I see Thee standing by.

When holy friendship shakes the hand,
He stands between them too;
He pours the nectar in mother's kiss
And the baby's sweet gmama h.
Thou wert my God with prophets old;
All creeds do come from Thee;

The Vedas, Bible, and Koran bold
Sing Thee in harmony.

"Thou art", "Thou art" the Soul of souls
In the rushing stream of life.
"Om tat Sat om". Thou art my God.
My love, I am Thine, I am Thine.[4]

As an unparalleled aesthetic thinker and practitioner in religion, Shri Ramakrishna has shown his devotion and esteem to every religion. To him, religion is Truth. Where Truth is, religion is existent in perfect efflorescence of Goodness and Beauty. So any religion representing any opinion, idea, concept or vision well backed by Truth, Goodness and Beauty cannot but be an ideal path to follow for ascent and excellence. This is a straightforward, clear, simple, easy, generous and altruistic aesthetic philosophy of religion of Shri Ramakrishna which poignantly attracted the attention of Vivekananda who has characteristically observed:

> I happened to get an old man to teach me, and he was very peculiar. He did not go much for intellectual scholarship, scarcely studied books; but when he was a boy he was seized with the tremendous idea of getting truth direct. First he tried by studying his own religion. Then he got the idea that he must get the truth of other religions; and with that idea he joined all the sects, one after another. For the time being he did exactly what they told him to do— lived with the devotees of these different sects in turn, until interpenetrated with the particular ideal of that sect. After a few years he would go to another sect. When he had gone through with all that, he came to the conclusion that they were all good. He had no criticism to offer to any one; they are all so many paths leading to the same goal. And then he said, gThat is a glorious thing, that there should be so many paths, because if there were only one path , perhaps it would suit only an individual man. The more the number of paths, the more the chance for every one of us to know the truth. If I cannot be taught in one language, I will try another, and so on. h Thus his benediction was for every religion.[5]

The true identity of man in relation to God as Shri Ramakrishna unfolds before us has no parallel in exposing the aesthetic philosophy of Truth. How to be enlightened with this aesthetic vision? One might recall in this connection

Shri Ramakrishna's most practical and soul-stirring anecdote on the concept of God who is our most endearing One:

> "I and mine. This alone represents right knowledge—' O God! Thou alone art doing everything, and Thou alone art my own. All these houses, buildings, family, relatives, friends, the whole world —everything belongs to Thee!' And I am doing everything; I am the householder. My room, building, family, children, friends, properties — all these are fiction.
>
> "The Master was explaining this to his disciple. God is yours and mine, none else is your very own. The disciple said, 'But, Sir, the mother and the family caress so much; if they don't see us, they encounter darkness; how much they love us!' The Master said, ' O that's an error of your mind. I'm showing you, none is yours. Keep these medicinal tablets with you. Returning home, take these and go asleep. People will think that you are dead. But you will maintain all external sense, you will be able to see and listen to everything, and, at that time, I'll be present there.'
>
> "The disciple accordingly did so. Reaching home, he took those tablets and became senseless. His mother, wife and all others in the house began to cry. At that time the Master appeared there in the guise of a physician. Hearing everything, he said, 'Well, there's a medicine — he will be alive again. But there's a condition. This medicine will have to be taken first by a person of his very own, and only then this will be delivered to him. The person as such who would take that tablet, would die. Now, his mother or his wife are all present here. There is no doubt that any one of them would take that medicine. Then this person will be alive again.
>
> "The disciple is listening to all this. The physician first called the mother. Being shocked in grief, she was rolling on the ground and weeping. 'Mother', said the physician, 'weep no more. Take this medicine. Then your son will be alive. But for that, you will die.' With the medicine in her hand, the mother began to think. Thinking much, she said crying, 'My son, I have a few more sons and daughters. I'm also thinking what would happen to them after my death. Who would look after or feed them?' Then the medicine was delivered to the wife of the disciple. The wife was also greatly crying. Taking the medicine in her hand, she also began to think, and heard that if she

would take it, she would die. Then she started weeping and said,' O whatever is to happen to him has already happened. Tell me what would happen to my hapless children now. Who would save them? How can I take that medicine?' At that time, the disciple has been free from the intoxication of the medicine. He understood that no one is meant for anybody. All on a sudden, he rose up and departed with the Master. The Master said, 'The only one close to you is God.'[6]

The aesthetic vision of God as Shri Ramakrishna unfolds above is very simple and practical, easily accessible and applicable in any religion that stands for fullness and perfection. The I of devotion must be the I as a servant, the I in quest of unending erudition and the I of a boy who is beyond all qualities. It embraces reality side by side with divinity. It is in eternal quest for the nectar. Indeed, Shri Ramakrishna strongly believed and translated in his life the great aesthetic truth:*Raso vai sah. Rasang hovayang lavdhanandi bhavati. / Ko hyevanyat kah pranyat. Yadesha akasa anando na syat.* (Taittiriyopanishat)

To taste the nectar of Hari, the All Divine, is to be a taster, and to be a true taster is to be a servant of the All Divine. Referring to the role of Prahlad, he reminds us:

"Prahlad sometimes visualised, I am He, and sometimes, again, remained like a servant. If devotion is not accepted, with what does the devotee remain? So service is to be sheltered as a servant —Thou art the Lord, I am the servant in order to taste the nectar of Hari. The idea of nectar and the taster of the nectar is — O God, Thou art the nectar. I am the taster of the nectar.

"I am of devotion, I am of erudition, I am of the boy — there is no blame in it. Sankaracharya kept the I of erudition in order to impart mass education. There is no complexity in the I of a boy. The boy is above quality, not a slave to any quality. Just now he is angry; again, nothing of the sort is there in him. Just now he has built the playhouse, at the next moment he forgets everything; just now he is loving players, but in their absence from the eyes, he forgets all. The boy is not under the yoke of any quality like *Sattva, Rajah or Tamah.*

"Thou art God, a devotee am I — this is the idea of a devotee, this 'I' is the 'I of devotion'. Why does the I of devotion protect us? It has a meaning. 'I' is never to depart. So let that silly 'I' remain as a 'slave I' or the 'I of the devotee'.

"Judge a thousand times, the 'I' is never eliminated. It is a pitcher in

> the form of I. Brahma is, as it were, a sea-water everywhere. Water is inside and outside the pitcher as well. Water is spread everywhere. Yet the pitcher is there. That is the real identity of the I of a devotee. So long as the pitcher is existent, there are you and I. Thou art God, a devotee am I; Thou art the Lord, a slave am I; this is also existent. Assess a thousand times, there is no chance for elimination of this. If there is no pitcher, then it will be a different story."[7]

Elsewhere, Shri Ramakrishna elucidates the concept of 'I' in terms of aesthetic efflorescence of emancipation almost in the same way:

> "After *Samadhi,* somebody is in possession of 'I' – 'the slave I', 'the I of the devotee'. Sankaracharya kept the 'I of erudition' for mass education. The 'slave I', 'the I of erudition', 'the I of the devotee' –these are named as 'the ripe I'. Do you know what the green I is? I am the head, I am the son of a very rich man. Learned and wealthy as I am, who dares say so?—such is the temperament. If anyone steals in the house, if he is caught, all the articles are at first snatched away from him. Then the owner beats him and later on hands him over to the police. Then he proclaims,'Doesn't he know whose belongings he has stolen?'
>
> "When one is in unison with God, his behaviour turns out to be just like that of a five year old boy. 'The I of the boy' and 'the ripe I'. The boy is not under the control of any quality. Beyond the three qualities. Not under any of the three qualities: *Sattva-Rajah-Tamah.* Behold, the boy is not under the spell of *Tamah.* Just now he quarrelled and immediately afterwards how endearing, how playful with the same playmates! He is not even under the control of the quality of *Rajah.*[8]

Self-belief and joy are the two aesthetic watch words in the success of any work to be accomplished. Unless there is a positive approach strengthened by these two components, we cannot succeed. Shri Ramakrishna clarifies this point very lucidly:

> Any work prenecessitates a belief. Along with that, remembering the thing, joy prevails. Only then the person for that work associates with it. There is a pitcher full of treasure underground —first, this knowledge and belief are required. Thinking about the pitcher, the mind gets joy. Then digging is done. While doing so,if there is a tinkering sound of the pitcher, joy is aggravated. Thereafter, the edge

> of the pitcher is seen. Then joy is more intensified. In this way, joy gradually increases.[9]

At the same time, one cannot but recall Shri Ramakrishna's viewpoints on the world of the aesthetic vision very often vitiated by devaluation of devotion:

> There was a jewellery shop. The owner was a great devotee, a sincere Vaishnav with a garland around the neck, *tilak* on the forehead, and in the hand the garland for counting the name of Hari. Believing him, every one came to that very shop, thought that those were all great devotees and would never try to cheat.
>
> When a group of customers had come, he would see that a certain jewellery worker hailed, 'Kesav, Kesav'. Another worker was naming, 'Gopal!' 'Gopal'! Sometime afterwards, another jewellery worker was pronouncing 'Hari, Hari'. Thereafter, someone else uttered, 'Hara, Hara'. Therefore, listening to the name of God, the customers would easily think that the jeweller was a very good man. But do you know the real matter? The idea of the person who said 'Kesav, Kesav!' is: Who are these (customers)? The words of the person who said 'Gopal, Gopal!' signifies: I looked at these and found them to be a herd of cows. The meaning of the words 'Hari, Hari' is : if these is a herd of cows, then let's steal. One who said 'Hara Hara' wanted to mean: then, of course, steal. A herd of cows these customers are![10]

Admittedly, Shri Ramakrishna has kept our mind wide open to assess the true aesthetic vision of religion where dogma, delusion or myth has no room for welcome or appreciation. The difference between knowledge and ignorance as he spells out in terms of aesthetics is not only unique but also simple and transparent. How to know Brahma, God Absolute? Here is his answer:

> "See, cross the bridge between knowledge and ignorance. Then it is possible to know Him. Ignorance is the name of different knowledge. The pride of pedantry is also ignorance. In every living being, One God exists. Knowledge stands for this absolute intelligence. To know Him in particular is called specific knowledge or science. For instance, the leg is thorn pricked. To remove it, another thorn is required. After removal of the thorn, both the thorns are thrown away. First, the thorn of knowledge is brought to wipe out the thorn of ignorance. Afterwards, both the thorns— one of knowledge and the other of knowledge – are to be thrown away. Beyond knowledge and ignorance,

He is. Lakshman said, 'Ram, how wonderful it is! Vasishthadev, so vastly learned, cried restlessly in bereavement of his son.' 'Brother', said Ram, 'one who has erudition has also ignorance. One who has knowledge of one has also knowledge of many. One who has the sense of light, has also the sense of darkness. Brahma is beyond knowledge, virtue and vice. Religion and irreligion, purity and impurity'."[11]

Shri Ramakrishna himself practised this aesthetic cohesion of antithesis as above in terms of devotion. Citing an example of the incomparable devotee, Ahalya, he poignantly describes:

"After Ahalya's emancipation from the curse, Ramchandra said to her, 'Pray for boon to me.' Ahalya said, 'Ram, if you want to bless me with the boon, then give me this boon: if I am born in the womb of a swine, there is no harm; but O Ram! let my mind lie in Thy lotus-feet.

"I wanted devotion only to the Mother. Offering flowers at the lotus-feet , I said with folded hands, 'Mother, take this Thy ignorance, take this Thy knowledge, give me pure devotion. Take this Thy purity, take this Thy impurity, give me pure devotion. Take this Thy vice, take this Thy virtue, give me pure devotion. Take this Thy good, take this Thy evil, give me pure devotion. Take this Thy religion, take this Thy irreligion, give me pure devotion.'[12]

That purity is inherent in impurity, virtue in vice, knowledge in ignorance, light in darkness and vice versa is a great aesthetic philosophy of ascent and marvel which Shri Ramakrishna translated in his natural and altruistic practice of perfection. He shows us not to suffer from any antagonism, narrowness of vision and accomplishment whatsoever or howsoever, but deep in our heart of hearts there must be the endless quest for perfection and beyond that. That is aesthetic devotion. That also is the emancipation of man.

Suri Ramakrishna's aesthetic world stands for fulness and the beyond. It is an endless quest for encounter with the All Beautiful, an untiring and steadfast journey for meeting the All Good, and an abiding mission for seeking the avenue of the All True by plunging deep into the sea of nectar . The Jnana-Yoga in perfect cohesion with the two other paths of self-purity and self-emancipation viz. The Bhakti-Yoga and the Karma-Yoga leads one to the lotus-land of divinity.

The way to encounter with the All Good as Shri Ramakrishna has aesthetically described and experienced is manifold. As he clearly spells out:

See, there are endless paths to go to the sea of nectar. It is to be united with this sea by any means whatsoever. Suppose, there is a reservoir of nectar. Whether you yourself plunge into that reservoir or take a bit of it by getting down slowly or somebody push you down to it, you will be deathless by sipping a bit through the mouth. The result is the same. If you taste a little of the nectar, you will be death-defying.

Knowledge, action and devotion— in whatever endless path you tread on, if you are sincere, you will encounter God.

The Jnana-Yoga— the wise wants to know Brahma, and assesses everything negatively. Brahma is True, the world is false — this is the assessment that he makes. He assesses what is existent and what is non-existent. Where assessment ends, Samadhi takes place there and the knowledge of Brahma is attained.

The Karma-Yoga-- to be devoted to God by action. Whatever you are teaching indicates that. Unattached *pranayama* and meditation and so on are Karma-Yoga. Being unattached, if worldly people submit to God for the result, have devotion to Him and perform worldly activities, that also is Karma-Yoga. To submit the result to God and perform activities like worship, japa and so on also stand for Karma-Yoga. To attain God is the end-in-view of Karma-Yoga.

The Bhakti-Yoga — to keep the mind closely attached to God by glorifying His name through songs and hymns etc.[13]

That Bhakti-Yoga is the touchstone for aesthetic unison with the All Existent, All Pervading *Sachchidananda* is what Shri Ramakrishna reminds us in a very simple way. He does not consider the world apart from citadel of devotion. It is the world that serves as the cathedral of the All True, All Beautiful and All Abiding. As he elegantly describes:

"If you are blessed with the blessings of the Mother of the world, you will also be blessed with devotion and knowledge."[14]

To revisit the aesthetic world of Shri Ramakrishna is to re-illuminate the eternal world of joy. It is the world that blesses us with consciousness, wisdom and self-abnegation. It is also the world that teaches us how to eliminate the so-called distinction between 'you' and 'I' and merge into the 'I' that stands for all by eliminating the little 'I' in everyone of us. It is the most aesthetic worship of man the Divine and All Beautiful. To Shri Ramakrishna and to everyone of us to lead a life is to lead it aesthetically and to lead aesthetically is to qualify oneself with the extinction of personality. A great aesthetic visionary like Shri Ramakrishna has shown us the way of the ascent of man by means of reducing ourselves to a blob. It is *samadhi* – a perfection through encounter with the All Knowledge, All Existence and All Bliss.

When are we in the quest for *sachchidanandamoy* as Shri Ramakrishna is a timeless aesthetic visionary?

REFERENCES

1. Swami Vivekananda: *The Complete Works of Swami Vivekananda,* Advaita Ashrama, Kolkata, Mayavati Memorial Edition, 1989, Vol. VII, p. 8.
2. In a letter written to Swami Shivananda, Vivekananda pays his tribute to his Master: Whether Bhagavan Shri Krishna was born at all we are not sure; and Avataras like Buddha and Chaitanya are monotonous; Ramakrishna Paramahamsa is the latest and the most perfect— the concentrated embodiment of knowledge, love, renunciation, catholicity, and the desire to serve mankind. So where is anyone to compare with him? He must have been born in vain who cannot appreciate him! My supreme good fortune is that I am his servant through life after life. A single word of his is to me far weightier than the Vedas and the Vedanta. *Tasya dasadasadasoham*— Oh, I am the servant of the servants of his servants. But narrow bigotry militates against his principles, and this makes me cross. Rather let his name be crowned in oblivion, and his teachings bear fruit instead! Why, was he a slave to fame? Certain fishermen and illiterate people called Jesus Christ a God, but the literate people killed him. Buddha was honoured in his lifetime by a number of merchants and cowherds. But Ramakrishna has been worshipped in his lifetime—towards the end of this nineteenth century by the demons and giants of the university as God incarnate.—*Ibid.,* pp. 483-484.
3. *Ibid.,* pp. 17-18.
4. *Ibid.,* pp. 451-452.
5. *Ibid.,* Vol. VIII, pp. 78-79.
6. Shri M: *Shri Shri Ramakrishna Kathamrita,* Reflect Publication, Kolkata, 1983. Translated by us.
7. *Ibid.,* p. 290. Translated by us.
8. *Ibid.,* pp154-155. Translated by us.
9. *Ibid.,* p. 169. Translated by us.
10. *Ibid.,* p. 168. Translated by us.
11. *Ibid.,* p. 173. Translated by us.
12. *Ibid.,* pp. 174-175. Translated by us.
13. *Ibid.,* p. 115. Translated by us.
14. *Ibid.,* p. 115. Translatd by us.

18

Ramakrishna on human values

Raghunath Ghosh

The paper deals with some comments of Ramakrishna Paramhamsa addressed to his disciples which emphasizes the glorification of human values. If these values are inculcated seriously in our society, many social problems can be eradicated.

In order to fulfil this mission in life, each and every action performed by us should be for a good cause; for the sacrifice of our little self and for the good of all humanity. Our body is of no use if it is not engaged in the well-being of others. In the same way, the mind which we possess is of no consequence if it is not applied to the well-being of others. Similarly, the sense organs too are stated as having no causal efficacy if they are not associated with the welfare of others.[20] This reminds one of the following *mantra* of the Kenopanisad:

Srotrasya srotram manaso mano yad
Vâco ha vâcam sa u prânasya prânah;
Caksusascaksur-atimucya dhîrâh
Pretyâsmâl-lokâd-amrtâ bhavanti.

Since he is the Ear of the ear, the Mind of the mind, the Speech of the speech, the Breath of the breath and the Eye of the eye, the wise men, knowing Him, giving up the wrong notion of self or dispelling egoism, attain immortality.

This *mantra* can be interpreted in the light of Ramakrishna's philosophy as follows: the eye becomes the eye in the true sense of the term if it can see to the welfare of all (not only of one's own). In the same way, the mind can be described as mind if it can think of others' well being. If someone understands the functions of the sense-organs also in this way, he can easily forsake his egotism and can extend his own self to overlap others, which is described as attaining immortality. The eye, mind, etc. of such a person become cosmic.

Considering this aspect of human value, Ramakrishna says that an individual, when born as a human being, should leave an indelible mark in the world *(janmechhis jakhan dag rekhe ja).* That mark is to become a transformed personality with a cosmic identity.

The above-mentioned standpoint may be substantiated with the concept of *Sat* in Indian tradition. An individual having *sattva* element is called *Sat* in as much as the term *sattva* is derived from the term *sat* and hence a balanced person can also be described as *sat* due to possessing the balanced quality of *sattva*. The literal meaning of the term *sat* is 'existent' or 'that which is existing'. One who is existent is called *Sat.* From this it follows that a man who has justified his existence is called *sat.* If a man does not perform any positive act, his existence is not justified in the sense that he has not made his existence meaningful. If, on the other hand, a man justifies his existence by way of performing many social works, he is called *sat* in the true sense of the term. The *satta* of an individual does not mean his mere physical existence. Those who are negatively famous or negatively prove their existence are called *asat.* In fact here an individual's existence is *socially* denied. Through the performance of duties in various spheres of life towards our family members, social members etc. by way of performing good works, social welfare, service to humanity etc. our existence is justified and hence we are called *sat* who is otherwise known as honest. The physically existent person who does not perform his duties for the sake of harmony is *asat.* Considering this aspect a father who is annoyed upon his son not performing duties properly is found lamenting with the word: 'I have no son though he exists'. A man, on the other hand, being satisfied with the service rendered by a stranger with whom he has no blood connection is found saying-' I am endowed with son though actually I have not.' In the former case the son has got physical existence, which is tantamount to not having a son. In the latter case the son having no physical existence is taken as equal to having a son after keeping the duties performed by the individual in mind. The Buddhists, I think, believed in this concept of existence. To them an object is to be understood as *sat* if it has got some causal efficacy *(arthakriyâkâritva)*. An object is called *sat* if it has got the capacity of serving others. If the same object fails to do so, it is called *asat.* The objects like jar etc. come under the first category as they bear the above-mentioned capacity while the sky-flower etc. belong to the second category due to not having the above-mentioned capacity of serving some purpose. Such a theory can be extended to other fields also. Behind the formulation of such notions of *sat* and *asat* some idea related social good or welfare is very much related. Following this line it can be said that an individual is consider as really existing after considering what type social welfare has been done by him. It is only the justification or *arthakriyâkâritva* for his existence, which is described by Vivekananda as indelible mark. Even to adopt *maitrî, karuòâ* etc is to be taken as the mark of our existence. Our existence endowed with such causal efficacy in the positive sense is called *sat.* Otherwise he is called *asat.* Hence *sattâ* or *asattâ* of an object as well as of an individual is determined in terms of its causal efficacy or otherwise respectively. To the Buddhists our human body is nothing but an object. As it is a human body, the *sattâ* of it is determined by the causal efficacy connected with human value or social value which is again connected with *maitrî, karuòâ* etc. If a person claims himself as *sat* due to his high post or family etc., he is not taken as *sat.* A person may become self-luminous through his auspicious deeds and hence he is called *sat.* We find an echo of this principle in the following religious poem composed by Kabira:

> *"Vada huya to kya hoya yaisa vadi khejur,*
> *Panthoko chaya nahi phal lagi atidur"*

That is, what is the use of being born in a high family? Just as big date-palm tree has no significance to the society in as much as it does not provide the travellers with shadow and as the fruits exist in a such a high altitude that they cannot be collected by the social beings, a person born in a high society or having higher education is insignificant to the society if he does not perform social welfare etc. It is known to us that a man proves his real existence by way of doing auspicious works like social welfare etc., but not through his birth in the high family or race etc. Such an idea has been expressed by Bhartrhari in his *Nîtiúataka.* The *sloka* runs as follows:

> "Eke satpurusâh parâthaghaþakâh svârthân parityajya ye,
> Sâmânyâstu parârthamudyamabhstâ svârthâvirodhena ye,
> Temî mânavaraksasâh parahitam svârthâya nighnanti ye,
> Ye tu ghnanti nirarthakam parahitam te ke na jânîmahe."
>
> (Verse no.64)

The above-mentioned *œloka* has been translated by Swami Ranganathananda in his *Eternal Values of a Changing Society* in the following manner: "There are some *satpurusas*, good people, who engage themselves in the good of others sacrificing their own self-interest; the *Samanyas,* the generality of people, on the other hand, are those who engage themselves in the good of others so long as it does not involve the sacrifice of their self-interest. There are those others, the *Manavaraksakas,* devilish men, who sacrifice the good of others to gain their selfish ends; but alas, what am I to say of those who sacrifice the good of others without gaining thereby any good to themselves or to any one else." (P.580, Bombay, 1971). The *satpurusas* or good men have got their overwhelming goodness not vitiated through the selfish motive and they have really glorified their existence. If they try to fulfil their own self-interest without paying any heed to the welfare of others, they are not called *sat* in the true sense of the term. The people who destroy others' welfare in order to get more pleasure in their own lives are called *mânavarâksakas*, the devilish men. They are so called because at this stage they try to satisfy their biological needs, but fail to develop their morality. Such persons try to fulfil their narrow interest at the cost of others and that is why, they are called devils in the form of men. In order to highlight this aspect of the true nature of man Ramakrishna Paramahamsa told that a true human being should have both sense of honour (*mân*) and carefulness about the welfare of other fellow beings (*hunœ).* An individual maintaining these two should be considered as a true human being who has justified his existence.

In practical life Sri Ramakrishna also advised Narendranath to be balanced in behaviour after keeping both the extreme situations in view. He narrated a beautiful story. Once the Master asked his snake – disciple to forsake violence. Hence, the snake decided to remain quiet all the time without injuring others by injecting its venom. It could not gather food and grew weak. Cowherds pelted stones at it in order to have some fun. This happened everyday. Once, on repeated questioning by his Master, the snake informed him about the situation also adding that the little boys were not to blame, as they did not know its change in attitude. The Master thereupon told the snake that he had asked it to adopt non-violence, but had not dissuaded it from frightening others with the hissing sound if there was a need for it. That is, an individual living in the world should avoid extremes in order to live peacefully. If someone adopts either extreme, of resistance or of non-resistance, he will no doubt suffer due to the absence of balance. Excessive attachment to food, clothes and the tending of the body and dressing of the hair should be avoided. Selfishness is always to be avoided in order to adhere to the status of balance. In the *Bhagavad-gita* we may find the echo of this theory. It is said that one who extremely enjoys something from others without giving them any thing in return is a thief (... *apradâyaîbhyo yo bhunkte stena eva sa* 3/12*)*).

Another practical aspect of Ramakrishna's philosophy is not mere tolerance but the acceptance of other religious paths. Religious life is a journey from truth to truth, from lower truth to higher truth. We should look upon others with love. So, the Advaita Vedanta of Swami Vivekananda accepts and respects all religious approaches as different paths leading humanity to the same ultimate goal. In the words of Sri Ramakrishna, 'As many faiths so many paths' *(yata mat tato path).*

It is said by Ramakrishna that a human being who is tolerant remains in this world and he who is intolerant is ruines *(Je sai se rai, je na sai se nash hai).* The *Gopis* are tolerant in the sense that they have endured much trouble for getting Krishna. Hence good always comes out of evils which are taken as Divine Sports (*lîlâ).*

Simplicity should be the mark of a man. It means to be transparent among what we think, what we act and what we speak (*Man muck ek hao*). This simplicity is equivalent to Divinity. Simplicity is the abode of Brahman as endorsed in the Kenoponisad. It is better to be as simple as a child (*'shishur mato saral') (Sri Sri Ramakrishnakathamrita,*Ananda, 1983, pp.176-177)

No man is a sinner. One who thinks himself sinner becomes really a sinner (*'Je pap pap sarvada kare se papi haye jai'*). A human being is the son of the Immortal (*Am°tasya putrâh*).

A human should keep himself in aesthetic enjoyment or joy which is nothing but Divinity (*raso vai sah*). Ramakrishna was full aesthetic bliss and always pray to Goddess to keep him amidst such pleasure (*amai rasebaœe rakhis ma suska sannyasi karis ne*).

There are many practical utilities of the advices given by Ramakrishna. Excepting the *Bhâva-samâdhi* part I find no mysticism in his life. At the level of *bhavasamadhi* Ramakrishna had many experiences which are to be taken as purely mystical.

Ramakrishna was more interested in human welfare and human good, which is reflected in the above-mentioned paths like practicing simplicity, adopting transparency among what we think, speak and act, thinking human beings as the son of Immortal (not sinner), adhering to the good virtues like tolerance, acceptance of all religions etc. If such practices prevail in the society, no problem would remain unsolved leading to social peace and harmony.

REFERENCES

1. Gupta, Mahendra Nath. The Gospels of Sri Ramakrishna, tr. by Swami Nikhilananda, Sri Ramakrishna Math, Mylapore, Madras, 1981
2. Gambhirananda, Swami . Holy Mother Sri Sarada Devi, Ramakrishna Math, Chennai, 2004.
3. Rolland, Romain , The Life of Ramakrishna, E F Malcolm-Smith(trans.), Advaita Ashrama, Kolkata, 2008
4. Ghanananda, Swami , Sri Ramakrishna and His Unique Message, Advaita Ashrama, Kolkata, 2005.

19

Kathamrita: Thy nectar

Sk. Makbul Islam

The world has witnessed series of scriptures and religious texts during the last several thousand years. Words that have indoctrinated human mind into God-consciousness found expression through the *Vedas*, *Puranas*, *Dhammapada*, Bible, *Al-Quran*, *Guru Granthsahib* - etc. We all know about these scriptures. Sri Ramakrishna's *Kathamrita* is one among such texts which has taught the world not only God-consciousness, but also has given adequate space to the philosophy and essence of all the previous scriptures. From this point of interpretation, the *Kathamrita* occupies a distinctly unique position amongst the scriptures of the world.

The Perspective of Sri Ramakrishna and Contemporary Time

When we read the *Kathamrita*, we come across with the same 'truth' which was pronounced by the prophets of the other parts of the world. Nevertheless, the words of *Kathamrita* enable us to transgress the limitations of 'religion' stimulating our inner-soul to realize '*Dharma*' and spirituality in its true sense. Before I enter into the main domain of discussion, it is essential to say some relevant points about Sri Ramakrishna, who with his limitless kindness had pronounced the words of *Kathamrita*.

1. Sri Ramakrishna was born in colonial period when India was dominated by the British.
2. The nation started searching for new 'identity' in terms of freedom which had both political dimension and spiritual dimension. Sri Ramakrishna's spiritual dimension added a new force in the dry arteries of our nation (which continued through Ma, Vivekananda and Ramakrishna order).
3. He had profound knowledge of '*Shastra*', yet there is no proof that he knew (or learnt) the *Shastra* through any so called formal education system (I believe he had learnt the essence of *Shastra* from the traditional process of oral communication; the 'folk process' that more depended on transmission

of the context and cognition indoctrinating people to act in conformity to 'Dharma' than that of mere theoretical knowledge.)

4. It can be presumed that he never trod to 'school' as was formulated by the foreign education system. But consequently he himself became the pioneer or of a distinct school of vision (the Ramakrishna Order).
5. As he himself personifies the *Shastriya* concept of '*Brahmin*' in true sense, his mind and heart were broad enough to perceive man and society from the point of '*Sat-Chit-Ananda*'. He always went in conformity to 'tradition' (*Aithiya*) grossly rejecting all narrowness that were detrimental to '*dharma*' and humanity.
6. He was appointed as a priest in the temple of '*Ma-Bhabatarini*' in the native state of an indigenous queen 'Rani Rasmoni' (who was considered as a 'woman' of 'low caste' in the then society). This temple was established on 31st May 1855 A.D. This temple became the hub of liberal vision from where the message of spiritual liberty was transmitted only because of Sri Ramakrishna, his disciples and well wishers.
7. Sri Ramakrishna settled in Dakshineswar which was not purely a town (Kolkata) and not purely a village from which he originated. But his connection with the elites of town (Kolkata) was quiet frequent.
8. Though he had no fame as 'literate' (or 'educated') yet he had close relation with the cream of the 'educated' of the then society and was highly respected by them.
9. How Sri Ramakrishna taught people? He himself was an instance of having profound faith in God and an evidence of having been realized God. His life taught nation the lesson of '*Dharma*' in a renewed manner.
10. He himself had never written anything for bringing about reform in the society. But his words (written by Sri Mahendranath Gupta / 'M'), has paved a way of reformation in the 'thought process' of the then society.
11. Sri Ramakrishna practiced almost all the major 'religions' like Islam, Christianity, Shikhism etc. Besides he practiced all the major branches of 'Sanatan Dharma' like – Shaivism, Vaishnavism, Tantra -etc.
12. To Sri Ramakrishna, all these practices were certainly secondary. The most important point is that he had perceived God and His creation from the perspective of 'One Absolute Consciousness' where only God is 'Truth' and being 'Truth' God is present everywhere. In this cosmic creation, God is present in man and matter.

13. He taught that God is to be 'realized' in the core of one's own heart, and one should surrender unto God to get His blessing. One should feel God with faith and devotion. It would be a foolish endeavour on the part of man to measure what God is and what not (as we do it in case of measuring any 'matter').
14. Sri Ramakrishna's life demonstrated a liberal version of the *Sanatan Dharma* in its proper connotation. He had shown us that spirituality (spiritual realization) is different than that of the rituals of 'religion'. He also showed that 'magic' (exercise of supernatural power) is not an integral part of *Dharma Sadhana*. He himself being a doubtless example had shown us a purified form of *Dharma Sadhana* and interpreted the concept of *Dharma*.
15. He never deviated from the path of *Sanatan* order. For his own practice he made some reformation, but ultimately Sri Ramkrishna stayed an embodiment of *Sanatan Dharma*. This is a commendable fact in his life. He never had deviated form the *Sanatan path*.
16. The uniqueness of his *Sanatan* practice was that he had included all the faiths and sects into the fold of his *Sanatan Sadhana*. That is why he loved Islam, Christianity and other religions too, strengthening the process of human integrity and amity in a new direction entirely from the perspective of spirituality.
17. There is no actual 'difference'. Everything is 'Brahma'. He manifests Himself in different forms. This philosophical approach of Vedanta was very much prominent in Sri Ramakrishna and Swami Vivekananda. Such an approach had paved the way of integrity, harmony, mutual-friendship amongst us. This was also a kind of reformation (in thought process).

All the points together mentioned above reflect the perspectives of Sri Ramakrishna and his *Kathamrita* too. The main objective of this write up is to analyze some salient points of the *Kathamrita* as well as to observe how the teachings of *Kathamrita* has accelerated the process of human amity in the context of Sri Ramakrishna's contemporary time and even beyond. Issues that have been discussed here are:

i. About God

ii. About Guru

iii. Incarnation

iv. About Sadhu-Sannyasi

v. Types of Guru
vi. Bhakti Yoga in Kaluyug
vii. Sri Ramakrishna's God: Sociological Relevance
viii. Knowledge and beyond
ix. About Islam
x. *Kathamrita*: an alternative enlightenment

3.1. About God

Doubt and uncertainty have led some people to confusion, resulting in gross disbelief in God (or in supreme power). Some of our doubts have been liquidated with the help of scriptures (like Gita, Dharmapada, Bible, Quran etc.). The 19th and 20th century Bengal too has seen multiple uncertainty and confusion in many aspects of social and spiritual life. The collective mind of the then intelligence was divided into many. In such an age of multi-idealism, Sri Ramakrishna himself beyond all doubts stood out a witness of God grossly advocating 'certainty' in existence of God. This was really unique in Sri Ramakrishna.

Swami Vivekananda aspired to realize God. But he had some doubts. Sri Ramakrishna liquidated all his doubts. He asked Sri Ramakrishna – "Have you seen God? Sri Ramakrishna promptly replied – Yes, I have seen God. I have seen closer than I see you" (Gambhirananda, Vol-1, pg. 83). The age has heard Sri Ramakrishna say: 'Yes, I have seen God'. There was no confusion. There was no doubt. Sri Ramakrishna was doubtless about God. This became true in Swami Vivekananda's life too.

What was Sri Ramakrishna's view on God? In *Kathamrita*, Sri Ramakrishna had mentioned countless points. Some significant lines necessary for our study is quoted below:

1. "God can be seen" (*Kathamrita*, p.111, 205; Translation: Author)
2. "God is perceptible with pure heart and pure mind" (*Kathamrita*, p.111; Translation: Author)
3. "After purifying one's own mind and after having devotion, one can see God by His blessing" (*Kathamrita* , p. 111; Translation: Author).
4. "One is unable to get God if he has any earthly desires." (*Kathamrita*, p.134; Translation: Author).
5. "A man devoid of 'desire' is capable to see Himself." (*Kathamrita*, p.134; Translation: Author)

6. "None and nothing is Pure but He – the One." (*Kathamrita*, p.134; Translation: Author)
7. "God is truth. This world is temporal." (*Kathamrita*, p.200, 356, 382; Translation: Author).
8. "God is the doer, everything happens by His will." (*Kathamrita*, p.204; Translation: Author)
9. "It needs '*sadhan*' to see God." (*Kathamrita*, p.205,318; Translation: Author)
10. "A *simple-hearted* man can get God quickly." (*Kathamrita*, p.230; Translation: Author)
11. "Be in truth, you can obtain God." (*Kathamrita* , p.234; Translation: Author)
12. "The aim of human life is to achieve God." (*Kathamrita*, p.318; Translation: Author)
13. "It is possible to realize God by giving up ego and designation." (*Kathamrita*, p.356; Translation: Author)
14. "God is to be realized only in truth." (*Kathamrita*, p.417; Translation: Author)
15. "God realization is not possible until we surrender our mind unto Him." (*Kathamrita*, p.427; Translation: Author)

These points may seem more theoretical. But to Sri Ramakrishna God was not any theoretical speculation. To him, God is perceived 'truth'. His God-concept is extended to the concept of 'Guru' (the Spiritual Master). Without understanding this, Sri Ramakrishna's concept of God can hardly be understood in conformity to Ramakrishna's sense. To Sri Ramakrishna God and 'Sat-Guru' are same, equal and identical. It would be worthwhile to mention Sri Ramakrishna's concept of '*Guru*' by exploring the text of *Kathamrita*.

3.2. About Guru

'*Guruvada*' or '*Guru-parampara*' (succession of Gurus) is a very significant doctrine in Indian philosophy and religious tradition. In spite of absence of the technical epithet – 'Guruvada', dependence on spiritual masters is available in almost all the major religions of the world in different forms. However, in Indian continent Guru has exclusive prime role in arousing spiritual knowledge and God-consciousness among the devotees. Guru in its true connotation is equated with God. God is 'Param-Brahma'. The original Sanskrit mantra says:

> "*Gururbrahma gururvishnu gururdeva maheshswara*
> *Gurureva param brahma, tasmoi sri Gurove namah*" [1]

Meaning

Guru is Brahma, Guru is Vishnu. Gurudeva is Maheshwara.
Guru himself is Param-Brahma, I bow down to Guru.
(Translation: Author)

If we analyze this single verse on Guru, we must understand that Guru occupies the position of God. This is because Guru is capable to bestow spiritual vision on devotee's eye. Guru 'opens the blind eyes' of devotee and brings 'light' into them. Here these expressions are symbolic. Here blindness is *ignorance*[2]. The light implies '*spiritual knowledge*'[3]. When one's eyes are opened with *spiritual consciousness* or God-consciousness, the eyes become *divine eye*[4]. Guru is the threshold of God. That is why the doctrine of Guru is so important in *Sanatan Dharma*. The principal concepts of Guru and its importance are referred to in '*Guru-Gita*'[5] compiled by Swami Raghubarananda.

I am not going to bring forth any detailed discussion on the doctrine of Guru as described in Indian philosophy. My aim is to present Sri Ramakrishna's view on Guru and to evaluate Sri Ramakrishna as 'Guru' (*Spiritual Master*).

Who is Guru? Sri Ramakrishna's unambiguous reply was: "*Sacchidananda* only is Guru. He alone will teach..." (*Kathamrita*, p. 91). Sri Ramakrishna made it clear that only God is Guru. Some men in the world can pretend like Guru, but they are not at all Guru in true sense. If a man gets the blessing of God Almighty he can act as Guru in conformity to God's direction. Without receiving any revelation from God man can neither become a Guru nor become worthy to give spiritual lesson to common people.

> "Taking the task of Guru as *profession* is similar to prostitution. Money is useless, selling oneself for getting popularity and physical pleasure makes no meaning. God can be attained with this body and soul. It is not wise to sell this body and soul for the cause of narrow end" (*Kathamrita*, Translation: Author, p.795).

Sri Ramakrishna also added that

> "Man can never become Guru by his own. Everything happens by the will of God" (Kathamrita, Translation: Author ,p. 647).

Whom Sri Ramakrishna considered to be Guru must be an incarnated. In this connection, Sri Ramakrishna's sayings on incarnation may be discussed here.

3.3. Incarnation

One of the basic tenets of Hinduism is that it believes God is incarnated as Guru. That is why Sacchidananda and Guru are 'one'. Srimadbhagabat Gita taught us that God himself descends in this world to establish 'Dharma'[6]. In *Kathamrita* Sri Ramakrishna said –

> "To teach lesson to common-folk, God is incarnated as Guru in different age" (*Kathamrita*, Translation: Author, p.37)
>
> In another reference of Kathamrita he mentioned:
>
> "To teach common-folk lesson Samadhista Purush descends and speaks (to us)" (*Kathamrita*, Translation: Author, p.50)

The point which I subscribe to in this context, *God, Guru* and *Incarnation* are the three *key words* to understand the relationship between God and human beings.

A sannyasi is also 'sad-Guru'. Sannyasi is also empowered to teach lesson to people. Sri Ramakrishna opined:

> "A saintly man's sacrifice teaches other people to learn sacrifice... sannyasi is sad-Guru" (*Kathamrita*, Translation: Author, p.142)

Since sannyasi is also Guru, that is why he has to undergo extreme restriction to set an example before common people. (*Kathamrita*, Translation: Author, p.142)

3.4. About *Sadhu-Sanyasi*

Sri Ramakrishnadev considered a Sanyasi to be Sad-Guru. This is because Sanyasi teaches common folk sacrifice by setting instance of sacrifice himself. In *Kathamrita* Sri Ramakrishna said

> "People will learn to sacrifice by seeing a Sanyasi's selfless sacrifice. Otherwise the common people will totter. Sanyasi is Sad-Guru." (*Kathamrita*, p. 142, Translation: Author)

I would like to add that the Sanyasi parampara initiated by Sri Ramakrishna is also a Guru-parampara. Sri Ramakrishna wanted it to happen that 'Naren will teach the common folk'. The same task is being carried out by the Sanyasis of Sri Ramakrishna's order. This is what I personally subscribe to.

4. Types of Guru

In *Kathamrita* Sri Ramakrishna had used two words: '*Sad-Guru*' (Guru in true sense) and '*Kancha-Guru*' (novice Master; *Kathamrita*, p.119). A novice

Guru is unable to emancipate his devotee (*Kathamrita*, p.119) But a *Sad-Guru* can easily make his disciples emancipated (*Kathamrita*, p.119). "A fully enlightened Guru can show the right way" (*Kathamrita*, p.337).

Sri Ramakrishna said that if one's sense of ego is wiped out by the grace of Guru then he can realize God (*Kathamrita*, p.120). Sri Ramakrishna emphasized faith on Guru's words. He mentioned that *Sadhana* is essential (*Kathamrita*, p.217). Faith in Guru's words is also a form of *Sadhana*.

Sri Ramakrishna clarified that God himself descends as Guru in different ages to 'teach common folk'[7] (*Kathamrita*, p.37). Sri Ramakrishna further added that if man attains consciousness then it should be known that Almighty *Sacchidananda* has appeared in the form of a human (*Kathamrita*, p.180). That is why Sri Ramakrishna added that if anybody takes initiation from human-Guru and thinks him to be 'common man' then he will have no achievement. One has to think Guru to be God. This faith is enough (*Kathamrita*, p.272). We find similar words in other places of *Kathamrita*, such as: "Faith in Guru's word is essential. By following his words one can realize God" (*Kathamrita*, p.536).

After attaining 'faith' in Guru's words, one has to obey the advice of Guru. According to Sri Ramakrishna, executing Guru's advice is *Karma Yoga*. He mentioned:

> "Attention and Karma-Yoga. Offering puja, pilgrimage, service to mankind according to the advice of Guru implies Karma-Yoga (*Kathamrita*, p.736)."

5. Bhakti Yoga in Kali Yuga

Sri Ramakrishna considered *Bhakti Yoga* to be the Dharma of this age. *Karma Yoga*, *Jnana Yoga* are also ways, but they are sometimes difficult to perform. That is why he prescribed *Bhakti Yoga* for our time. Some of his quotations may be referred to here to get the essence of his points:

a. "*Bhakti Yoga*, chanting God's name and prayer is best in Kali Yuga. *Bhakti Yoga* is the religion of this age." (*Kathamrita*, p. 93; Translation: Author)

b. "One can achieve *Brahma-jnana* by the way of *Bhakti*." (*Kathamrita*, p. 122; Translation: Author)

c. "*Bhakti Yoga* is better in *Kali Yuga*. One can achieve Him by *Bhakti*." (*Kathamrita*, p. 138; Translation: Author)

d. "The power of *Kulakundalini* arises through *Bhakti*. God cannot be realized if the power of *Kulakundalini* is not awaken within." (*Kathamrita*, p. 356; Translation: Author)

e. "*Bhakti Yoga* – one has to fix his mind on God by chanting and singing His name. *Bhakti Yoga* is an easy way in *Kali Yuga*." (*Kathamrita*, p.470; Translation: Author)

f. "*Bhakti Yoga*, *Jnana Yog*a both are true ways. You can realize God through any of the ways. But the way of *Bhakti* is easier. The way of 'knowledge' ('jnan') is rather difficult." (*Kathamrita*, p. 485; Translation: Author)

If we analyze Sri Ramakrishna's life we must understand that he himself was a *Bhakti Yogi*. His confession in *Kathamrita* in this context is most significant. Sri Ramakrishna said:

> "Everything can be achieved through *Bhakti Yoga*. I earnestly cried to my Mother 'Please make me know what Yogis have known through Yoga, what wise men have known by judging'. Mother has shown me all. If devotees cry before Her with an earnest inclination she makes them know everything. What are there in *Veda-Vedanta, Puran, Tantra* - Mother made me know everything." (*Kathamrita*, p.406; Translation: Author)

In Srimad Bhabat Gita we find Karma-yoga, Jnana-yoga and Bhakti-yoga. Sri Chaitanyadeva started *Bhakti-Movement* in Bengal. The medieval India has witnessed Bhakti-Movement in many points of her territory. Sri Ramakrishna also spoke in favour of *Bhakti*. But the prime question is – why Sri Ramakrishna gave emphasis on Bhakti? What I understood is that *Bhakti* contains deep love and faith which knowledge may lack. One can have knowledge about God. But knowledge is not necessarily followed by faith. In spite of logical understanding, knowledge sometimes gives birth to multiple views and 'ism' which may not converge to a singular acceptable 'truth'. But, *Bhakti* has the potential to bring about diverse notions to 'one realization'. This is also an underlying logic of *Bhakti*. The mind of 19th century Bengal was divided into 'many' views. Education was there bookish-knowledge from east and west was there but the collective mind was not crystallized giving birth to any *unified- heart* due to lack of 'faith'. Sri Ramakrishna had set an example of faith and *Bhakti* in his own life. When plurality results 'difference', *Bhakti* seems to be a practicable solution to bring about '*spiritual oneness*'. Sri Ramakrishna proved it in his life. There were difference between the *Shaktas* and the *Shaivas*; there were difference between the Hindus and the Muslims. But Sri Ramakrishna's vision of *Bhakti* could pronounce - *all the paths lead to*

God. Bhakti and spirituality can provide the power to transgress 'difference'. The 19th century needed this. That's why Sri Ramakrishna told *Bhakti Yoga* is prescribed in *Kali Yuga*. Apart from its religious and spiritual implication, it has some sociological implication too.

6. Sri Ramakrishna's God: Sociological Relevance

Sri Ramakrishna said:

> "God can be attained through many paths and through many religions..." (Kathamrita, p.38; Translation: Author)

These words of Sri Ramakrishna have immense significance in the context of 19th century. We have seen many religious sects trying to speak in that period. The Shaktas, the Vaishnavas, the Islam, the Christianity, the Bauls, the Brahmas – all were searching God. In spite of their objective of search being one (God), these sects and religious communities could not come together to form a 'collective mind'. Everybody thought their way is the only way nurturing a hidden idea that the other's way is 'incorrect'! This psyche created some social disagreements among the communities and invited quarrel and even bloodshed. Historically it is true that the Brahmas tried to bring integrity in religious practice. In this context Sri Ramakrishna's view "all religions are true" and "God can be achieved through all paths" was a clear pronouncement of a liberal vision. There is no doubt that Sri Ramakrishna's time has learnt the lesson of liberalism in a new manner from his words and deeds. He stood to be an admirer of all religions. This was indeed exclusive in his life. His consciousness of 'One-God' prompted him to perceive Hindu-Muslim-Christian-Shikh as 'one human community'. India needed this oneness at that time and even today. This sociological relevance need to be underlined in our time to come out of man's created narrowness with the help of spirituality and God-consciousness.

7. Knowledge and Beyond

'What knowledge is' and 'how do we get knowledge' - are of course two important questions which are much discussed in philosophy. But how traditional philosophy of both orient and occident perceives knowledge is not my concern in this discussion. I would like to draw near readers' attention to Sri Ramakrishna's conclusion of knowledge with the textual references of *Kathamrita*.

To the best of my appreciation, Sri Ramakrishna's concept of knowledge has an underlying hierarchy. He used to use three words - '*ignorance*' *(Agnan)*, '*knowledge*'*(Jnan)* and '*absolute realization*' *(Bijnan)*. We start from '*ignorance*', we pass through '*knowledge*' and ultimately attain '*absolute realization*'. Sri Ramakrishna said 'ignorance' is an integral part of 'knowledge'. We have to give up both 'knowledge' and 'ignorance' to attain the '*absolute realization*'. Absolute realization can throw both 'knowledge' and 'ignorance' overboard.

Sri Ramakrishna had explained his ideas in a simple manner. He said:

> "*Bijnan* implies specific realization. Somebody has heard about milk, somebody has seen milk, somebody has drunk milk. He who only has heard (about milk) is 'ignorant' (Ajnan). One who has seen (milk) has 'knowledge' (Jnan), but he who has drunk (milk) could attain 'absolute realization' (Bijnan). Absolute realization implies seeing God and having close communion with Him" (*Kathamrita*, p. 415, Translation: Author)

Sri Ramakrishna clarified his idea in another way. He said:

> "Ignorance, knowledge, absolute realization. He who has knowledge perceives that He exists. He is the creator – He creates, sustains and destroys. He who has absolute realization feels that He has manifested Himself as this cosmic universe. (*Kathamrita*, p. 437, Translation: Author)

Again, regarding knowledge Sri Ramakrishna said –

> "God is the absolute creator, not me –such realization is knowledge." (*Kathamrita*, p. 167, Translation: Author)

And what ignorance is? Sri Ramakrishna said:

> "Not-knowing God implies ignorance."
>
> (*Kathamrita*, p. 18, Translation: Author)

and

> "The ego of a *pandit* (scholar) is also ignorance" (*Kathamrita*, p. 974, Translation: Author)

Sri Ramakrishna suggested Baburam to transgress both 'knowledge' and 'ignorance'. Thakur mentioned:

> "He who has knowledge has ignorance. Brother (Baburam), you transgress knowledge-ignorance both" (*Kathamrita*, p. 757, Translation: Author)

However, it is to be noted that traditional philosophy considers 'knowldege' to be the prime destination to reach. But Sri Ramakrishna pointed that man can go beyond 'knowledge' through his 'realization'. Or in other words, 'knowledge is fulfilled in realization. Sri Ramakrishna in *Kathamrita* taught us to march forward from '*Jnana*' to '*Binana*'; i.e, knowledge to realization. This is the threshold of Bhakti.

8. About Islam

Sri Ramakrishna Deva's appreciation of Islam was purely spiritual and beyond all confinements. Above all, Sri Ramakrishna himself was a spiritual-bridge between Hindu and Muslim, in a wider sense 'Vedanta' and 'Islam'. In conformity to such logic of understanding, I would like to throw light on Sri Ramakrishna's view and vision of Islam.

Sri Ramakrishna ascertained that God can be achieved by practicing any religion or order. He said:

> "He can be achieved through all religions. All religions are true." (*Kathamrita*, p. 59, Translation: Author)"

Sri Ramakrishna once told Mani Sen (on 22nd October, 1882) that he had to practice all the religions. In *Kathamrita* we find Sri Ramakrishna saying:

> "I had to embrace all religions - Hindu, Muslim, Christian, again Shakta, Vaishnav, Vedanta, I had to tread all the paths. I have seen the same God – everybody is coming to Him through different paths, (*Kathamrita*, p.77, Translation: Author)"

Sri Ramakrishna clearly declared that each and every path of religion leads man to Ultimate God. The paths may differ but God is one. Such a monotheistic vision had opened up a new way of inter-religious amity in the age of Sri Ramakrishna.

Another interesting point is that Sri Ramakrishna had seen Mother Bhabatarini (Kali) in the guise of a Muslim girl. In *Kathamrita* we find Sri Ramakrishna's utterances:

> "Another day (Mother Kali) in the guise of a Muslim girl came to me. She had a '*tilak*' on her forehead. She was '*digambari*'- devoid of garments. A girl of 6 or 7 years roamed with me and made pranks. (*Kathamrita*, p.131, Translation: Author)"

These textual references of *Kathamrita* have shaken me from within and became a prime cause for initiating one pertinent question in my mind. Why Sri Ramakrishna perceived Mother Kali as a Muslim girl? What message did Sri Ramakrishna want to convey? As I take it into consideration Sri Ramakrishna tried to overleap the so called conceptual boundary of Hindu and Muslim that existed in the mind of the then society. On one hand Kali is supposed to be an alien goddess to the concept of the Muslims, on the other hand to the Hindus, Muslim girl has never been associated with any goddess in Hindu religious history. Interestingly Sri Ramakrishna by perceiving Kali as a Muslim girl has broken the conceptual confinement of both Hinduism and Islam. This is how he brought about a dynamic, flexible and liberal vision where both inter-religious and trans-religious bond have become highly significant.

In this context, I would like to add one reference from the life of Swami Vivekananda. When Swamiji was in Srinagar (Kashmir), he worshipped an 8 year old Muslim girl as *Kumari*. She was the daughter of the owner of a houseboat where Swamiji stayed in Dal Lake. Sister Nivedita has given description of this incident in her book 'Swamijir Sahit Himalaye'. The date of Swamiji's Kumari puja was 12th or 13th August 1898. It is needless to mention that Swamiji followed the path of his guru – Sri Ramakrishna who also perceived goddess Kali as a 7 or 8 year old Muslim girl.

Another incident is described in *Kathamrita*. One bearded Muslim brought rice in a dish and Sri Ramakrishna had tasted some rice (*Kathamrita*: p.259). This incident is again mentioned in slightly different way in other parts of *Kathamrita* (*Kathamrita*: p.796). This incident to the best of my perception has two fold meaning. The first one is its transcendental meaning. In this world there is no discrimination in God-consciousness. The ultimate sustainer, the '*Sacchidananda*' Himself is manifest as Englishman or Muslim, low caste etc. The original text of *Kathamrita* is quoted here:

> "One day I have seen, one consciousness – undivided… Again came one bearded Muslim holding a plate in his hand. Some rice were there in it. He put a little rice on everyone's mouth. I too tasted it." (*Kathamrita*: p.259, Translation: Author)

The same idea is elaborated in other part of *Kathamrita* which goes like this:

> "The tree of drumstick and a basil used to appear equal. My capacity to perceive distinction was ceased. When I was in meditation under a banyan tree, I was shown a bearded Muslim who brought some rice in a plate and stood in front of me. He gave me some rice after serving some of its portion to the untouchables. Mother showed me there is none except the ultimate one. Sacchidananda Himself is manifested in different forms…" (*Kathamrita*: p. 796, Translation: Author)

Interestingly Sri Ramakrishna portrayed a saintly Muslim in *Kathamrita*. The text goes like this:

> "Once a woman became attached to a Mussalman and invited him to her room. But he was a righteous person; he said to her that he wanted to use the toilet and must go home to get his water-jar for water. The woman offered him her own, but he said: 'No, that will not do. I shall use the jar to which I have already exposed myself. I cannot expose myself before a new one.' With these words, he went away. That brought the woman to her senses. She understood that a new water-jar, in her case, signified a paramour." (Gospel: p.519)

Why Sri Ramakrishna told us about a saintly Muslim? Perhaps he tried to portray the character of an alternative Muslim in the context of his contemporary time when people perceived Muslim with the traditional obsession of casteism. He never appreciated Muslim from any derogatory sense. The high moral value of self control was imposed by him in a Muslim. If we compare the contemporary psyche of the society regarding the Muslim we must find that Sri Ramakrishna set an example of bright exception.

Sri Ramakrishnadev had minutely noticed Muslim's sincerity towards offering *Namaz*. He admired such inclination. He told:

> "At dusk put aside all duties and pray to God. One is reminded of Him by darkness. At the approach of darkness one thinks: 'I could see everything a moment ago. Ho has brought about this change?' The Mussalmans put aside all activities and say their prayers [*Namaz*] at the appointed times." (Gospel: p. 588)

If we try to explain *Namaz* from the Sanatan view, *Namaz* is a form of Yoga. Namaz helps to develop a transcendental communion between God and man. A devotee can realize Almighty Allah through *Namaz*. That is why Sri Ramakrishna appreciated sincerity for offering *Namaz*. In this context I would like to add that Sri Ramakrishna also offered *Namaz* in the mosque near to Dakshineshwar Kali temple. Another incident is that Sri Ramakrishna once went to the Idgah (the ground of Namaz) of Mandaran. He came to see the Id Namaz. We get this information from the description of Sheikh Umed Ali, a friend from Sri Ramakrishna's boyhood. (Islam: p.94)

I have cited some selected examples here to uphold Sri Ramakrishna's point of view about the Muslims. Initially he taught the contemporary age not to perceive Muslims or Islam religion from any narrow notion. He believed that God can be realized through Hindu, Muslim, Christian, Shakta or Vaishnava order. Whosoever is inclined to God with pure heart and mind will realize

God. There is no doubt about it. He himself embraced Islam-*sadhana* and took 'Allah's name' from Gobinda Ray (Wazed Ali Khan). Sri Ramakrishna said:

> "I took initiation in *Allah -mantra* from Gobinda Roy." (*Kathamrita*, p. 584; Translation: Author)
>
> and
>
> "I used to chant *Allah-mantra* at that time." (*Kathamrita*, Islam: p.89)

Sri Ramakrishna's Islam-sadhana is really unique in the history of several thousand years of Hinduism as well as one and a half thousand years history of Islam. After studying Sri Ramakrishna's *Kathamrita* I felt that Sri Ramakrishna himself was a bridge between Hinduism and Islam.

I find many striking points in the *Kathamrita* of Sri Ramakrishna which have inspired the nation to revaluate some conventional notions. What I have understood as a humble reader of '*Kathamrita*' is presented here in brief.

9. Kathamrita: The Voice of Alternative Enlightenments

Historical interpretation says that Raja Rammohan Roy had brought about enlightenment in Bengal in the 18th and 19th century. If we take the time from Raja Rammohan to Sri Ramakrishna, we see some major changes in the thought process. I may try to analyze the changes with the following arguments. Though my effort is to make a comparative analysis of the history, yet I don't want to present Rammohan and Ramakrishna in any contradictory oppositional model. I rather would like to interprete the differences in terms of continuity. This technical note needs to be spelt out clearly that it may not lead readers to further confusion. Now we can enter into our discussion by presenting the following points:

1. In Rammohan we can observe a confluence of eastern and western ideologies. His psyche was developed with the help of Vedanta and Bentham. Sri Ramakrishna, in his contemporary time grasped Sanatan wisdom rather than any western ideology. Inclination towards Sanatan wisdom as we found in Rammohan, flourished more vividly in Sri Ramakrishna.
2. Rammohan Roy had profound formal study on religion and philosophy. He had to do it because he had to form argument for many issues. This prompted him to 'write' many things with his hidden faith.

   Sri Ramakrishna depended more on 'faith' than argumentation. In spite of presenting 'faith' and 'arguments' through 'writing' his process of communication depended on 'orality' (the folk process) and himself stood the very example of what he had taught. He himself was Sanatan wisdom personified.

3. The term 'reformation' makes distinct meaning in Rammohan and Ramakrishna's life. Rammohan's time prompted him to go for social reform. He took initiative for prevention of burning Sati.

   Sri Ramakrishna continued Reformation in another way. He wanted to bring about structured changes in the thought process of the mass. If the thought pattern of the society changes, the society will undergo corresponding changes. This is also an alternative way of reformation.

4. Raja Rammohan Roy's mind was wide enough to study Al-Quran and he paid respect for Islam religion. Sri Ramakrishna marched forward far ahead and did 'Islam-Sadhana' by taking initiation from Wazed Ali Khan (Gobinda Roy). To Sri Ramakrishna, Islam was not a subject of 'study', like all paths Islam was his 'Sadhana' too.
5. Both Rammohan and Ramakrishna wanted to advocate the spirit of religious integrity and harmony. This was really commendable. What was started by Rammohan fully flourished in Ramakrishna.
6. Rammohan Roy had formulated 'Brahma Dharma' which appears to be a departure from 'Hindu' Dharma as such. There is no doubt that 'Brahma Dharma' was also a fruit of reformation. Interestingly Sri Ramakrishna stayed within the fold of Hinduism and spoke of re-formation of mind so as to open enough space for reformation within the mind-set.
7. Thakur-Ma-Swamiji altogether became source of inspiration of an alternative enlightenment and *Kathamrita* was both its manifests and constitution as well.

Alongwith this historical perspective we may consider the *Kathamrita* as a 'text' that reflects the contemporary history and dialectics of the age. The doubts, debate, questions and complexities of the time are reflected in *Kathamrita.* But unlike any 'report' *Kathamrita* presents questions and complexities along with their reconciliation. In *Kathamrita* 'problem' is not the last word but solution; contradiction is not the last word but reconciliation. Here *Kathamrita* is exceptional, exclusive and of course an alternative way.

Notes

1. Guru Pranam Mantra, Ref: Guru Gita, Verse-26 (See: Raghuvarananda, p. 47)
2. Ignorance: In traditional Sanskrit verse, ignorance is symbolized as '*tamasa*' – darkness.

3. Spiritual knowledge: the knowledge that makes us aware of God Almighty – the Supreme One.
4. Divine eye: The term 'divya chakshu' is mentioned in Bhagabat Gita. Original quotation is: '*divyam dadami te chakhuh......*' (Gita, 11:8).
5. Guru Gita: See Reference: Raghubarananda
6. Dharma: It is difficult to find an exact word in English to suggest the actual meaning of the word – '*Dharma*'. The connotation needs to be understood in conformity to *Sanatan* tradition.
7. To teach common folk: Sri Ramakrishna used the word 'lok-siksha' (Ref: *Kathamrita*, p. 37)

REFERENCES

1. Swami Gambhirananda, '*Juganayak Vivekananda*', Udbodhan Karyalay, Kolkata, 1373 Bangabda
2. Sri Ma, Sri Sri Ramakrihna Kathamrita, Udbodhan Karyalay, Kolkata, 2003
3. Swami Jagadiswarananda (Edited), Srimad Bhagavad Gita, Udbodhan Karyalay, Kolkata, 1985
4. Swami Nikhilananda (Translated),The Gospel of Sri Ramakrishna, Sri Ramakrishna Math, Mylapur, Madras, 1942
5. Sk. Makbul Islam, Sri Ramakrisha Balay O Islam Dharma, Bangiya Sahitya Samsad, Kolkata, 2013
6. Swami Raghuvarananda (Compilation), Gurutattva O Guru Gita; Udbodhan Karyalay, Kolkata, 2004

20

Sri Ramakrishna as a social leader

Prosenjit Biswas

In order to spread spiritual knowledge among the masses one needs to have a clear understanding of their lifestyle at a given period of time. Having had that faculty in himself, Thakur succeeded in presenting God according to the needs of the modern man of the nineteenth century.

Thakur occupies the pivotal position in the various nineteenth-century religious discourses mentioned in the 'Kathamrita'. It is true that his concepts were original as his ideas about the Almighty were inspired by the long-established cannons of Indian spirituality. But his originality lies in the way he applied these concepts. The 'Kathamrita' shows the novelties of his spiritual thoughts.

Sri Ramakrishna's treatment of the experiences of his personal life is important. From the 'Kathamrita' it is clear that one of the tools utilised by Thakur for mass education was the repertory of his daily experiences, which he used as stories. He painted pictures of pieces from the goings-on of regular life before people and thus made comprehensible a subject as intense and demanding as the perception of God. He also tried to end the common misunderstandings related to this subject. He emphasized most on the human mind; he said, 'In thrall in mind, in mind set free. Your mind will take on the hue with which you dye it. Like clothes in a washman's house: red if dyed red, blue if blue. Don't you see, reading a bit of English makes one begin to speak English words. Foot-fat, it-mit (everybody laughs). Then would follow wearing boots, whistling songs, et cetera et cetera. If you keep your mind in bad company then you would talk and think bad- if you keep it with the devout, it will think of God and His name'[1]. The human mind is a container which does not have its own identity at first, information derived from the surrounding world defines it. Therefore Thakur urged everyone firstly to decide which identity or education they would choose for themselves. Although he maintained that the mind will follow God if one chooses to think properly, his language in describing the results of learning English shows that merely following God's path does not bring one close to Him; otherwise he would not have described an English student in terms of superficial mimicry (wearing boots, whistling songs). In fact he also wanted to say that the mind should be submerged correctly and entirely. The clothes get disfigured by spots if not properly dyed- he wanted to say that as well.

His transcendental humanism is also important. He struck at the roots of the established communal systems of perceiving God. Since ancient times religious teachers have persuaded people to accept their own religion as the only true path, established themselves as middlemen between God and Humans by claiming to be God's favourites and reinforced the image of God as a controller of men's day-to-day prayers and wants. Thus began an exchange in God's name. The priests delivered the common people's prayers to God in exchange for certain gifts. Hindu Brahmins, Muslim Maulavis, Christian Clerics- none were exempt from it. This practice gave rise to a couple of notions about God in people's minds: firstly, that it is possible to attain God by following the ways prescribed in the scriptures and secondly, that God takes care of men's wants by using His supernatural powers. As a result most people imagined God as someone like the genie of Aladdin who could replace their disappointments and deprivations with happiness.

On the other hand Sri Ramakrishna dismissed all rules and regulations on the way of attaining God and said, 'Every religion leads to God if one is sincere. The Vaishnavites will have Him, the Shaktas will have Him, the Vedantics, the Brahmos, Muslims and Christians will also have Him. Every sincere person will have Him'[2]. Contemporary spirituality took on the first non-communal tinge through this comment of Thakur's. He made the subject of the priests' long-established monopoly universal. Another point to be noted is that unlike other religious leaders, he did not assure people of material gains. To him attainment of God meant attainment of the ultimate 'Truth'. It was that very 'Truth' he hinted toward in a secular style.

To the people of India supernaturalism is a subject entangled with religion and spirituality. Supernatural tales often sneak into the lives of the great. From Jesus Christ to Vidyasagar none is free from it. Even today, in the twenty first century, one comes across a widespread marketing of supernaturalism in various public media like books, art and advertisements. Viewers of TV serials are always eager to watch Gods in their supernatural best and in the rural parts ghosts and other supernatural beings 'impersonating people' are common. Black or white magic- whatever it may be, the human desire for sudden gains outside the logic of causality is apparently everlasting, and always in excess. This is why the Theosophists were able to exercise a remarkable influence over the common people of the nineteenth century. Thakur did not confine himself in the supernatural. According to him, "I saw an expert in Deb Mondal's house. He could summon Spirits at his will. They brought him lots of things. Now what would I do with such supernatural power? Does it help in attaining God? If it does not then it is rubbish."[3] Here Thakur did not explain the kind of supernatural power involved, but only hinted at how the supernatural might prove to be an obstacle to people's success in getting close to God. The supernatural can help only in material gain. It has nothing to do with God. That is why Thakur called it 'rubbish'. To him God is the only truth. Thakur tried to spread that truth among the common people through his teachings and at the same time tried to free them from the obsession with the supernatural.

Thakur did not always look down upon the sensuous nature of worldly people. His opinion that renunciation cannot come if indulgence is not over is repeated in many places in the 'Kathamrita'. To a member of the Brahmo Samaj at Sinthi he said, "...if indulgences like money, fame and physical pleasure are not consummated at least once- if the will to indulge is not over- then the desperation for God does not arise in everyone."[4] In order to attain true renunciation or concentration in God one needs at first to have a thorough understanding of all potential setbacks. Naturally the nineteenth-century Bengali people welcomed his views. It was because contemporary Calcutta was mired in indulgence and sensuousness. Thakur felt in his heart that these people would never be able to concentrate in God if they are told to keep away from the instruments of indulgence. That is why he said, "One cannot tell the people of Calcutta, 'Renounce everything for God'-one has to say, 'Renounce in mind'." This is how he made God's entrance into the post-indulgence lives of contemporary sensuous and worldly Bengalis easy. The following story by Thakur found in the 'Kathamrita' helps in elucidating this point–

> Two friends were going along a road. In a place there was a gathering where a man was reading out from the Bhagvad. One of the friends said, "Come, let us listen for a while." The other man peeped in and went his way to a whorehouse. There after some time he became disgusted. He told himself, "Shame on me. My friend is listening to

the name of God, and I am perishing down here." The man who was listening to the Bhagvad also felt ashamed of himself. He thought, "What a fool I am, listening on to mutterings of gibberish! And that friend of mine is having fun." When these people died, the man who was listening to the Bhagvad was taken by a messenger of Yamraj[6]. The man who went to the whorehouse was taken to Vaikunth by a messenger of Vishnu[7]."[8]

Thakur here talks about three issues. Firstly, he shows what the nature of true devotion is. Secondly, he shows that a mind immersed in material indulgence is unfit for spirituality. Thirdly, he also shows how such a mind might turn to God once its desire for indulgence is fully satisfied. Thus he bound together appearance and internal desire. One does not attain God if in spite of using His name one's mind stays focused on the desire for material objects.

Thakur informed us of an essential characteristic of human life which even he himself could not sacrifice. He surrendered everything of his own life before the Divine Mother but could not give up truth. In the 'Kathamrita' Thakur sacrificed wisdom, ignorance, purity, impurity, the good and the bad to Mother and prayed only for unblemished devotion, but could not sacrifice truth. "...when I said all these things, I could not say, 'Mother! Take your truth, take your untruth.' I gave Her everything, but could not give truth."[9] Thakur urges people to have this quality first. This is the path in which everything in life, including God, can be attained. One may think at first that Thakur did not sacrifice truth to the Mother, does it mean truth is greater than God! But actually truth is something without which the attainment of God becomes impossible; again from another point of view it might be said that God and truth are the same thing.

Even after all this discussion a doubt may arise in the common mind that Thakur was an incarnation of God[10] or a sage with a very high calibre- in other words, that he is not common like most people. His abilities and disabilities have absolutely nothing to do with those of the common people. As Thakur understood his time, he brought forth some mistakes of his own life. In a conversation with Mahendranathhe says-

I have told her, "Mother! Make me well; I will not eat kulpi anymore." Then I have said again, "Nor will I eat ice..." As I told that to Mother I cannot eat those things. But sometimes I make mistakes. I said once,

"I will not have fish on Sundays." But I ate one on a Sunday recently by mistake. But I never do it knowingly..."[11]

This 'mistake' by a sage whose fame has spread outside India to the whole world suddenly brings him close to us. Common people relate to Thakur and become able to consider the mistakes of their own lives and think- they too will succeed some day. Thus Thakur established himself as a precedent. But he bound his 'mistakes' tightly. His 'mistakes' are all born of ignorance, because he never made 'mistakes' knowingly. He lets the common people embarking on a quest for truth rectify their ignorant mistakes, but pretensions of the wise are contemptible to him.[12]

Thakur's methods to create bridges to reach out to common people is an worth mentioning point. Similes make up most of it. Thakur used Kamarpukur-born Gadadhar Chattopadhyay's experiences of rural environment, of listening to the teachings of the Vedas and the Upanishads from various people, of living at Dakshineshwar, of visiting other places to spread God's name- as similes to present spirituality before the nineteenth century.

It takes a little primary care to cultivate any thought. Likewise when the mind first turns to spirituality it needs to be guarded. When the thought matures, however, the guarding does not need to remain that rigorous. About this Sri Ramakrishna said, "A sapling needs the protection of a fence. Without it, it will be eaten by goats or cows."[13] Or again "Devotion needs quiet. In order to get butter you need to curdle milk in quiet. It will not curdle if you move it around. Once the curd is ready, you have to churn it in quiet leaving every other work. Only then you will have butter."[14]

God's diversity is a very important subject. At its root are a person's growing up, education, subjective thinking etc. Differences of environment, difference among education systems and the subjects of learning help people think differently from each other. This is how people have different dresses, food, language and customs. But in certain aspects all forms of diversity are true. So it is with respect to religious beliefs. Different regions, familiar customs and beliefs cause people develop different concepts of spirituality and in related circumstances all of these are true. To clarify the diversity of religious thoughts among people Thakur said, "A mother has five sons. One day they have fish for lunch. The mother cooks different items with fish- for each what suits him best. For one she cooks fish polao; for another, fish with lemon juice; yet others have fish curry or fish fries. Each gets what suits him best- do you see?"[15]

How to live in this world? In other words, if someone with an inclination towards spirituality has to lead a regular life,how should he do it? To make this point clear Thakur used a number of similes:

1. "Live like an eel. It lives in mud but has got no mud on its body. Also live like a prostitute who is always thinking of her paramour."[16]
2. "A housemaid in a rich household does all work of it but is always conscious of her own home in the country. She still takes care of her master's sons as her own sons. She calls them 'my Ram', 'my Hari', but knows very well in her mind- they are nothing to me."[17]
3. "A tortoise swims in water, but do you know where her mind is? It is on the banks where her eggs are. Do every work you have in the world, but keep God in your mind."[18]

There are many religions in our nation. Every religion is again divided into many sects. This differentiation from each other gives birth to communal thought which is one of the key problems of the world at present. Man can revere his own religion or his particular mode of spirituality but cannot treat other religions likewise. In many cases he becomes intolerant. Thakur solves this problem by reminding people of the duties of the ideal mistress at the centre of a joint family- "The wife serves all the brothers of her husband with water to wash their feet, cushions to sit etc. but does not serve them as she serves the husband himself. Her relationship with her husband is at a different level."[19] Having respect for other religions is not forbidden even if one honours one's own religion most because every religion leads to a path towards the absolute truth. From this viewpoint the different religions of the world make up a structure like a joint family where other religions are like the 'brothers of one's husband'.

Thakur's spirituality did not constitute solely of revelations concerning the lives and duties of devotees- he also had things to say about the operations of God. In his talks all these took on the forms of extraordinary allegories. "Mother is cooking. Her infant son is lying by her side. Mother has given him a toy; when the baby throws away the toy and starts crying, his mother leaves her works and gives him suckle."[20] In other words, when the worldly human sees through his everyday works and wants to know the ultimate truth, then God feels compelled to be attentive to him. These are examples of Thakur's manipulation of regular Bengal life. Different aspects of popular culture also served to enrich it. An example is popular sports. Perhaps God does not want humans to be spiritual from the beginning. He wants humans to attain Him through evolution.Thakur said, "In the game of hide-and-seek the thieves are to be found by the police. The thieves are not satisfied if they are found too soon. Likewise, God also wants the game to go on for a while."[21] Besides this, popular beliefs such as white magic to catch real thieves and offerings to God in hope of someone's recovery (like Thakur's offerings of coconut and sugar to the Divine Mother for Keshab's recovery) are also found in the 'Kathamrita'.

Calcutta was not neglected in Thakur's teachings. In order to explain the difference between living a worldly life and leaving civilization for concentrating in God, i.e. that the feelings of joy, sorrow, disappointment etc. engulf a worldly mind but cannot affect a mind away from such considerations, Thakur said- "as long as you are under the Monument you can see cars, horses, white men and women etc. But once you go to the top you see only the sky like a sea, empty and vast. Then you don't like the thought of houses, horses, cars and people; these look like ants."[22]

To have God's grace or to have a place at His lotus-like feet it is necessary to seek His shelter, to pray to Him. Thakur merged this process of praying to God with the gas-office at Sealdah. "Every house has a tube for gas supply. You get gas by asking the gas company. Ask it and they will supply it- you will have light at your house. Their office is at Sealdah."[23]

Again it is not right to think God will be pleased as soon as one calls Him if the caller does not surrender himself. Thakur compared the desperation for God with a clerk's desperation for his job. "The way a clerk becomes desperate if he loses his job. The way he goes from office to office and asks, 'Sir, is there a vacancy?'"[24] Thakur asks for that level of desperation. In order to measure man's urge to attain God he said elsewhere, "If a wife's attraction towards her husband, a miser's attraction towards his wealth and a mother's attraction towards her child are combined, then He can be attained."[25]

In early parts of his quest to get close to God a devotee may face difficulties. But that penance awaits the highest possible achievement. What is there to worry about once God's grace is obtained? In this respect Thakur held up the toils of service life and the comforts of the pension that follows it: "Always keep your mind concentrated in God. At first you will have to toil a bit. Then you will enjoy the pension."[26]

The 'Kathamrita' also touches upon the topic of circus, in order to explain the act of contemplating God. "You have to practice regularly. I saw a galloping horse in a circus, on which a girl was standing. It certainly took a lot of practice."[27] Pointing out a girl who stood upon a galloping horse at a circus Thakur wanted to say, "You can", but you need practice.

In the question of the method of leading a worldly life Thakur held up the case of the railway guard in the urban context. The guard can get on to and get down from a train whenever he wants. He is not bound to stay there for any length of time. Likewise, Thakur forbade people from getting completely immersed into worldly affairs because it is an obstacle in the path to God. But he never advised people to skip their essential duties to the world, he rather forbade it. That topic will be discussed later.

According to this priest of the Dakshineshwar Kali Temple, the most essential ingredient for attaining God is faith. In certain systems of philosophy logic is given priority over faith. But even after having logic on his side, man can succeed in every step of his life only if deep down he is faithful. Moment by moment faith orientates him towards achievement. To elucidate the nature of this faith Thakur held up the topic of Hanuman's faith in the name of Lord Ram, "The Puranas say that Lord Ram, who was a part of Narayan Himself, had to build a bridge to reach Lanka. But Hanuman with his absolute faith in Ram's name crossed the sea in one big leap. He did not need a bridge."[28] In other words, faith is an instrument which helps to attain even apparently impossible goals. In the quest for spirituality Thakur held up the deep faith of Hanuman as the ideal. The prevalent notion that there are different ways to attain God, i.e. different sets of rules and regulations which one must follow if he is to get close to God was also challenged by him; he reminded people of Hanuman's words: "Hanuman said, 'I don't care about days, phases of the moon or the stars- I only think of Lord Ram.'"[29] No matter which path you choose, faith and devotion are the true catalysts of man's success.

Thakur, however, did not encourage the notion that the perceptible world hinders us from the path to God or that the world is a place of degradation. He brought forth the value of the world with the help of the Puranas. The world is God's creation and therefore everything is actually manifestations of God Himself; He became everything. The world is nothing but Him. "Ramchandra became motivated for renunciation after reading the Vedas at his Guru's place. He said, if the world is a dream then it is best to get away from it. Dasharath was frightened. He sent Guru Vashishtha to make Ram understand. Vashishtha said, Ram, why do you say you want to get away from the world? Make me understand that the world is without God. Ram could not answer him."[30]

Thakur drew upon rural, regular Bengal, its people, their customs and beliefs, the whereabouts of Calcutta, its features, its business, the Puranas, even popular codes of conduct and popular sports. A question arises concerning his objective in using all these elements to decorate his teachings. Why did he not make tough Sanskrit shlokas filled with complex information like the long-established tradition of systematized religion and theologians? It was because that method was not suited to his time. In order to inform Thakur of people in a colonized nation Trailokyanath said, "Sir, they have no time; they have to work for the English."[31] It is for this lack of time that people want to understand a subject like theology in an easy way. Mani had told Thakur about it:

> Mani- Sir, the whole, the part, the art- I can't understand these things much. But I understood very well the round hole in the wall that you talked about.
>
> Sri Ramakrishna[32]- So tell me what it is?[33]...

In those days the educated middle class, moving away from a feudal society towards a capitalist one and busy with their clerks' jobs could not find time for thinking about religion. To turn their heads to God in such a state required an effort to make God familiar to them. Thakur drew upon the common Bengali life to utilize this very method. The advantage of presenting people with something familiar to them is that they can make out the significance of the presentation very easily. As a result they can easily accept and assimilate it. Precisely for this, life in Bengal was his chosen subject. Krittibash Ojha painted The 'Ramayana' from a Bengali perspective for the same reason. In his writings Lord Ram is quite perceptibly the first-born son of a Bengali family, Sita a wife devoted to her husband. Krittibash even turned the state of Ayodhya into a mirror-image of the natural and cultural atmosphere of Bengal. Simplicity is a key requirement of acceptability. The spell-bound Shyam Bose called Thakur's words 'sugar-coated' for their simplicity. And again, because of these references the 'Kathamrita' carries with itself signs of Bengal's regional features. For readers from the other provinces of India, a clear knowledge of Bengal is most necessary before reading this book. A complete understanding is not possible otherwise. This feature of the 'Kathamrita' also presents all readers with an opportunity of learning about contemporary Bengal.

Another point to be noted about Thakur's use of similes is that these are taken from every level of the society. It does not reflect the specific details of any one class, proving Thakur's modern mindset and revealing before us his abilities as a sociologist.

The sage will be entirely absorbed in his thought of God and will be indifferent towards life and the world at large- this is a concept familiar to the common man, because the most widely taught theology, the Advaita Vedanta, says that only the Brahma is true and everything else is false. It would not have been difficult either for Sri Ramakrishna because he too advised people to keep God in mind in spite of leading worldly lives and told them to believe in the essentiality of God. Historian Sumit Sarkar said about the Divine Love of Sri Ramakrishna that "he considered the organized efforts for the development of society wasted"[34]. It is to be noted that the creed Sumit Sarkar follows does not believe even in the existence of God. On the other hand Thakur believed solely in God. If two persons belong to entirely opposite belief systems and one of them describes another according to his own set of values, it might help in forming an argument but the acceptability of it in the wider perspective remains doubtful. On his second meeting with Mahendranath, Thakur tells him, "Pratap's brother came and stayed here for a few days. He has no work. He said, I will stay here. I heard he has a wife and a number of children. He had left them all at his in-laws'. I gave him a good scolding. Did he expect people from that locality to feed his family and bring his children up? Does he have no shame...I scolded him a lot, and told him to find work. Then did he wish to go his way."[35] Thakur never supported concentrating on spirituality at the cost of injustice to one's family. He considered someone's neglecting of his primary duties to attain God untimely.

In the social structure of nineteenth-century India the distance between people belonging to different castes and races were maintained like ancient times, the description of which can be found in Sunil Gangopadhyay's novel 'Shei Shomoy'. Chandranath, the son of prostitute Hira Bulbul could not obtain a seat in the Hindu College despite being meritorious. The reaction of other pupils' households on his coming to the college on the first day- "that day every other student of the third standard had to bathe and sprinkle Ganges water on their heads after returning home. The clothes worn by them were thrown out on the streets. The guardians were extremely upset. It was like the whole nation was on the brink of collapse. How abominable! How very abominable! At Shovabazar in the mansion of Radhakanta Deb, at Jorasanko in the house of Debendranath Tagore and at Taltala in the house of Rajendranath Dutta meetings were held separately among the aristocracy"[36]. Even the teacher Mahendranath was in doubt on his way to the house of Balaram Bose, "who knows whether these rich people would let...in"[37] - Thakur felt these problems in his heart. His tonic for the abolishing of such communal problems-

> There is a way of ending the caste system. That way is devotion. The devotee has no caste. With the emergence of devotion one's body, mind and soul gets purified immediately. Gour (Sri Chaitanya) and

> Nitai took shelter in the name of Sri Hari, and provided it for people from every caste.[38]

Thakur wanted the end of the caste problem through devotion. History also teaches us that the excess of devotion during the time of Sri Chaitanya brought all strata of the Bengal society at one level: an event unparalleled in the history of Bengal. Thakur wishes to use the same weapon to abolish the hierarchical system.

Thakur himself was unattached. He could not collect anything. He might be called a monk with a home. He embraced civilization from the outside, and although internally he believed God only to be essential, he did not forbid common people from collecting worldly things. He knew they could not lead a life like his. Therefore considering their point of view he even put forth questions such as how will a man provide for his family if he does not make money. By drawing upon the image of a bird he said, collecting things or making money is natural for common people. "Only the monk will not collect. 'Birds and hermits' do not collect. But birds do when they have offspring. They collect food for their babies"[39]. It is an usal practice that sages are giving up their homes for the path of realization. The Buddha or Sri Chaitanya was no exceptions. But Thakur talked about concentrating in God while maintaining one's home; thus providing homely people who were keen for God but could not leave their duties with a new solution. Sadarwala was very pleased for this and gleefully said, "The very words that it is not necessary to leave my home, that one can attain God even from within the home brought peace and joy to my mind."[40]

Thakur never made any distinctions between people who came to visit him. Everyone is made of some good and some bad, so people who are revered as pundits might also have follies. Likewise people who are marked as idiots might have in-depth knowledge of certain things. In the 'Kathamrita', to make us conscious of this truth Thakur held up the topic of Shankaracharya's taking lessons from a lower-caste chandal. The chandal carrying a load of meat touched the just-bathed body of Shankar and he said, -"Hey, you touched me! The chandal replied, 'revered sir, neither did you touch me, nor did I touch you'. The Soul is not the body, nor the five elements, nor the twenty four theses."[41] Thus Shankar realized the truth. It means that the social demarcations like caste do not represent a person's complete identity. The beginning of the enlightenment of the Shudras that spread across the nation with Swami Vivekananda in the following years can be found in this speech of Thakur's.

Man obtains faith in God when that faith is based on the bedrock of logic. It means that in order to have love for God or to think that God is the essence it is necessary to start with a framework of logical arguments. Gradually this framework gets dissolved in faith. Therefore Thakur does not consider the Guru's words or any sage's teachings to be the only acceptable ones at the moment of establishing faith in one's mind. He also scolded a Brahmo devotee for this-

> Sri Ramakrishna- If it is not a kind of energy, why did so many people obey Keshab? The Gita says that whoever commands the respect of the masses, be that for education, or for music, or for lectures, or for anything else- be assured that God's energy is manifested in that person.
>
> Brahmo devotee (to Sadarwala)- you don't accept what he says!
>
> Sri Ramakrishna (to Brahmo devotee)- what kind of man are you! Obeying without believing! That is cheating! I see that you are an imitation necklace!
>
> The Brahmo devotee was much ashamed.[42]

Sri Ramakrishna did not talk about living illogically. He always advised to accept what was evidently true. But Sumit Sarkar says, "He (Sri Ramakrishna) did not bother much about logic and reason."[43] That Thakur not only supported logic but also liked arguments have been pointed out by the writer of the 'Kathamrita' many times. It is here a sage who tells people to be mindful of God but also to do their duties to the world, who asks faith to be primarily guarded by the 'fence' of logic. Worldly people at that time got a new chance to receive God through him.

These two subjects are inseparably entangled with social life. From a distance they cannot be separately recognized. Corruption in the mask of nobleness is present everywhere. Thakur revealed the nature of such corruption in page after page of the 'Kathamrita'. Perhaps as a social leader he had realized that the nation needs to be rescued from the wrong path to the right one. He himself was on the right path since his childhood. In the 'Kathamrita' Thakur talked about his early days, "if I heard someone was reading out from the Ramayana or the Bhagvad I sat down and listened. But if the reader was pretentious I made caricatures of him and told others."[44] In other words, he did not like the manipulation of one's voice solely to render the reading of holy texts acceptable without the realization of their internal truth. The truth-seeker Thakur's mimicry of fake readings holds up before us the unadulterated nature of his devotion.

The mushroom-like sprouting of a number of religious teachers in Bengal and the rest of India was also called into question by him. People often become gurus without the qualifying attributes of one. It is said about Thakur in the book titled 'Kaliyug, Service and Devotion: Sri Ramakrishna and His Times' that he wanted to become a 'new type of guru'[45] to the educated middle class. But in the 'Kathamrita' His opinion about gurus is, "being a guru is like prostitution. - selling oneself for trivia like money, fame and the comfort of the body."[46] Even in his personallife he shared his feelings about God with others. He asked for their opinion and never presented himself as the guru. He clearly distinguished renunciation from pretended renunciation. The result is that there is a chance of a mixture of these two even among people who visited him for the 'shelter of God'. Pratap's brother who came to Thakur to avoid his responsibilities to his family. So Thakur says-

> Renunciation is of three or four kinds. Some wear saffron after burning in the fires of the world. This kind of renunciation does not last long. Some slip into a saffron robe and go to Kashi when they can't get a job. Three months later they write to their families, 'I got a job, will return home after a while, do not worry.' Again there are those who have everything, yet they do not feel well. They weep for God in seclusion. *This* is sincere renunciation.[47]

Thakur never supported pretensions of renunciation. He also held up the hypocrisy of those who think merely uttering God's name will take one to Him. He said, "I know someone, I will not name him, he took God's name all the time, but was bearing false witness for ten thousand rupees. That's why I say; if there is renunciation it affects desire for every worldly thing."[48] Michael Madhusudan Dutt in his play 'Is This Civilization?' painted a character in similar colours. Another character named Kali says about this fraud, "I was shocked to see how the Vaishnavite behaves. The rogue makes much of his Tulsi garland with one hand, and takes bribes liberally with the other to lie! That rogue is the biggest hypocrite I ever saw."[49] As a matter of fact, people stuck in the maze of codes of conduct and intent upon advertising their love for God outnumber those who truly surrender themselves before Him. These frauds try to conceal their insincerity with elaborate prayers and visits to temples. In his 'Life of Madhusudan Dutt', Yogindranath Bose wrote, "the Hindu society was degraded not only through the practices of the Anglicized youth; the characterless hypocrites pretending to carry forward the ancient traditions ruined it a hundred times more completely...routines of many such people consisted of praying outside and keeping prostitutes in secret. Although they made much of traditional Hindu customs, their character and behaviour in effect brought those customs to shame."

Thakur did not spare the economic functions of the priests in our country. Although he did not oppose Brahmin priests taking donations after their acts of worship, he did not approve of them when they made a mockery of that act. He tells Ishaan, "Go to Brahmin pundits no more. All they care about is silver...I have seen Brahmins come to worship, reading out from the Chandi or something else. I have seen them skip half the pages (everybody laughs)."[50] In fact, Thakur always stood by the truth. He never accepted anything else.

The colonial Calcutta was like a private property of the English and the newly rising 'babus' of Bengal. They used this region as they pleased. As a result of its nascent Capitalism, life in contemporary Calcutta was naturally full of indulgences of various kinds. The following excerpt is from the periodical 'Somprakash' (August 1862, Srabon 1269)-

> A very clever group has formed among the zamindars. In order to digest their bad deeds they establish schools and hospitals. They have learnt this from a sect of our ancients. There is no misdeed which these people do not do. Visiting others' wives, taking bribes, gobbling up others' wealth by treachery- they are averse to none of these. There is an antidote to all their misdeeds. It is, bathing in the Ganges and wearing a namavali.

Kaliprasanna Singha writes about Calcutta in 1862 in his 'The Observant Owl', "Going to prostitutes is regarded as a deed of valour and an essential pastime for the aristocracy in this city nowadays". To these Babus who were the results of a society based on the omnipotence of money and formed out of the remnants of a rural economy, immoralities, miming the English andfrequenting whorehouses were all honourable deeds. In the 'Kathamrita' as well, Narendra and Mahendranath worry about the young generation. According to Narendra-

> From what I myself have seen it seems that everything is going to collapse. Chicken fights, crude jokes, conceited displays of wealth, dropping out of schools- these are rampant. I have even seen them visit bad places.[51]

Thus Western consumerism alienated Bengal from its indigenous culture. As a result of the logic, education and 'freethinking' of the British, the Bengali could figure out the fallacies of the conservatisms of Hinduism but maintained its caste-based hierarchy carefully. Thakur with his followers has come to the house of a devotee named Adhar who is a goldsmith. When the time for dinner has arrived, Thakur asks Mahendra and Priyanath 'Mukherjee', "Will you not eat? They answered, 'not now, sir'." Thakur never accepted this caste discrimination. He himself often ate at devotees from lower castes. When it became known that Thakur himself accepted food there (at Adhar's house), the discrimination slowly became obsolete[52]. Narendranath was a Kayastha, and he dared to test the flexibility of castes by smoking Muslims' hookah in his childhood. For this, he was liable to be marked as an outcaste by the conservative Brahmins. Thakur also accepted Kamarni as his firstprovider of alms[53] and took up the duty of a priest at a temple established by a Shudra lady. He also worshipped Goddess Kali according to his own wish, disregarding the proceedings mentioned in the scriptures.

The Bengalis divided themselves not only according to caste, but according to region as well, a discrimination present even today. Even now the term 'bangal' for people from eastern Bengal and the term 'ghoti' for those from Western Bengal are well known. These two groups do not like each other. The 'ghotis' have a bit of snobbery. The 'Kathamrita' talks about it. On July 3rd, 1884 Mr. Chowdhury was supposed to visit Thakur. Manmohan said, "Chowdhury will not come. He said, that bangal from Faridpur (Shashadhar) will be there- I will not go."[54] Bengalis can never forget the acid rivalry between 'East Bengal' and 'Mohun Bagan'. Besides all these, another different kind of discrimination sat in the midst of the base of contemporary society. It was the financial discrimination. Common people from middle class or poor backgrounds dared not face people from influential groups. That is why Mahendranath hesitated when Thakur proposed a visit to Balaram Bose's house; because "rich people- what if they don't let me in"[55]. Such doubts always plagued common people. With Thakur's influence these social anomalies began to give way one by one. Although an ardent believer in God's essentiality, he never looked down on people. He hailed man's infinite power with reverence- "man is much". He not only tried to demolish the hierarchy in the mainstream of society, but went out of his way to honour contemporary stage actors and actresses of Bengal. The pride that dramatists and actors of Bengal feel today were sown by Thakur in the end of the nineteenth century. He had seen the Divine Mother in actresses (who were then prostitutes by profession). He accepted the regards of every actress at the end of the play 'Dakshayajna'. At that time even the common people shuddered at the thought of them; they were untouchables. Thakur smiled and told them, "That will do, mothers, get up now, you are distributing joy to all who live with your art, now go and put on your make up."[56] The higher castes could not honour Chandranath (of 'Shei Shomoy') but it was them who caused the births of people like him. On the other hand the Vinodinis achieved salvation through Thakur. Girish Ghosh, Suren Mitra, Dana-Kali, Actress Vinodini, poor Latu, Brinde the housemaid, Chinu the dealer in conch-shells, Rashik the sewer-worker, Manmath the goon- every one of these people got his shelter. He hailed humanity through them all; he did not shrink even from accepting food from a 'fallen woman'[57]. Thakur did not permit Girish to leave the stage because it would help in mass-education. Besides, he accepted leftovers from the downtrodden, drank lemonade in Dakshineshwar temple and ate ice cream offered to him by a 'man with a long beard' at the house of Keshab Sen without a bit of hesitation. According to the standards of contemporary social life each of these was equivalent to heresy. An account of the views of contemporary Hindus on soda, lemonade, biscuits and white bread can be obtained from the autobiography of Bipin Chandra Paul[58]. In the following years Deshbandhu Chittaranjan Das' ideal of caring about the poor and Mahatma Gandhi's Harijan Movements were influenced by Thakur's teachings.

Rammohan Roy, Keshab Sen, Vidyasagar, David Hare, and Beaton are considered the leading figures of women's liberation movement in India today. But coming after them, Sri Ramakrishna turned the very concept of women's position in society upside down. When he went to Balaram Bose's house on 12th of April, 1885, a number of women devotees also came to witness his visit but 'they are watching him from behind a curtain'[59]. Women's liberation in nineteenth-century Bengal was confined within curtains. Vidyasagar or the Brahmo Samaj wanted an end to women's sorrows. The establishment of women's leadership was not on their agenda. Even Bankim Chandra Chatterjee, in spite of bringing women to the battlefield in his 'Ananda Math' (1884), reinforced the notion that attending to her husband's household and managing homebound affairs is the sole duty of woman in 'Devi Chowdhurani' (1884) and 'Sitaram' (1887)[60]. Thakur worshiped the benevolent Goddess Kali, the Tantric nun Bhairavi was one of his gurus. None of the incarnations before him made Shakti his most revered deity or accepted a woman as his teacher.

According to Swami Vivekananda, "The acceptance of a female guru, the cultivation of the feminine spirit and the dissemination of the spirit of the Divine Mother through the Ramakrishna incarnation are all for women's liberation"[61]. Thakur even viewed his wife as a manifestation of the Divine Mother. To his disciple Harinath he said, "Do not look down on women. Respect them properly and your sins will be washed away. But if you loath them you will always remain sinful"[62].

REFERENCES

1. 'M', 'Sri Sri Ramakrishna Kathamrita' (The Gospel of Sri Ramakrishna), Complete, Udbodhan Karyalaya, Kolkata, 2011, p. 87.
2. Ibid, p. 151.
3. Ibid, p. 110.
4. Ibid, p. 179.
5. Ibid, p. 136.
6. Yamraj's designation in the Hindu pantheon is somewhat dubious. He is seen as the God of death, of the underworld and even as the supreme distributor of justice. It is generally agreed that he sends the souls of all sinners to different layers of Hell according to the magnitude of their sins.
7. Vishnu sustains Creation. Vaikunth is the abode of Vishnu.
8. Ibid, p. 167.
9. Ibid, p. 297.
10. By that time a portion of Bengal had accepted Thakur as an incarnation of God.
11. Ibid, p. 838.
12. "But I never do it knowingly. The other day I asked someone to come to Jhautala with a pitcher of water. Now he had gone to relieve himself, so he sent someone else. I came back from toilet and saw there was someone else with the pitcher. I could not use that water. What to do? I had to stand there with soil in hand till the man I had asked came with water."(the 'Kathamrita', p.839)
13. Ibid, p. 19.
14. Ibid, p. 20.
15. Ibid, p. 19
16. Ibid, p. 215.
17. Ibid, p. 20.
18. Ibid, p. 20.
19. Ibid, p. 365.
20. Ibid, p. 211.

21. Ibid, p. 437.
22. Ibid, p. 134.
23. Ibid, p. 168.
24. Ibid, p. 191.
25. Ibid, p. 21.
26. Ibid, p. 173.
27. Ibid, p. 139.
28. Ibid, p. 26.
29. Ibid, p. 343.
30. Ibid, p. 394.
31. Ibid, p. 662.
32. i.e. allegorical stories are more acceptable.
33. Ibid, p. 904.
34. Sarkar, Sumit, 'Kaliyug Chakri Bhakti: Ramakrishna and His Times', Seriban, South 24 Parganas, December 2010, p. 10.
35. 'M', 'Sri Sri Ramakrishna Kathamrita' (The Gospel of Sri Ramakrishna), Complete, Udbodhan Karyalaya, Kolkata, 2011, p. 17.
36. Gangopadhyay, Sunil, 'Shei Shomoy', Ananda Publishers, Kolkata, 1414 (bn.), p. 215.
37. 'M', 'Sri Sri Ramakrishna Kathamrita' (The Gospel of Sri Ramakrishna), Complete, Udbodhan Karyalaya, Kolkata, 2011, p. 32.
38. Ibid, p. 107.
39. Ibid, p. 108.
40. Ibid, p.661.
41. Ibid, p. 217.
42. Ibid, p. 659.
43. Sarkar, Sumit, 'Kaliyug Chakri Bhakti: Ramakrishna and His Times', Seriban, South 24 Parganas, December 2010, p. 10.
44. 'M', 'Sri Sri Ramakrishna Kathamrita' (The Gospel of Sri Ramakrishna), Complete, Udbodhan Karyalaya, Kolkata, 2011, p. 208.
45. Sarkar, Sumit, 'Kaliyug Chakri Bhakti: Ramakrishna and His Times', Seriban, South 24 Parganas, December 2010, p. 11.
46. 'M', 'Sri Sri Ramakrishna Kathamrita' (The Gospel of Sri Ramakrishna), Complete, Udbodhan Karyalaya, Kolkata, 2011, p. 795.
47. Ibid, p. 158.
48. Ibid, p. 716.
49. Dutt, Madhusudan, 'Madhusudan Rachanabali', Sahitya Samsad, Kolkata, March 2009.

50. 'M', 'Sri Sri Ramakrishna Kathamrita' (The Gospel of Sri Ramakrishna), Complete, Udbodhan Karyalaya, Kolkata, 2011, p. 272.
51. Ibid, p. 70.
52. Ibid, p. 519.
53. In the custom of Upanayan which is a sort of religious initiation in the life of the Brahmin boy, a Brahmin lady is usually chosen as the first provider of alms. Kamarni, of course, was not a Brahmin.
54. Ibid, p. 498.
55. Ibid, p. 32.
56. Chattopadhyay, Ramlal, 'Theatere Dakshayajna Dekhte Jawa', Swami Chetanananda (ed.), 'Sri Ramakrishnake Je Rup Dekhiyachhi', Udbodhan Karyalaya, 1998, p. 33.
57. Dutt, Bhupendranath, 'Swami Vivekananda', Nava Bharat Publishers, Kolkata, 1383 (bn.), p.189 and Sri Durgapuri Devi, 'Sarada- Ramakrishna', Sri Sri Saradeshwari Ashram, Kolkata, 1386 (bn.), pp. 90-92.
58. Paul, Bipin Chandra, 'Seventy Years' (Biography), Yug Yatri Prakashak Limited, Kolkata, 1362 (bn.), pp. 79-83, 121.
59. 'M', 'Sri Sri Ramakrishna Kathamrita' (The Gospel of Sri Ramakrishna), Complete, Udbodhan Karyalaya, Kolkata, 2011, p. 793.
60. For detailed discussion look up: 'Biplaber Pratik Sri Sri Ma Sarada Devi', pp. 68-69, 80-85.
61. Swami Vivekananda, 'Bani o Rachana', 7th part, Udbodhan Karyalaya, Kolkata, 1384 (bn.), p. 244.
62. Isherwood, Christopher, 'Ramakrishna o Tar Shishyogon' ('Ramakrishna and His Disciples'), trans. Ravi Shekhar Sengupta, Mandal Book House, Kolkata, 1388 (bn.), p. 195.

Contributors

1. **Swami Prabhananda,** Vice-President, Ramakrishna Math and Mission, Belur Math, West Bengal.
2. **Swami Mukhyananda,** Ramakrishna Mission, Belur Math, West Bengal.
3. **Basab Chaudhuri,** Vice Chancellor, West Bengal State University, Kolkata.
4. **Swami Vedatitananda,** Ramakrishna Mission Polytechnic College, Belur Math, West Bengal.
5. **Subhas Chandra Saha,** Former Vice-Chancellor: Assam (Central) University, Silchar, Assam and Rajiv Gandhi (State) University, Itanagar, Arunchal Pradesh.
6. **Ratnabali Banerjee,** Former Joint Secretary, University Grants Commission, India.
7. **Pranab Ranjan Ghosh,** Former Professor, Department of Bengali, University of Calcutta, Kolkata.
8. **Swami Kamalasthananda,** Principal, Ramakrishna Mission Vivekananda Centenary College, Kolkata.
9. **Br. Shrutichaitanya,** Ramakrishna Mission Vivekananda Centenary College, Kolkata.
10. **Somnath Bhattacharya,** Associate Professor, Department of Mechanical Engineering, Jadavpur University, Kolkata
11. **Tarit Kumar Bandyopadhyay,** Former Associate Professor, Raja Peary Mohan College, Kolkata.
12. **Anupam Jash,** Assistant Professor, Department of Philosophy, Bankura Christian College, West Bengal.

13 **Mamata Kundu,** Associate Professor, Department of Philosophy. Kaliyaganj College, West Bengal.

14 **Goutam Ghosal,** Professor, Department of English & Other Modern European Languages, Visva Bharati, Santiniketa, West Bengal

15 **Sarani Ghosal Mondal,** Assistant Professor in English, National Institute of Technology, Goa.

16 **Swami Chandrakantananda,** Ramakrishna Mission, Belur Math, West Bengal.

17 **Mohit Chakrabarti,** Former Professor of Education, Visva-Bharati, Santiniketan, West bengal.

18 **Sobdo Chakrabarti,** Assistant Professor, Department of English, Burdwan Raj College, Burdwan, West Bengal.

19 **Raghunath Ghosh,** Former Professor, Department of Philosophy, University of North Bengal, West Benal.

20 **Sk. Makbul Islam,** Associate Professor, Department of Bengali, St. Paul's Cathedral Mission College, Kolkata.

21 **Prosenjit Biswas,** Ramakrishna Mission Vivekananda University, Belur Math, West Bengal.